Kant and
Applied Ethics

Kant and Applied Ethics

The Uses and Limits of Kant's Practical Philosophy

Matthew C. Altman

WILEY-BLACKWELL

A John Wiley & Sons, Ltd., Publication

This edition first published 2011
© 2011 John Wiley & Sons Inc.

Wiley-Blackwell is an imprint of John Wiley & Sons, formed by the merger of Wiley's global Scientific, Technical and Medical business with Blackwell Publishing.

Registered Office
John Wiley & Sons Ltd, The Atrium, Southern Gate, Chichester, West Sussex, PO19 8SQ, UK

Editorial Offices
350 Main Street, Malden, MA 02148-5020, USA
9600 Garsington Road, Oxford, OX4 2DQ, UK
The Atrium, Southern Gate, Chichester, West Sussex, PO19 8SQ, UK

For details of our global editorial offices, for customer services, and for information about how to apply for permission to reuse the copyright material in this book please see our website at www.wiley.com/wiley-blackwell.

The right of Matthew C. Altman to be identified as the author of this work has been asserted in accordance with the UK Copyright, Designs and Patents Act 1988.

Library of Congress Cataloging-in-Publication Data
Altman, Matthew C.
  Kant and applied ethics: the uses and limits of Kant's practical philosophy / Matthew C. Altman.
      p. cm.
  Includes bibliographical references (p.) and index.
  ISBN 978-0-4706-5766-9 (hardcover : alk. paper)
  1. Kant, Immanuel, 1724-1804.   2. Applied ethics.   3. Ethical problems.   I. Title.
  B2799.E8A47 2012
  170.92–dc22
                                    2011015489

A catalogue record for this book is available from the British Library.

This book is published in the following electronic formats: ePDF
ISBN 978-1-118-11412-4; Wiley Online Library ISBN 978-1-118-11416-2;
ePub ISBN 978-1-118-11413-1; mobi ISBN 978-1-118-11415-5

Set in 10/12 pt Sabon by Toppan Best-set Premedia Limited
Printed and bound in Malaysia by Vivar Printing Sdn Bhd

1   2011

Contents

Preface   vi

Note on Sources and Key to Abbreviations   viii

Introduction: Why Kant Now   1

Part I.   Applying Kant's Ethics   11

1. Animal Suffering and Moral Character   13
2. Kant's Strategic Importance for Environmental Ethics   45
3. Moral and Legal Arguments for Universal Health Care   71
4. The Scope of Patient Autonomy   90

Part II.   Kantian Arguments against Kant's Conclusions   115

5. Subjecting Ourselves to Capital Punishment   117
6. Same-Sex Marriage as a Means to Mutual Respect   139

Part III. Limitations of Kant's Theory   165

7. Consent, Mail-Order Brides, and the Marriage Contract   167
8. Individual Maxims and Social Justice   194
9. The Decomposition of the Corporate Body   217
10. Becoming a Person   241

Conclusion: Emerging from Kant's Long Shadow   283

Bibliography   289

Index   311

Preface

For better or worse, Immanuel Kant casts a long shadow over contemporary Western thought. The philosophical and historical importance of Kant's ethics can hardly be overestimated, yet Kant's legacy for the wide variety of issues in applied ethics still has not been fully and fairly appreciated. The admittedly ambitious goal of this book is to look comprehensively at Kant's moral philosophy as it relates to key debates in contemporary applied ethics. By analyzing how we have inherited Kant's ideas, we will not only begin to fulfill the fundamental demand of philosophy – to know ourselves – but we will also examine these issues more carefully and open up unfamiliar possibilities for resolving what can seem like intractable moral problems. I will defend Kantian positions on many of these topics – his emphasis on freedom, dignity, and mutual respect is particularly compelling – but I will also stake out the limits of his practical philosophy, the ways in which Kantian presuppositions lead us astray or restrict our vision by, for example, giving us a distorted picture of moral agency. Thus, *Kant and Applied Ethics* addresses both the strengths and the weaknesses of Kant's ethics, demonstrating the value of his approach for making informed judgments and interrogating the theoretical bases of Kant's theory through the lens of applied ethics.

Of course, it would be foolhardy and historically ignorant for a philosopher to claim that his work is the first or last word on any subject. Kant scholarship is teeming not only with close readers of Kant, but also with such innovative thinkers as Christine Korsgaard, Allen Wood, and Barbara Herman, who are taking Kant's philosophy in new and interesting directions. Furthermore, the controversies that this book addresses – physician-assisted suicide, health-care allocation, abortion, and others – have been and will continue to be hotly debated. What follows, then, is an attempt to begin a series of conversations – among Kant scholars, of course, but also among other philosophers and nonphilosophers – about our Kantian inheritances. By coming to grips with Kant's legacy, we will be able to work through these contemporary debates more productively.

Work on this volume started innocently enough, when I began writing an essay on capital punishment without the intention of involving Kant. However, Kant's relevance for the paper quickly became apparent as I considered the unreasonableness of committing ourselves to a system in which innocent people could be (and have been) executed. From that first essay, a series of others followed: on same-sex marriage, corporate responsibility, social justice, and so on. Not coincidentally, the topics of these early papers corresponded to the themes of the annual Conference on Value Inquiry, where versions of several of these chapters were first presented. I delivered talks based on other chapters and parts of chapters at meetings of the North American Kant Society, the Association for Practical and Professional Ethics, and the Northern Illinois Ethics Consortium, as well as the Northwest Philosophy Conference, the International Social Philosophy Conference, and the Inland Northwest Philosophy Conference. I would like to thank the participants at these conferences, especially Patrick Frierson and Ron Wilburn, who presented commentaries on my work, and Sharon Anderson-Gold and Stephen Latham, who referred me to important scholarly sources.

The editors and publishers of three journals have been kind enough to grant permission for me to use previously published material. Versions of chapters 5, 6, and 9 originally appeared, respectively, in *Public Affairs Quarterly*, *Kant-Studien*, and the *Journal of Business Ethics*.

A number of students and former students provided helpful feedback on the manuscript. I am especially grateful to my research assistants: Phillip Downes, whose copious notes prompted weeks of revisions; Casie Dunleavy, whose expertise in applied ethics was an invaluable resource; and Noah Simons and Sofia Bernstein, who spent hours checking sources and proofreading. Ruth Ann Stacy, Human Protections Administrator at Central Washington University, also made several important suggestions regarding the Introduction.

My wife and colleague, Cynthia Coe, has contributed her insights at every stage of the book's production. Cindy has shaped my thinking in countless ways, and she has made me a much better philosopher, writer, and teacher than I otherwise would be.

Finally, I want to thank my parents, Doug and Sheryl, and my sister, Lisa, for their continuing support.

Ellensburg, Wash.   M.C.A.
April 2011

Note on Sources and Key to Abbreviations

Frequently cited works by Kant are referenced in the text parenthetically, using the abbreviations listed below. When available, I have used the standard English translation. Where there is no mention of an English version, the translation is my own. Unless otherwise indicated, italics in quotations appear in the original sources. Works cited only in the notes are given with their full publication information. The complete list of sources is collected in the bibliography.

As is standard in Kant scholarship, references to Kant's writings cite the page numbers of the Royal Prussian Academy edition (*Kants gesammelte Schriften*), which are included in the margins of the translations. At the end of each of the following entries (when applicable), I list the volume number of *Kants gesammelte Schriften* in which the German version appears.

A   *Anthropology from a Pragmatic Point of View* (1798). Trans. Robert B. Louden. In *Anthropology, History, and Education*. Ed. Günter Zöller and Robert B. Louden. Cambridge: Cambridge University Press, 2007. (VII)

Ak   *Kants gesammelte Schriften*. 29 vols. Ed. Deutschen Akademie der Wissenschaften. Berlin: de Gruyter, 1902. References to the Academy edition are given in the form Ak 5:47, indicating volume and page number(s). Where applicable, I have also included the number of the *Reflexion* (R).

CB   *Conjectural Beginning of Human History* (1786). Trans. Allen W. Wood. In *Anthropology, History, and Education*. Ed. Günter Zöller and Robert B. Louden. Cambridge: Cambridge University Press, 2007. (VIII)

CJ   *Critique of the Power of Judgment* (1790). Trans. Paul Guyer and Eric Matthews. Ed. Paul Guyer. Cambridge: Cambridge University Press, 2000. (V)

CPR   *Critique of Pure Reason* (1781, 1787). Trans. and ed. Paul Guyer and Allen W. Wood. Cambridge: Cambridge University Press, 1998. (III, IV)

CPrR   *Critique of Practical Reason* (1788). In *Practical Philosophy*. Trans. and ed. Mary J. Gregor. Cambridge: Cambridge University Press, 1996. (V)

DR   *On the Different Races of Human Beings* (1775). Trans. Holly Wilson and Günter Zöller. In *Anthropology, History, and Education*. Ed. Günter Zöller and Robert B. Louden. Cambridge: Cambridge University Press, 2007. (II)

G   *Groundwork of the Metaphysics of Morals* (1785). In *Practical Philosophy*. Trans. and ed. Mary J. Gregor. Cambridge: Cambridge University Press, 1996. (IV)

LE   *Lectures on Ethics*. Trans. Peter Heath. Ed. Peter Heath and L. B. Schneewind. Cambridge: Cambridge University Press, 1997. (XXVII, XXIX) From this volume, I draw on the lecture notes of J. G. Herder (1762–64) (27:3–78), Georg Ludwig Collins (the *Moralphilosophie Collins*, 1784–85) (27:242–471), and Johann Friedrich Vigilantius (1793–94) (27:479–732).

LM   *Lectures on Metaphysics*. Trans. and ed. Karl Ameriks and Steve Naragon. Cambridge: Cambridge University Press, 1997. (XXVIII, XXIX) From this volume, I draw on *Metaphysik L_1* (mid-1770s) (28:167–350), *Metaphysik Volckmann* (1784–85) (28:355–459), *Metaphysik L_2* (1790–91?) (28:525–610), *Metaphysik Dohna* (1792–93) (28:615–702), and *Metaphysik Mrongovius* (1782–83) (29:747–940). In-text citations of LM refer to the volume and page number of the Academy edition.

MM   *The Metaphysics of Morals* (1797). In *Practical Philosophy*. Trans. and ed. Mary J. Gregor. Cambridge: Cambridge University Press, 1996. (VI)

OBS   *Observations on the Feeling of the Beautiful and Sublime* (1764). Trans. Paul Guyer. In *Anthropology, History, and Education*. Ed. Günter Zöller and Robert B. Louden. Cambridge: Cambridge University Press, 2007. (II)

P   *Prolegomena to Any Future Metaphysics That Will Be Able to Come Forward as a Science* (1783). Trans. Gary Hatfield. In *Theoretical Philosophy after 1781*. Ed. Henry Allison and Peter Heath. Cambridge: Cambridge University Press, 2002. (IV)

PP   *Toward Perpetual Peace* (1795). In *Practical Philosophy*. Trans. and ed. Mary J. Gregor. Cambridge: Cambridge University Press, 1996. (VIII)

Rel   *Religion within the Boundaries of Mere Reason* (1793). Trans.
       George di Giovanni. In *Religion and Rational Theology*. Ed. Allen
       W. Wood and George di Giovanni. Cambridge: Cambridge
       University Press, 1996. (VI)

SRL   "On a Supposed Right to Lie from Philanthropy" (1797). In
       Practical Philosophy. Trans. and ed. Mary J. Gregor. Cambridge:
       Cambridge University Press, 1996. (VIII)

TP   "On the Common Saying: That May Be Correct in Theory, but It
       Is of No Use in Practice" (1793). In *Practical Philosophy*. Trans.
       and ed. Mary J. Gregor. Cambridge: Cambridge University Press,
       1996. (VIII)

WE   "An Answer to the Question: 'What Is Enlightenment?'" (1784).
       In *Practical Philosophy*. Trans. and ed. Mary J. Gregor. Cambridge:
       Cambridge University Press, 1996. (VIII)

Introduction:
Why Kant Now

It is ironic that Immanuel Kant's ethical theory is so often accused of formalism, of being too abstract to be relevant for real-life decisions, and yet we appeal to Kantian concepts in almost every important debate in applied ethics. G. W. F. Hegel was the first to claim that the categorical imperative yields only empty tautologies and gives us no guidance without assuming specific facts about the agent's material and historical circumstances. Similar criticisms have been advanced by Max Scheler, Bernard Williams, Annette Baier, and others.[1] Still, Kant's ethics remains a touchstone. His ethical concepts are ingrained in our moral discourse, such that moral reasoning seems only to be possible against the background of Kant's practical philosophy.

As an example, consider the use of human subjects in medical research. The discussion of research ethics began as a response to the atrocities committed by Nazi doctors in concentration camps, and the ethical standards that were subsequently adopted at their trial are known collectively as the Nuremberg Code. In the United States, the mistreatment of human subjects was especially egregious in the Tuskegee syphilis study, where the disease was allowed to progress in a group of African American men even when, in the 1950s, penicillin became widely available and accepted as the standard therapy. Subsequently, the Belmont Report was written in order to identify the basic principles that ought to govern the treatment of human research subjects. Both the Nuremberg Code and the Belmont Report, the two most important documents on the ethics of human subject research, are deeply informed by Kantian principles.

First, for Kant the object of moral consideration and moral judgment is the individual person, whose humanity is distinguished by the ability to

Kant and Applied Ethics: The Uses and Limits of Kant's Practical Philosophy, First Edition.
Matthew C. Altman.
© 2011 John Wiley & Sons Inc. Published 2011 by Blackwell Publishing Ltd.

decide what he or she will do. Unlike animals and other nonrational things, human beings have wills – that is, they are able to choose on the basis of principles, including ethical principles, rather than being entirely motivated by natural desires and impulses (G 412; MM 392). This gives human beings an inherent dignity and incomparable worth. Accordingly, we must treat them as free beings rather than things. We should not deceive or coerce people because that fails to respect their capacity to choose, and we cannot use them merely as means for the achievement of some end, no matter how laudable (G 428–9).

The Nuremberg Code and the Belmont Report both reflect Kant's focus on the individual agent and respect for personal autonomy. The Belmont Report lists "respect for persons" as a basic ethical principle, claiming that "individuals should be treated as autonomous agents."[2] Among other things, this justifies the need for voluntary consent that is listed as the first principle of the Nuremberg Code.[3] The forced use of prisoners in experimentation during the Holocaust was morally reprehensible not only because the experiments caused intense pain, disfigurement, and often death, but also because human beings were used as mere instruments for the production of scientific data. The risks and harms were imposed on them without their free and informed consent, which violated the respect they deserved as self-determining agents. As we will see in chapter 7, it is very difficult to specify the conditions of consent, particularly because of Kant's philosophical assumptions. Nonetheless, it suffices to note at this point that self-determination is a basic goal for Kant, and that it ought to be preserved out of respect for the person.

The Belmont Report notes that people with diminished capacity are especially in need of protection.[4] Historically, researchers have often targeted vulnerable populations, including unsuspecting and uninformed members of the general public, military personnel, prisoners, the handicapped, and ethnic minorities.[5] The Tuskegee syphilis study, conducted with impoverished African American men, is a classic case of using such people merely as means. Deceptive practices that were used during the Tuskegee study did not allow the men to make informed decisions. For example, the participants thought that they were undergoing treatment, when in fact they were only being monitored while the disease was allowed to take its course. Lying to patients amounts to choosing for them, in the sense that they are being manipulated into doing something rather than being given the full information necessary to decide for themselves. Thus they are not being respected as people with the capacity to choose. The Belmont Report says that it "show[s] lack of respect for an autonomous agent . . . to withhold information necessary to make a considered judgment."[6] In effect, the doctors in the Tuskegee study chose on behalf of the test subjects, deciding to expose them to risks to which they had not consented.

Like Kant, most people distinguish between research on humans and research on animals. Because human beings are rational agents with the capacity to consent, they have an absolute worth that ought to be respected in our treatment of them. By contrast, animals can be used merely as means to promote human welfare, so testing on animals is acceptable if it reduces the danger to humans. The Nuremberg Code states that human subject research should proceed only after the risks have been identified using animal test subjects.[7] Of course, most people object to the gratuitous suffering of animals,[8] but generally their necessary sacrifice in medical experiments is thought to be justified – a Kantian idea. Chapter 1 will address whether Kant would approve of such animal suffering to advance human interests, especially if there are alternatives to animal testing that are as effective. Still, humans and animals are not morally considerable in the same way. From a Kantian perspective, then, one of the most disturbing elements of the Tuskegee study is that African American men were treated as lab rats. Their mistreatment reflected a dehumanizing racism that is contrary to mutual respect for autonomous beings.

This dehumanization has two aspects: full informed consent was not sought or secured, and the experiment did not establish acceptable risk levels through animal controls. Even if the patients had consented to the procedure knowing the risks and the benefits, it would not have been enough to ensure that it was a rational, fully autonomous decision. Patients have duties to themselves that would be breached if they were to engage in reckless behavior that threatens their health with little or no benefit. Whether the Tuskegee experiment posed such risks had not been determined by seeing the effects of untreated syphilis on animals, so it would have been wrong even to solicit consent for such an experiment prior to assessing the level of danger on nonhuman subjects.

This is where Kant diverges from the purely liberal model in which informed consent is sufficient for free choice. Without the standard requirement that animals be used to prevent needless harm and suffering for human beings, even informed consent cannot settle the issue of whether the patient is treating himself in accordance with his dignity as a person. Requiring informed consent can only protect the person against being used merely as a means by others. Legal restrictions on how we treat others can set the stage so that people are not used in this way, but a person could still choose wrongly and consent to things that he should not. Consent on its own is only a necessary condition for autonomous self-determination. Free choices must also be rational, manifesting a commitment to right principles.

When Kant says that a choice must be free, he means that it must be made based on reasons that are justifiable to others, not based on inclinations that a particular person happens to have. If I decide to participate in a dangerous and worthless experiment because I like to spend time with lab technicians, that risks something that has absolute worth, my very self, for the sake of satisfying a desire that is specific to me. Kant claims that, despite my consent, such an action cannot be right because the moral law must constrain rational beings universally and necessarily. My decision must be shareable by all rational beings if it is to be autonomous – that is, based on reason rather than what I happen to want – and only then is it morally permissible. Kant formulates this principle as the first version of the categorical imperative, the formula of universal law, which states that one should not adopt a subjective principle of action (maxim) that one cannot also will as a universal law (G 421). That is, I should not do something that depends on others acting differently; I cannot make an exception of myself (G 424).

In the ethics of human subject research, the importance of universalizability manifests itself as a concern for fairness. Researchers are asked to put themselves in the position of the human subjects. The Nuremberg Code takes this literally when it comes to experiments that pose substantial risks to test subjects: such experiments are prohibited "except, perhaps, in those experiments where the experimental physicians also serve as subjects."[9] Although the categorical imperative is not equivalent to the golden rule, they share the insight that when one acts, one must put oneself in the place of those who are being affected. If the researchers were test subjects, what information would they expect or want to have in order to make an informed decision? Is it absolutely necessary to mislead the subjects in order for the experiment to be successful? Would knowing the information make the subject less likely to participate? In short, is the deception justifiable, or does it amount to a kind of coercion? These sorts of questions are routinely asked by institutional review boards.

According to Kant, we have moral duties to all people by virtue of the fact that they are rational moral agents. We should refrain from thwarting others' capacity to act, but we should also help them to achieve their purposes (G 430). Hence, we have a duty of beneficence in addition to the duty of nonmaleficence. The Belmont Report lists beneficence as the second ethical principle governing research on human subjects, from which it follows that harms must be minimized, benefits must be maximized, and the benefits must outweigh the risks. Although testing on human subjects is supposed to benefit society as a whole (by providing new knowledge), "the risks and benefits affecting the immediate research subject will normally carry special weight." Typically, the test subject himself must benefit from the treatment, unless the value of the test for society is so great that risks to the subject are justified. But even then, the test can only proceed on the condition that "the subjects' rights have been protected."[10] In other words, the person can be treated as a means, but not *merely* as a means (G 428–9). Thus, the Kantian demand that we respect the dignity of persons also implies that we should not expose test subjects to extreme risks regardless of the benefits: according to the Nuremberg Code, "no experiment should be conducted where there is an *a priori* reason to believe that death or disabling injury will occur."[11]

It is also important that the risks be equitably distributed. Justice is the third and final principle adopted under the Belmont Report, and it implies that, in the selection of test subjects, researchers must not target a specific population because they are more easily pressured into participating. The Tuskegee study was not only wrong because of the use of deceptive practices, but it was also unjust because it exclusively targeted poor black men. People who are in a vulnerable position because of social or physical circumstances should not bear the burdens of research unfairly while more advantaged populations receive the benefit. It is contrary to the spirit of the categorical imperative that some people should be treated differently from others because of something such as their race, which is irrelevant to their humanity.[12] According to Kant, what matters is a person's capacity to act rationally: to set and pursue ends, and to be able to act on the basis of (moral) principles. Prisoners, the poor, and ethnic minorities have a dignity that ought to be respected, and they should not be used as test subjects "solely for administrative convenience, or because they are easy to manipulate as a result of their illness or socioeconomic condition."[13]

The ethics of research on human subjects is only one example of Kant's continuing presence in contemporary moral issues. The concepts of autonomy, dignity, fairness, and duty arise over and over again in issues as diverse as physician-assisted suicide, animal rights, same-sex marriage, and corporate ethics. These concepts are central to our common moral vocabulary, whether we are professional philosophers or not.

This book is an attempt to appreciate the full scope of Kant's relevance for the various fields of applied ethics, both the power of Kantian concepts and their limitations. There are three major sections. In the first part, I use Kant's philosophy to analyze several important topics in medical and environmental ethics. The second section shows that Kant's moral theory yields positions that contradict Kant's own stated views; Kantian insights are preserved at the expense of Kant's culturally specific prejudices. Finally, in the third part, I explore some of the problems with Kant's theory, and specifically how Kantian concepts have limited its application when it comes to some contemporary moral issues.

With this overall structure, the arc of *Kant and Applied Ethics* moves from the practical usefulness of Kant's ethics to what may be called a disenchantment with some of his theory's basic assumptions. Kant's moral framework has deeply shaped the major ethical debates of Western society, and we should recognize that influence in order to assess its continuing legitimacy. Much of what Kant has to tell us about the importance of autonomy and fairness should continue to guide our moral deliberations, as it does in the field of research ethics. However, this should not foreclose a critical examination of the theory's limitations. As we will see, many of Kant's conclusions and even some of his primary concepts need to be challenged and revised. This study of Kant's philosophy is not only a historical exercise, to get clear about what Kant said and to demonstrate his relevance for applied ethics, but it is also an exercise in self-scrutiny in which we come to evaluate – sometimes positively, sometimes negatively – the Kantian concepts that we have internalized.

Each chapter of the book focuses on a particular area of moral controversy in applied ethics. In chapters 1 and 2, I examine Kant's relevance for evaluating our treatment of animals and the environment. Kant's philosophy is a paradigm case of anthropocentrism: only human beings (or, more specifically, rational beings) are directly morally considerable. Attempts have been made to modify Kant's strict position, a kind of "Kantianism" (broadly construed) rather than an application of Kant's own theory. However, I will show that, if we follow the letter of Kant's position, we can nonetheless justify the advancement of animal welfare and numerous environmental protections. Kant has a lot to contribute to environmental ethics. Most importantly, his contributions are more likely to speak to us given our enduring anthropocentrism – which, of course, is also one of Kant's legacies.

In chapter 3, I turn to bioethics and the issue of health-care distribution. On both moral and political grounds, Kant's ethics justifies health care as a basic right that is necessary to support people's capacity to set and pursue ends. The corresponding duty we have extends not only to our fellow citizens but beyond our borders. We ought to support health-care initiatives in other countries as well.

Chapter 4 addresses more personal issues in bioethics, including physician-assisted suicide, the refusal of life-saving medical treatment, and organ donation. Here the basic question concerns patient autonomy and which actions best accord with our capacity for self-determination. Physician-assisted suicide and the right to refuse treatment are often considered paradigm cases in which a person ought to have the freedom to choose to die. However, Kant's philosophy shows how a restriction of people's freedom in these cases actually sustains their autonomy. Furthermore, while it is true that people should not be forced to donate their organs, a public policy in which people would be required to "opt out" of donating – that is, a policy that assumes people's consent, unless they say otherwise – is more conducive to morally permissible action. In chapter 4, then, we see the contours of Kant's conception of autonomy and the difference between acting reasonably and acting capriciously.

Chapters 5 and 6 focus on very different topics: capital punishment and same-sex marriage. What the chapters share is a deep distrust of Kant's own conclusions on these issues. I argue that, if Kant is to be consistent, he ought to condone same-sex marriage and prohibit use of the death penalty. With regard to the death penalty, the possibility of wrongly convicting someone of a capital offense means that we cannot be duty-bound to fulfill the law of retribution. We should not administer death as a punishment because we know that we may inadvertently kill the innocent. In chapter 6, I show that, if we disregard Kant's failed condemnation of homosexuality as "unnatural," then same-sex marriage must be recognized as an important institution to ensure that homosexual couples can have a healthy and fulfilling sex life while continuing to respect one another's personhood.

Beginning with chapter 7, I begin to stake out the limitations of Kant's theory. I examine mail-order marriages as a case study in why Kant cannot adequately understand how coercive social conditions affect personal responsibility (chapter 7); I demonstrate that the reasonableness of some maxims depends on their interpretation in a social context, which validates something like Hegel's formalism charge (chapter 8); I show that Kant's theory of moral subjectivity cannot make sense of collective responsibility, which limits his relevance for business ethics (chapter 9); and I explain how Kant's approach to the problem of abortion is philosophically inadequate and leads to the kind of stalemate that we face in the abortion debate today (chapter 10). These last four chapters test Kant's theory of subjectivity (the criteria of personhood) as well as his focus on the rational individual who is, in principle, separate from a community of deliberators.

Covering so many topics in one book means that each one cannot receive as much attention as it deserves. I am especially brief in discussing the public policy implications of my ethical analyses. Still, each chapter provides an important insight into both Kant's moral theory and the different areas of applied ethics. It becomes clear that Kant's philosophy provides a compelling model of moral discourse and moral value that helps us to resolve many charged ethical debates. There are reasons why Kant's theory has had such a lasting impact and why his philosophical assumptions remain (for the most part) our own assumptions. However, we will also discover that working within a Kantian framework in some cases stifles progress on important moral issues.

This book has two major aims. First, it is an attempt to rethink some of the major ethical debates in the West. Kant's philosophy deeply informs our moral thinking, so examining his approach to various topics in applied ethics will help us to reflect on and evaluate our own positions. My hope is that understanding Kant's ideas in more complex ways will allow us to deploy them differently and, where those ideas limit our thinking, to consider alternatives.

The book's second, related, aim is to defend Kant as far as he can be defended, and no further. Kant's critics are wrong to reject his philosophy outright as overly rule-based or inflexible, as dismissive of nonrational beings such as animals and nature, or as incapable of addressing complex moral issues. Nonetheless, over the course of this book, it will become clear that Kant's moral philosophy has its limitations. We will discover that Kant's almost exclusive focus on the individual agent as the subject of moral responsibility and the object of moral duties, and his failure to appreciate the extent to which social and historical circumstances affect what we are obligated to do, reveal themselves to be untenable premises on which to base a moral philosophy. As alternatives, toward the end of the book I briefly explain how Hegelianism and communitarianism may be particularly well suited to resolve some of the problems left to us by Kant.

Thus, *Kant and Applied Ethics* not only shows how to apply Kant's ideas to practical issues. It also uses a study of these practical issues to show the limits of Kant's theoretical assumptions. As we will see, a careful study of Kant's practical philosophy inspires us to move beyond the strict confines of Kantian moral theory, to embrace what we can of Kant but to be clear that doing ethics and applied ethics amounts to more than a simple exegesis of Kantian ideas.

Notes

1   See Max Scheler, *Formalism in Ethics and Non-Formal Ethics of Values: A New Attempt toward the Foundation of an Ethical Personalism*, 5th rev. edn., trans. Manfred S. Frings and Roger L. Funk (Evanston, Ill.: Northwestern University Press, 1973); Bernard Williams, *Moral Luck: Philosophical Papers 1973–1980* (Cambridge: Cambridge University Press, 1981), and *Ethics and the Limits of Philosophy* (Cambridge, Mass.: Harvard University Press, 1985); and Annette C. Baier, *Moral Prejudices: Essays on Ethics* (Cambridge, Mass.: Harvard University Press, 1994).

2   National Commission for the Protection of Human Subjects of Biomedical and Behavioral Research, "The Belmont Report: Ethical Principles and Guidelines for the Protection of Human Subjects of Research" (1979), Part B, ohsr.od.nih.gov/guidelines/belmont.html. Another important document in research ethics, the Declaration of Helsinki, also emphasizes the incomparable value of the autonomous subject: "It is the duty of physicians who participate in medical research to protect the life, health, dignity, integrity, right to self-determination, privacy, and confidentiality of personal information of research subjects" (World Medical Association, *Declaration of Helsinki: Ethical Principles for Medical Research Involving Human Subjects* (1964), Article 11, www.wma.net/en/30publications/10policies/b3/index.html).

3   "The voluntary consent of the human subject is absolutely essential" (*Trials of War Criminals before the Military Tribunals under Control Council Law No.*

10: Nuremberg, October 1946–April 1949 [Nuremberg Code] [Washington, D.C.: Government Printing Office, 1949], 2:181). The requirement that test subjects give full informed consent is central to all of the most important documents in research ethics: not only the Nuremberg Code, but also the Belmont Report (Part C), the Declaration of Helsinki (Articles 24–9), and the 1971 guidelines issued by the U.S. Department of Health, Education and Welfare (later the Code of Federal Regulations [CFR], Title 45, Subtitle A, Part 46) (§46.116), www.hhs.gov/ohrp/humansubjects/guidance/45cfr46.htm.

4   "The Belmont Report," Part B. See also the Declaration of Helsinki, Article 9, and the CFR, Title 45, Subtitle A, Part 46, §46.111.

5   Famous (or infamous) examples include, respectively, the "Green Run," when radioactive materials were released from the Hanford nuclear facility in Washington state (1949); a series of experiments performed by the U.S. Army's Chemical Warfare Service, in which thousands of military trainees were exposed to mustard gas (1942–45); project MK-ULTRA, in which the CIA administered hallucinogenic drugs to prisoners (early 1950s–late 1960s [or later]); the Willowbrook hepatitis study, in which healthy, mentally disabled children were injected with the hepatitis virus (1963–66); and the Tuskegee syphilis study, in which researchers allowed the disease to progress in a group of African American test subjects (1932–72).

6   "The Belmont Report," Part B.

7   "The experiment should be so designed and based on the results of animal experimentation and a knowledge of the natural history of the disease or other problem under study that the anticipated results will justify the performance of the experiment" (*Trials of War Criminals before the Military Tribunals* [Nuremberg Code], 2:181). See also the Declaration of Helsinki, Article 12, and the CFR, Title 45, Subtitle A, Part 46, §46.204a, which specifically recommends that studies on pregnant animals precede studies on pregnant women.

8   Although the Declaration of Helsinki enumerates principles governing human subject research, it also states in passing that "the welfare of animals used for research must be respected" (Article 12).

9   *Trials of War Criminals before the Military Tribunals* (Nuremberg Code), 2:182.

10 "The Belmont Report," Part C.

11 *Trials of War Criminals before the Military Tribunals* (Nuremberg Code), 2:182.

12 Kant himself struggled with this, as we will see in chapter 8.

13 "The Belmont Report," Part C.

Part I

Applying Kant's Ethics

Kant's practical philosophy continues to speak to us for a number of reasons. His emphasis on autonomy in ethics and personal freedom under the law resonates with modern liberalism. The absolute worth of humanity restricts how we can be treated by others and how we can treat ourselves, and employing this idea avoids some of the pitfalls of rival ethical theories such as utilitarianism. Kant also gives a compelling argument for why moral constraints must apply to everyone equally in similar circumstances.

One of the purposes of this book is to demonstrate the usefulness of Kant's moral and political theories, and to show that they do not yield only empty tautologies. A moral concern for autonomy and the value of persons has important implications for environmental ethics and medical ethics. As we will see in chapters 1 and 2, Kant does not believe that animals and the environment are morally considerable in their own right, but he does justify their protection by appealing to the value of humanity. Despite his anthropocentrism, or even because of it, Kant is an ally in the defense of animal welfare and environmental conservation.

Chapters 3 and 4 focus specifically on personal autonomy in an effort to address some issues in bioethics from a Kantian perspective. First, I claim that Kant's practical philosophy warrants our commitment to universal health care. We must support others' existence as rational beings and preserve civil society, so we are obligated, morally and legally, to support their health by providing a basic level of care. Then, in chapter 4, I apply Kant's theory to physician-assisted suicide, the refusal of life-saving medical treatment, and the procedures for consenting to donate organs. Valuing patient autonomy does not mean that patients can do whatever they want as long

Kant and Applied Ethics: The Uses and Limits of Kant's Practical Philosophy, First Edition.
Matthew C. Altman.
© 2011 John Wiley & Sons Inc. Published 2011 by Blackwell Publishing Ltd.

as it only affects them. For Kant, there are constraints on the actions we take as rational beings. By addressing these three issues in medical ethics, chapter 4 illuminates what we are ethically required to do and what we ought to be allowed to do under the law. Kant's conception of rational autonomy becomes clearer, and we begin to see what is implied by our own commitment to patient self-determination.

1

Animal Suffering and Moral Character

Kant has had little impact on the field of environmental ethics. When his work is not simply ignored, it is often dismissed as a paradigm of morally corrupt anthropocentrism. Like many other Western philosophical and religious traditions, Kant places human beings at the center of the moral universe and does not directly consider the well-being of plants, animals, and ecosystems. Instead, they are only indirectly morally relevant, to the extent that they advance rational beings' capacity to set and pursue ends; nonrational things can be used merely as means for the satisfaction of human needs. Because of this, many philosophers – Holmes Rolston III, J. Baird Callicott, Peter Singer, and others – conclude that Kant's intellectual legacy is partly responsible for the environmental crises that we now face.

Kant's theory has often been misconstrued as implying that animals and nature are valuable only as resources to satisfy unreflective human wants. For Kant, however, properly relating to the environment is an important part of a fully moral life. Our treatment of animals affects who we are, so we are obligated to treat them well even when we use them to accomplish our ends; and, as we will see in chapter 2, the appreciation of natural beauty prepares us to act rightly, without a concern for our personal interests. Although we are distinguished from animals and plants by our rationality, we must understand ourselves to be the products of nature's teleological development, and so we should not view nature merely as a thing to be used and discarded. This change in our intellectual orientation, as well as the recognition that our treatment of the environment and nonhuman animals affects our moral character, have the combined effect of justifying a number of animal and environmental protections. Thus the conclusions of Kant's moral philosophy converge in many ways with those who believe in advancing animal welfare or preserving the environment due to their intrinsic worth.

Kant and Applied Ethics: The Uses and Limits of Kant's Practical Philosophy, First Edition. Matthew C. Altman.
© 2011 John Wiley & Sons Inc. Published 2011 by Blackwell Publishing Ltd.

Because of this convergence, environmental ethicists have been wrong to exclude Kantian anthropocentrism from the debate over how and why we ought to protect animals and the environment. Our legal and moral traditions are steeped in anthropocentrism, and typically restrictions on our behavior are justified by noting the effect that animal cruelty and environmental degradation have on human flourishing. Given our intellectual heritage – the fact that in general people *are* anthropocentric – and in the absence of convincing evidence for the intrinsic worth of animals and nature, we should accept Kant's moral philosophy not as *the* correct environmental ethic (although it may be), but strategically, as a discursive resource to achieve the practical aims of environmentalism.

Kant's Logocentrism

Kant claims that human beings, by virtue of their capacity to reason about and decide what to do, have an incomparable worth and dignity. They choose the subjective principles upon which they act, and because of this, they are distinguished from nonrational things that are moved to act by gravity or by their own instincts: "Everything in nature works in accordance with laws. Only a rational being has the capacity to act *in accordance with the representation* of laws, that is, in accordance with principles, or has a *will*" (G 412; see also MM 392). Christine Korsgaard describes this as a kind of "reflective distance" between what one is naturally inclined to and what one decides to do.[1] Animals follow their strongest desire – to eat, to avoid harm, to reproduce, etc. – and heliotropic plants respond to the position of the sun, but neither animals nor plants are capable of acting on the basis of reasons.

What Kant means by humanity – what gives us dignity and makes us worthy of respect – is the capacity to act autonomously, the ability to do what is right simply because it is right. Because of this, we sometimes hold people morally and legally responsible for their actions. Although animals' actions are attributable to them – dogs and horses *do* things, after all – animals are not held accountable for what they do. To be sure, some animals act in ways that may initially look like they are motivated by an ethical concern for their fellow animals. For example, chimpanzees help one another, have complex social structures, and ostracize members of the group that engage in antisocial behavior. However, reactive social formations do not indicate moral deliberation and judgment about the wrongness of an action. The needs of the group members are valued (in some broad sense of valuing), but they are at best evolutionary precursors of what becomes in human beings a thoughtful concern for other people's rights and dignity. Even Frans de Waal, who has spent his career showing how closely humans and primates are related, stops short of attributing moral agency to them.

He claims that, although some animals (such as chimpanzees) have the building blocks of a moral life – sympathy, cooperation, the ability to follow social rules – they do not engage in what could properly be described as autonomous moral reasoning:

> Even if animals other than ourselves act in ways tantamount to moral behavior, their behavior does not necessarily rest on deliberations of the kind we engage in. It is hard to believe that animals weigh their own interests against the rights of others, that they develop a vision of the greater good of society, or that they feel lifelong guilt about something they should not have done.[2]

For Kant, following or not following social norms is not "tantamount to moral behavior." Only rational beings are capable of the reflective deliberation that is necessary for moral agency, and because of this only human beings are directly morally considerable. Kant equates the class of moral patients, those to whom we have direct obligations, with the class of moral agents, and he limits moral agency to human beings.[3] Nonrational animals are not persons in the morally relevant sense of the term.

Moral agency is also different from a being's capacity merely to think or to reason more generally. Although some animals have more intellectual capabilities than human infants – for example, chimpanzees form mental representations of themselves, have rudimentary languages, can empathize with others, and can discern cause-and-effect relationships[4] – Kant does not claim that intelligence makes someone worthy of moral consideration. Being able to think in this sense is not the same thing as the reflective distance by which one is capable of acting for the sake of duty.[5] For Kant, it is the latter capacity that makes someone worthy of respect.

When rational beings are responsible for what they do, they decide which ends to pursue. For something to be good for me, it is not enough that I want it. I have to decide that it is something that I ought to try to get. As Kant puts it, I am the sort of being who sets my ends. Because I must decide that I ought to pursue something in order for it to be good for me, the capacity to decide things and determine what is good is a condition of all other goods, and therefore has absolute value. This leads to the version of the categorical imperative known as the formula of humanity: "*So act that you use humanity, whether in your own person or in the person of any other, always at the same time as an end, never merely as a means*" (G 429).[6] Persons have intrinsic worth because they are rational, whereas the worth of nonrational things is relative to human needs and tastes, insofar as they can be used to advance human purposes (G 434–6, 427–8). Apart from humanity, nothing in nature is good in itself; all nonrational beings are (or may be) only instrumentally good.

By claiming that only humanity has intrinsic worth, Kant seems to be advancing a form of anthropocentrism, which values human beings over all other species. However, Kant is not privileging human beings per se, but the capacity to reason that many human beings have. Therefore, Kant's view is better characterized as what Allen Wood calls "logocentrism," a position "based on the idea that rational nature, and it alone, has absolute and unconditional value."[7] Of course, the implications of logocentrism are (for the most part) the same as those of anthropocentrism: human beings are included but plants, animals, and ecosystems are excluded from direct moral considerability. For Kant, rainforests and chimpanzees are morally equivalent to bricks and chairs, in the sense that all of them are in the same class, nonrational things, "with which one can do as one likes" (A 127). Kant echoes the biblical idea that animals are "gifts of nature" given to human beings by God:

> The first time [the human being] said to the sheep: *Nature has given you the skin you wear not for you but for me*, then took it off the sheep and put it on himself (*Genesis* 3:21), he became aware of a prerogative that he had by his nature over all animals, which he now no longer regarded as his fellow creatures, but rather as means and instruments given over to his will for the attainment of his discretionary aims [*beliebigen Absichten*]. (CB 114)

According to Kant, we have obligations only to ourselves and other rational agents, so we can use plants, animals, and whole ecosystems as resources to accomplish any human purposes and satisfy any human desires – our "beliebigen Absichten" – without restriction. Environmental ethics is an oxymoron.

Kant's Justification for Our Duties (with Regard) to Nonrational Animals

Because of the absolute value of humanity, a rational being has moral duties toward himself, such as developing his talents and not committing suicide, and toward others, such as acting beneficently and not lying (G 421–3, 429–30). Although we have *direct* duties only to rational beings, Kant also claims that we have a number of *indirect* duties, and it is here where we see how Kant restricts our behavior in ways that are consistent with non-anthropocentric positions in environmental ethics.

With regard to animals in particular, Kant begins by noting that our treatment of them has an impact on our character. To use Kant's more technical terminology, how a person behaves toward animals affects his disposition (*Gesinnung*), "the first subjective ground of the adoption of the maxims," which orders his given incentives according to adopted standards of practical self-determination (Rel 25). Because our moral choices are the result of our character, and because our character is shaped (among other things) by how we treat nonrational animals, behaving cruelly toward animals would ultimately affect the kind of people we are and the principles upon which we choose to act. Hence, we have duties to animals, but only indirectly – that is, because of how our behavior toward animals impacts us:

> Any action whereby we may torment animals, or let them suffer distress, or otherwise treat them without love, is demeaning to ourselves. It is inhuman, and contains an analogy of violation of the duty to ourselves, since we would not, after all, treat ourselves with cruelty; we stifle the instinct of humaneness within us and make ourselves devoid of feeling; it is thus an indirect violation of humanity in our own person. (LE 710; see also MM 443; LE 459)

To say that we have indirect duties to animals is a bit misleading. Properly speaking, we have indirect duties to persons through our treatment of animals. We should not treat animals cruelly because doing so coarsens our sensitivity to others' suffering, a view that psychologists now call the "violence graduation hypothesis."[8] If the pain we cause sentient beings (including some animals) does not arouse our sympathy, if we become more desensitized to it the more we inflict it, then it becomes less likely that causing a person pain will concern us. Parallel cases include shooting a dog or allowing a horse to starve when they have served us well over the course of their lives (LE 459, 710). A lack of gratitude toward such animals reflects and reinforces a similar feeling toward people to whom we are indebted. Despite many differences, animals are similar enough to human beings that treating animals badly progressively undermines our consideration for human animals. Animal cruelty ultimately erodes our moral virtue.[9]

Our obligations regarding the treatment of animals are often similar to our obligations to rational beings – refraining from gratuitous cruelty, for example – but the fundamental difference is that we can only have direct duties to rational beings, and to animals indirectly because of our duty to ourselves. I should not unnecessarily harm other people because I ought to respect them. I should treat animals well because if I do not, I will become callous to suffering, which undermines my attempt to develop a virtuous character. This is a crucial premise in Kant's argument for indirect duties to animals, and there is evidence to support it.[10]

I will be more likely to harm other people if I enjoy making animals suffer, and this is morally significant. However, Kant is most concerned with how enjoying or ignoring the suffering of animals corrupts *me*. It makes me a bad person who, incidentally, is also more likely to disregard others' feelings, which I ought to consider when I make a moral decision. As Barbara Herman puts it, we ought to refrain from unnecessarily harming animals "because indifference and insensitivity are hostile to reason, to getting things right, and therefore not part of justified ways of acting."[11] If I disregard others' suffering, then I am not deliberating correctly. The right treatment of animals, if it is done for the right reason, reflects a kind of self-respect rather than a respect for the animals themselves.[12]

When someone confuses these kinds of duties and believes that animals themselves are worthy of respect, Kant says that the person is committing "an *amphiboly* in his *concepts of reflection*," or a logical fallacy that results from an ambiguous use of terms (MM 442).[13] There is an ambiguity in saying that we have duties to animals, and those who claim that animals (or plants, or ecosystems) have intrinsic worth play on this ambiguity. As Kant puts it, we can have duties *"with regard to [in Ansehung]"* animals but not *"to [gegen]"* animals, which Kant classifies as merely *"(nonhuman) objects"* (MM 442). So, there are moral reasons to treat animals well (or at least not badly), but it would be a mistake to conclude from this that animals themselves constrain us, independently of how our treatment of them impacts our dispositions.

Implications of Kant's View for Our Treatment of Animals

Defenders of animal rights and utilitarians who promote animal welfare – typically represented by Tom Regan and Peter Singer, respectively – do not accept Kant's approach precisely because it protects animals only to encourage human virtue. Still, it is important to emphasize that Kant does think animals are deserving of moral consideration; the treatment of animals is not a conceptual blind spot within his practical philosophy. Even though the duties are indirect and "with regard to" animals, we have moral duties nonetheless. It is cruel to cause sentient beings unnecessary pain, whether or not they are rational agents. While it is not wrong apart from its impact on us, the cruelty of the act *is* wrong. Like Regan and Singer, Kant criticizes the mistreatment of animals in strong and morally significant terms.

In fact, the conclusions Kant reaches concerning our specific duties coincide with much of what is advanced by Regan and Singer. Kant claims that we ought to be concerned with the pain and comfort of animals, and that we ought to minimize their suffering even when doing so serves no immediate human purpose. For example, Kant says that we should not "strain [domestic animals] beyond their capacity" (MM 443). Even if working animals to death would maximize profits and make our lives a lot easier, we have a moral obligation that overrides these desires. We ought to be concerned with their comfort and well-being. Kant also says that hunting animals for sport is immoral (LE 460). The fact that a person takes pleasure in it is irrelevant.

Additionally, Kant's position on animal testing is fairly strict: "agonizing physical experiments for the sake of mere speculation, when the end could also be achieved without these, are to be abhorred" (MM 443).[14] Kant would not prohibit the use of animals in all experiments – neither would Singer[15] – but it is important to note that the pain animals feel puts the justificatory burden on those who want to engage in animal testing. Human interests do not automatically trump animal interests.[16] Killing or maiming animals to develop such things as cosmetics is prohibited, because this end is even less important than "mere speculation." It is possible to develop a cruelty-free product. Having no concern for the intense suffering of animals that undergo routine poisoning in testing labs, and thinking that such suffering is worth it because we desperately need yet another kind of lipstick, clearly seems hard-hearted. Medical testing may have greater potential benefits than cosmetic testing, but it is crucial to determine whether animal suffering is avoidable. If we can get the same results without killing countless animals in painful experiments, then endorsing such tests amounts to a callous disregard of others' pain. If there are often alternatives to painful medical testing, as some now claim there are,[17] then Kant would rule out animal testing in most cases, even when health benefits for persons could be achieved.

Whether we can kill animals for food is less clear. Kant certainly thinks that there are restrictions on how we treat animals that we eat: he says that they must be killed as quickly and painlessly as possible (MM 443). Kant would condemn the deplorable conditions around factory farming. Livestock animals produced through breeding and genetic engineering experience chronic pain, disease, and premature death; crowded pens and feedlots do not allow animals to express their natural instincts, causing stress and self-injurious behavior; and all of this is followed by the cramped and cold transportation to the slaughter plant, then electrical stunning, putting bolts through their brains, hanging animals upside down and slitting their throats, etc. The fact that many people are unaware of the conditions under which their meat is produced does not exempt them from moral criticism. As Dan Egonsson notes, "if you are a deliberate meat eater, that does not automatically mean that you practise cruelty to animals in a direct fashion. But you will in one way *accept* the fact that animals are treated the way they are in the animal factories." Willful ignorance does not excuse people from their moral duties. If we have an indirect duty to make sure that animals are not mistreated, then we have an obligation to determine whether the meat we are eating comes from mistreated animals. Egonsson extends Kant's claim that "he who is cruel to animals becomes hard also in his dealing with men" (LE 459) to insist that "he who accepts cruelty to non-human animals will eventually accept cruelty also to people."[18]

Kant would condemn sacrificing animals simply because we like the taste of meat. We would be overlooking the pain of animals for our own pleasure, the essence of a callous disregard for others. If meat were necessary to keep us alive and healthy, then killing animals humanely would be justified in order to advance our existence as rational and natural beings. But most of us, who have access to nutritionally equivalent alternatives, can live just as healthily with a vegetarian diet. If we tacitly support incredible amounts of animal suffering because of a shallow desire for the taste of animal flesh, it dulls our moral sensitivity, as it does that of butchers who, Kant says, become "inured to death" (LE 459–60).[19] Arguably, this limitation on meat-eating, short of absolute prohibition, is consistent with Singer's own position.[20] Kant condemns neglecting our duties in order to satisfy our inclinations, the latter of which are only conditionally good. If accepting the cruel treatment of livestock damages a person's character, and if we only eat animals because we like to do so, then most of us ought to become vegetarians.

As I said, Kant does not rule out the killing of animals in principle. For example, indigenous peoples in isolated lands would be allowed to hunt animals in order to survive. If a developing country had to choose between putting money into more expensive but more humane agricultural practices and investing in adequate health care or nutrition for human beings, the human beings are privileged. However, the implications of Kant's position here do not contradict animal rights and animal welfare theories. Regan discusses so-called lifeboat scenarios in which the choice is between saving an animal and saving a person, and he argues that the human should be saved in such cases because of the miniride principle: if someone's rights must be harmed, then we must do what we can to minimize the harm. Because opportunities for preference satisfaction are greater for the person than for the animal, the person's death would be a greater *prima facie* loss.[21] Kant reaches the same conclusion. Therefore, by explaining why we should minimize animal suffering based on anthropocentric principles, Kant's views go a long way toward eradicating meat-eating in many developed nations, making the practice more humane in others, and (like Singer and Regan) explaining why it is justified in rare circumstances.

Of course, most of us are unaware of the conditions under which animals are housed and slaughtered. That is why Singer's *Animal Liberation* was and is a life-changing book for many people: it makes them aware of the cost in animal suffering caused by their predilection for meat. However, it also poses a problem for Kant. If we are ignorant of what goes on in factory farms, then our character would not be affected by what happens there. Egonsson says that we would be "accepting" animal cruelty, and in a sense we would be, since we would not be condemning it and our meat purchases would be financing it. However, in another sense, we are not approving it either, because most of us are simply unaware of it or do not think about it. It is a tacit acceptance, but that does not necessarily mean that we embrace it or that this kind of acceptance actually corrupts our character. If we do not consider it at all, then animal cruelty in the meat industry would seem to have no effect on our moral attitudes. Kant's position would seem to imply that ignorance is a good thing in this case, because while we remain ignorant, we can satisfy our desires by using nonrational creatures, and without any negative side effects for us. The more hidden from view animal slaughter is, the better it is in a moral sense. This seems like an odd implication for Kant's position.

There are two different responses that the Kantian vegetarian could make to this line of argument. One response the Kantian could *not* give is to say that it is wrong to remain ignorant of animal suffering, because animal suffering is bad in itself and we ought to become aware of it as a first step in ending a wrong. If, as Kant claims, we have only indirect duties to ourselves through animals, then there is nothing morally objectionable about animal suffering unless it affects our character and, because of that, we treat other rational beings poorly. We have no obligation to become aware of something that is in itself morally neutral.

So, how would remaining ignorant of or unconcerned with animal suffering affect our character in a negative way? First, cultivating this lack of concern with animals whose suffering is not immediately apparent to us may encourage this kind of blindness with regard to the suffering of humans whose plights are not brought to our attention, and this does have an impact on our virtue. Although this psychological connection is not as clear or well documented as the violence graduation hypothesis, not caring about the suffering of nonrational creatures may affect our attitudes toward the suffering of others, especially those who have traditionally been thought to be less than fully rational, such as women and people in the so-called Third World.[22] If we encourage ignorance of animal suffering, then we may also encourage ignorance of human suffering in places such as Africa, which gets relatively little media attention in the West. The latter ignorance is morally blameworthy.

Second, supporting the meat industry financially through one's food dollars also supports jobs for people who kill the animals and whose sensitivity to others' suffering is being coarsened. I have an obligation to improve my own character, but I also have an obligation not to corrupt others. For those who slaughter the animals and those who are aware of animal suffering and do nothing about it, the meat industry is morally dangerous. When I buy meat, I am funding an industry that pays people to, for the most part, disregard animal harm. My direct duty not to further those people's morally inappropriate ends may imply that I have an indirect duty to protect the animals they would kill. Of course, this argument, however plausible, is more tenuous than Kant's earlier claims about our duty not to mistreat animals that we affect directly with our own actions. Still, it shows that Kant is not entirely silent even regarding such recent inventions as factory farms.

Kantians Revising Kant: Wood and Korsgaard

Allen Wood rejects Kant's approach to animal welfare because, he says, it fails to capture "why most of us think we should cherish natural beauty and care about the welfare of other living things" – namely, that nature and animals deserve to be valued for their own sake. Wood also worries that Kant's prohibition on wanton cruelty rests on a contingent premise that, conceivably, could change our obligations depending on what we are like:

> if it happened to be a quirk of human psychology that torturing animals would make us that much kinder toward humans (perhaps by venting our aggressive impulses on helpless victims), then Kant's argument would apparently make it a duty to inflict gratuitous cruelty on puppies and kittens so as to make us that much kinder to people.[23]

To avoid Kant's "repugnant" argument strategy, Wood presents an alternative that is Kantian in spirit but rejects what Wood calls the "personification principle": the idea that every duty must be to a person, because only persons have humanity.[24] Instead, Wood claims we also ought to respect things that are not themselves rational, but that "bear the right relations to rational nature" – that is, things that have "fragments," "necessary conditions," or "the infrastructure, so to speak, of rational nature."[25] Many animals experience pleasure and pain, and such animals have preferences (in some sense) for pleasure over pain. This is part of the "natural teleology" that human beings share with animals. By satisfying the natural desires that we have – the desire for food and drink, the basic will to live – we protect our physical integrity and maintain our existence as rational beings. But that means that the conditions that make possible our rational existence are good. In addition, acting on preferences is part of or similar to what it means to be an end-setter. One pursues what one takes to be good. Such natural purposiveness ought to be advanced in both persons and nonrational things because it is the "infrastructure" of our own rational nature.[26] In short, Wood claims, human beings ought to respect animals that resemble rational beings in the correct, morally relevant way.

Christine Korsgaard also tries to extend Kant's philosophy to justify direct duties to animals, and in a way that goes beyond Wood's position. While Wood thinks that we ought to give animals moral consideration because they have elements or necessary conditions of rationality, Korsgaard claims that animals are valuers in the relevant sense of the term:

> in general, although not infallibly, an animal experiences the satisfaction of its needs and the things that will satisfy them as desirable or pleasant, and assaults on its being as undesirable or unpleasant. These experiences are the basis of its incentives, making its own good the end of its actions. In that sense, an animal is an organic system to whom its own good matters, an organic system that welcomes, desires, enjoys, and pursues its good. We could even say that an animal is an organic system that matters to itself, for it pursues its own good for its own sake. . . . When we say that something is naturally good for an animal, we mean that it is good from its point of view.[27]

Here Korsgaard says that, because animals have a "point of view" on their own well-being, they and human beings value things in a similar way. Although nonhuman animals are not rational, they have a sense of good and bad, and they are capable of pursuing one and avoiding the other on the basis of incentives. Korsgaard even goes so far as to say that "pain [even in animals] is the perception of a *reason*."[28] That is morally relevant. Elsewhere Korsgaard compares animals to what Kant calls "passive citizens," people such as women and children who are not allowed to participate in forming legislation but who nonetheless are protected under the law (MM 314–15).[29] Animals do not give themselves the moral law – they are not self-legislating agents – but they are worthy of moral consideration by those who do. This is so because, as organisms, they maintain themselves in such a way that things can be good or bad with regard to their own teleological development, and they are aware of this. Like Regan, who calls animals "subjects of a life," Korsgaard says that some animals have a "sense of self," or that being an animal is "a way of being someone."[30]

Korsgaard admits that what is good for an animal is not intrinsically good; value depends on our determining that something is valuable. But we do take our continued existence as animal beings to be (conditionally) good. We cannot commit suicide or starve ourselves to death without undermining what we affirm to be good in willing at all – that is, in willing, we take our capacity to will, and our existence as a willing being, to be a good thing. But if we and nonrational animals share this capacity for things to matter to us, then, according to Korsgaard, our affirming the pursuit of natural goods extends both to rational and nonrational beings:

> The strange fate of being an organic system that matters to itself is one that we share with the other animals. In taking ourselves to be ends-in-themselves we *legislate* that the natural good of a creature who matters to itself is the source of normative claims. Animal nature is an end-in-itself, because our own legislation makes it so.[31]

Ironically, Korsgaard accepts Kant's claim that value is the result of our reasoning about what ends we will pursue and deciding what is worthwhile, yet she rejects the argument that, as a condition of all other goods, humanity alone is an end in itself. Instead, she says that valuing the capacity to reason commits us to valuing our natural existence, which is a good thing for us, and that valuing our natural existence commits us to valuing the natural existence of other organisms that, like us, care about their well-being. Korsgaard thus follows Wood by appealing to the fact that an organism's natural development can be thwarted, and by inferring from this a normatively constraining conception of good and bad for the organism itself.

Wood and Korsgaard disagree in some ways. In particular, Wood criticizes Korsgaard for intimating that natural purposiveness is sufficient for something to be a valuer.[32] Wood also does not go so far as to claim that animals are moral subjects or ends in themselves. However, Wood's and Korsgaard's positions overlap on the most important point, namely that the purposiveness of organic beings makes them directly morally considerable.[33] While Korsgaard claims that "life is a form of morality" because striving for some good is a kind of valuing,[34] Wood claims that we ought to promote natural teleology even in nonrational beings because it is part of the "infra-structure" of rational nature:

> If respect for the rational nature served by this natural teleology requires that it not be thwarted or frustrated, then once we are free of the restrictions of the personification principle it seems reasonable to extend this argument and claim that respect for rational nature requires similar constraints regarding the natural teleology in nonrational living things.[35]

The differences between Wood and Korsgaard, then, are not so great. Korsgaard says that an animal *is* a valuer because of inner purposiveness, and Wood says that an animal *is like* a valuer because of inner purposiveness. From the fact that animals have this natural teleology – that things can be good or bad with regard to their preferences, or that things matter to them – both Wood and Korsgaard conclude that animals are deserving of direct moral consideration. Such purposes do not support moral reasoning in nonhuman animals, but for Wood and Korsgaard that is not important. What is important is that, because this natural teleology supports *our* rational nature, it ought to be respected *in general*.

Problems with Wood and Korsgaard

Plants also have the natural teleology to nourish themselves and reproduce, so plants would also seem to be objects of direct moral concern. Korsgaard agrees that things can be good or bad for a plant, although not in as deep a sense as they can be for an animal, since plants do not have a "point of view" on how they are affected. They have no preferences per se. Korsgaard concludes that plants may also have moral standing, but to a lesser degree.[36] If Wood believes that a plant's striving for self-preservation is not robust enough to be considered a "fragment" of rational nature, he does not give any reason for why that is.

By isolating natural teleology as a sufficient condition of moral considerability, Wood and Korsgaard are appealing to the fact that something that develops or lives and grows continues to do so only under certain conditions, and that undermining those conditions thwarts the achievement of its aim. They follow the logic of environmental ethicists who claim that animals, species, and ecosystems have intrinsic value because things can be good or bad for them, given their organization and development. For example, in his defense of biocentrism, Paul Taylor characterizes animals and plants as "teleological centers of life," each with its own point of view: each organism "carr[ies] on its existence in the (not necessarily conscious) pursuit of its good."[37] Holmes Rolston III says that value makes sense with regard to plant activity because of their purposiveness, regardless of the fact that they are not aware of it: "though things do not matter *to* plants, things matter *for* them."[38] Kenneth Goodpaster goes so far as to say that living organisms such as plants have interests – not only things that are good and bad for them, but actual interests, just as human beings have interests – and that this is sufficient for them to be directly morally considerable.[39]

Following this line of thinking, Wood says that we are obligated not to frustrate a thing's "natural teleology," and Korsgaard says that "a living thing is a thing for which the preservation of identity is imperative."[40] Anything that maintains itself is an independent source of value, because things can be good or bad with regard to its own purposive activity. Therefore, animals have preferences and, perhaps, plants have interests, just as human beings have preferences that advance their existence as natural beings. If natural purposiveness is what is morally relevant, then all living organisms are directly morally considerable because things may frustrate or promote their teleological development. Although most environmental ethicists accept this, it takes us a long way from Kant.

Of course, Korsgaard and Wood do not simply reject Kant's ethics in favor of utilitarianism or some opposing theory, as someone such as Singer does. They begin with the very Kantian idea that rational nature must be valued, but they extend that to include animals that are enough like us that they too ought to be part of the moral community. Animals' lives have intrinsic value because they have preferences that they try to satisfy, or because they are aware of how they are affected, negatively or positively. The latter criterion (at least) is not shared by plants. Such characteristics are similar enough to the valuing that we engage in as rational beings, and that makes it a bad thing for animals to suffer, or for their ends to be thwarted. For Wood and Korsgaard, as for Kant, man is the measure of all things: rational beings remain the paradigm case of ends in themselves, and animals only have value "because our own legislation makes it so."[41]

Wood and Korsgaard are Kantians, or at least they try to remain Kantians. However, their attempts to revise Kant jettison something that is central and foundational to Kant's moral theory as a whole – namely, Kant's anthropocentrism. The categorical imperative states that humanity is an end in itself, and Kant defines humanity in terms of the capacity to act autonomously (G 435). Kant strictly contrasts this with natural purposiveness. Being able to act in accordance with principles is what separates rational beings from mere things, including nonrational animals, whose behavior is entirely determined by natural laws (G 412). Jacques Derrida claims that modern philosophy defines what is proper to persons by distinguishing us from animals, by constructing our concept of animals such that they lack the characteristics required for moral consideration.[42] Kant is no exception. Humanity is defined by its ability to free the subject from animal inclinations; our animal nature is a constant threat to what reason requires us to do. The appeal to an organism's natural development, then, is directly opposed to a foundational assumption of Kant's ethics. Wood and Korsgaard claim that animals are directly morally considerable because they are like us, but Kant contends that we are moral agents with dignity precisely because we are *not* like animals. Korsgaard's and Wood's approaches are Kantian only in the very broadest sense: rational autonomy is still the standard for moral considerability. What matters is not that animals suffer (as it does for the utilitarian), but that their activity is enough like rational activity to make them matter. Kant's moral theory, however, is predicated on the idea that being self-motivated is not equivalent to choosing one's ends.

The "infrastructure" or "conditions" of reasoning are not important for their own sake, but as means to the only thing that is an end in itself: our humanity. The natural teleology of human beings is worth promoting because it *does* in fact support our capacity to be entirely motivated by rational constraints. For example, Kant says that we have a natural desire for food and drink, and that this natural desire should not be abused, either by depriving ourselves or by indulging too much, *because* doing so would impair our rational faculties (MM 427). Eating and drinking are not good simply because we are naturally inclined to them, but because they support our capacity to reason. Reason is what makes us capable of acting autonomously, and it is that by virtue of which we have dignity (G 435–6). Where the capacity to act for the sake of duty is absent – in cows, clams, and ferns – there is no morally relevant value.

Kant's Response to Wolff: The Difference between Animal Choice and Moral Agency

It should be noted that Kant is not oversimplifying what it is for animals to act, as if they are wholly determined by fight-or-flight reflex. Kant rejects Descartes's assertion that animals are mere machines, and he grants that they act on the basis of representations of the world (Ak 2:60; LM 28:449, 690; CJ 464n). Kant even says that animals share with us a capacity to choose (LE 344; MM 442; Ak 28:117). But animal choice is very different from rational self-determination. Indeed, Kant claims that our difference from animals is what distinguishes us, makes us moral agents, and gives us our dignity. Without delving too deeply into Kant's philosophical predecessors, it is instructive to explain Kant's own theory of freedom as he contrasts it with the work of Christian Wolff, for Kant's response to Wolff clarifies how Kant conceives of and values so-called "animal choice."

Following G. W. Leibniz, Wolff claims that the soul possesses the power of forming representations, which facilitate its knowledge and move it to action. What determines the soul is its desire for perfection, which Wolff defines as the ability of some combination of parts to work toward a unified purpose – for example, the parts of an eye functioning to achieve faultless vision. Through God, the most perfect being, all things in the world have some degree of perfection, and the soul perceives it either confusedly through sensuous desires or clearly through higher desires. Because the soul necessarily strives to realize the greatest degree of perfection, its representation of perfection is both the cause and motive of the will. The soul is formally self-determined through its own representations of the world, and the content of its rational choices is determined by the perfection of things in the world. For example, we form an opinion about how perfect vision is achieved, and based on that opinion we are compelled to try to accomplish that end. In other words, while the decision to maximize perfection comes from individual agents and their interpretation of what is given to them, the ends that they pursue are given from without. What makes vision faultless depends on the natural properties of things. The structure of being necessitates us to act in certain ways given the nature of the rational soul.[43]

Wolff's account of human freedom sounds a lot like Wood's and Korsgaard's descriptions of animal activity. According to Wood, natural teleology is an inner principle that motivates animals to achieve what they take to be good (or more perfect, to use Wolff's terminology). An animal tries to satisfy its preferences in order to thrive. Similarly, Korsgaard claims that "experiences are the basis of [an animal's] incentives" – she could have easily have said "representations" instead of "experiences" – and that the animal "pursues its good" in response to those experiences.[44] Like human beings, animals evaluate the world and act on the basis of those evaluations, even if, unlike human beings, animals are necessitated by their biological drives. Kant concedes that this is a kind of choice because an animal's behavior is not random and it is determined by the animal's own biological drives, based on its representations, rather than by external causes. In fact, he says that, like all living things, animals have "a faculty for practicing actions in conformity with one's representations" (LM 28:594). Animals are end-directed, just as human beings are.

Although the Wolffian agent chooses, the agent is constrained by a material end (perfection) that is given to the will rather than being self-legislated. Kant gives two reasons why such an approach to agency precludes the possibility of moral activity. First, the action is traceable to the agent's inner life, but the agent is not responsible in the sense that he could have done otherwise. An animal's action is biologically determined by instinct in conjunction with what is presented to the animal in experience: "This choice is not free, but necessitated by incentives and *stimuli*" (LE 344; see also LM 28:594). Moral agency is different. A person's action results from reasoning about what ought to be done and setting his end, sometimes contrary to his inclinations or natural teleology. As Kant phrases it, stimuli have "necessitating power" with animals, but with human beings they have only "impelling power" (LM 28:255).

The second reason why the Wolffian agent is incapable of morality is because the agent's choice results from the nature of the soul, so his behavior is governed by "rules that are subjectively necessitated" (LE 344). The agent's pursuit of perfection depends on how his soul is constituted as an empirical fact, but natural laws are not strictly necessary, even if they do apply to all actual agents. As Kant demonstrates in the *Groundwork of the Metaphysics of Morals*, only an objective moral law, which constrains rational beings as such, is suited to be the supreme principle of morality (G 408). The appeal to perfection can only give us a hypothetical imperative: *if* one wills perfection, *then* one ought to act in a certain way. By contrast, the moral law constrains rational beings as a categorical imperative, necessarily and universally. The good will gives itself a formal constraint – that maxims be universalizable – rather than being heteronomously conditioned by the nature of the soul or by biological drives (G 443–4).

Kant calls the Wolffian subject an "*automaton . . . spirituale*" that is "driven by representations," and he characterizes this kind of freedom as predetermined spontaneity, "the freedom of a turnspit" (CPrR 97; see also Ak 17:313–14 [R 3855]). A being who attempts to maximize perfection has the capacity for choice (*Willkür*), because it discriminates among possible ends and acts based on its preferences. However, such a being has only what Kant calls "*arbitrium brutum*" or "animal choice" (MM 213; CPR A534/B562; LM 28:254–6). When a representation exerts a pull on an animal so that it is moved to act for the sake of that end, the animal acts on the basis of what it represents to be best: whatever preserves itself, the species, or its capacity to enjoy life (MM 420). The animal is "pathologically necessitated" by such given, natural ends and is unable to act otherwise than to pursue these ends, just as the Wolffian rational agent is necessitated by the desire for perfection (CPR A534/B562; see also LE 266–7).

Although animals choose to act based on their representation of and desire for given ends, rational beings are capable of *free* choice (*"arbitrium liberum"*) because they can determine their actions based on what their own reason requires of them, "independently of necessitation by sensible impulses." Kantian agents are "pathologically affected," in that they want things that they desire (such as happiness and perfection), but they are able to be motivated purely by duty (CPR A534/B562; LM 28:254–6). To the extent that rational beings can act in accordance with principles, they have wills (*Wille*) in addition to the power of choice (*Willkür*) (G 412).

Wood and Korsgaard imply that animals value things in a way that is morally relevant, because it makes them enough like human agents that they ought to be directly morally considerable. But for Kant, the capacity to represent the world and to act on the basis of those representations is not equivalent to reflecting on those representations and determining what one ought to do on the basis of rational principles. Kant concludes that animal instinct is not merely a lesser degree of reason, as Korsgaard and Wood seem to imply, but is qualitatively distinct from moral judgment (Ak 2:60; LM 28:594, 689–90). Humans and animals are different in kind.

Kant grants that animals have a mental life and that at least some animals are capable of a kind of choice. They represent the world to themselves and pursue what is taken to advance their preferences. Korsgaard is right to say that this amounts to a kind of valuing. But like the Wolffian agent, animals evaluate possible actions against a given end or set of ends and perform the actions that are necessary given their empirical makeup, or their natural teleology. By contrast, rational beings act on principles that are freely chosen, independently of determination by natural law. This distinguishes the humanity in persons and makes them worthy of moral respect. Kant concludes that "if all creatures had [only animal] choice, tied to sensory drives, the world would have no value" (LE 344). This conclusion is not simply the result of a bias in favor of human beings, a "personification principle" that can be discarded, but is rather a reflection on the morally salient differences between rational beings and animals.

Evaluating Pain and Pleasure

Both human beings and some animals have the capacity for feeling pleasure and pain, and this is very relevant to understanding our indirect duties regarding animals. It is precisely because of their similarity to us in this respect that indiscriminately harming animals would retard our empathy for others' pain. It would corrupt our character. However, we must be careful here not to make an unjustified logical move – an amphiboly – and say that pain is somehow wrong in itself, and that we have a duty to minimize animals' pain for its own sake. Richard Dean takes Kant in this direction: because we view our own pain as something to be avoided, and because we empathize with nonhuman animals that are also capable of pain, "it seems almost irrational to be aware in this way of the extreme similarity between different beings' pain and not regard the pains in a similar way."[45] The problem with this view is that, although the pains are similar, that pain is bad *in a moral sense* does not follow simply from the fact that it is unpleasant to a sentient being. Whether pain is bad depends on its relation to our moral capacities, and particularly whether the pain undermines our ability freely to do what is right. Of course, there may be other reasons to minimize animal pain. For example, we may not like the idea of animals being in pain unnecessarily; we may feel for them, and we may feel happier when they are protected. But this is merely a preference. If this were the only consideration and our awareness of animal pain had no impact on our character, then the mere fact of their being in pain would be morally insignificant.

For Kant, we have dignity because of our autonomy, not because we are sentient or have the capacity for preferences. As James Skidmore points out, there are a number of conditions of autonomy for us, including the ability to digest food,[46] but no one would claim that an elaborate machine whose sole function is to break down food and use its nutrients is for that reason worthy of respect. In addition, there are plenty of things that make it possible for us to exist as rational beings, but are not necessary for rational nature in general. God is perfectly rational and has a holy will that is necessarily in conformity with the moral law, but without a body God has no sense of pleasure and pain – that is, God is not like humans and other vertebrates in that God is not sentient. If there is such a thing as a divine preference, it is much different from any kind of desire satisfaction had by humans and animals. In what sense, then, are these things some of the "necessary conditions" of rational nature, rather than part of a human nature that also happens to be rational? This gets to the crux of the issue for Wood's interpretation. The ability to digest food *is* necessary for us to exist as rational beings, yet it is *not* part of the "infrastructure" of rational nature. Sentience is *not* a necessary condition of rational nature, yet Wood says that it *is* in the right relation to rational nature (only in us?). By trying to expand the value of rational autonomy to include the "fragments" of rational nature, Wood gives us no clear criteria by which to distinguish beings who are directly morally considerable from those who are not.

Kant agrees with Wood that nonrational animals are like human beings in certain ways; he says that "animals are an analogue [*Analogon*] of humanity" (LE 459). It is precisely because they are like us – dogs have a sense of loyalty, chickens are aware of pain and pleasure – that our treatment of them has an impact on our character, and thus we have indirect duties not to abuse them. But to say that we have direct duties to nonhuman animals is, as Kant himself says, to commit a logical mistake.

Animal nature is valued by human beings because it supports our capacity to set and pursue ends, not because it has an inner purposiveness. Appealing to natural teleology alone commits the naturalistic fallacy: because something is natural, it is therefore good. Kant himself avoids this error by claiming that desires, even natural desires,[47] are only conditionally good. In fact, the goodness of any of the ends that we or other organisms pursue depends on the presence of a good will (G 393–4). Only a good will has absolute worth and is the proper object of morality; acting for the sake of duty constrains the agent on the basis of reasons rather than what is given by the inclinations. Korsgaard makes much of the fact that animals act on the basis of "incentives," but for Kant it is the ability to be motivated purely by a concern for duty, to have a particular *kind* of incentive – a pure incentive – that gives people dignity.[48] We do not deserve direct moral consideration because we can be motivated, but because we can be motivated *in the right way*.

This is why we have a duty of beneficence to other rational agents. We ought to help people to achieve their goals provided that they are acting in ways that are morally appropriate. However, animals do not hold themselves to the moral law. To treat animals as ends in themselves, as Korsgaard instructs us to, would mean that we must advance their ends, but because such ends are "pursued by animals heteronomously, pathologically, and reactively . . . that would make our actions heteronomously motivated."[49] In short, we cannot be morally bound by the ends that are set by nature. Kant demonstrates as much in the *Groundwork*. Such ends are conditionally good depending on what reason requires, which means that we only have indirect duties regarding animals depending on how our treatment of them affects us.

Wood and Korsgaard attempt to remain in the spirit of Kantianism, but end up advancing inadequate positions that contradict the basic tenets of Kant's moral philosophy. The question then arises as to why they find it necessary to devise new arguments that diverge from Kant's own avowed position – by rejecting the personification principle, for example – given that Kant endorses many of the most important policies of animal rights and animal welfare philosophies. Kant's ethics prohibits wanton cruelty toward animals, strictly limits animal experimentation, and, arguably, obligates us to become vegetarians. Why extend direct moral consideration beyond those with the capacity to set and pursue ends (humanity) to animals that have "fragments" of rational nature or animals for which their "own good matters"?

Kant's Practical Appeal

Wood and Korsgaard believe that there must be some value to animals apart from how their treatment affects humans, such that we have direct duties to advance their welfare. The idea that there must be something intrinsically wrong with harming animals is, according to many theorists, simply common sense, and if Kant cannot accommodate this, then so much the worse for his moral theory.[50] As mentioned earlier, Wood imagines a hypothetical case in which a person's character is not adversely affected by animal cruelty.[51] Alexander Broadie and Elizabeth Pybus complain that indirect duties regarding animals apply only to human beings (with our particular psychological associations) rather than to rational beings as such, so animal cruelty may be acceptable for rational beings who are not constituted as we are.[52] All of these critics of Kant are objecting to the fact that his prohibition on animal cruelty rests on what Martha Nussbaum calls "fragile empirical claims about psychology": Kant's assertion that not caring about animals' well-being tends to make us callous toward other persons.[53] Purposely harming animals would be acceptable to Kant if we or other rational beings were not affected by it – if, for example, someone could be kind to other persons while burning stray dogs to death in his spare time.[54]

Although it is true that people who are radically different psychologically would not have duties to animals, it is unclear how this is an objection to Kant's position, given the fact that it *is* the case that unnecessarily harming animals corrupts us morally. Many things would have to be different for our indirect duties regarding animals to change: our bodies and behavior and other animals' bodies and behavior would have to be dramatically dissimilar (that is, there would have to be no analogy between humans and animals), our constitution would have to be such that we fail to identify or sympathize with animals, our character would have to be unaffected or improved by their suffering, and so on. Although the categorical imperative is discovered *a priori*, Kant is explicit in claiming that the particular duties that follow from it depend on our physical nature, our psychology, and our social circumstances (G 388–9, 410–12; MM 214–18). And empirical data supports Kant's claim that mistreating animals affects how we treat other human beings.[55] Complaining that, on Kant's view, our duties to animals rest on a contingent psychological premise is like complaining that, if people did not mind being punched and shoved to the ground, then Kant would approve of assault and battery. This is not the case, so it is irrelevant.

Nearly every moral theory depends on empirical and psychological facts to justify its condemnation of animal cruelty: utilitarianism would permit torturing animals for fun if animals felt pain less acutely and if it did not influence us to harm others, virtue ethics would condone it if it made us more charitable and benevolent people, etc. It is hardly an objection to any ethical theory that it cannot make some action wrong in every possible world, under any possible circumstances, and with every conceivable agent. Presumably, claiming (against Kant) that animals should be directly considered is meant to make sure that animals are considered even when our moral character is not affected. But if it is affected, whether we are inflicting cruelty on animals or simply allowing it to happen, then we have a number of obligations to animals that involve dramatically reforming our current behavior. We are just as obligated by indirect duties as we are by direct duties. Therefore, Kant's appeal to indirect duties has no adverse practical implications for how we treat nonrational animals.[56]

Of course, this response does miss the point a bit. Presumably, those objecting to Kant are claiming that, even if Kant arrives at the same conclusions as those who defend animal welfare, he is doing so for the wrong reasons. Kant's position lacks what J. Baird Callicott calls "moral truth," because it does not base its moral judgments on the intrinsic value of non-humans.[57] The rights of animals and the satisfaction of their preferences should matter for their own sake. If this is true, then Kant's anthropocentrism is inadequate.

Kant's position is defensible. It is based on a particular conception of value, and the fact that we are the sorts of beings who set our own ends. The capacity to do so has absolute value, because it is a condition of anything being (taken to be) good for us. This is not some nonsensical prejudice. Rather than argue with Singer and Callicott about the merits of anthropocentrism and what makes someone or something morally considerable, however, it is sufficient for our purposes to emphasize that there are many points of convergence between Kant and animal welfare theorists when it comes to policy and personal behavior. Instead of rejecting Kantianism out of hand, defenders of animal welfare ought to look to Kant as a strategic ally. The main reason is that Kant's and similar anthropocentric views have been more influential in Western legal and moral thinking than those that refer to animals' intrinsic, non-instrumental value.

Historically, most jurisdictions have appealed to human interests to justify anti-cruelty laws, and they have treated animals as property rather than as things that are directly morally considerable. In Great Britain and the United States, animal cruelty legislation was first passed in the 1800s, and the stated reason for it was because of the morally corrupting influence that animal cruelty has on human decency, for those who harm animals and those who witness it.[58] In some cases this was stated explicitly in the statutes, and in others it was affirmed by the courts. For example, in one of the famous Stage Coach Cases involving Henry Bergh, founding president of the American Society for the Prevention of Cruelty to Animals (ASPCA), the court concluded:

> This kind of legislation . . . truly has its origin in the intent to save a just standard of humane feeling from being debased by pernicious effects of bad example – the human heart from being hardened by public and frequent exhibitions of cruelty to dumb creatures, committed to the care and which were created for the beneficial use of man.[59]

Note the biblical reference, used by Kant as well (CB 114), that animals are given by God for us to use. Because of the anthropocentric assumptions here, the mere killing of an animal was not punishable unless it was in conjunction with cruel treatment. While previous legislation had only protected animals as people's property that should not be damaged, new laws in the 1800s were thought to be a great advance in that animals' suffering was morally important – but again, only indirectly, because of how it affects our character. This kind of reasoning remains the dominant justification for anti-cruelty laws in the United States. In her wide-ranging survey of such laws, Margit Livingston concludes that "the 'equality' view" – that is, the view that animal interests are, like human interests, important in themselves – "arguably has had little effect on laws relating to animals," and that this view "finds only limited acceptance in our culture and laws."[60] Despite appeals to common sense by those who defend animal welfare and animal rights, the idea that animals are morally considerable in themselves is largely absent from Western philosophical, religious, and legal thought. We tend to talk about how causing animal suffering or allowing it to continue affects human psychology – noting, for example, that serial killers often begin by torturing animals,[61] or that people who abuse their pets tend also to abuse children and spouses. The latter concern has prompted many U.S. states to enforce animal cruelty laws more strictly in an effort to prevent domestic violence.[62]

The moral privileging of humanity, or at least a focus on the interests and rights of persons, is a common assumption underlying most people's ethical reasoning. Mary Warnock reports that, despite the many disagreements among the members of her commission on embryo research, they all accepted anthropocentrism, and in fact rejected the claim that it is merely an unjustified prejudice: "We all believed, on that contrary, that it would require justification *not* to prefer one's own species to another. Those who thought that an argument was needed to explain why they would save a human rather than a dog or a fly would themselves be guilty of prejudice."[63] Other philosophers have claimed that moral reasoning only makes sense within accepted value paradigms, including the anthropocentric paradigm. Whether anthropocentrism can be justified is secondary, because moral reasoning takes place within the system of valuing according to which humanity is privileged.[64] This is why it sounds so intuitive to talk about humans versus animals rather than human animals versus nonhuman animals. In our language, there is a deep distinction in value that is made clear when people are considered different in kind from animals. According to Richard Posner, pro-animal arguments, especially utilitarian arguments, seem "bizarre" within the linguistic conventions and conceptual paradigms that form the starting point for moral reasoning.[65]

Such conventions and paradigms should be critically scrutinized. Not doing so would imply our blind acceptance of the status quo, an embrace of relativism, and a refusal to reason our way to more morally justifiable beliefs.[66] But the fact that people *do* think this way, as a matter of convention or something else, poses a question of strategy that is not simply theoretical. Given many people's latent or explicit anthropocentrism – how else could people think that the mass slaughter of chickens, pigs, and cows is justified simply to satisfy our taste? – the more reasonable response by animal welfare theorists would not be to reject Kant's position (as Singer and Regan do) or to revise it (as Wood and Korsgaard do), but to adopt it when necessary as a coherent argument strategy that makes a convincing case for why our current policies toward animals ought to be reevaluated. In other words, those who are concerned about animal welfare should draw on our existing values in order to justify the more humane treatment of animals. In a culture that still largely tolerates unnecessary animal testing, abominable conditions in factory farms, and the deaths of billions of animals every year for food, the anthropocentric argument is more likely to carry moral weight. Whether Kant is in fact right or wrong – and, as I said, there are strong reasons behind his anthropocentrism – his assumptions are our assumptions. Bringing Kant into the conversation as a defender of animal welfare has the potential to improve our attitudes and behavior toward animals in morally significant ways.

Final Thoughts for the Nonanthropocentrist

Of course, the debate over whether we have direct duties to animals should continue, as should the debate as to whether Kant's approach is more effective in changing our behavior. One could argue, for example, that Kant's basic anthropocentric assumptions overshadow the animal-friendly implications of his position. If we emphasize that rationality belongs only to human beings and that this is the basis of direct moral considerability, it may make our awareness of the analogy between animals and humans less likely, and it may undermine the recognition of how our treatment of animals affects us. Perhaps the analogy between rational beings and animals is submerged under Kant's logocentrism, leaving us only with the idea that the crucial differences between us and them give us "dominion over nature." In this case, Kant's philosophy would not be practically useful in advancing the aims of animal welfare.

This is a psychological thesis that needs as much empirical support as the purported link between animal cruelty and human cruelty. But it is important to recognize that such a debate over Kant's usefulness occurs *within* the field of animal welfare ethics. We should evaluate the truth and the practical value of Kant's ethics, but the fact that Kant is an anthropocentrist does not by itself imply that his views are contrary to the values and aims of animal welfare theory, or that Kant has nothing to contribute to debates over environmental policy.

In environmental ethics generally, anthropocentrism is often used as a kind of slur, similar to racism or sexism. As we have seen, however, Kant's anthropocentrism is not some baseless prejudice, but is actually backed up by a sophisticated value theory. There are good reasons to be an anthropocentrist, at least in one's moral foundations. And if we look closely at Kant's own applications of his theory, we can see that this sort of foundational anthropocentrism does not disregard the suffering of nonhuman animals. In fact, Kant's ethics can be a solid and politically effective basis for advancing their interests.

Notes

1   Christine Korsgaard, *The Sources of Normativity* (Cambridge: Cambridge University Press, 1996), 49–130.

2   Frans de Waal, *Good Natured: The Origins of Right and Wrong in Humans and Other Animals* (Cambridge, Mass.: Harvard University Press, 1996), 209. Some recent books on animal behavior attempt to blur the line between humans and nonhuman animals when it comes to morality. They claim that all of us, humans and animals alike, feel empathy for others, engage in cooperative relationships, and have a commitment to justice, in the sense that we are expected to adhere to social expectations or else risk punishment, usually ostracism from the group. See especially Marc Bekoff, *The Emotional Lives of Animals: A Leading Scientist Explores Animal Joy, Sorrow, and Empathy – and Why They Matter* (Novato, Calif.: New World Library, 2007), and Marc Bekoff and Jessica Pierce, *Wild Justice: The Moral Lives of Animals* (Chicago: University of Chicago Press, 2009). Like de Waal, however, these authors distinguish between morality (or "prosocial" behavior) and ethics. Morality is the

set of rules that govern social cooperation and is synonymous with culturally relative, or "species-relative," customs and manners. For Kant, such rule-following is not what it means to engage in practical reasoning. The categorical imperative is not a social norm, but a self-legislated constraint on the maxims that we choose to adopt. Research into animal cognition and behavior does not support the idea that nonhuman animals engage in such reasoning or are responsible in the requisite sense. Peter Carruthers has emphasized this distinction, arguing that animals are incapable of the long-term planning, representation of different possible futures, and conceptualization of social rules that are requisite for rational agency (*The Animals Issue: Moral Theory in Practice* [Cambridge: Cambridge University Press, 1992], 122–45). For a different view of animals, one that attributes reflection and deliberation, even a degree of autonomy, to some higher animals, see David DeGrazia, *Taking Animals Seriously: Mental Life and Moral Status* (Cambridge: Cambridge University Press, 1996), esp. 166–210.

3 Christina Hoff calls this the "patient–agent parity thesis." See Hoff, "Kant's Invidious Humanism," *Environmental Ethics* 5, no. 1 (1983): 63–70. For a fuller treatment of the implications of this view, see chapter 10.

4 Stephen M. Wise, *Rattling the Cage: Toward Legal Rights for Animals* (Cambridge, Mass.: Perseus, 2000), 179–237.

5 It is common for critics of Kant's ethics to confuse the ability to think with the ability to decide what to do – that is, to confuse rudimentary problem-solving with engaging in practical reasoning. For example, see Christina Hoff, "Immoral and Moral Uses of Animals," *New England Journal of Medicine* 302, no. 2 (10 Jan. 1980): 115–18 (p. 115).

6 Christina Hoff and David DeGrazia both overlook this argument in support of the categorical imperative's formula of humanity. They think that human dignity is merely asserted, that Kant puts forward as an axiom the idea that rational beings are ends in themselves, in contrast to animals. See Hoff, "Kant's Invidious Humanism," 66, and DeGrazia, *Taking Animals Seriously*, 67–8. However, Kant justifies his position by appealing to a particular conception of value and the idea that human beings have incomparable worth because they set their ends. There is an argument here.

7 Allen W. Wood, "Kant on Duties Regarding Nonrational Nature," *Proceedings of the Aristotelian Society for the Systematic Study of Philosophy*, supplement 72 (1998): 189–210 (p. 189).

8 The label was coined by Arnold Arluke, Jack Levin, Carter Luke, and Frank Ascione in "The Relationship of Animal Abuse to Violence and Other Forms of Antisocial Behavior," *Journal of Interpersonal Violence* 14, no. 9 (Sept. 1999): 963–75.

9 The cruel treatment of animals corrupts us because animals are like us in certain important ways – animals are sentient, we are capable of feeling sympathy for them, etc. – not because they have intrinsic value. If we come to ignore the cries and protests of an animal, we are more likely to ignore the cries and protests of a person. Thus Kant has an answer for Mary Anne Warren, who poses what is supposed to be a rhetorical question: "if there were nothing inherently wrong with needlessly harming animals, then why would we expect

it to damage the agent's moral character?" ("Moral Status," in *A Companion to Applied Ethics*, ed. R. G. Frey and Christopher Heath Wellman [Oxford: Blackwell, 2003], 439–50 [p. 440]).

10   There is overwhelming evidence that animal cruelty is *linked* to other forms of interpersonal violence, especially domestic violence. Children who abuse pets are much more likely to begin other abusive behaviors as they grow older. See Kimberly D. Becker et al., "A Study of Firesetting and Animal Cruelty in Children: Family Influences and Adolescent Outcomes," *Journal of the American Academy of Child and Adolescent Psychiatry* 43, no. 7 (July 2004): 905–12, and Benita J. Walton-Moss et al., "Risk Factors for Intimate Partner Violence and Associated Injury Among Urban Women," *Journal of Community Health* 30, no. 5 (Oct. 2005): 377–89.

Although some psychologists claim that cruelty to animals is merely symptomatic of a preexisting disposition to violence, a number of compelling psychological studies support the claim that engaging in animal cruelty actually *causes* people to be more violent toward other people. See especially Alan R. Felthous and Stephen R. Kellert, "Violence against Animals and People: Is Aggression against Living Creatures Generalized?" *Bulletin of the American Academy of Psychiatry and the Law* 14, no. 1 (1986): 55–69; Randall Lockwood and Frank R. Ascione, eds., *Cruelty to Animals and Interpersonal Violence: Readings in Research and Application* (West Lafayette, Ind.: Purdue University Press, 1998); Kathleen M. Heide, *Animal Cruelty: Pathway to Violence against People* (Lanham, Md.: AltaMira, 2003); Suzanne E. Tallichet and Christopher Hensley, "Exploring the Link between Recurrent Acts of Childhood and Adolescent Animal Cruelty and Subsequent Violent Crime," *Criminal Justice Review* 29, no. 2 (2004): 304–16; and Frank R. Ascione, *Children and Animals: Exploring the Roots of Kindness and Cruelty* (West Lafayette, Ind.: Purdue University Press, 2005).

Some researchers have challenged the contention that torturing animals leads to other kinds of violence. They claim that children tend to grow out of such violent behavior when they develop impulse control and a greater capacity to empathize with others. For example, see C. E. Climent, M. S. Hyg, and M. D. Ervin, "Historical Data in the Evaluation of Violent Subjects," *Archives of General Psychiatry* 27 (1972): 621–4; R. Langevin et al., "Childhood and Family Background of Killers Seen for Psychiatric Assessment: A Controlled Study," *Bulletin of the American Academy of Psychiatry and the Law* 11, no. 4 (1983): 331–41; and Suzanne R. Goodney Lea, *Delinquency and Animal Cruelty: Myths and Realities about Social Pathology* (El Paso, Tex.: LFB Scholarly Publishing, 2007).

Although the evidence does not conclusively establish a causal link between animal cruelty and interpersonal violence, such a link is widely accepted in the psychiatric community. For a consideration of the different methodologies that may account for the divergent findings, as well as references to other studies, see Alan R. Felthous and Stephen R. Kellert, "Childhood Cruelty to Animals and Later Aggression against People: A Review," *American Journal of Psychiatry* 144, no. 6 (June 1987): 710–17, and Catherine Miller, "Childhood Animal

Cruelty and Interpersonal Violence," *Clinical Psychology Review* 21, no. 5 (July 2001): 735–49.

11   Barbara Herman, *Moral Literacy* (Cambridge, Mass.: Harvard University Press, 2007), 272.

12   There is some debate over whether we have indirect duties to animals because of our duties to ourselves or because of our duties to other people. Lara Denis believes that there are two kinds of indirect duties at work: *"perfect duties to ourselves as animal and moral beings,"* because we should maintain our natural "susceptibility to love and sympathy"; and *"imperfect duties to others* (i.e., *duties of love*) or . . . *imperfect duties to oneself,"* because we should foster "dispositions that help us practically express morally required appreciation and concern for others" and should also perfect ourselves, particularly our moral dispositions ("Kant's Conception of Duties Regarding Animals: Reconstruction and Reconsideration," *History of Philosophy Quarterly* 17, no. 1 [2000]: 405–23 [pp. 408–9]). By contrast, Barbara Herman and Paul Guyer claim that all of our duties regarding nonrational things (animals, nature, etc.) are imperfect duties to oneself. See Herman, *Moral Literacy*, 271–2, and Guyer, *Kant and the Experience of Freedom* (Cambridge: Cambridge University Press, 1993), 318–30, 373–82. It would go beyond the scope of this chapter to sort this out, although Kant's claims at LE 710 and MM 443 seem to support Herman's and Guyer's view. That is the position I adopt here.

13   Kant focuses on amphibolies in which two divergent terms are thought to be equivalent. In the *Critique of Pure Reason*, Kant identifies amphibolies in which we confuse an empirical claim with a transcendental claim, or in which a concept of reflection is misapplied either to sensibility or to the understanding (CPR A260/B316–A268/B324).

14   See also CPrR 160 and LE 459, where Kant praises G. W. Leibniz for sparing an insect and returning it to its leaf after examining it under a microscope.

15   "If one, or even a dozen animals had to suffer experiments in order to save thousands, I would think it right and in accordance with equal consideration of interests that they should do so. This, at any rate, is the answer a utilitarian must give" (Peter Singer, *Practical Ethics*, 2nd edn. [Cambridge: Cambridge University Press, 1993], 67). See also Peter Singer, *Animal Liberation*, rev. edn. (New York: HarperPerennial, 2002), 85.

16   In the *Moralphilosophie Collins*, Kant makes it clear that there is no absolute prohibition on our use of animals in experiments, because only rational beings must always be treated as ends: "So when anatomists take living animals to experiment on, that is certainly cruelty, though there it is employed for a good purpose; because animals are regarded as man's instruments, it is acceptable . . . " (LE 460). We may test on animals, but our use of them is limited by what is necessary to promote the "good purpose" of advancing human well-being. In the *Metaphysics of Morals*, Kant seems to restrict what could be considered to be a *good* purpose.

17   For example, see Jean Swingle Greek and C. Ray Greek, *What Will We Do If We Don't Experiment on Animals? Medical Research for the Twenty-First Century* (Victoria, B.C.: Trafford, 2006), and the various publications available

at the Center for Alternatives to Animal Testing at Johns Hopkins University (caat.jhsph.edu).

18   Dan Egonsson, "Kant's Vegetarianism," *Journal of Value Inquiry* 31, no. 4 (Dec. 1997): 473–83 (p. 477). This echoes Ralph Waldo Emerson's condemnation of meat-eating: "You have just dined, and however scrupulously the slaughterhouse is concealed in the graceful distance of miles, there is complicity" (*The Conduct of Life*, vol. 4 of *The Collected Works of Ralph Waldo Emerson*, ed. Alfred R. Ferguson [Cambridge, Mass.: Belknap, 2003], 4).

19   There is some empirical evidence for this claim. See Temple Grandin, "Behavior of Slaughter Plant and Auction Employees toward the Animals," *Anthrozoos* 1, no. 4 (1988): 205–13, and Amy J. Fitzgerald, Linda Kalof, and Thomas Dietz, "Slaughterhouses and Increased Crime Rates: An Empirical Analysis of the Spillover from 'The Jungle' into the Surrounding Community," *Organization and Environment* 22, no. 2 (June 2009): 158–84. See also James Serpell, *In the Company of Animals: A Study of Human–Animal Relationships*, rev. edn. (Cambridge: Cambridge University Press, 1996).

20   R. M. Hare claims that "responsible" meat-eating, where animals are subject to more humane forms of animal agriculture such as biodynamic ranching and free-range practices, would actually decrease the aggregate animal pain more than calls for complete abstinence ("Why I Am Only a Demi-Vegetarian," in *Singer and His Critics*, ed. Dale Jamieson [Oxford: Blackwell, 1999], 233–46). Singer responds that this kind of farming would continue to encourage attitudes toward animals that lead to their widespread mistreatment. With no principled objection to killing animals, including animals that are capable of forming desires for the future, we would be less vigilant, such that abusive practices would reemerge (Peter Singer, "A Response," in *Singer and His Critics*, 325–7). See also Singer, *Animal Liberation*, 229, and Singer, *Practical Ethics*, 134.

21   Tom Regan, *The Case for Animal Rights* (Berkeley: University of California Press, 1983), 324–5.

22   In chapter 7, I will address Kant's complicity in this tradition.

23   Wood, "Kant on Duties Regarding Nonrational Nature," 194–5. See also Mary Midgley, *Animals and Why They Matter* (Athens, Ga.: University of Georgia Press, 1983), 52.

24   Wood, "Kant on Duties Regarding Nonrational Nature," 196.

25   Ibid., 197, 198, 200. See also Allen W. Wood, *Kantian Ethics* (Cambridge: Cambridge University Press, 2008), 101–5.

26   Wood, "Kant on Duties Regarding Nonrational Nature," 201, and Wood, *Kantian Ethics*, 102.

27   Christine M. Korsgaard, "Fellow Creatures: Kantian Ethics and Our Duties to Animals," *Tanner Lectures on Human Values* 24 (2004): 79–110 (pp. 103–4). See also Korsgaard, *Sources of Normativity*, 152–60. The Neo-Friesian Leonard Nelson defended a similar interpretation of Kant many years before Korsgaard did. Nelson claimed that all beings with interests are persons and that all persons have rights that ought to be respected. Because nonhuman animals have interests, they also have rights. Therefore, we have direct duties to both

humans and animals. Whenever animal interests are in conflict with human interests, we ought to weigh the interests themselves against one another. The kind of being that has the interests, whether human or animal, is irrelevant. This is very similar to what Korsgaard argues, although Nelson goes beyond saying that animals are valuers to claim that animals are in fact full-fledged persons with dignity. See Leonard Nelson, *System of Ethics*, trans. Norbert Guterman (New Haven, Conn.: Yale University Press, 1956), 97–8, 136–44. The problem is that Kant does not value acting on interests, but the ability to choose among competing interests and the ability to be motivated by a pure interest of reason.

28   Korsgaard, *Sources of Normativity*, 149; emphasis added.

29   Korsgaard, "Fellow Creatures," 96. I discuss Kant's views on women and children in chapters 7 and 10, respectively.

30   Regan, *Case for Animal Rights*, 243–8; Korsgaard, "Fellow Creatures," 103; and Korsgaard, *Sources of Normativity*, 156. There are many similarities between the views of Regan and Korsgaard. Like Korsgaard, Regan refers to the fact that things can be good or bad for (some) animals, and he claims that they are valuers with both self-consciousness and the ability to act on their preferences: "like relevantly similar humans, animals have a life of their own that fares better or worse for them, logically independently of their utility for others. . . . Moreover, while it is admittedly true that animals lack the kind of autonomy required for moral agency, it is false that they lack autonomy in any sense. For animals not only have preferences, they can also act, on their own, to satisfy these preferences" (Regan, *Case for Animal Rights*, 178, 182). Being self-motivated in one's actions, however, is not what is morally relevant for Kant. The agent must be able to be motivated in the right way.

31   Korsgaard, "Fellow Creatures," 105–6.

32   Wood, "Kant on Duties Regarding Nonrational Nature," 209n11.

33   J. Baird Callicott notes that this extension of moral considerability beyond rational beings to all conative beings appears in the work of Arthur Schopenhauer, who (like Wood and Korsgaard) took himself to be properly interpreting Kant's philosophy (*In Defense of the Land Ethic: Essays in Environmental Philosophy* [Albany: State University of New York Press, 1989], 144). Schopenhauer claims that humans, animals, and indeed all natural things are phenomenal manifestations of the thing in itself, which he identifies as the Will. We overcome the illusion of individualism and separateness by having compassion for the suffering of others, including animals.

34   Korsgaard, *Sources of Normativity*, 152.

35   Wood, "Kant on Duties Regarding Nonrational Nature," 201.

36   Korsgaard, "Fellow Creatures," 102, 106n69.

37   Paul W. Taylor, *Respect for Nature: A Theory of Environmental Ethics* (Princeton, N.J.: Princeton University Press, 1986), 119–29.

38   Holmes Rolston III, "Value in Nature and the Nature of Value," in *Philosophy and the Natural Environment*, ed. Robin Attfield and Andrew Belsey (Cambridge: Cambridge University Press, 1994), 13–30 (p. 18).

39   Kenneth E. Goodpaster, "On Being Morally Considerable," *The Journal of Philosophy* 75, no. 6 (June 1978): 308–25 (pp. 319–20).

40   Wood, "Kant on Duties Regarding Nonrational Nature," 201, and Korsgaard, *Sources of Normativity*, 152.

41   Korsgaard, "Fellow Creatures," 105–6.

42   Jacques Derrida, *The Animal That Therefore I Am*, ed. Marie-Louise Mallet, trans. David Wills (New York: Fordham University Press, 2008).

43   Christian Wolff, *Von der Menschen Thun und Lassen, zu Beförderung ihrer Glückseeligkeit*, ed. Hans Werner Arndt and Jean École (Hildesheim: Olms, 1976), and Christian Wolff, *Von Gott, der Welt und der Seele des Menschen, auch allen Dingen überhaupt*, ed. Charles A. Corr and Jean École (Hildesheim: Olms, 1976).

44   Korsgaard, "Fellow Creatures," 103–4.

45   Richard Dean, *The Value of Humanity in Kant's Moral Theory* (Oxford: Clarendon Press, 2006), 188.

46   J. Skidmore, "Duties to Animals: The Failure of Kant's Moral Theory," *The Journal of Value Inquiry* 35, no. 4 (Dec. 2001): 541–59 (p. 546).

47   What it means for a desire to be natural or unnatural is conceptually problematic. All desires we have occur in nature, in the sense that they are had by human beings and are not implanted in us by some supernatural entity. Saying that some desires are unnatural typically either masks an appeal to divine law, which Kant would reject as a basis of moral prescriptions, or it reflects a mere social prejudice, which most ethical theorists (including Kant) think is morally irrelevant. Typically, when people say that something is unnatural, they simply mean that it is bad, but that again commits the naturalistic fallacy. Kant himself makes this mistake when he condemns homosexuality, as I discuss in chapter 6.

48   Korsgaard, "Fellow Creatures," 103–4.

49   Holly L. Wilson, "The Green Kant: Kant's Treatment of Animals," in *Environmental Ethics: Readings in Theory and Application*, ed. Louis P. Pojman and Paul Pojman, 5th edn. (Belmont, Calif.: Thomson Wadsworth, 2008), 65–72 (p. 71).

50   Henry Sidgwick gives clearest voice to this sentiment: "there is general agreement that we ought to treat all animals with kindness, so far as to avoid causing them unnecessary pain; but it is questioned whether this is directly due to sentient beings as such, or merely prescribed as a means of cultivating kindly dispositions towards men. Intuitional moralists of repute have maintained this latter view: I think, however, that Common Sense is disposed to regard this as a hard-hearted paradox, and to hold with Bentham that the pain of animals is *per se* to be avoided" (*The Methods of Ethics* [New York: Dourer, 1966], 414).

51   Wood, "Kant on Duties Regarding Nonrational Nature," 194–5.

52   Alexander Broadie and Elizabeth M. Pybus, "Kant's Treatment of Animals," *Philosophy* 49 (Oct. 1974): 375–83 (p. 382).

53   Martha C. Nussbaum, *Frontiers of Justice: Disability, Nationality, Species Membership* (Cambridge, Mass.: Belknap, 2006), 330. See also Heather Fieldhouse, "The Failure of the Kantian Theory of Indirect Duties to Animals," *Animal Liberation Philosophy and Policy Journal* 2, no. 2 (2004): 1–9.

54   This example is from Hoff, "Kant's Invidious Humanism," 67.

55 See note 10 above.

56 Onora O'Neill puts it this way: "in allowing that harming non-human animals is an *indirect* violation of duties to humanity Kant endorses more or less the range of ethical concern for non-human animals that more traditional utilitarians allowed" ("Kant on Duties Regarding Nonrational Nature," *Proceedings of the Aristotelian Society for the Systematic Study of Philosophy*, supplement 72 [1998]: 211–28 [p. 223]). Margit Livingston notes that, because of the violence graduation hypothesis, the anthropocentric approach justifies the same kinds of legal protections that an appeal to animal rights would: "One need not believe that animals have a 'right' to be free from torture and neglect to promote legal reforms directed at reducing the overall incidence of animal abuse. In identifying and treating young abusers especially, society arguably diminishes the likelihood that such abusers will progress to violent acts against humans" ("Desecrating the Ark: Animal Abuse and the Law's Role in Prevention," *Iowa Law Review* 87, no. 1 [Oct. 2001]: 1–73 [p. 42]).

57 J. Baird Callicott, "Intrinsic Value in Nature: A Metaethical Analysis," *Electronic Journal of Analytic Philosophy* 3 (spring 1995), ejap.louisiana.edu/EJAP/1995.spring/callicott.1995.spring.html.

58 John Lord Campbell thought that, while animals had no legal rights, "any malicious and wanton cruelty to animals in public outrages the feelings, – has a tendency to injure the moral character of those who witness it, – and may therefore be treated as a crime" (*Lives of the Lord Chancellors and Keepers of the Great Seal of England from the Earliest Times Till the Reign of King George IV*, 5th edn. [London: John Murray, 1868], 9:22–3). In the United States, animal cruelty was typically classified along with things like adultery and blasphemy as an "offense against chastity, decency, and morality." For example, see Mich. Rev. Stat. 8.22 (1838), N.H. Rev. Stat. 219.12 (1843), Minn. Stat. 96.18 (1858), and Pa. Laws tit. IV, 46 (1860). For a thorough history of anti-cruelty laws in the nineteenth century, see David Favre and Vivien Tsang, "The Development of Anti-Cruelty Laws during the 1800's," *Detroit College of Law Review* 1 (1993): 1–35.

59 *Christie v. Bergh*, 15 Abb. Pr. (n.s.) 51 (N.Y. 1873). A similar thought is expressed in a Mississippi case: "Cruelty to [animals] manifests a vicious and degraded nature, and it tends inevitably to cruelty to men. . . . Human beings should be kind and just to dumb brutes, if for no other reason than to learn how to be kind and just to each other" (*Stephens v. State*, 3 So. 458–9 [Miss. 1887]). Both cases echo Kant's reasoning, especially at LE 459.

60 Livingston, "Desecrating the Ark," 21, 72.

61 The FBI, for example, includes a history of animal abuse in its profile of the typical serial killer or serial rapist. See Randall Lockwood and Ann Church, "Deadly Serious: An FBI Perspective on Animal Cruelty," in *Cruelty to Animals and Interpersonal Violence*. In 1987, the American Psychiatric Association added physical cruelty to animals as one of the diagnostic criteria for conduct disorder (*Diagnostic and Statistical Manual of Mental Disorders*, 3rd rev. edn. [Washington, D.C.: American Psychiatric Association, 1987], 55).

62 Frank R. Ascione, "Battered Women's Reports of Their Partners' and Their Children's Cruelty to Animals," *Journal of Emotional Abuse* 1, no. 1 (July

1997): 119–33; Charlotte A. Lacroix, "Another Weapon for Combating Family Violence: Prevention of Animal Abuse," *Animal Law* 4 (1998): 1–32; Frank R. Ascione and Phil Arkow, eds., *Child Abuse, Domestic Violence, and Animal Abuse: Linking the Circles of Compassion for Prevention and Intervention* (West Lafayette, Ind.: Purdue University Press, 1999); Lisa Anne Zilney, *Linking Animal Cruelty and Family Violence* (Youngstown, N.Y.: Cambria, 2007); and Charles Siebert, "The Animal-Cruelty Syndrome," *New York Times Magazine*, 13 June 2010, 42–51.

63   Mary Warnock, "Do Human Cells Have Rights?" *Bioethics* 1, no. 1 (Jan. 1987): 1–14 (p. 10).

64   See, for example, Tony Lynch and David Wells, "Non-Anthropocentrism? A Killing Objection," *Environmental Values* 7, no. 2 (May 1998): 151–63.

65   Richard Posner, "Animal Rights: Legal, Philosophical, and Pragmatic Perspectives," in *Animal Rights: Current Debates and New Directions*, ed. Cass R. Sunstein and Martha C. Nussbaum (Oxford: Oxford University Press, 2004), 51–77 (p. 60).

66   Singer has responded strongly to Posner, emphasizing the relativistic implications of Posner's position. See Peter Singer, "Ethics beyond Species and beyond Instincts: A Response to Richard Posner," in *Animal Rights: Current Debates and New Directions*, 78–92. See also Elisa Aaltola, "The Anthropocentric Paradigm and the Possibility of Animal Ethics," *Ethics and the Environment* 15, no. 1 (spring 2010): 27–50.

2

Kant's Strategic Importance for Environmental Ethics

Kant's concern for animal welfare depends on animals' similarity to human beings. Because animals feel pain as we do, harming them will desensitize us to others' pain, corrupt our character, and impact our treatment of other people. We have no direct duties to animals because they are incapable of autonomous self-determination, and so they lack the humanity that would give them intrinsic value.

Like animal behavior, the course of nonsentient nature is also causally determined; plants and ecosystems do not set their ends. More importantly, plants and ecosystems do not experience pain, so we cannot use the same reasoning as we did in chapter 1 to justify indirect duties to nature. Singer has been criticized because his sole focus on sentient beings seems to preclude a larger environmental ethic. An anthropocentric theory has even stricter limitations.

Many environmental philosophers claim that animal welfare ethics and ecocentric ethics have incompatible justificatory strategies. The individualistic focus on particular sentient beings contradicts a holistic concern for species, ecosystems, or nature in general, and the latter is thought to be the hallmark of an environmental ethic.[1] Kant's philosophy seems like it would be especially unhelpful in understanding our obligations to nature as a whole, since it is not only anthropocentric but individualistic, in that it focuses on autonomous agents each of whom must be treated as an end in himself. This kind of atomistic view of human nature supports a political theory that treats people as individual rights-bearers, a view that, according to people such as Garrett Hardin, leads to the exploitation of nature held in common: resources are depleted as individuals seek to enlarge their personal claims on them, polluted waterways distribute harm to others, the population increases unsustainably, and so on.[2]

Kant and Applied Ethics: The Uses and Limits of Kant's Practical Philosophy, First Edition. Matthew C. Altman.
© 2011 John Wiley & Sons Inc. Published 2011 by Blackwell Publishing Ltd.

We saw in chapter 1 that a moral concern for rational beings, even if those are the only things to which we have direct moral obligations, implies that we also ought to support the well-being of animals. In this chapter, I will argue that Kant can justify a morally grounded concern for the environment based on the need to improve ourselves and a more generalized commitment to human flourishing. Anthropocentrism does entail that we ought to protect nature because it can help us to advance our ends, but that is only one reason that nature is morally significant. We also have duties to protect the environment for future generations. In addition, Kant explains how a noninstrumental approach to the environment, aesthetically and in other ways, can help us to progress as moral beings. Therefore, the environment is not only or even primarily a source of raw materials. When we appreciate nature apart from our interest in using it, we can develop the kinds of attitudes that are conducive to Kantian virtues. On this basis, Kant can develop a sophisticated environmental ethic based on anthropocentric principles, which nonetheless avoids the tragedy of the commons and converges in important ways with biocentrism.

Natural Purposiveness in the *Critique of Judgment*

Most theories in environmental ethics are predicated on the fundamental unity of humans and the natural world, and typically this is construed as a challenge to the Cartesian/Kantian picture of us as beings who are able to distinguish ourselves from nature through our capacity to reason. As we saw in chapter 1, for Kant rational beings are not simply higher animals, but different in kind when it comes to moral agency and responsibility. In the *Critique of Pure Reason*, Kant shows that the concept of causality only applies to phenomena. Although we are determined as natural things, when we consider ourselves as noumenal beings, it is possible that we are free and capable of moral agency (CPR Bxxii–xxx, A532/B560-A558/B586). The reality of freedom (as opposed to merely its possibility) is then demonstrated in the *Critique of Practical Reason*, where Kant appeals to the immediate sense of moral constraint (the fact of reason) to demonstrate that we are in fact free, albeit from a practical perspective (CPrR 47). Our sense of being so constrained proves that we are moral agents, and therefore that we ought never to be treated merely as means.

This dualistic and hierarchical approach to the world has led some people to claim that Kant's anthropocentrism is morally repugnant, an "invidious humanism" in which nature is subordinated to reason, culture, and human ends.[3] But this interpretation fails to realize that the divide between reason and nature is not simply accepted by Kant, but poses a problem that must be resolved. As an imperfectly rational being, a human being is not only a self-legislator but also a natural being. The question then becomes how to conceive of the whole of nature and our relation to it. Nature is composed of causally determined phenomena, but is there some point to it all? If there is, what role do we play as free but pathologically affected agents?

Kant attempts to address these issues in the *Critique of Judgment*, where he explores the basis and justification for thinking of nature in terms of ends or purposes. Kant agrees that explaining nature as a purposive system is not theoretically justified. We know events in the world only as causes and effects, not as means and ends. However, teleological judgments serve an important role as "regulative principle[s] for the reflecting power of judgment" (CJ 457–8; see also CJ 375). That is, they do not indicate some fact of the matter (as "constitutive principles" do), but seeing natural events as if they are purposive does help us to achieve a complete and systematic knowledge of nature as a whole. They are "regulative principles for research" (CJ 387).

Kant begins the *Critique of Teleological Judgment* with an analysis of organic life, which can be understood in terms of what he calls "intrinsic purposiveness." What defines an organism is how its parts are related to one another and to the whole: "*An organized product of nature is that in which everything is an end and reciprocally a means as well.* Nothing in it is in vain, purposeless, or to be ascribed to a blind mechanism of nature" (CJ 376; see also Ak 8:181). The parts of an organism support the organism itself, and they depend on the whole organism to function properly. The heart pumps blood to the body, and the body supplies the heart with the nutrients it distributes, both to the rest of the body and to the heart itself. This is very different from a causal account, because theoretically we can only make sense of progressive causation, where events give rise to events in the future – the cue ball knocks the eight ball into the pocket. By contrast, we can only make sense of an organism *qua* organism by appealing to a regulative principle whereby there is reciprocal purposiveness – the heart supports the body, and the body in turn supports the heart.

Kant then claims that, once we identify particular organisms as the products of nature, we are led to conceive of nature itself in purposive terms, as a single teleological system (CJ 380–1). Unlike organisms, however, nature as a whole is not a natural thing but the class of natural things. Reciprocal purposes do not make sense on this scale, because the different parts of nature are not parts of one organism. Therefore, we must relate different natural things, both organic and inorganic, by means of *extrinsic* purposive relations, "in which one thing in nature serves another as the means to an end" (CJ 425).

How are we to relate the various parts of nature as means and ends within the system as a whole? First, Kant claims that inorganic beings must be understood as means, because only organic beings exhibit intrinsic purposiveness and can thus be considered as ends. Once we distinguish living from nonliving things, however, there is no obvious reason why any particular organism should be given priority over other organisms. Kant says that human beings could be seen as the ultimate end because they eat the carnivores that eat the herbivores that eat the plants, but he says that we could just as easily interpret things differently: humans are the means to establish a "balance" among the carnivores and herbivores by eating some of the predators (CJ 426–7). According to this naturalistic interpretation, all living things support one another and no living thing is more valuable than another. Such an approach gives us the concept of an ecosystem, in which different species are related to one another as means and ends of one another's existence, and it forms the basis of a biocentric conception of the world.[4] Aldo Leopold, for example, identifies chains of dependence in the land pyramid, through which energy is conducted in both an "up-circuit" and a "down-circuit," neither of which has priority in maintaining the biota.[5]

Kant does not stop there, of course. Ultimately, the naturalistic perspective is inadequate. It fails to make sense of the world because it fails to unify the various natural purposes under one "ultimate end" (CJ 426). If each part of nature existed for the sake of some other thing, there would be a series of ends but no point to the natural system as a whole. It would not be a system per se, because there would not be any order to the means–ends relationships. In short, there would be particular purposes for the various natural things, but there would be no purpose of nature itself. Once we conceive of nature as a teleological system, there must be a hierarchy of ends in which some are subordinated to others.

As can be expected, Kant says that the human being is the ultimate end of nature. This is "because he is the only being on earth who forms a concept of ends for himself and who by means of his reason can make a system of ends out of an aggregate of purposively formed things" (CJ 426–7). Rational beings are the only ones who have the reflective capacity to decide what they ought to do – that is, they "act *in accordance with the representation* of laws" (G 412) – but they are also the only ones who can conceive of nature as a teleological system. In both cases, we are making judgments about values – the value of our own ends or the value of nature relative to its purpose – and the capacity to make such judgments is what sets us apart from the rest of nature and establishes our worth as nature's ultimate end.

Furthering Nature's Purposes: The Stewardship Model

Kant has arrived once again at anthropocentrism. Nature has no intrinsic value – that is, it is not good for its own sake, regardless of who (if anyone) is affected by it. Instead, nature is valuable instrumentally, only insofar as it achieves its final purpose of producing and sustaining human beings: "without human beings the whole of creation would be a mere desert, existing in vain and without a final end" (CJ 442). Many environmental philosophers, most notably Richard Sylvan, believe that this contradicts the foundational principles of environmental ethics, which, they claim, must begin with the assumption that nature has its own value even apart from (rational) evaluators.[6]

Such a line in the sand is unnecessary, however, if environmentally minded philosophers have as their goal to protect and preserve the natural world. One can make the case that an environmental ethic is essentially characterized by its practical implications, not its theoretical underpinnings, and if this is so, then we should reconsider Kant's relevance for the field. Kant's approach to animals is consistent with much of animal welfare theory. Similarly, the practical import of Kant's approach to nature converges with the environmental policies of those who claim that we have direct moral obligations to living things in general. By conceiving of human beings as the result of nature's teleological development – indeed, as beings who depend on nature for their existence – Kant relates us to the system of nature in a way that mitigates the seemingly negative implications of anthropocentrism. He prohibits the exploitative destruction of nature to accomplish our arbitrary purposes.

The idea that all other natural ends are subordinate to human beings as nature's highest end seems to be a holdover of a Judeo-Christian model of the universe according to which we have dominion over nature. In chapter 1, I quoted from Kant's *Conjectural Beginning of Human History*, where, explaining a passage in Genesis, Kant says that animals (and presumably the rest of nature) are "means and instruments given over to [the human's] will for the attainment of his discretionary aims" (CB 114). From a moral perspective, it is true that only rational beings have absolute worth and that all other things have worth only relative to our ends. However, in the *Critique of Judgment*, Kant modifies this position and says instead that, since we are also natural beings, we must value and promote nature's ends even apart from their usefulness for us.

In defense of what is often called the stewardship model of environmental ethics, Kant claims that our place as nature's ultimate end implies that we have an obligation to support nature's functioning. We are morally responsible for our actions in a way that trees and gazelles are not, and we are able to conceive of nature as purposive. These abilities distinguish us from the rest of nature and place a special burden on us not to upset its systematicity. As Allen Wood puts it, "it is only to beings with rational ends that nature could appear as a system requiring to be fostered or preserved."[7] Because we can understand nature as a cohesive system with an ultimate purpose – the existence of rational end-setters – we have a responsibility to maintain nature as a means to that end.[8]

As long as it is in accordance with the moral law, rational beings must advance nature's ends; our ends must harmonize with the ends of nature because we are part of nature. That means we are obligated to preserve nature or to restore its functioning when necessary. For example, exploiting natural resources to the point where ecosystems are damaged conceives of nature's health as irrelevant to us. Destroying species undermines biodiversity and, in doing so, disrupts nature's ability to achieve its purposes. We have a negative duty to refrain from excessively harming nature.

A number of anthropocentric considerations support environmental conservation. For example, protecting a wilderness area from development contributes to the lives of future people who will then have a chance to experience its unique space, plants, and wildlife. Transforming too many open spaces would make the wilderness less accessible and would drive people to other recreational areas. The resulting overcrowding would have an impact on the aesthetic experience of the visitors. In cases such as this, human interests coincide with nature's interests, so, in a sense, we serve as surrogates for plants and animals. That is, we advance nature's aims by advancing our own.

We also have a positive duty to mitigate our negative impact on nature through restoration. The ethics of restoration is a matter of debate among environmental philosophers,[9] but generally Kant would support it. Naturally evolved systems do not have more value than benevolent restorations simply because the latter are in some sense human artifacts. First of all, in the *Critique of Judgment* Kant conceives of humans as part of nature; he rejects the strict distinction between nature and culture/artifact.[10] In fact, culture is one of nature's purposes, in the sense that nature's ultimate goal is to produce the conditions under which rational beings can decide what to do and can use nature as a means to achieve what they take to be valuable (CJ 430–1). Second, if natural beauty or the health of an ecosystem can be restored through human efforts, then we would be protecting the value of nature by maintaining its integrity as a system. To the extent that we can remedy damage to the environment, then restoring nature is analogous to our duty of reparation to other people. In both cases, when we clean up an oil spill or repay someone the money we have stolen, we are freeing people to realize their ends – by returning the property for them to use or, in the case of the oil spill, by protecting people's land and health. In some cases at least, restoration helps nature to achieve its ultimate purpose – that is, by making the world more supportive of human flourishing. Therefore, we have an indirect duty to restore nature, just as we have a direct duty to repair the wrongs we have committed against other people.

Of course, Kant's moral philosophy provides no justification for the belief that nature in its pure state, apart from the sometimes devastating effects of human action, is somehow better simply because it is more natural. For Kant, the fact that something is natural or unnatural carries no moral weight. The question regarding nonrational things is how they affect the lives and well-being of rational agents, and it is very possible that Kant would accept some environmental degradation if it were the result of activity that advances our aims and supports our happiness. For example, some environmentally deleterious manufacturing would be acceptable provided that the consequences were not catastrophic and the products were useful. I hasten to add, however, that such a position is inconsistent only with environmentalists who criticize *any* human impact on nature, and such an extreme form of environmentalism grates against not only Kant's anthropocentric theory but a wide variety of approaches in the mainstream environmental movement.

The Value of Nature for Humanity

Although our capacity to reason distinguishes us from much of the natural world, we should not treat nature badly for the obvious reason that we are also natural beings, and our health and well-being depend a great deal on the health and well-being of the environment. Among other things, treating people as ends in themselves means not undermining the conditions that make possible their existence. Therefore, we have indirect duties to nature because of how our treatment of nature affects us. As Onora O'Neill claims, we are not prohibited from using nature for our own benefit, but we are restricted in what we can do based on how our actions impact the human population:

> By this standard it might not be wrong to irrigate a desert or to bring land under plough – unless, for example, the cost of so doing is the permanent destruction of habitats, of species and of bio-diversity, which might lead to systematic or gratuitous injury to agents (and inevitably harms many other sentients). It might not be wrong to use an industrial process – unless, for example, that process would damage conditions of life, such as the ozone layer or the CO_2 level, in ways that will injure agents (and inevitably harm many other sentients). In acting in disregard of such considerations we at the very least risk injuring agents gratuitously and at worst actually injure them systematically.[11]

Directly harming the environment indirectly harms rational beings. Water contamination from pesticides can affect human health by causing cancer; damage to the nervous system, liver, and reproductive system; and low birth weight. Climate change causes extreme weather that leads to death and disease: it allows mosquitoes and rodents to spread, infecting people with malaria, dengue fever, and encephalitis; it threatens agricultural production worldwide, risking greater malnutrition; and it causes floods and droughts that reduce the availability of clean drinking water. One of the reasons we must protect the environment is that doing so supports people's psychological and physical health.

There are also larger environmental concerns, based entirely on anthropocentric interests, that support vegetarianism, or at least the reformation of factory farming. Chapter 1 approached this issue through its effect on our character – accepting so much animal suffering desensitizes us – but large-scale meat production profoundly impacts human health as well. Beyond the fact that raising meat is inefficient in its use of resources (especially water and petroleum), the demand for feed-crops leads to deforestation (to produce new grazing lands) and the use of toxic pesticides and fertilizer, both of which cause land degradation and the loss of biodiversity. In addition, the large amounts of manure produced in factory farms lead to nitrogen pollution of land and water and the release of ammonia, which contributes significantly to acid rain and the acidification of ecosystems. The hormones and antibiotics given to factory-farmed animals make their way into the water supply and, of course, into the human food supply, and this causes antibiotic resistance, among other things. In 2006, the United Nations Food and Agriculture Organization found that the livestock sector of the economy is the largest source of water pollution and is responsible for 18 percent of greenhouse gas emissions, which is more than the share produced by the world's automobiles.[12] Because of the negative impact on our land, air, water, and climate, and the subsequent harm to human health, Kant can mount a moral argument against meat-eating on environmental grounds, without appealing to its effects on human character and all the while retaining his anthropocentrism.

The implications of Kant's moral theory extend beyond the obvious prohibition against poisoning our air and water. Since the appearance of Leopold's *Sand County Almanac* in 1949, which set out a form of holistic biocentrism and (arguably) founded the field of environmental ethics, philosophers in the West have begun to recognize that humans are not separate from nature and that the disruption of ecosystems can have unintended consequences for human health.[13] An ecosystem consists of all of the living things (animals, plants, microorganisms) and nonliving things (soil, rocks, water) that are related to one another in a given environment, and it is difficult to determine how such a complex system sustains life and what kinds of human activity could impede its proper functioning. Among other things, ecosystems produce soil and nutrients for plants; adjust the concentration of oxygen, carbon dioxide, and water vapor in the atmosphere; and regulate global precipitation and temperature. We are also beginning to learn the advantages of biodiversity, which tends to limit the emergence and spread of infectious diseases by maintaining an equilibrium among predators and prey, hosts and parasites.[14]

Upsetting ecosystems or causing species to become extinct may have unexpected consequences for human beings. In Kantian terms, someone who adopts a maxim that would substantially damage the environment cannot plead ignorance given our current understanding of how intimately our well-being is related to the well-being of species and ecosystems. Such a person would be disregarding the human cost of environmental degradation and thus would be using people merely as means. Because the natural environment supports human life, we have an indirect duty to nature because of our direct duty to human beings. The natural world supports beings who have the capacity to value, so nature itself has value.

Considering Future Generations

Of course, climate change and many other human-caused environmental problems will primarily affect future generations, so Kant's theory must be able to make sense of duties to others that extend beyond our own lifetime. His kind of individualism seems to make this particularly problematic. If I have as my maxim *not* to minimize my emissions of CO_2 and other greenhouse gasses, there is no clear violation of the formula of universal law. Maxims are morally impermissible if they cannot be made into coherent laws of nature (contradiction in conception), or if I cannot will that everyone adopt the maxim without contradicting my own ability to act on it (contradiction in the will) (G 424).[15] Although the universalization of this maxim would be devastating, such an action is logically consistent, so there is no contradiction in conception. And there seems to be no contradiction in the will, since even if the maxim is universalized, it will not undermine *my* capacity to adopt it and carry it out. If none of us regulate our greenhouse gas emissions, the effects could conceivably harm me, but if the most dramatic impact of global warming would not be felt until the next generation, then it is unclear how it would affect my willing.

The formula of humanity seems like the obvious route to go here. If our damage to the environment causes harm to people in the future, then our environmental irresponsibility would be undermining their capacity to set and pursue ends. We would be damaging their health and depleting the natural resources that they could use as means. We would not be treating future people in accordance with their dignity as rational agents.

As intuitively attractive as this approach is, it seems odd to say that we ought to respect people who do not exist, and indeed whose very existence depends on the actions we take. The "non-identity problem," first recognized by Derek Parfit, is that we cannot determine our behavior based on the interests of future individuals, because our behavior determines the individuals who will exist in the future as well as their interests.[16] There is a paradox here. It seems that I have obligations to people who will exist and be affected by my actions, but also that I cannot have such obligations since future people are a kind of moving target. There is no duty to them if the very actions I take may mean that there are no such people. And if such people never come to exist, then I have not wronged anyone.

Consider this example: a woman who abuses harmful recreational drugs is injuring herself, but it is unclear if we should blame her for harming her future children because she may not get pregnant and, if she does, she may not carry the embryos to term. If she does have children, she risks making them physically and mentally impaired because they ingested the drugs *in utero*. However, we do not know whether she is guilty of disregarding the well-being of other people unless and until she actually has children. Criticizing environmental harm because of its effects on future generations is susceptible to this same kind of uncertainty, writ large.

Parfit's paradox problematizes individualistic moral theories such as utilitarianism and rights ethics. For example, the utilitarian cannot easily consider the consequences of environmental policies for future persons because the people who will exist and will be affected change depending on decisions we make now regarding reproduction and environmental sustainability. However, Kant's moral theory avoids this paradox precisely because it does not settle moral questions with reference to an action's impact on future individuals. Kant does not judge the morality of an action based on its consequences, or its effects on actual persons (G 394, 399–401). Instead, the focus of moral judgment is the agent's maxim, and the agent's attitude toward the value of rational beings is expressed in the maxim. A policy of consumption that leads to unsustainable levels of global warming would harm future generations, but what is crucial for Kant is instead the principle upon which we as consumers would be acting. Such a maxim does not distinguish between existing and future persons.

Of course, it matters that *some* future people will exist and will be affected by our actions, and we can assume that this will be the case. Future generations are morally significant because they are composed of rational beings with absolute worth. This affects how the current generation of consumers treats the environment. Kant can make sense of such an obligation to future generations without requiring that we specify *particular* people who will be affected, so Parfit's non-identity problem is not in fact a problem for Kant.

With this in mind, Kant can claim that serious, future-directed environmental harm is morally wrong. Unbridled consumption would amount to treating persons as expendable things that can be harmed as a byproduct of my own pursuit of a comfortable life – like speeding dangerously through pedestrian crosswalks so that I can get home to watch the Cubs game, setting a bomb to go off in Times Square in eighty years because I enjoy doing it, or storing toxic waste carelessly because it costs my company less than disposing of it properly. In all of these cases, the adopted maxim would be something like this: "I will harm or risk harming others when doing so makes my life more pleasant." The fact that people are only potentially harmed or that they do not yet exist is irrelevant to the formulation of my maxim, which cannot be phrased so specifically as not to include me (but only future generations). That would violate the spirit of the categorical imperative.[17] The metaphor of environmental catastrophe as a ticking time bomb is apt: like a bomb, we are intending to harm because we are aware of the harm we will cause, even if it does not occur during our lifetime. When we focus on the maxim rather than the effects of the action, it becomes clear that needlessly harming future people not only treats them merely as a means, but also cannot be universalized because doing so produces a contradiction in the will. Were I to will a maxim of disregarding others' welfare as a universal law of nature, my ability to act would be thwarted by those who are carelessly pursuing their own happiness. When I harm the environment to the extent that it negatively affects human health, I make an exception of myself: my acting depends on my not being impaired or dying as a result of environmental catastrophe, yet environmentally destructive actions lead to just such a catastrophe. Acting in this way is unreasonable. Hence, I have an obligation not to pursue environmental policies whose most deleterious effects will be felt by future generations.

Not only do we have a negative duty not to harm future generations (nonmaleficence), but we also have a positive obligation to provide them with the resources they need (beneficence). To fulfill this obligation, we must advance what Barbara Herman calls people's "true needs," the things that make it possible for us to set and pursue ends. In addition to ourselves and other persons, Herman points out that we also need things, including private property and natural resources.[18] I act wrongly when universalizing my maxim would undermine those needs and thus deny the conditions of free agency. Plundering the earth's useful resources is prohibited because this would deprive future generations of the means to accomplish their ends.[19]

In order to fulfill our duty of beneficence, we must refrain from damaging the environment when possible, and we must repair environmental harms so that natural resources are available for others. For example, clearcutting forests exposes bare soil, increasing erosion and flooding (by eliminating buffer zones that absorb water), and it leads to a loss of biodiversity due to the loss of habitat. Therefore, we should restock depleted woodlands with native trees in order to reduce environmental harm and restore the environment for future generations. Of course, this remains a form of anthropocentrism – the environment is valuable because it can be used to further human purposes – but considering the interests of future persons nonetheless restricts how and to what extent we can use nature as a means.

Beauty as a Symbol of Morality

Nature provides us with resources for the accomplishment of human purposes, but for Kant, that is not its only value. In fact, Kant claims that nature can be valuable in some cases precisely because it is not useful. Our appreciation of natural beauty in particular serves to develop our capacity for what Kant calls "disinterested pleasure" (CJ 209–11). Kant explains his aesthetic theory in first part of the *Critique of Judgment*, the *Critique of Aesthetic Judgment*: When we make a judgment of taste, we are not bringing particular experiences under some general rule as we are when we make a theoretical judgment. Our inability to bring the experience under a concept of the understanding results in the free play of the imagination; we cannot categorize what is given to our sensibility. Although we cannot discover some overarching rule that makes sense of the beautiful thing, it seems as if the different elements were put there for a reason. Because of this, Kant says, beautiful things have the quality of being purposive without having a purpose (CJ 213–36).

A beautiful thing – a painting, a sculpture, a landscape – is not merely something that we happen to like because of our personal feelings; it is not something that satisfies some inclination that we have. Instead, it is something that everyone should appreciate given our common (shared) way of apprehending the world, purely for its own sake (CJ 237–40). A beautiful thing resists categorization. Despite its lack of purpose, it gives us pleasure. By developing our capacity to appreciate natural beauty, then, we learn to detach ourselves from our personal desires and a consideration of nature's usefulness for achieving some contingent end.

Although it is still a subjective feeling, aesthetic appreciation is nonetheless like our ability to love what is morally good, in the sense that neither aesthetic judgments nor moral judgments depend on our inclinations, and both command universal assent. We do not do what is right in order to promote our self-interest, and we do not love what is beautiful in order to make a profit or satisfy some personal feeling. Instead, both the beautiful and the good are valued for their own sake. The experience of beauty is an experience of freedom, in the sense that the free play of the imagination is like the freedom of the will in acting purely for the sake of duty. Because of these similarities (and despite their differences[20]), Kant concludes that beauty is a symbol of morality (CJ 351–4; see also Ak 15:354 [R 354]).

Kant's conception of aesthetic judgment as disinterested pleasure and the similarity between the aesthetic feeling and our esteem for the good have implications for how we ought to treat nature. Because beauty is a symbol of morality, learning to love nature without reference to its usefulness can help us to love goodness for its own sake (CJ 267). Harming nature unnecessarily reflects a disregard for what does not advance our own personal interests. In short, appreciating natural beauty helps us to become better people. As with animals, Kant claims that we have a duty to nature indirectly because of our direct duty to ourselves – that is, our duty to develop a character that is more virtuous, more prone to do what is right apart from personal gain:

> A propensity to wanton destruction of what is *beautiful* in inanimate nature (*spiritus destructionis*) is opposed to a human being's duty to himself; for it weakens or uproots that feeling in him which, though not of itself moral, is still a disposition of sensibility that greatly promotes morality or at least prepares the way for it: the disposition, namely, to love something (e.g., beautiful crystal formations, the indescribable beauty of plants) even apart from any intention to use it. (MM 443; see also CJ 433–4)

Of course, Kant's claim here depends on his particular aesthetic theory. And unlike the link between animal cruelty and later violence toward humans, the psychological thesis that an appreciation of natural beauty encourages a virtuous character has, as far as I know, never been empirically tested.[21] Nonetheless, Kant's claim is important because he can consistently remain an anthropocentrist and still attribute moral value – albeit indirect moral value – to the preservation of nature. As Paul Guyer says, "as far as our duty concerning mineral and vegetable nature is concerned, it is clear that our duty must be to conserve beautiful instances thereof in their natural state, so far as possible."[22] Kant's moral philosophy, by way of his aesthetic theory, provides us with a conservation ethic.

Preserving the Sublime

Kant's understanding of the sublime provides additional support for conservationism. Nature need not be beautiful; it can be overwhelming and awesome. As examples of what can cause the feeling of the sublime, Kant mentions "shapeless mountain masses towering above one another in wild disorder with their pyramids of ice, or the dark and raging sea, etc." (CJ 256). The boundlessness of these things outstrips any attempt by the understanding to bring them under determinate concepts, and this causes us pain. But the imagination's attempt to represent them shows that we are capable of more than what is captured by the limits of the understanding. It discloses to us our capacity to reason, which distinguishes us as free beings who are not merely bound by the constraints of nature: "That is sublime which even to be able to think of demonstrates [*beweisen*] a faculty of the mind that surpasses every measure of the senses" (CJ 250). The feeling of the beautiful helps develop the character to overcome our personal desires, while the feeling of the sublime reveals that we are the sort of beings who are capable of rational autonomy. Like beauty, the sublime is a symbol of morality.[23] Therefore, the domestication of nature, through the overuse or "management" of its resources, would undermine the opportunities to become fully aware of our capacity to reason. We are obligated to preserve not only natural beauty, but nature that is overpowering.

Developing Kantian Virtues

It should be clear by now that Kant does not only value nature insofar as it is useful for human beings. The appeal to human interests may entail a number of environmental protections, but of course it need not do so. It is conceivable that destroying an old-growth forest to put in a housing development would actually improve our lives more tangibly. Not all thoughtless destruction of nature has catastrophic consequences for human well-being. Nonetheless, it is the very thoughtlessness of some natural destruction that Kant would oppose. A healthy respect for the natural environment reflects and encourages character traits that are conducive to morality.

Thomas Hill argues that, although anti-environmentalists may treat people well, a disregard for the natural world "often signals the absence of certain traits which we want to encourage because they are, in most cases, a natural basis for the development of certain virtues."[24] Hill singles out humility, self-acceptance, an aesthetic sense, and "the natural roots of gratitude" as four characteristics that are lacking in someone who has no concern for nature except insofar as it affects human beings.[25] Kant explicitly praises these qualities, as when he says that one should not shoot a dog that "has served his master long and faithfully": "that is an analogue of merit; hence I must reward it" (LE 459). The "roots of gratitude" can be encouraged or discouraged depending on how we treat nonrational things, including animals that serve us and nature that sustains us.

A person who sees nature as merely a resource does not fully comprehend that we are natural beings. Of course, Kant emphasizes that, because of our dignity, we are distinguished from the rest of nature. But as nature's final end, we are also dependent on nature. Not recognizing ourselves as parts of a teleological system amounts to a failure of understanding regarding who we are. We share many of the needs and limitations of the natural world of which we are a part. Although we need not attribute intrinsic value to nature for this reason – Hill is careful not to draw the kind of conclusion about nature that Wood and Korsgaard do about animals – neglecting nature amounts to a lack of self-acceptance.

Disregarding natural beauty is not only evidence of an inability properly to appreciate what is aesthetically pleasing. There are a number of qualities that someone must have in order to value the beautiful: "curiosity, a mind open to novelty, the ability to look at things from unfamiliar perspectives, empathetic imagination, interest in details, variety, and order, and emotional freedom from the immediate and the practical."[26] As we saw earlier, the latter qualities are particularly important to Kant, because they strengthen our ability to care about things in which we have no sensuous interest, which is crucial to having a moral character. Ultimately, Hill claims, we ought to have some concern for nature itself because not doing so evinces a kind of callousness. We would be disregarding nature, which helps to give our lives value, as soon as it fails to serve our immediate interests. Having this attitude as part of our character is morally blameworthy and may affect how we treat other people – actual ingratitude, manifesting the "roots" of ingratitude.[27]

In the *Doctrine of Virtue*, Kant defines virtue as "the moral strength of a *human being's* will in fulfilling his *duty*" (MM 405). Virtuous agents are able to overcome obstacles, such as inclinations, that tempt them away from doing what is right. We have a duty to develop our virtue insofar as we have a duty to improve ourselves, including our moral character. Therefore, we are indirectly obligated to have a proper regard for nature because of our direct duty to take on characteristics that help us to become virtuous people. The traits listed by Hill tend to support our ability to make the kinds of choices that a Kantian agent ought to make.

It is important to remember that Kantian virtue theory is a complicated field of Kant studies. Kant does not espouse a virtue-based ethics, at least not as it is typically defined. Rather, Kant claims that the virtues we ought to have are derived from our duties, and those duties are to rational beings, both ourselves and others. However, for Kant, the focus of moral judgment is an agent's maxim – not a specific action, but the general principle that structures the agent's behavior. A person's disposition or character (*Gesinnung*) governs the specific choices that she makes. As a result, some expositors of Kant argue that a person's character *is* nothing but her most general or fundamental maxim.[28] If this is correct, then the categorical imperative applies to our character as well as our more specific principles of action. Kant thus blurs the distinction between judging the action and judging the agent, the latter of which is the hallmark of a virtue-based ethics. Insofar as our maxims must reflect virtues such as humility and self-acceptance, and these virtues help us to have the strength to act as we should, a proper regard for nature is morally required of us.

Norton's Convergence Hypothesis and Light's Practical Pluralism

Philosophers such as J. Baird Callicott and Tom Regan worry that, without an appeal to independent values, nature will be treated merely a resource to satisfy humans' unreflective desires. Ultimately, our approach to the environment will collapse into nothing but cost-benefit analyses: would we enjoy this forest more if it were left alone for hiking or if we plowed it over and used the wood to build a shopping mall?[29] However, the supposed need to appeal to nature's intrinsic value, like the supposed need to appeal directly to animal rights or animal welfare, is not felt within the Kantian framework, in the sense that there are no egregious practical ramifications for our treatment of the natural world. As we have seen, biocentrism and Kant's anthropocentrism arrive at similar prescriptions regarding the protection of animals and environmental conservation and restoration.

This has important implications for how we evaluate Kant's ethics. By emphasizing the worth of natural beauty, Kant denies that the environment is only instrumentally valuable insofar as it is used by human beings to satisfy their desires. Instead, it has value when it serves no such purpose. This attitude toward nature prompts us to treat it differently (because we do not see it merely as a means), but as Marc Lucht notes, it may also lay the groundwork for a theory of value that is nonanthropocentric:

> What Kant offers – perhaps against his own intention – is a way of thinking about how to cultivate the very attitude that would dispose one to consider seriously the possibility that natural beings could in fact deserve respect. The disinterestedness of taste is an attunement in which something like an ecological imperative might first speak to us, an attunement that could render us initially receptive to the claim that nonhuman beings may well make upon us.[30]

To be sure, Kant is not a nonanthropocentrist. Natural beauty is valuable only in relation to human needs, desires, and disinterested feeling. However, what we see here, as we did with Kant's treatment of animals, are signs of convergence between Kant's views and the views of those who believe that nature has intrinsic value. The specific imperatives that follow from Kant's aesthetics include, among other things, the obligation to restore the natural beauty of damaged ecosystems and the presumption that nature should not be harmed unnecessarily. Of course, there will be disagreements between

Kantians and nonanthropocentrists, especially when they debate what counts as a "necessary" harm to the environment, but the gap between the two parties is not as great as is often assumed.

Bryan Norton has recently made the case for what he calls the "convergence hypothesis": anthropocentrism can be used to justify a number of environmental protections that are advanced by those who appeal to nature's intrinsic value, provided that we seek to fulfill considered (or rational) preferences over felt preferences.[31] Norton concedes that *strong* anthropocentrism may lead to environmental degradation, because this view values the satisfaction of any and all human desires (felt preferences). In other words, according to strong anthropocentrism, nature can be used merely as a resource as long as people have not discovered a reason to protect it, even if good reasons exist. However, if we instead emphasize *considered* preferences, desires that result from deliberation and are brought into conformity with a rational world view, the resulting *weak* anthropocentrism has practical implications that are consistent with nonanthropocentrism.

Norton focuses on two different lines of argument that weak anthropocentrists could use to justify extensive environmental protections, and both of them are supported by Kant's moral philosophy. First, Norton says, once we recognize the fundamental unity of human beings and the natural world, then it becomes obvious that living contrary to the aims of nature is actually a self-destructive act:

> to the extent that environmental ethicists can make a case for a world view that emphasizes the close relationship between the human species and other living species, they can also make a case for ideals of human behavior extolling harmony with nature. These ideals are then available as a basis for criticizing preferences that merely exploit nature.[32]

As we saw earlier, Kant supports such a view by recognizing our place in the teleological system of nature. The wanton destruction of the environment would reflect not only an ignorance of how crucial a healthy environment is for human flourishing, but also a dualistic conception of man and nature that contradicts our understanding of natural teleology. Because human beings are nature's ultimate purpose, to say that we ought to advance our humanity is equivalent to "extolling harmony with nature" and provides the means to criticize actions that lead to environmental degradation.

According to Norton, weak anthropocentrists may also value nature if it contributes to character formation. In particular, nature may help us to become the kind of rational deliberators who seek to satisfy considered preferences rather than felt preferences:

> To the extent that environmentalists can show that values are formed and informed by contact with nature, nature takes on value as a teacher of human values. Nature need no longer be seen as a mere satisfier of fixed and often consumptive values – it also becomes an important source of inspiration in value formation.[33]

To value the satisfaction of considered preferences, we must recognize such preferences, which means that we must be capable of deliberating and reasoning about the long-term desirability and moral permissibility of our felt preferences. In Kantian terms, we must reflect on our inclinations in order to determine whether they are in accordance with the moral law, and when necessary we must resist what we want to do and act rightly. As we saw, this capacity to be motivated purely by a concern for morality is, Kant says, facilitated by our appreciation of beauty, including natural beauty. Beauty is a symbol of morality. Respect for the natural world also promotes traits that are conducive to moral virtue. Therefore, we are obligated to protect the environment because of its function in forming valuers who are capable of acting rightly – that is, who are capable of looking beyond their felt preferences to what is rational.

The bottom line is that, although Kant values nature only in terms of how it affects human beings, his anthropocentrism has environmentally friendly policy implications regarding such things as the preservation of wilderness, resource management, pollution control, the restoration of damaged ecosystems, climate change, biodiversity, and nuclear waste disposal, just to name a few. As O'Neill says, what follows from Kant's anthropocentrism "is likely to have numerous anti-speciesist corollaries."[34] To be sure, Kant is not challenging the basic metaphysical assumptions that underlie the Cartesian distinction between reason and nature, a distinction that deep ecologists such as Arne Naess believe has led to environmental degradation. And a case could be made that our traditional interpretations of Kant have reinforced our view of the world as an expendable resource. But as we have seen over the course of this chapter, unpacking Kant's teleological, aesthetic, and moral theories yields strong environmental protections. The practical aims of Kant's shallow ecology converge with the aims of philosophers and activists who appeal to intrinsic natural values.

Many theorists have tried to limit the kinds of approaches that, they claim, can give us an adequate environmental ethic – for instance, rejecting a focus on individual animals in favor of a holistic concern for species and ecosystems, or appealing to intrinsic value in nature while dismissing anthropocentrism as inadequate. In this intellectual climate, Andrew Light argues for a position called "practical pluralism." Where there is theoretical disagreement, we ought to think strategically and accept different approaches that speak to different people in order to achieve shared environmental goals: "Because people find nature valuable for so many different reasons, 'practical' pluralists argue that no single ethical theory could be made attractive to a sufficient number of people to generate the support for meaningful environmental change." Therefore, we ought to "acknowledge the practical importance of developing alternatives to nonanthropocentrism so long as these alternatives could be used to justify the same policy ends."[35] For both anthropocentrism and nonanthropocentrism to be acceptable under practical pluralism, we must demonstrate that they both arrive at similar recommendations for how we ought to treat the environment – Norton's convergence hypothesis. Given the overlap in policies between Kant's view and biocentrism, Light's practical pluralism suggests that environmental ethicists should not reject Kant out of hand, but should adopt Kant's position when it is useful to do so – assuming of course that Kant's anthropocentrism does not contradict common sense, and that it can provide compelling reasons for some people to act more responsibly toward the environment.

The Appeal to Common Sense

A number of environmental ethicists have argued that anthropocentrism is counterintuitive. Consider the following thought experiment, which is a variation on Sylvan's famous "last man argument": There is only one human being alive on earth, and she will die shortly. Would it be wrong for her to spend her last few moments killing animals and destroying whole ecosystems for the fun of it?[36] Because this would not affect any human beings, some claim that the only way to explain the wrongness of such an act is by appealing to nature's intrinsic value. In destroying those things, she wrongs the animals and the ecosystems. If we want to condemn the last person on earth for her anti-environmentalism – and most of us would condemn her – then common sense seems to be telling us that nature has value apart from human purposes.

Before I address this specific claim, it should be noted that appeals to common sense do not get us very far. There is no way to adjudicate between two contradictory positions simply by gesturing at an unverifiable sense that is attributed, wrongly, to everyone. So, the fact that most of us would criticize a last man or woman who thoughtlessly destroys the natural environment carries no moral weight. Even if Kant's conclusions contradict what we take to be true, that may force us to revise our position rather than reject Kant.

Having said that, we should also not assume that Kant's ethics yields a counterintuitive conclusion in this case. Kant and Kantian defenders assert that Kant's views accord with common sense (CPR A807/B835; G 394). Regarding the last man argument, Kant would claim that gratuitously destroying the natural world reflects a mistaken view of human existence, the idea that we are somehow separate from nature and its purposes. Although Kant would not criticize the effects of the action – the fact that nature is destroyed – he would conclude that the person's maxim reflects or is evidence of a bad character, one that has no regard for natural beauty or animal life. Hill claims as much: "if someone really took joy in the natural environment, but was prepared to blow it up as soon as sentient life ended, he would lack this common human tendency to cherish what enriches our lives."[37] A last man or woman with no concern for nonhuman life lacks humility, empathy, and the roots of gratitude.

Imagine that the last man were not destroying nature but a building. The building is not particularly beautiful, and there is no reason to reduce it to rubble. The person simply enjoys breaking things: smashing windows, crashing cars, and blowing up houses. Many people would object to such wanton destruction, yet that does not imply that buildings (or glass or Toyotas) have intrinsic value. Rather, the person is failing to appreciate the architectural know-how and effort that went into producing the building, he is wasting cultural artifacts (even if he does not have immediate use for them), and almost certainly there are better, more worthwhile ways that he could spend the last moments of his life. Like tearing up the natural world, taking pleasure in breaking things simply in order to render them useless betrays a person's lack of virtues such as, perhaps, gratitude, thrift, and industriousness.

The last man example also shows why it is crucial that Kant is concerned with how our character is affected rather than how that affects our treatment of other people. Abusing animals undermines our capacity for moral virtue. It is incidental, but of course also important, that it indirectly impacts our behavior toward our fellow human beings. Similarly, the wanton destruction of nature corrupts us; Hill gives a compelling Kantian interpretation of why. We may subsequently harm other people, but that is not the primary issue. Therefore, the fact that someone is indeed the *last* man or woman is irrelevant. One's virtue is harmed, which is important regardless of whether the person can impact others through his or her actions.

Kant's interpretation of our environmental responsibility is justified by appealing to the incomparable worth of human life and the moral demand that we develop a good character. These foundational claims cannot be easily dismissed by critics. In the absence of a clearly correct or intuitive nonanthropocentric view, and apparently without any negative implications of his anthropocentric approach, the question then becomes: should we adopt nonanthropocentrism or Kant's weak anthropocentrism in order to achieve our practical aims regarding the environment?

I should mention in passing that practical pluralism is not the sort of position that Kant himself would ever accept. If Kant is right and his moral theory is *the* moral theory, then accepting other theories to accomplish some desired end would not be tolerated. In the *Groundwork*, Kant says that "morals themselves remain subject to all sorts of corruption as long as we are without the . . . supreme norm by which to appraise them" (G 390). The hallmark of practical pluralism is that it has no "supreme norm," only some practical aim. It is a strategy rather than a moral theory per se. For Kant especially, the value of any end is conditional on the goodness of the will that achieves it. Our reasons for promoting animal welfare or protecting the environment must be based in a concern for the value of rational beings as ends in themselves. Protecting animals or the environment for the wrong reasons would not be morally praiseworthy. Kant would not accept the variety of reasons that environmental activists have in their pursuit of a common cause.

Kant's Place in the Debate over Environmental Policy

The appeal to practical pluralism will not win over any Kantians, but it is not meant to. Instead, chapters 1 and 2 have brought us to two separate conclusions for two separate audiences – the Kantians and the biocentrists. First, Kant's version of anthropocentrism has environmentally positive implications for our treatment of animals and nature. This is relevant to the contemporary Kantian theorist who wants to do applied ethics. Kant has something to contribute to the conversations going on in environmental ethics, because he finds a sure and accepted basis – the value of rational human beings – for justifying the promotion of animal welfare and the conservation of the environment.

Norton contends that environmentalists are not defined by some value theory that they hold. The philosophical distinction between anthropocentrism and nonanthropocentrism is not made by most people, including most environmental activists. When environmentalists do espouse views on such theoretical issues, they usually hold what philosophers would consider to be contradictory positions: for example, claiming to value nature for its own sake while also wanting to conserve nature for use as a resource by future generations. According to Norton, environmental conservationists and preservationists are distinguished by their behavior toward the environment, specifically their support for conservation and preservation, rather than their underlying philosophies.[38] Because Kant justifies similar environmental policies, he may be more of an environmentalist than we tend to think he is.

The second conclusion of this chapter is that rejecting Kant out of hand actually hampers the environmental movement. Insofar as environmentalists want to form a coalition of people who hold different principles but share the same goals regarding animals and the environment, they ought to draw on Kantian ideas in order to advance their aims. Ironically, it is because of his anthropocentrism that Kant serves an important practical purpose, even for biocentrists.

With its emphasis on the absolute value of rational beings, anthropocentrism, particularly Kant's version, has shaped our understanding of the value of animals and the environment. In chapter 1, we saw how the relevant case law in the West has been influenced by the idea that animal cruelty corrupts our moral character. Historically, the worth of natural formations, plants, species, and ecosystems has also been understood in terms of how they are related to what we value. The United States government, for example, justifies conservation and preservation by appealing to the aesthetic value of nature for us rather than the intrinsic value of nature itself. In 1992 the U.S. Supreme Court found that "the desire to use or observe an animal species, even for purely aesthetic purposes, is undeniably a cognizable interest for purpose of [legal] standing" – that is, legally, causing the extinction of a species injures us because we can no longer appreciate it aesthetically.[39] Healthy ecosystems are valued because of their support (or potential support) for human life and the benefits they provide to society – so-called "ecosystem services."[40] And biodiversity is often protected because threatened plant species may serve as resources for the production of lifesaving medicines, and animals may serve as research models to understand human diseases and develop cures.[41]

Given our intellectual inheritance, Kant's philosophy can speak to us in a way that nonanthropocentric positions cannot. Most people are more likely to be convinced that we should not destroy the rainforests if we can show how it harms us and future generations, rather than merely invoking the worth of the trees themselves and the value of the habitat for endangered species. Given the convergence between the environmental policies of nonanthropocentrism and Kant's anthropocentrism, it becomes clear that Kant's philosophy does not offend against common sense, nor does it undermine our moral responsibilities to animals and nature. Despite caricatures of his practical philosophy, Kant has important contributions to make to environmental ethics.

Notes

1   The debate was instigated by J. Baird Callicott, "Animal Liberation: A Triangular Affair," *Environmental Ethics* 2, no. 4 (winter 1980): 311–28. See

also Eric Katz, "Is There a Place for Animals in the Moral Consideration of Nature?" *Ethics and Animals* 4, no. 3 (Sept. 1983): 74–87.

2 Garrett Hardin, "The Tragedy of the Commons," *Science* 162 (13 Dec. 1968): 1243–8. Richard Sylvan (Routley) also claims that liberalism is at the core of much of Western ethics, and that its anthropocentrism, or "basic (human) chauvinism," is contrary to an environmental ethic. See Sylvan, "Is There a Need for a New, an Environmental, Ethic?" in *Proceedings of the XVth World Congress of Philosophy*, vol. 1, *Philosophy and Science, Morality and Culture, Technology and Man* (Varna, Bulgaria: Sofia, 1973), 205–10.

3 Christina Hoff, "Kant's Invidious Humanism," *Environmental Ethics* 5, no. 1 (1983): 63–70. Kant's normative dualism between humans and nature is the basis of Jeanna Moyer's claim that "Kant's philosophy is antithetical to the aims of ecofeminism." See Moyer, "Why Kant and Ecofeminism Don't Mix," *Hypatia* 16, no. 3 (summer 2001): 79–97.

4 Holly L. Wilson, "Rethinking Kant from the Perspective of Ecofeminism," in *Feminist Interpretations of Immanuel Kant*, ed. Robin May Schott (University Park: Pennsylvania State University Press, 1997), 373–99 (pp. 386–7).

5 Aldo Leopold, *A Sand County Almanac and Sketches Here and There* (Oxford: Oxford University Press, 1987), 214–20.

6 Sylvan, "Is There a Need for a New, an Environmental, Ethic?" 205–10.

7 Allen W. Wood, "Kant on Duties Regarding Nonrational Nature," *Proceedings of the Aristotelian Society for the Systematic Study of Philosophy*, supplement 72 (1998): 189–210 (p. 205).

8 In a note written in his personal copy of *Observations on the Feeling of the Beautiful and Sublime*, Kant emphasizes how important this responsibility is: "Man's greatest concern is to know how properly to fulfill his station in creation and to understand rightly what one must be in order to be a human being" (Ak 20:41).

9 See especially the essays in Paul H. Gobster and R. Bruce Hull, eds., *Restoring Nature: Perspectives from the Social Sciences and Humanities* (Washington, D.C.: Island, 2000), and William Throop, ed., *Environmental Restoration: Ethics, Theory, and Practice* (Amherst, N.Y.: Humanity, 2000).

10 This is one of the strategies employed in Yeuk-Sze Lo, "Natural and Artifactual: Restored Nature as Subject," *Environmental Ethics* 21, no. 3 (fall 1999): 247–66.

11 Onora O'Neill, "Environmental Values, Anthropocentrism and Speciesism," *Environmental Values* 6, no. 2 (May 1997): 127–42 (p. 137).

12 Henning Steinfeld et al., *Livestock's Long Shadow: Environmental Issues and Options* (Rome: Food and Agriculture Organization of the United Nations, 2006).

13 Of course, this oversimplifies the emergence of environmental consciousness. Ancient Greek philosophers recognized that we are natural beings who share many things with animals and plants. Many Eastern philosophies do not draw a strict distinction between people and the world. Native Americans had a much more inclusive worldview. During the Industrial Revolution, people expressed concern about the effects of modern industry on human health. These and many other movements have challenged the idea that humans are

separate from and unaffected by the environment, and they pre-date *A Sand County Almanac*. I am claiming here only that Leopold gave rise to a distinct field of philosophy known as environmental ethics.

14   Eric Chivian, "Environment and Health: 7. Species Loss and Ecosystem Disruption – the Implications for Human Health," *Canadian Medical Association Journal* 164, no. 1 (Jan. 2001): 66–9 (p. 68). See also Robert Costanza et al., "The Value of the World's Ecosystem Services and Natural Capital," *Nature* 387 (15 May 1997): 253–60.

15   For detailed discussions of the contradiction in conception test and contradiction in the will test, see Onora Nell [O'Neill], *Acting on Principle: An Essay on Kantian Ethics* (New York: Columbia University Press, 1975), 59–93, and Barbara Herman, *The Practice of Moral Judgment* (Cambridge, Mass.: Harvard University Press, 1993), 45–72, 113–58.

16   Derek Parfit, *Reasons and Persons* (Oxford: Oxford University Press, 1986), 351–80, and Derek Parfit, "Energy Policy and the Further Future: The Identity Problem," in *Energy and the Future*, ed. Douglas MacLean and Peter G. Brown (Totowa, N.J.: Rowman and Littlefield, 1983), 166–79. See also Bryan G. Norton, "Environmental Ethics and the Rights of Future Generations," *Environmental Ethics* 4, no. 4 (winter 1982): 319–37.

17   The problem of how to formulate our maxims has been discussed for many years in the secondary literature on Kant. At this point, the consensus seems to be that maxims should be very general. Maxims that identify the particular people who would be affected would be too specific and would seem to permit obviously wrong actions. A maxim that picks out a particular person who is not me would not affect me were it to be universalized, because it would only affect the specified person. See Rüdiger Bittner, "Maximen," in *Akten des 4. Internationalen Kant-Kongress*, vol. 2, pt. 2, ed. Gerhard Funke (Berlin: de Gruyter, 1974), 485–98; Otfried Höffe, "Kants kategorischer Imperativ als Kriterium des Sittlichen," *Zeitschrift für philosophische Forschung* 31 (1977): 354–84; Onora O'Neill, *Constructions of Reason: Explorations of Kant's Practical Philosophy* (Cambridge: Cambridge University Press, 1989), 83–9, 129–31; and Herman, *Practice of Moral Judgment*, 64–5, 116–17. In chapter 8, I will discuss some of the problems that confront Kant's philosophy when it comes to properly formulating maxims.

18   Herman, *Practice of Moral Judgment*, 53.

19   Martin Schönfeld phrases it like this: "sustainable behavior patterns concern offspring and are guided by the predictable resource needs of all those who can be expected to be born. Respect for humankind is consequently also the respect for future generations" ("The Green Kant: Environmental Dynamics and Sustainable Policies," in *Environmental Ethics: Readings in Theory and Application*, ed. Louis P. Pojman and Paul Pojman, 5th edn. [Belmont, Calif.: Thomson Wadsworth, 2008], 57). Although Schönfeld properly understands how harming the natural environment undermines our humanity, his interpretation of the formula of universal law is a bit strange. Kant has us act *as if* our maxim were made a universal law of nature through our willing. Schönfeld thinks of the moral law itself as a natural law. He says that "the moral law is . . . a historical product of a very long chain of processes in the network of

life" (55). This would make the moral law empirical and contingent rather than what Kant says it is: an *a priori* (strictly necessary and universal), formal constraint of reason. Schönfeld says that the moral law is the result of our historical evolution. However, even though we may progress toward conformity with the moral law, the law itself is not a historical artifact. Finally, Schönfeld seems to claim that the moral law simply *is* a call to sustainable development, since unsustainable development is "illogical and self-terminating" (57). The fact that the natural world as we know it would be hampered is not by itself wrong unless we relate it to the original maxim and explain why it leads to a contradiction in conception or a contradiction in the will. Kant cannot refer to natural sustainability without relating it to rational beings' capacity to set and pursue ends. Schönfeld talks only about nature as a continuing system.

20 The main differences between the beautiful and the good regard the different ways that we are pleased by them and the kinds of judgments that are being made. The beautiful pleases us immediately/intuitively and without any interest; the morally good pleases us with reference to a concept and produces an interest – that is, a pure interest in doing what is right, which is what makes it possible for us to be motivated by respect for the law. In addition, aesthetic judgments concern the agreement of the beautiful and the understanding; moral judgments refer to "universal laws of reason." Finally, aesthetic judgments demand universal assent only because of a "common sense" (*sensus communis*), and thus are only empirically necessary; moral judgments refer to a universal concept that constrains rational beings as such, and thus are strictly necessary. See CJ 354 and Ak 16:159 (R 1928).

21 Anna Freud does make the connection between harming nature and generalized violence. She traces violence graduation through animal cruelty to the destruction of other things, which may include the environment. Freud thinks that a child's destructiveness is expressed in different ways when the child concentrates his aggressive impulses on substitutes for the mother: "With respect to aggression, the line would lead from the child's maltreatment of his own toys to the torturing of defenseless animals and from there to massive destructiveness turned against inanimate objects." Freud mentions specifically the desire to possess (and control) material goods. The treatment of nature as a mere resource could be interpreted as an unhealthy outlet for the aggressive impulse toward something that does not "take offense or retaliate" (Anna Freud, "A Psychoanalytic View of Developmental Psychopathology," in *The Writings of Anna Freud* [New York: International Universities, 1981], 8:66–7). Extreme forms of this aggressive impulse would include such things as fire-setting, which, along with animal cruelty and enuresis (bedwetting), is one of the triad of behaviors that is thought to be predictive of later violence.

22 Paul Guyer, *Kant and the Experience of Freedom* (Cambridge: Cambridge University Press, 1993), 326; see also 330.

23 Ibid., 252–4.

24 Thomas E. Hill, Jr., "Ideals of Human Excellence and Preserving Natural Environments," in *Autonomy and Self-Respect* (Cambridge: Cambridge University Press, 1991), 104–17 (p. 109).

25   Ibid., 115.

26   Ibid., 116.

27   Hill is careful to talk about the "roots of ingratitude" rather than ingratitude itself because, I believe, he thinks we cannot have full-fledged gratitude to an entity that is not a reason-giver. Here Hill follows P. F. Strawson, who characterizes gratitude as a "reactive attitude," which is intrinsically bound up with holding agents morally responsible (Strawson, "Freedom and Resentment," in *Studies in the Philosophy of Thought and Action*, ed. P. F. Strawson [Oxford: Oxford University Press, 1968], 71–96). We could only show ingratitude toward nature if nature were freely responsible for what it does.

28   For example, see Henry E. Allison, *Kant's Theory of Freedom* (Cambridge: Cambridge University Press, 1990), 140–3, and G. Felicitas Munzel, *Kant's Conception of Moral Character: The "Critical" Link of Morality, Anthropology, and Reflective Judgment* (Chicago: University of Chicago Press, 1998), 65.

29   See J. Baird Callicott, *In Defense of the Land Ethic: Essays in Environmental Philosophy* (Albany: State University of New York Press, 1989), 157–63, and Tom Regan, "The Nature and Possibility of an Environmental Ethic," *Environmental Ethics* 3, no. 1 (spring 1981): 19–34.

30   Marc Lucht, "Does Kant Have Anything to Teach Us about Environmental Ethics?" *American Journal of Economics and Sociology* 66, no. 1 (Jan. 2007): 127–49 (p. 136).

31   See Bryan G. Norton, "Environmental Ethics and Weak Anthropocentrism," *Environmental Ethics* 6, no. 2 (summer 1984): 131–48, and Bryan G. Norton, *Toward Unity among Environmentalists* (Oxford: Oxford University Press, 1991), 187–243.

32   Norton, "Environmental Ethics and Weak Anthropocentrism," 135.

33   Ibid.

34   O'Neill, "Environmental Values, Anthropocentrism and Speciesism," 137.

35   Andrew Light, "The Case for Practical Pluralism," in *Environmental Ethics: An Anthology*, ed. Andrew Light and Holmes Rolston III (Oxford: Blackwell, 2003), 229–47 (p. 230).

36   Sylvan, "Is There a Need for a New, an Environmental, Ethic?" 205–10.

37   Hill, "Ideals of Human Excellence," 117.

38   Norton, *Toward Unity among Environmentalists*, esp. 69–73.

39   *Lujan v. Defenders of Wildlife* (90–1424), 504 U.S. 555 (1992).

40   For example, see Costanza et al., "The Value of the World's Ecosystem Services and Natural Capital," and the report from the United Nations Millennium Ecosystem Assessment Board, titled *Ecosystems and Human Well-Being: Current State and Trends*, vol. 1, ed. Rashid Hassan, Robert Scholes, and Neville Ash (Washington, D.C.: Island, 2005).

41   See especially Eric Chivian and Aaron Bernstein, eds., *Sustaining Life: How Human Health Depends on Biodiversity* (Oxford: Oxford University Press, 2008).

3

Moral and Legal Arguments for Universal Health Care

The first two chapters have demonstrated that Kant's theory justifies a number of duties regarding animals and the environment. That is a surprising conclusion, but one, paradoxically, to which we are driven because of our respect for ourselves and other people. Applying Kant's ethics to some of the major debates in bioethics should be much easier and more straightforward. For one thing, bioethics concerns the health and well-being of rational human beings, to whom we have direct moral obligations. Furthermore, we saw in the introduction that some of Kant's key concepts are central to bioethics, specifically research ethics. Kant's philosophy is also relevant more generally to debates in the clinical and public policy settings. For example, physician-assisted suicide and the right to refuse life-saving medical treatment are typically supported by appealing to patient autonomy, and the fair distribution of scarce medical resources begins with the assumption of people's fundamental dignity and equality. How can health-care professionals best advance human flourishing while respecting a person's right to decide for herself?

Although Kantian concepts are prevalent in bioethics, a case must still be made for how Kant's philosophy, because of its supposed formalism, is relevant to the more complex issues in medicine. Kant can explain why stealing or lying is wrong, but many of our current debates in bioethics blur the distinction between legality and morality, public and private, in ways that test the theory's applicability. The health-care debate, in particular, seems to pose a host of problems for Kant. Assuming that we have a moral duty to help others, why must we support access to health care, as opposed to other goods? Is the proper role of government to assist people or merely to keep them from harming one another? How would we weigh a supposed

Kant and Applied Ethics: The Uses and Limits of Kant's Practical Philosophy, First Edition. Matthew C. Altman.
© 2011 John Wiley & Sons Inc. Published 2011 by Blackwell Publishing Ltd.

right to health care against the right to property, since state-provided universal health care would be funded with forcibly extracted tax revenues? What are a government's obligations internationally, to the health of people who are not its own citizens? An *a priori* moral theory that conceives of us in abstract terms – that is, only as imperfectly rational end-setters – seems ill equipped to answer such questions.

Despite these concerns, Kant's moral and political philosophies have important contributions to make in the debate over health-care allocation. Out of respect for others' humanity, we have a personal obligation to help people be and remain healthy. In addition, a government's protection of its citizens' freedom implies that it not only ought to stop people from interfering with one another, but must also promote their capacity to act by providing adequate health care for all its citizens. Finally, the obligation of the state to join a cosmopolitan league of nations means that it must assist other countries in becoming and remaining republics, where elected representatives govern according to established laws that are generally respected by the citizens. Because adequate health care is necessary for a country's political and social stability, the ideal of perpetual peace requires that we support international health initiatives through public funds. All of these conclusions highlight the extent to which Kant diverges from classic liberalism and embraces a rational ideal to which we are driven by means of the law.

The Moral Duty to Assist Others in Their Health Care

With regard to our personal moral obligations, whether and how we ought to assist people depends on what follows from the categorical imperative. Among other things, respecting another person's humanity means not harming her (without justification) and not stealing her property. By harming her, we would undermine her capacity to set and pursue ends. A person cannot do as much if she is hampered by a broken arm. And if we did not respect her rightful ownership of property, we would not be allowing her to achieve her goals by using the things she has.[1] Barbara Herman lists three kinds of means for the achievement of ends: ourselves (as we have abilities and skills), things (both animate and inanimate), and other persons (given their capacity to adopt our ends as their own).[2] Among other things, the rational demand that we promote our capacity to set and pursue ends commits us to developing our talents, not wasting our resources, and helping others.

Kant claims explicitly that we have a positive duty to help; nonmaleficence does not exhaust our interpersonal obligations. In the *Groundwork*, he poses this as a question: Is it morally permissible for me to ignore others' suffering, even if I agree to forgo their assistance in return? In short, can I simply leave people alone, neither helping nor harming them? Drawing on the formula of universal law, we would rephrase the question like this: Can I rationally will that everyone adopt the maxim of nonbeneficence? With the stipulation that I do not expect help from anyone else, I am not contradicting myself in any obvious way. The concept of universal indifference is logically consistent, in the sense that such a world is possible. However, Kant claims that a maxim of nonbeneficence cannot be universalized because, in willing such a maxim, I would undermine one of the conditions of my willing. As a finite being, I often need others' help to accomplish things. If I will that all people refuse to help one another as a universal law, then I deprive myself of one of the means to achieve my ends. There is a contradiction in the will here (G 423; see also MM 453).

The formula of humanity brings us to the same conclusion. By refusing to help others, I am not fully respecting them; I am not treating them as ends in themselves. I have a duty not only to refrain from thwarting their goals, but also to further the ends they set for themselves. I cannot carelessly push someone down as I rush to an appointment, but I must also help a person to his feet if someone else knocks him down. Nonbeneficence is impermissible; beneficence is morally obligatory (G 430). In fact, Herman makes a convincing case that positive duties to relieve others' suffering and to promote just social relations are integral to Kant's moral philosophy.[3]

That we have a duty of beneficence is clear under Kantian ethics, but as an imperfect duty, it is unclear how exactly we ought to discharge our responsibility. Whose ends am I obligated to adopt as my own – only those in my community who are directly impacted by my actions, or all rational beings, many of whom are only indirectly affected by what I do? How should I decide which purposes are most morally pressing, given the great amount of suffering in the world? What should I do to help, given that I am only one person, with limited time and resources? Such casuistical questions are difficult to answer, even if we use the categorical imperative to guide our deliberations (as Herman suggests). It seems obvious, for example, that those who have the ability to help others without unduly depriving themselves of resources ought to give to charity, but there is no general rule for how much they ought to give and the kind of charity they must promote, whether it sustains social workers to help the less fortunate, provides the destitute with things they need (such as food and clothing), or educates them so that they can succeed through their own efforts – the three kinds of means identified by Herman.

In chapter 8 I will address charitable giving in more detail and discuss the problems for determining how to make appropriate moral judgments about beneficence. However, even on a cursory examination, the importance of adequate health care stands out as serving one of the true needs that Herman describes.[4] Bodily integrity is a condition of setting and pursuing any ends whatsoever, so it is particularly pressing that people have a minimum level of health and well-being. Mending a broken arm, treating a debilitating illness, providing critical care after a heart attack – all of these (and more) are necessary to maintain our functioning as agents. Because health care sustains people in this way, we have a moral duty to provide access to medical assistance for people who cannot help themselves. We ought to support people's health as part of treating them in accordance with their dignity.[5]

Many philosophers, even some Kantians, would resist this conclusion. Kant's restriction of moral concern to the maxim one chooses rather than the consequences of one's actions leads some Kantian theorists to diminish the relevance of the body for our humanity. Although we affect the world and other people through our actions, the results of our actions do not matter when we are evaluated as agents. Intentions only are the object of moral judgment. Bernard Williams and Thomas Nagel have characterized this as an attempt to exclude luck from moral evaluation.[6] A poor person with a treatable disease but without health care cannot be held responsible for her infirmity or the limits on her ability to act. What she accomplishes is irrelevant, only that she wills that it be accomplished. Certainly, the will must involve "the summoning of all means insofar as they are in our control," but the lack of ability through ill health can be chalked up to "the niggardly provision of a stepmotherly nature" (G 394). A person is not culpable if physical circumstances thwart the achievement of her ends. Therefore, health is not necessary to maintain a person's autonomy, and it is irrelevant to whether the person's actions have moral worth.

Although it is true that, for Kant, consequences are morally irrelevant for determining the worth of the agent or the action, an extreme distinction between reason and the body neglects the extent to which our ability to choose and act freely is affected by our physical circumstances. Edmund Pellegrino and David Thomasma offer a particularly compelling explanation of how illness leads to a loss of autonomy. They say that the sick body seems foreign to us as it obstructs the fulfillment of our purposes: "In illness the body is interposed between us and reality; it impedes our choices and actions and is no longer fully responsive. The body stands opposite to the self." They call illness an "assault on the ontological unity of body and self." When we are ill, we are in a state of "wounded humanity," because what makes a person most human – the ability to reason about alternatives, decide what to do, and then do it – is undermined.[7]

Kant recognizes how deeply the mind and the body are related, so he emphasizes the importance of physical health for maintaining rational agency: "The body must first be disciplined, because in it there are *principia* by which the mind is affected, and through which the body alters the state of the mind" (LE 378; see also LE 369). Kant's texts are littered with examples of people whose agency is threatened by a lack of physical well-being: the woman who is "consumed" by a troubled pregnancy (MM 359), the poor person who "partially murders" himself by selling a tooth for money (MM 423), the glutton whose overconsumption puts him into a "passive condition" (MM 427). Since Kant claims that the ability to set and pursue ends is what essentially defines rational beings, being unable to act because of illness or infirmity is a threat to personhood. To use Herman's terminology, when one's health is compromised, then so is one of the three means of accomplishing one's ends.

According to Kant, personhood involves not only the power to set ends, but also the ability to act on the basis of our decisions. Establishing this with regard to moral action is one of the primary tasks of the *Critique of Practical Reason*, where he shows that we can be motivated purely by respect for the moral law.[8] In addition to the lower faculty of desire (*Begehrungsvermögen*) that we share with animals, we also have a higher faculty of desire by which "respect for the moral law [serves] *as of itself a sufficient incentive to the power of choice*" (Rel 27). Because we can act on the basis of what we determine to be rationally required of us, we are not only rational but "*responsible [zurechnungsfähig]*" beings (Rel 26). To respect ourselves and others as persons in a moral sense, we must further the ability to do what we and they choose to do, and that involves supporting a certain basic level of health care for everyone.

Health Care Should Be Provided by the Government

We have a moral duty to help others. From this it follows that, because bodily integrity is so important to autonomous action, we ought to do what we can to make adequate health care more accessible to those in need. Even if we grant this basic claim, which admittedly is quite vague – whom do we help? how much do we give? which medical procedures are necessary? etc. – this by itself does not imply anything about the government's responsibility to its citizens. Debates over whether health care should be publicly funded are often hampered by a failure to distinguish these issues. In the United States, for example, many people on the political right are willing to grant our moral obligation to help others while denying that the government ought to redistribute wealth. People on the left often misconstrue this as a lack of concern for others' well-being rather than a disagreement about the state's proper role.

To discover Kant's position on whether the government ought to provide health care for its citizens, we must answer a few basic questions: What is the role of government, according to Kant? Does rational consent to a social contract commit citizens collectively to support the less fortunate through tax money? Should property be taken from its rightful owners, under threat of punishment, and redistributed to the poor?

It is important to realize that Kant strictly distinguishes legality from morality. This will be particularly relevant when I discuss capital punishment in chapter 5. For now, it is enough to know that the formal conditions of rational willing constrain the maxims that we adopt, while the law deals only with our actions and how they affect others. What motivates us to obey the law is irrelevant. What matters only is that our actions are in accordance with what the law requires us to do (MM 219). By contrast, motivation is everything for Kant's moral theory. I must act out of respect for the law (for the sake of duty) if my action is to have any moral worth. If I refrain from stealing because I fear being caught and punished, then legally I am blameless, but morally my actions are not praiseworthy, because they are motivated by self-interest rather than duty.

Furthermore, pure moral philosophy abstracts from all empirical concepts in considering the moral agent simply as a rational being with a will. However, Kant's *Doctrine of Right*, in which he derives the legal constraints to which we ought to consent, fills out the conditions under which we are acting. Specifically, it considers us as finite rational beings in relation with other finite rational beings, and it enumerates the legal constraints that ensure everyone's ability to act as he or she chooses. As Kant puts it, "right is . . . the sum of the conditions under which the choice of one can be united with the choice of another in accordance with a universal law of freedom" (MM 230; see also LL 539). The law restricts my actions when they inhibit the actions of others.

Here is where we see how moral and legal constraints are similar, although they apply to different things. Morally I ought to adopt maxims that can be universally held by rational beings, and legally I am bound to act in ways that, were others also to act in that way, my free action would not be hindered. In other words, wrong maxims undermine my own or others' ability to set and pursue ends, and illegal actions undermine my own or others' ability to act on the basis of what I or they choose to do. Relations of right are justified by our obligation to respect persons as rational end-setters, just as moral obligations are. What distinguishes legality and morality is that the law is concerned with agents' actions, but ethically we must evaluate their maxims. Thus, Kant can distinguish legal obligations from moral obligations even as he claims that "true politics can therefore not take a step without having already paid homage to morals" (PP 380). What we are legally bound to do reflects in large part the actions we ought to take in accordance with the moral law, and they follow from the same reasoning: we must act in ways that are consistent with others' freedom. If my actions undermine other people's ability to act, then they violate the demands of justice.

Kant scholars, and indeed Kant himself, tend to focus on the negative legal obligations we have to one another: there are laws against stealing, assault, murder. Kant's emphasis on personal freedoms is consistent with the liberal emphasis on rights and the limited role of government. Indeed, several liberal and libertarian thinkers have looked to Kant for inspiration. In his defense of the minimal state, Robert Nozick claims that it is wrong to violate people's liberty in order to advance larger social goods. Forcibly redistributing wealth to the poor treats people merely as a means to support the well-being of others, because doing so takes what they rightfully own without their consent. Nozick says that we ought not to violate one another's rights, but that this restriction serves as merely a "side constraint" on the pursuit of our own personal goods: "Side constraints upon action reflect the underlying Kantian principle that individuals are ends and not merely means; they may not be sacrificed or used for the achieving of other ends without their consent."[9] A government that confiscates some people's property in order to advance the aims of others turns the rich into mere instruments. Kant would not approve of this, any more than he would approve of my mugging someone to fund my daughter's trip to the hospital. Like Nozick, Friedrich Hayek says that, in the context of the law, Kant's categorical imperative serves as a "negative test" that excludes what is unjust without requiring positive duties to advance the cause of justice.[10] Nozick's and Hayek's Kant gives little credence to the claim that we have social obligations, which should be legally enforced, to provide others with basic goods that support human flourishing. In order to understand the legal implications of Kant's approach, then, we must first address this common misinterpretation.

Three important points need to be made against selective readings that portray Kant as a kind of proto-libertarian. First, Kant believes that the protection of individual freedom involves more than simply leaving others alone. For Kant, the law is ultimately justified in moral terms, and a government is instituted to help us pursue a rational ideal. We are not only morally obligated to refrain from undermining a person's pursuit of ends (nonmaleficence), but we also have a positive duty to further the ends they set for themselves (beneficence). Likewise, we have positive legal obligations to support people's capacity to act. The law forces us (through the threat of coercion) not to limit others' freedom, but it also forces us to help our fellow citizens in time of need. Kant argues that the rich are obligated under the law to assist the poor:

> The general will of the people has united itself into a society which is to maintain itself perpetually; and for this end it has submitted itself to the internal authority of the state in order to maintain those members of the society who are unable to maintain themselves. For reasons of state the

government is therefore authorized to constrain the wealthy to provide the means of sustenance to those who are unable to provide for even their most necessary natural needs. (MM 326)

Of course, the law cannot force people to be beneficent; the rich may help the poor only to avoid going to jail. However, because the law is concerned with our freedom – albeit our "outer freedom" (or capacity to act), as opposed to our "inner freedom" (or choice of maxims) – it can compel us to advance the ends of others in a way that is in accordance with our duty to respect them (MM 396). So, just as morally we ought to support people's access to health care, since a minimum level of well-being is necessary for acting at all, we also have the legal obligation to "maintain" them through our tax money. And the state can "constrain" its citizens to fulfill this obligation.

The justification for this legal requirement, the reason why helping others is needed to maintain society, is a matter of debate. However, Alexander Kaufman argues convincingly that the equality required for and by a republican constitution depends on helping the poor. If some members of the population are so poor that they cannot enjoy even a basic level of health without private charity from other individuals, this would make them susceptible to coercion. Their choice would be either to die or to do what the provider demands. The government, however, must preclude such an asymmetric power relation. Of course, this does not mean that the rich and poor must have equal access to health care or equal amounts of goods. Complete equality is not necessary, only the basic equality that allows people to advance without the help of others. To draw on a contemporary metaphor, the state levels the playing field, providing equality of opportunity rather than equality of outcome, and thus works "to preserve the *rightful condition* of civil society perpetually."[11]

There is also the broader point that the rich, like all members of society, could only have thrived in a stable system that provided for their education, health, and security. People are able to become successful and maintain comfortable lives because their property rights are protected and because even the poor consent to laws that keep them from simply taking what they need. The rich thus have an obligation to give something back to society: "The wealthy have acquired an obligation to the commonwealth, since they owe their existence to an act of submitting to its protection and care, which they need in order to live; on this obligation the state now bases its right to contribute what is theirs to maintaining their fellow citizens" (MM 326). This obligation to support the society that has supported them means that the rich must help fund the activities of the government, but it also means that they must support their "fellow citizens." The state is comprised of individual members whose unity makes the state possible. The survival of the people is important, since no legitimate state would exist without a community of free individuals who rationally consent to abide by the law.

The second important point in Kant's argument is that the state is not confiscating our property against our will. Instead, Kant claims that we *have* consented to help others by engaging in the social contract. By agreeing to a lawful arrangement, we commit ourselves to support the health of the state. Because the state's viability is dependent (in part) on the fact that its citizens can survive, at least minimally, taxation must be used in order to fulfill "their most necessary natural needs" (MM 326). If Kant is correct here, then Nozick is wrong to claim that the rich are being used merely as a means when their tax money is redistributed to the destitute. It is true that the rich are used as a source of revenue, but the fact that they have agreed to maintain the state, and therefore also its citizens, means that they are treated as rational beings with the power to consent. The rich are treated as a means, but they have previously committed themselves to their fellow citizens, so they are not being treated *merely* as a means.

Kant does not stop there. Not only are the rich obligated to maintain the state to which they have consented, but they are also personally indebted to the poor. Welfare assistance to the poor is not an act of beneficence, nor is it only an attempt to keep the state functioning. According to Kant, the rich have "previously snatched away" benefits from the poor, so the rich must support them financially in order to pay back the debt:

> One may take a share in the general injustice [*Ungerechtigkeit*], even though one does nobody any wrong by civil laws and practices. So if we now do a kindness to an unfortunate, we have not made a free gift to him, but repaid him what we were helping to take away through a general injustice. For if none might appropriate more of this world's goods than his neighbour, there would be no rich folk, but also no poor. Thus even acts of kindness are acts of duty and indebtedness [*Pflicht und Schuldigkeit*], arising from the rights of others. (LE 416)

The moral duty to support the less fortunate is not based simply in the fact that they need support and that the rich have the ability to help. The duty also arises because the rich person *owes* the poor person, as if the former had taken something from the latter and must return it in order to "make reparation [*ersetzen*]" for what the rich person has "unjustly obtained" (LE 416). Supporting the poor is an act of compensatory justice – it may not "really deserve to be called beneficence at all" – so the state has an obligation to redistribute wealth, just as it would if it forced a thief to make restitution to his victims (MM 454).[12]

Many people, especially those on the political right, would object to this characterization of inequality. There is creation of wealth in a capitalist system, not simply the distribution of some static amount of which the wealthy are amassing a bigger share. One person's gain need not come at the expense of some other person, so the rich are really not taking anything from the poor. These are good points, and I cannot settle this debate here. However, Kant's claim can be given a more charitable interpretation: capitalism can only function if there are a number of unemployed people because that helps regulate the labor market. Specifically, there must be competition for new jobs so that wages stay at a reasonable level. Because the wealthy benefit from an economic system that depends on others who are destitute and willing to work for low wages, the wealthy are indirectly indebted to the poor. And of course, this line of reasoning can be given a stronger, Marxist interpretation: business owners increase their wealth by unjustly exploiting workers – that is, by not paying them the full value of their work – so redistributive taxation helps to pay workers for the surplus labor that they invest in their products.

In total, Kant gives three reasons why committing ourselves to a just state obligates us to help the poor through government assistance: the duty to maintain the state, to support our fellow citizens, and to give them what we owe. The state follows through on that commitment by forming redistributive tax laws, and the people adhere to the law by relinquishing a part of their income. Forcibly taking money from a person does not violate the person's rights as a rational being, but instead carries out what he has consented to do. Given the importance of physical health for remaining a free and active citizen, the duty to help the poor commits us to fund a minimum basic level of health care for all.

Of course, this leaves aside the question of how publicly supported health care ought to be provided – whether there should be socialized medicine (as in Great Britain), a single-payer system (as in Canada), a nonprofit multi-payer system (as in France), a government-regulated system of private insurers, with tax credits and subsidies for mandated purchases (as in the United States),[13] or some other alternative. I also have only hinted at how we ought to weigh the need for health care against other needs of the poor – for housing, food, education, job training, and other goods. These are important public policy issues. However, none of these practical decisions affect the fact that the government has an obligation to maintain the health of its citizens, nor are they specific to the health-care debate. Fulfilling our personal moral obligations involves the same kind of strategizing. For example, if I had so little food that I could help someone financially only at the cost of starving myself to death, I would not be obligated to help the person. This does not imply that I have no duty of beneficence. Similarly, if a government could provide health care to its citizens only by making the entire population otherwise destitute, then funding such a scheme would be counterproductive to the end of supporting its people. Nonetheless, when it is feasible given its other commitments, the state should provide health care for its citizens. This follows directly from the function of the government to ensure the greatest freedom for each person in a way that is consistent with freedom for all, because it supports people's capacity to act and helps them to avoid coercion by others.

The Duty to Provide Truly Universal Health Care

Establishing our moral and legal obligations to help the needy still leaves the question open as to whom we owe this assistance. With regard to our moral duties, this is easily settled. For Kant, what is important is that someone is a rational being. We should respect the humanity in all persons; one's race or country of origin is morally irrelevant. Therefore, because we have a duty to help others (to further their ends), we have a duty to support people in foreign countries through international charities.[14] We do not have special or more pressing moral obligations to our fellow citizens for the reasons that Peter Singer gives in his famous essay "Famine, Affluence, and Morality": in the information age, we are just as aware of humanitarian crises overseas as we are of poverty in our own country, and the abundance of international organizations that can come to their assistance gives us the ability to help them even if they are far away.[15] In light of this, Herman's claim that "we can take on very little of a stranger's end" and that the duty of beneficence is "relationship-sensitive," such that we can privilege those close to us, seems factually inaccurate (given the reach of international charities) and morally inappropriate (given the greater need of people in the so-called Third World).[16]

In fact, one could argue on strictly deontological grounds that foreigners have more of a claim on our assistance than our fellow citizens. Thomas Pogge, for example, has argued that that we have a very compelling, negative duty to repair harms caused by unjust social and economic relations. A person's nationality is insignificant if our actions directly or indirectly affect the person's prospects: "injustices and other wrongs we commit against foreigners have the same weight as like injustices and other wrongs we commit against compatriots." And if, as Pogge claims, "foreigners . . . are being harmed through a badly slanted global order in whose continuous shaping and coercive imposition we are materially involved," then we practice maleficence when we decline to give to international charities. We do not merely fail to practice beneficence.[17]

People in the so-called First World have obligations to people in developing countries that they do not have to their fellow citizens, not only because the First World has contributed to economic insecurity in the global South, but also because the needs of the global poor are more critical. Providing vaccines for African children is at least as important as providing vaccines for American children, and it is more morally significant than helping American children get new toys at Christmas. Someone closer to me may have a better chance of pulling at my heartstrings, but the fact that I am affected in this way does not mean that they are more deserving of my support. We are not limited in our knowledge or our ability to help, so our duties of beneficence and nonmaleficence are not restricted to those who are near us.

Whether a government ought to support health initiatives in other countries is more controversial. For Kant, we must provide for our fellow citizens because we have consented to a social contract. Our legal duty to help the poor follows from the fact that "the general will of the people has united itself into a society which is to maintain itself perpetually" (MM 326). Our commitment under the law does not extend beyond our own borders, where the reach of the social contract ends. When we recognize the health crisis in Africa, with malnutrition, the lack of immunizations, and the spread of AIDS, we each have a moral duty to assist the African people, say, by donating time and money to the Red Cross or other non-governmental organizations. However, we normally believe that the government has no direct duties to non-citizens.

A case could be made, in fact, that this would amount to misappropriating tax money, given that we are legally obligated to one another because we agree to be bound by the laws that reason prescribes – that is, we agree (under threat of coercion) to act in ways that respect one another's humanity. We are obligated to help the poor members of our own society because we and they are part of a general will. But in the United States, for example, citizens have no social contract with Africans. If the purpose of the welfare state is "to maintain [the society] perpetually," then forcibly taking resources from its citizens to distribute to people outside of the society would go beyond the government's mandate and would amount to an unlawful violation of its citizens' property rights (MM 326). To borrow Nozick's language, this would treat people merely as a funding resource to assist others, whom they have not engaged in a social contract.

Although Kant is a social contract theorist, he also takes a broader view of relations of right. We establish a system of law in order to secure our freedom to choose and to pursue a way of life that is consistent with others' freedom. The problem is that our freedom remains under threat as long as the only people who are constrained not to harm us are our fellow citizens. We will more effectively safeguard our property and our well-being if we also protect ourselves against aggression from other countries, and we will maintain a more stable system of international relations if we help to prevent other countries from collapsing into chaos. But how can we achieve these aims? Kant believes that an international model based on a balance of power – a Hobbesian system in which peace is maintained through deterrence alone – will never succeed in bringing about perpetual peace (TP 312–13). Instead, states must form a cosmopolitan league of nations committed to universal law and peaceful coexistence, in accordance with the rational demand that we respect one another's external freedom – that is, so that individual citizens and states commit to noninterference.

Kant scholars disagree about how to interpret Kant's cosmopolitan ideal, whether we must form a world republic under a global government or merely a federation of free states.[18] If it were truly a world republic, then the obligation of each state to assist the others would clearly follow from the respect for personal freedom that justifies the formation of the republic in the first place. An individual state must further its citizens' capacity to act by providing a basic level of health care; by the same token, a world republic must support the freedom of all within what Kant calls "a universal state of mankind" (PP 349n). We maintain the individual republic by supporting the citizens of the state who are least well off; we maintain a world republic by supporting the world citizens who are least well off. Americans and Africans would be jointly represented by the cosmopolitan government and would enjoy its protection equally.

Even if there were no world republic, however, the obligation of a particular government to help people beyond its borders follows from the obligation to join a cosmopolitan federation. A treaty in which despotic or lawless states participate is as unsustainable as a Hobbesian balance of power. For a perpetual peace to be established, Kant claims that participants in a league of nations must be republican governments – that is, representative governments bound by justified legal constraints (PP 349–53). How can we encourage foreign countries to establish and maintain legitimate, republican systems, and thus be capable of playing a part in world government? One important way to promote republican self-rule in less stable nations is for wealthy nations to assist them in providing adequate health care to their citizens. If we will an end, we must also will the means to that end – this is the hypothetical imperative. Because we must establish perpetual peace through a federation of states, we must also help those states to function as republics. And we can best achieve this goal by supporting the health of their people in times of scarcity.

Numerous researchers have identified the lack of basic health care as a cause of political instability. The U.S. government has issued a variety of reports that confirm the need to support global health. In a CIA-commissioned study of 113 cases of state failure over 38 years – that is, cases in which the government loses effective control over its territory – the State Failure Task Force found that high infant mortality is one of the three factors that tend to correlate with the collapse of the state.[19] Of course, political chaos may be one of the causes of restricted access to health care, but the reverse is also the case: without medical resources to combat infectious diseases and other health problems, social and political instability is much more likely.

There are a number of explanations for why the lack of basic health care affects a state's political climate so dramatically. The National Foreign Intelligence Board blames the struggle for scarce resources,[20] while Georgetown University's O'Neill Institute for National and Global Health lists other key factors:

> The mechanisms and causal relationships between health and political instability are uncertain, and appear to be inter-related with poverty and lack of education. It may be that citizens are left without political leadership; the military without strong soldiers; children without parents, education, or guidance; families without livelihood; and communities without social structure and order. But despite the complexity of the health-security relationship, extremely poor health is a significant contributing factor to the instability of States.[21]

The lack of proper health care undermines any state, but it threatens a republican state in particular because it weakens the general population and often gives rise to a chaotic struggle for survival. It is hardly surprising that people who are deprived of physical and intellectual resources face a difficult path to freedom and self-legislation. Without assistance for the poor, including a basic level of health care, extreme class divisions result. This lends itself to disorder or despotism.

If they are to encourage and maintain republican systems in foreign countries, the United States and other Western nations must support world health initiatives. The nonpartisan think tank Council on Foreign Relations arrives at the same direct and forceful conclusion: "Supporting public health worldwide will . . . promote democracy in developing countries and those in transition."[22] Encouraging stable, representative governments helps to support their participation in a league of nations, which in turn helps incrementally to further the cause of perpetual peace. Insofar as individual nations are obligated to advance that end, they are obligated to contribute to the improvement of people's health throughout the world. Although it is somewhat misleading (because states are not ends in themselves), there is an analogy between the obligations of the individual to other individuals under the law and the obligations of states to other states under a cosmopolitan system. The rich of a given country are legally obligated to help the poor and thus to further their capacity to act. Similarly, rich countries are obligated to help poor countries so that they can effectively participate in a league of nations.

Finally, there is an argument to be made that the same kind of indebtedness that rich individuals have to poor individuals within states also obtains with regard to states themselves, and thus that rich nations are obligated to support health initiatives among disadvantaged foreign populations. Kant says that the wealthy individual must make reparations to the poor for taking a larger share of the total wealth of the country (LE 416; MM 454). This is one way that he justifies redistributive taxation. Similarly, Pogge argues that rich Western nations have prospered because of a history of enslavement, colonialism, and genocide. The West advanced economically by exploiting the so-called Third World, and as a result, Western nations now have a duty to contribute to the alleviation of world poverty. The legacy of the West's unjust exploitation of other nations continues to be felt today in a number of ways that reinforce economic inequality: unequal business competence and bargaining power skew economic negotiations between rich and poor nations, domestic policies (quotas, tariffs, subsidies, etc.) are adopted that favor exchange among developed nations, and the global institutional order, including treaties and conventions, protects the markets of affluent countries by regulating cross-border investments and defending intellectual property rights. Affluent Western nations exert much greater power in formulating and enforcing international agreements that favor Western markets and Western producers, thus taking advantage of an already existing asymmetrical power relationship. In addition, Western nations' willingness to recognize a foreign government's rights over the country's resources encourages coups and supports illegitimate and oppressive governments even today. This hampers a country's progress toward democracy and its economic growth, despite the great value of and demand for its resources.[23]

If it is true that Western countries and Western governments have benefited from the exploitation of the Third World – and, at least as a historical claim, this is undeniable – then Kant would insist on their duty to repair this injustice. And one way to respond to an urgent need of the world's poor is for governments in the West to support international health initiatives. As Pogge claims, if these governments did not contribute, they would be practicing maleficence rather than merely failing to practice beneficence. They would be perpetuating an economic system that unfairly targets and takes advantage of non-Westerners.

Of course, it is difficult to negotiate the various legitimate demands that face Western nations. A Western government's duty to maintain the state would seem to have priority, and thus the health of its citizens would seem to be most pressing. But if, as Pogge claims, Western nations are in fact indebted to the so-called Third World, then the duty not to harm and to repair injustice would seem to validate a strong, perhaps even a stronger, commitment to international aid, especially given the relative affluence of most Westerners.

In addition, I have not specified which method of supporting global health is best, because there are many viable alternatives. Devoting resources to reducing severe poverty abroad could conceivably have a greater impact on improving global health than programs that are targeted at the specific medical needs of a given population. If we confront global poverty more generally, we could improve the social and economic conditions that increase rates of starvation, preventable diseases, and death. Furthermore, supporting the health of foreign citizens may not involve any direct government aid. Perhaps it would be best to offer tax incentives to private drug companies to make low-cost vaccines available, advise foreign governments on how to distribute social services more efficiently, or provide logistical support for non-governmental organizations. Regardless of the method, it is enough here to establish, on Kantian grounds, that Western governments have a duty to support international health initiatives. The obligation that nations have to treat one another as fellow participants in a system of cosmopolitan right demands that they support truly universal access to health care.[24]

Rejecting the Liberal Model

The conclusions drawn in this chapter shed light on the extent to which Kant's political philosophy diverges from classic liberal political theory. The right to noninterference is part of the law, as it is part of our respect for others – not to harm them or steal from them. For Kant, though, we are transformed under the law. I recognize other people as beings who are worthy of respect only by agreeing to limit my freedom and by consenting to coercion that would constrain my actions accordingly. Therefore, only as part of civil society do I take on the responsibility I have as a rational being. By consenting to the law, I agree to act in ways that are consistent with others' freedom. Although I may not be motivated by respect for them, my commitment to the law involves not only refraining from harming others – the legal equivalent of nonmaleficence – but furthering their capacity to act. A necessary condition of being able to act is having a basic level of physical well-being, and having access to adequate health care is an important part of that.

Contrary to liberalism, Kant is not only trying to give people the space to exercise their freedom. He also believes that the law should encourage us to act more rationally. By keeping us from acting contrary to reason, the hope is that the government will help us to develop good habits and eventually to do what is right as a matter of course – an Aristotelian idea. To that end, the law is coercive in keeping us from harming others, but it also forces us to "maintain those members of the society who are unable to maintain themselves" (MM 326). Hayek's and Nozick's interpretations of Kant fail to appreciate the state's positive obligations to advance people's prospects.

Of course, demonstrating that people and governments ought to provide universal health care is only a beginning. The next step is to put aside Kant's *a priori* metaphysics of morals and focus on specific human needs, our technological capabilities, and the logistics of distributing scarce medical resources. Though less ideologically charged than the conclusion reached in this chapter, the debate about how to fulfill our moral and legal obligations is likely to be where the most difficult work is done.

Notes

1 For Kant, this justifies the protection of property rights under the law. See MM 245–57.

2 Barbara Herman, *The Practice of Moral Judgment* (Cambridge, Mass.: Harvard University Press, 1993), 53.

3 Barbara Herman, *Moral Literacy* (Cambridge, Mass.: Harvard University Press, 2007), 254–75.

4 Herman, *Practice of Moral Judgment*, 53.

5 The American Medical Association draws on something akin to the formula of humanity to argue for universal health coverage. The AMA's Principles of Medical Ethics state that, as part of respecting the rights and dignity of patients, "a physician shall support access to medical care for all people" (www.ama-assn.org/ama/pub/category/2512.html).

6 Williams and Nagel conclude that luck invariably enters into our moral choices, and thus that Kant's conception of moral value and moral judgment are flawed. See Bernard Williams, "Moral Luck," in *Moral Luck: Philosophical Papers, 1973–1980* (Cambridge: Cambridge University Press, 1981), 20–39, and Thomas Nagel, "Moral Luck," in *Mortal Questions* (Cambridge: Cambridge University Press, 1979), 24–38.

7 Edmund D. Pellegrino and David C. Thomasma, *A Philosophical Basis of Medical Practice: Toward a Philosophy and Ethic of the Healing Professions* (New York: Oxford University Press, 1981), 208.

8 As I explained briefly near the beginning of chapter 2, Kant claims that the immediate consciousness of moral constraint (the fact of reason) demonstrates that our subjection to the moral law is "unavoidable," that our claim to be bound by it is intuitively warranted, and that our use of the concept of freedom in explaining our actions is self-justifying (CPrR 55).

9 Robert Nozick, *Anarchy, State, and Utopia* (New York: Basic Books, 1974), 30–1.

10 Friedrich A. Hayek, *Law, Legislation and Liberty*, vol. 2, *The Mirage of Social Justice* (Chicago: University of Chicago Press, 1976), 43. Hayek calls Kant, along with Friedrich Schiller and Wilhelm von Humboldt, the three "great

German liberals" (*The Trend of Economic Thinking: Essays on Political Economists and Economic History*, ed. W. W. Bartley III and Stephen Kresge, vol. 3 of *The Collected Works of F. A. Hayek* [Chicago: University of Chicago Press, 1991], 103–4).

11   Alexander Kaufman, *Welfare in the Kantian State* (Oxford: Oxford University Press, 1999), 25–34.

12   Kant originally makes the charge of injustice in the *Moralphilosophie Collins*, but he repeats it in the *Metaphysics of Morals*, albeit in a modified form. In the later work, Kant contends that the laws favor the rich, and therefore that the government is primarily responsible for economic inequality: "Having the resources to practice such beneficence as depends on the goods of fortune is, for the most part, a result of certain human beings being favored through the injustice of the government, which introduces an inequality of wealth that makes others need their beneficence. Under such circumstances, does a rich man's help to the needy, on which he so readily prides himself as something meritorious, really deserve to be called beneficence at all?" (MM 454). The results of both arguments are the same, however. Because the rich benefit from injustice, they have an obligation to help the poor, who are unfairly harmed.

13   This system is being instituted in the United States over several years as a result of the Health Care and Education Reconciliation Act of 2010 (Pub.L. 111–52, 124 Stat. 1029). The law is being challenged in court.

14   Properly speaking, we have a duty to give to *effective* international charities. In chapter 8, I will discuss the theoretical difficulties of determining our charitable obligations.

15   Peter Singer, "Famine, Affluence, and Morality," *Philosophy and Public Affairs* 1, no. 3 (spring 1972): 229–43 (p. 232).

16   Herman, *Moral Literacy*, 209–10.

17   Thomas Pogge, *World Poverty and Human Rights: Cosmopolitan Responsibilities and Reforms*, 2nd edn. (Cambridge: Polity, 2008), 139.

18   Sidney Axinn defends the claim that Kant envisions a world republic, and Fernando Teson interprets Kant as wanting a looser federation. See Sidney Axinn, "Kant on World Government," in *Proceedings of the Sixth International Kant Congress*, ed. Gerhard Funke and Thomas M. Seebohm, vol. 2 (Washington, D.C.: University Press of America, 1998), 243–51, and Fernando Teson, "Kantian International Liberalism," in *International Society: Diverse Ethical Perspectives*, ed. David R. Maple and Terry Nardin (Princeton, N.J.: Princeton University Press, 1998), 103–13.

19   Daniel C. Esty et al., "State Failure Task Force Report: Phase II Findings," in *Environmental Change and Security Project Report* (Washington, D.C.: The Woodrow Wilson Center, 1999), 49–72. The other two factors are lack of democratization and resistance to international trade.

20   "AIDS, other diseases, and health problems will hurt prospects for transition to democratic regimes as they undermine civil society, hamper the evolution of sound political and economic institutions, and intensify the struggle for power and resources" (John C. Gannon, "Defining U.S. National Security for the Next Generation," Conference on the Role of Foreign Assistance in Conflict

Prevention, United States Agency for International Development, 8 Jan. 2001, www.dni.gov/nic/speeches_definingsecurity.html).

21 Lawrence O. Gostin, "Meeting Basic Survival Needs of the World's Least Healthy People: Toward a Framework Convention on Global Health," *Georgetown Law Journal* 96 (2008): 331–92 (p. 358). See also Andrew T. Price-Smith, *The Health of Nations: Infectious Disease, Environmental Change, and Their Effects on National Security and Development* (Cambridge, Mass.: MIT Press, 2002).

22 Jordan S. Kassalow, *Why Health Is Important to U.S. Foreign Policy* (New York: Milbank Memorial Fund and the Council on Foreign Relations, 2001), www.milbank.org/reports/Foreignpolicy.html. See also Barack Obama, "Renewing American Leadership," *Foreign Affairs* 86, no. 4 (July/Aug. 2007): 2–16. Obama makes the case that providing foreign assistance, including increasing access to health care, will help to combat the social conditions that produce terrorism and conflict.

23 Thomas Pogge, "Severe Poverty as a Human Rights Violation," in *Freedom from Poverty as a Human Right: Who Owes What to the Very Poor?* ed. Thomas Pogge (Oxford: Oxford University Press, 2007), 11–53, and Pogge, *World Poverty and Human Rights*, esp. 18–26, 102–6, and 118–22. Contemporary Marxists extend this kind of thinking in their critique of Third World sweatshops: the wages of Western laborers are subsidized by the surplus labor of underpaid Third World workers, thus making Western laborers comfortable in their exploitation.

24 In the United States, when people talk about "universal" health care, they are talking about government-funded health care for all American citizens. This ignores the fact that there is a universe beyond U.S. national borders that is also populated by human beings.

4

The Scope of Patient Autonomy

Although we have positive obligations, exercised personally and through the government, to help those in need, Kant also defends the value of personal freedom, which in many ways forms the core of his moral and legal theories. In fact, Kant claims that we each have "*only one innate right*," "independence from being constrained by another's choice," a point that Nozick and Hayek both emphasize in Kant's work (MM 237). The idea that we ought to refrain from interfering with others' spheres of acting is one of Kant's philosophical legacies and one of the legacies of the Enlightenment more generally, central to the work of John Locke, Mary Wollstonecraft, and Thomas Jefferson, among others.

The importance given to personal freedom manifests itself in contemporary bioethics as an emphasis on patient autonomy in a clinical setting. Physicians are not supposed to decide unilaterally what would be best for their patients. Rather, physicians present patients with a range of possible treatment options so that patients can make informed choices based on their own value systems. Patients decide whether to undergo risky but promising surgeries, whether to take pain medication that affects their mental acuity, and whether to prolong their lives through extraordinary measures. Patients can refuse or withdraw from treatment, they must explicitly give their consent to donate organs after they die, and in some European countries and some U.S. states terminally ill patients can even request medication in order to end their own lives. In short, patients decide what treatments they will consent to, almost without restriction.

In response to the shortcomings of paternalism, many physicians and bioethicists have defended a nearly unfettered kind of patient autonomy. Hospitals and nonprofit health organizations often advertise "patient-

Kant and Applied Ethics: The Uses and Limits of Kant's Practical Philosophy, First Edition. Matthew C. Altman.
© 2011 John Wiley & Sons Inc. Published 2011 by Blackwell Publishing Ltd.

centered care," by which they mean that, after doctors fully inform them of their options, patients have the right to decide what will happen to them. The implication is that they will not be asked to justify their decisions, and that they can choose their treatments for any reason, including religious conviction, economic concerns, an aversion to pain, or even self-destructiveness.

Tensions arise, however, if we equate autonomy with being able to do whatever one wants to do. A Kantian approach shows that freedom is maintained only when a person's choices are morally and legally constrained. There are restrictions on what we can choose in order to choose rationally, instead of being guided by our own personal inclinations. Even when we are not coerced, our choices can be unfree if they are based on principles that contradict our rational nature.

The aim of this chapter is to reveal some of the ways in which our freedom ought to be limited in the medical context. This is not a matter of making the patient do what is in her own best interest; such a utilitarian argument could conceivably justify medical paternalism. Instead, Kant shows that valuing patient autonomy commits us to the promotion of an agent's capacity to set and pursue ends. As we will see, Kantian ethics rules out physician-assisted suicide, has a mixed view of the refusal of life-saving medical treatment, and justifies an organ donation policy that presumes consent. These restrictions do not undermine our freedom. Rather, they advance our personhood by protecting our capacity for rational self-determination. The prevalent conception of patient autonomy, as a kind of unlimited capriciousness, actually fails to safeguard our dignity. Ironically, we ought to limit what a patient can do *because* we value patient autonomy.

Physician-Assisted Suicide

A growing number of people support what they call a patient's "right to die," but it is important to pause and evaluate the ethics of physician-assisted suicide (PAS). Using Oregon's Death with Dignity Act (1994) as a model, in 2008 Washington state voters approved physician-assisted suicide with the passage of Initiative 1000, and groups in many other U.S. states hope to follow suit. Resistance is fierce among some members of the medical community, who believe that giving patients lethal medications is contrary to their role as healers. Opponents and advocates alike believe that the consequences of legalizing PAS justify their position. Either legalized suicide leads to a slippery slope such that poor, incompetent, non-consenting, and non-terminal patients will eventually be pressured into dying, or legal limitations succeed and allow rational adults to end their pain in a dignified manner and on their own terms. The actual impact is hard to gauge; the data is inconclusive, especially given the very different experiences and laws of, say, Oregon and the Netherlands.

Regardless of the consequences, the belief that PAS is a rights issue clearly seems to support the practice. We should not restrict people's right to free speech based on dubious appeals to bad consequences. Similarly, we should respect people's right to die despite fears of a slippery slope toward euthanasia and regardless of PAS's possible impact on our attitudes toward life and death. If we value patient autonomy, the patient should be able to decide the time and manner of his death, without obstruction by the state, the American Medical Association, or the personal views of his doctor.

Out of respect for the patient, the modern medical profession protects patient autonomy above even the physician's obligation to help her patients – that is, if there is a conflict, it is more important to respect the patient's wishes than to force the patient to do what is best for himself. For example, it is now seen as highly unethical if a physician withholds information from a patient, even if doing so protects the patient's well-being. This kind of paternalistic attitude now strikes us as coercive: if the patient chooses a prescribed course of treatment due to a lack of information, the patient is not consenting to the treatment; the doctor is consenting on the patient's behalf. The physician ought to respect the patient's autonomy, not try to maximize good consequences. This seems like characteristically Kantian reasoning. However, this argument depends on a conception of autonomy as unconstrained freedom, which is very different from the Kantian conception of autonomy as rational self-determination.

Because the patient is only harming himself, some people have concluded that he should be free to decide the time and place of his death, based on the right he has over his own body. Kant summarizes the liberal argument for the permissibility of suicide in the *Moralphilosophie Collins*:

> At first [suicide] has a seeming air of being allowable and permitted. The defenders of this view argue that, so long as he does not infringe the rights of others, a man disposes freely over the earth's goods. So far as his body is concerned, he can dispose over it in many ways. He can have an abscess lanced, for example, or ignore a scar, have a limb amputated, etc. and is thus at liberty to do anything in regard to his body that seems to him expedient and useful. Should he not, then, be also entitled to take his life, if he sees that this is the most useful and expedient course for him? (LE 369–70)

Each person has the right to use his property as he sees fit, since it is his property. A person's body is also a kind of property – this is a central tenet of Lockean liberalism – in that it is a thing that he can control and make decisions about, in a way that he cannot make decisions that affect other people's bodies.[1] The patient chooses generally how to live and which medical procedures are most beneficial to him. To respect the patient as a rights-bearing subject, it seems to follow that we should also respect his decision to end his own life when suicide is preferable to continuing to live with a debilitating terminal illness, provided that he is competent and not coerced.

There are limits to what one is free to do, of course, even within a rights ethic. Both Kant and Locke assert that our actions are limited by others' rights, such that we are not free to harm them unjustifiably. Arthur Dyck has argued that PAS is impermissible for just this reason: it shuts off family members' chances to relate to the person and is traumatic for them in a way that the patient's natural death would not be.[2] Kant says that suicide could be construed as a violation of duty to one's spouse, one's children, and one's fellow citizens (MM 422). Such objections are unconvincing, however, because they construe harm too broadly. My rights are not limited by *any* harm I cause people, or else it would violate my girlfriend's rights if I dumped her. In addition, Dyck mischaracterizes the effects of PAS, which often allow family members to come to terms with the patient's death better than an extended process of degeneration.

Suicide is a self-regarding act, in the sense that the dying person is, barring strange circumstances, the only one who is critically affected by it.[3] The question then becomes: What limits are there, if any, on what one can do to oneself? Jean-Jacques Rousseau claims that a person cannot voluntarily enslave himself, because doing so would undermine the right to self-determination that makes the choice possible in the first place.[4] Similarly, Locke says that having the right to self-determination does not imply that we can choose to give ourselves over to someone's unchecked rule.[5] Kant echoes this prohibition, claiming that someone who chooses to become a slave alienates his freedom and conceives of himself merely as a thing (LE 594, 601–2). In other words, we cannot consent to relinquish our capacity to consent. That contradicts the conditions of the initial choice and is therefore wrong.

Like slavery, suicide similarly (and more definitively[6]) cuts off one's capacity to choose and thus contradicts the conditions under which such a choice could be made. By killing himself, the patient relinquishes the very power to act or to consent to anything. In Kantian terms, the person treats himself as a thing rather a rational being; he uses himself *"merely as a means* to maintain a tolerable condition up to the end of life" (G 429). No one has a right to enslave himself, because that undermines the person's status as a rights-bearer. Similarly, no one should have the freedom to kill himself, because that undermines the person's freedom. The illegality of PAS thus has the effect of maintaining people's autonomy, not restricting it. Were they to participate in PAS, they would be undermining the rights that make possible free choice in the first place. As Kant puts it, "one's own consent [*Einwilligung*] means nothing here, because one has no will [*Willen*] to stop being anything at all" (Ak 19:165–6 [R 6801]).

When someone decides to commit suicide, the person makes a choice. Such a choice is free in the sense that it is not coerced, but it is not entirely free because the person chooses wrongly. By killing himself, the person gives himself over to what he wants as a physical being with inclinations. He allows himself to be determined by pain and pleasure rather than by what reason requires. Maxims that depend on my particular inclinations cannot be universalized; only rational choices are shareable by all rational end-setters. As agents, we are responsible for our choices, but we must choose in ways that are morally justifiable if, as Barbara Herman puts it, we are to act for reasons "all the way down."[7] Kant defines freedom not only as the power to choose, but also as the power to choose rightly: "Freedom consists only in this, that the agent utilizes his powers at his own choice, in accordance with a principle of reason" (LE 594). Defenders of the "right to die" miss this important distinction when they claim that suicide can be freely chosen. In some sense it can, but not in the morally weighty sense that is important in Kant's ethics.

According to Kant, my choosing to do something assigns value to that end; it becomes good for me when I endorse it. But if this is so, then in willing at all I am committing myself to the value of reason as a condition of other goods. In other words, by pursuing anything that I take to be good, the power to will on the basis of reasons is also affirmed to be a good thing. In choosing to commit suicide, I am implicitly valuing the capacity to choose, but I also cut off my power to choose by ending my life: "[Suicide] transcends all limits on the use of free choice, for the latter is only possible insofar as the subject exists" (LE 370). From the Kantian deontological standpoint, suicide is morally wrong because the decision to commit suicide (and end my existence as a rational being) is self-contradictory and irrational.

Michael Cholbi has argued that Kant mischaracterizes the motives of most suicidal people. Kant believes that the suicidal person rationally considers the options, weighing the good of living against the good of dying, and then chooses a course of action that maximizes happiness. However, Cholbi convincingly argues that, typically, people who are contemplating suicide are not driven by self-love and a desire for happiness, but rather experience a loss of personal identity and a sense of despair that they will ever be happy. Attempting suicide is thus the result not of some rational choice per se, but hopelessness, disengagement, and a loss of practical identity – "a diminished capacity to value ends of their own."[8] Many such agents are mentally ill, "and even when it is false and suicidal behaviour is unrelated to mental illness, it can be difficult, especially for non-professionals, to determine if a suicidal person is mentally ill."[9]

Cholbi's investigation into what motivates attempted suicide complicates Kant's analysis and calls into question Kant's characterization of the typical suicidal person. However, Kant's analysis is very appropriate when it comes to physician-assisted suicide in particular. The laws in Oregon and Washington target only terminally ill patients with less than six months to live precisely because such patients often face a choice between constant pain and drug-induced stupor. Such patients are not typical suicidal people, because when they decide whether to request a doctor's assistance in dying, they engage in thoughtful deliberations about quality of life. They recognize options and weigh reasons, often in consultation with their physicians and family members. In fact, only patients who are determined to be competent by medical professionals are allowed to consent to the procedure. They are rational and they set their ends freely, without the loss of personal identity that Cholbi describes.[10]

The terminally ill patient who chooses to die tacitly commits himself to the idea that the value of his life depends on how much pain or pleasure he experiences. This choice is imputable to the patient, but the patient is not acting autonomously because he allows his end to be set by his physical condition. A person is fully self-legislating only if he does what he ought to do – namely, respect himself as a being with incomparable worth. Whether we call it physician-assisted suicide or physician-assisted death – the latter moniker is preferred by defenders of the practice in order to remove some of its stigma[11] – it amounts to the same thing: ending the life of a rational agent (with intrinsic worth), usually in order to avoid pain (which is only conditionally bad). Suicide is contrary to the value that we are committed to in acting at all:

> A human being cannot renounce his personality as long as he is a subject of duty, hence as long as he lives; and it is a contradiction that he should be authorized to withdraw from all obligation, that is, freely to act as if no authorization were needed for this action. To annihilate the subject of morality in one's own person is to root out the existence of morality itself from the world, as far as one can, even though morality is an end in itself. (MM 423)

It cannot be moral to deny one's capacity for morality. One cannot rationally choose to thwart one's capacity to choose. A so-called "right to die" is inherently contradictory.

Kant has a lot to add to the conversation about PAS because he reminds us of the distinction between duties to oneself and duties to others. Critics of PAS often claim that people will come to distrust doctors because of their role in the death, that the suicide somehow wrongs other people by cutting off their relations with the patient (as Dyck says), or that PAS diminishes the worth of human life in general. In addition, if PAS becomes common practice, vulnerable people may be encouraged to die prematurely – the famous slippery slope. Kant does not draw on these kinds of objections, which talk about consequences for other people or society as a whole and which, incidentally, have varying degrees of merit. Instead, Kant brings our attention back to the patient himself – the person who is most affected by the decision to die – and argues that, even though the patient is choosing to do this, he is wronging himself above all. He is violating a duty to himself, not (or not primarily) his duties to others.

Not all forms of chosen death are necessarily wrong. There are reasons why a rational being may justifiably end or risk ending his own life. Kant wonders whether a martyr who sacrifices himself "for the good of all humanity" has done wrong (MM 423). The fact that, during Kant's time, pregnancy was especially dangerous for a woman's health does not mean that becoming pregnant was morally impermissible. Kant recognizes that being vaccinated against smallpox carries a risk of death, but it is done "*in order to preserve* [the person's] life" (MM 424). And of course, running into a burning building to save trapped children may result in the person's death, but such heroic self-sacrifice is morally praiseworthy. Kant recognizes that there are cases where people face the choice between killing oneself (or allowing oneself to be killed) and living a life without virtue or value. Kant mentions Cato, who killed himself to strengthen his people's resolve against Caesar; and Lucretia, who (Kant says) should have fought to the death rather than be raped (LE 370–1). For Kant, the consequence of the act – the mere fact that a death is self-caused – does not make the action wrong. Rather, physician-assisted suicide is wrong because of the reasons behind it, the attempt to minimize pain or reduce medical costs, neither of which is valuable enough to override the absolute value that rational beings have.

Although PAS seems like a clear violation of the duty to oneself, self-inflicted death may be justified when the value of life has been lost: Kant says that "I should seek to preserve my life only insofar as I am worthy to live" (LE 371). Because it is our humanity that gives us our dignity, Dennis Cooley claims that Kant would approve of suicide for people who are losing their rational capacity, specifically those facing the onset of severe dementia. Indeed, Cooley claims, such people are obligated to kill themselves in order to prevent themselves from reaching "a lower moral status."[12] With severe dementia comes a loss of personhood as Kant understands it – one lacks the ability to reason and is no longer responsible for one's actions – so suicide in this case would end what Cooley calls a person's physical life while "preserv[ing] her moral life."[13] According to Cooley, this is a laudable end that is achieved by suicide, and it does not treat the person merely as a means because, with severe dementia, the person no longer exists. Choosing to die would kill only an organism whose continued existence is degrading to the agent.[14] Suicide in this case is a form of self-respect, because the person sacrifices his physical life to avoid degenerating into a nonperson.

Cooley cites several cases in Kant's writings where a person is obligated to sacrifice his life for some moral good: for example, a wrongly convicted prisoner must choose execution over becoming a slave so that he does not become merely a tool of others, which is contrary to his dignity (LE 376).[15] However, in this case and in the case of dementia, Cooley overlooks an important distinction: involuntarily losing one's personhood is not morally equivalent to intentionally taking one's life. As noted earlier, the latter maxim is self-contradictory, whereas there is no contradiction either in being executed in order to avoid dishonor or in making the most of one's (rational) life as dementia approaches.

The real problem with Cooley's hypothesis is that a rational person would be choosing to commit suicide, which is not consistent for a rational end-setter to do. In other words, the suicide victim *is* a person, even if he will not be at some point in the future. With physician-assisted suicide in particular, it is a requirement under the laws in Oregon and Washington that the patient be competent. Similarly, for Cooley the person must still be rational so that he can decide freely to fulfill his (supposed) moral duty. Yet by killing himself, he would be treating a person – his pre-dementia self – merely as a means.

Furthermore, suicide would do nothing to preserve the "moral life" of the soon-to-be-demented person. With physical death comes death to the person, the exact fate that Cooley wants the person to avoid. Constance Perry notes the irony of Cooley's position:

> Death does not offer greater freedom. Death merely speeds up the progression of the disease, destroying all brain function immediately, rather than gradually. So death does not provide a chance for freedom in Kant's system. In actuality, living with the progression of the disease maximizes freedom because it eliminates the risk of premature suicide.[16]

It is true that, by killing himself, the patient would avoid the inevitable mental deterioration that will eventually rob him of his personhood – assuming that the diagnosis is correct. However, the suicide victim would still end up dead in a moral sense, and earlier than he would have been otherwise. That is, he will cease to be a person as soon as he kills himself. Only the non-demented individual can freely choose to commit suicide, but in doing so, he would end his life while he is still a person. Holding out against the disease is the only way to ensure that one does not shorten one's rational existence. And this is very important, given the absolute worth of humanity.

Cooley recognizes that a nonrational being has no absolute worth and that, conceivably, existing with dementia would be demeaning. People do not like the idea of losing their faculties. But it is not demeaning in the Kantian sense, because the person is not choosing slavery or otherwise allowing himself to be treated as a thing. Rather, the patient is affirming his rational existence by preserving himself, even as his personhood is taken. Stephen Latham points out that such a person is blameless from Kant's perspective:

> He does not surrender his humanity willingly, but has it stolen from him. He does not deny his autonomy as the slave does, but gradually loses it. . . . He may die many years before he perishes. But like a good Kantian he will die wishing not to – will die fighting perhaps, or will finally come to accept a death that was never his goal.[17]

There is a crucial difference between intending to kill oneself and intending to extend one's moral life as it slowly ebbs away. The person who succumbs to dementia is not demeaning himself. It would be demeaning, however, to kill oneself while one remains a rational being. Therefore, Kant would never condone suicide for the soon-to-be demented.

This leaves the question open as to how patients should be treated who have completely lost their faculties, such as those with full-blown dementia or those in persistent vegetative states where the higher brain is destroyed. Some people would be taken aback by the idea that euthanasia in these cases may be more acceptable than suicide before the change. One could give a Kantian defense, for example, of someone who arranges for a doctor to give him a lethal injection at whatever point in time he is too demented to count as a person. Setting aside the question of how to determine his state of dementia, a person who has lost his mind has died prior to receiving the lethal injection, to adopt Latham's terminology. If the person is gone – the rational, conscious being, what Cooley calls the "moral life" – then ending that life would destroy merely a physical thing rather than someone with dignity.[18]

Refusing Life-Saving Medical Treatment

Whether it is morally permissible for a person to refuse medical treatment and allow herself to die is a very different moral issue from physician-assisted suicide – or at least that is how it tends to be perceived. California passed the Natural Death Act in 1976, and it became a template for similar laws in other U.S. states. The California law criminalizes anyone (including doctors) who aids another person in committing suicide, but the law explicitly allows for patients to request that life-sustaining treatment be withheld or withdrawn. The American Medical Association (AMA) makes a similar distinction, claiming both that "physician-assisted suicide is fundamentally incompatible with the physician's role as healer"[19] and that respecting a patient's decision to forgo life-sustaining treatment is consistent with the "social commitment of the physician" to "relieve suffering."[20] In the refusal of treatment, neither the patient nor the doctor is intervening in order to cut short the patient's life. The illness is killing the patient. The doctor is merely letting the patient die – passive euthanasia, as opposed to active euthanasia.

A patient's decision to have the doctor withhold or withdraw life-saving medical treatment is, like physician-assisted suicide, thought to be consistent with patient autonomy. The doctor is not deciding for the patient what is best. By having the authority to refuse treatment, the patient is deciding for herself whether life is worth living. As we saw with physician-assisted suicide, however, there are limits to what a patient can rationally decide for herself. When a patient refuses life-saving medical care, it is usually because the quality of her life has declined so much that death is preferable, or because a series of uncomfortable resuscitations will only delay an inevitable, imminent death. For example, if a patient is in the final stages of terminal cancer, she may sign a "Do Not Resuscitate" (DNR) order that prohibits emergency medical technicians from reviving her using cardiopulmonary resuscitation. The burdens of living outweigh the benefits.

What matters for Kant is not the fact that the person is refusing treatment, but why the treatment is being refused. Ending one's life in order to avoid pain conceives of life merely as a means to pleasant experiences. For Kant, happiness is only conditionally good. Ending one's life out of self-love, whether actively or passively, is prohibited.

But patients who approach death with a debilitating illness often face a different choice. I spoke in chapter 3 about how illness obstructs autonomous activity. Prolonged incurable diseases often lead to the gradual and inevitable diminishment of personhood. In such cases, the refusal of life-saving medical treatment may be morally permissible. Modern medicine is advanced enough that there is always something else that doctors can do. A patient with failing kidneys can be put on dialysis, someone who can no longer eat can have a feeding tube inserted into her, and someone who cannot breathe can be given a tracheostomy so she can be kept alive on a ventilator even as her condition worsens and her consciousness fades. The purpose of medical technology is to prolong life. But not all life is equally valuable.

Kant is no vitalist; he does not value life simply for its own sake. Removing the feeding tube from someone who has permanently lost all the elements of personhood – someone like Terri Schiavo, without self-consciousness, the capacity to reason, or the capacity to act on reasons – would not be wrong, since there is no humanity in this case to be destroyed. So, we cannot conclude that we have a duty not to withdraw treatment in any circumstances, because withdrawing treatment from a nonperson is morally neutral.

Although it does not justify suicide for the soon-to-be demented, Cooley's argument becomes relevant here in deciding when it is appropriate to refrain from further medical treatment. To know whether allowing oneself to die is permissible, we would have to know the circumstances and motives of the action. Choosing to die in order to avoid pain is morally indistinguishable from self-regarding suicide. By contrast, a person who is in a persistent vegetative state (PVS) has already lost the basis of human dignity. At this point, the body functions without the person, and further interventions serve no moral purpose. A DNR order is appropriate.

Many people and organizations, including the AMA, believe that refusing treatment is significantly different from committing suicide – more acceptable, not as morally problematic. However, the supposedly crucial distinction between killing and letting die gets no traction with Kant. Both an action and a refusal to act are the result of maxims; both follow from subjective principles that the agent has adopted. Signing a DNR order is different from allowing oneself to be taken over by dementia because not being treated by trained medical professionals depends on the active intervention of the patient in refusing the treatment, whereas succumbing to an inevitable loss of mental acuity does not depend on the person. The latter passivity is different from the former in a morally significant way: refusing treatment results from a free decision on the part of the patient to end her life. What is important for Kant is not that someone is dying, but the reason that someone is choosing to die. Therefore, refusing treatment is more like suicide than natural death. Like James Rachels, who argues convincingly that active and passive euthanasia are morally equivalent, Kant believes that it makes no moral difference whether the patient is killing herself or allowing herself to die.[21]

There is an analogy here with our duties to others. As we saw in chapter 3, I am morally obligated not to harm others (nonmaleficence), but that is not enough. I also ought to help them to advance their ends (beneficence). We have similar duties to ourselves: I must not only refrain from killing myself (a negative duty), but I must also advance my capacity to set ends – by developing my talents so that I can better achieve my goals, and by getting the treatment I need in order to maintain my existence as a rational agent (positive duties) (G 421–3, 429–30). Although suicide and refusing treatment are different kinds of actions, they are both wrong if they are done for the same reason. That is, both suicide and the refusal of life-saving medical treatment are wrong if they follow from maxims whose aim is to destroy a person's humanity in an effort to avoid pain. If we can avoid death without compromising our moral integrity, then we are obligated to maintain our existence. After all, if neglecting my talents is morally wrong because it does not facilitate my pursuit of ends, then neglecting my health is morally wrong because it does not facilitate the existence that is necessary in order for me to set ends at all – provided, of course, that I still have my humanity.

This leads to an important question about what it would mean to fulfill this duty to ourselves. Must we do anything and everything that would extend our lives as persons? Chronic overeating and other bad habits have long-term effects on our health that limit what we can do and shorten our lives. Losing a lung to cancer after years of smoking or having a triple bypass after years of cheeseburgers seem just as bad as selling a tooth or having yourself castrated: Kant says that the latter actions "are ways of partially murdering oneself" (MM 423) and that "intemperance" is a kind of "subtle suicide" (LE 642). In order fully to respect our humanity, we ought to eat well and exercise. But how far must we take this?

Both the duty of beneficence and the duty to develop our talents are imperfect duties, in that we have certain latitude on how we fulfill them. We need not develop every talent, even though doing so would have a greater impact on our ability to accomplish our purposes. We need not give to every charity, even if each act of kindness were to have a positive impact on people. Similarly, we need not make the optimal health decision in every aspect of our lives. We must strengthen our bodies as we must develop our talents: there is some latitude in what we must do, as long as we are made "useful for all sorts of purposes" (G 423).

What is crucial in assessing the action is, once again, the maxim that best describes what the person is doing, the circumstances, and the reasons for doing it. Someone who eats an unhealthy meal may be having an isolated indulgence, or it may be part of a pattern that will lead to clogged arteries. Someone may not be exercising regularly because she has trouble finding the time for it given her work and family obligations, or she may be avoiding it because she has no concern for her own well-being. The latter action is morally blameworthy but the former is not, even though outwardly they seem to be the same action. When a patient refuses life-saving medical treatment, that is different from occasionally having a Big Mac. Both are detrimental to one's health, but a patient refuses treatment *in order to* die.

A patient's direct duties to herself depend on her state of health and her motives. In certain circumstances, a patient may refuse life-saving treatment. But there are other possible duties to consider here. For example, the Catholic Church claims that withdrawing treatment, even from patients in persistent vegetative states, makes us less respectful of persons.[22] It is the same kind of argument that, in chapter 1, showed that we are obligated to promote animal welfare. As we saw there, we have a duty to develop our moral character, so we should not engage in activity that undermines compassion and other traits that support an ethical life. If the withdrawal of treatment from any patient, including PVS patients, were inimical to the development of important virtues, then the Kantian would have reason enough to maintain the lives of the permanently incapacitated. If the Catholic Church's argument were sound, that would justify indirect duties to PVS patients, in addition to the direct duties we have to mentally competent adults.

The problem is that there is no evidence to support the claim that our character is corrupted when we withdraw treatment from PVS patients – for example, by removing Schiavo's feeding tube. PVS patients lack the capacities that most people think are crucial to being a person. They lack even the behavioral and physical characteristics that animals share with us and that form the basis of our duties with regard to animals. If we dismiss the Catholic Church's argument against withdrawing treatment even in the case of nonpersons – that is, if we assume that there are no such indirect duties to PVS patients – then the morality of withdrawing treatment depends on whether the patient is a person or the patient has been permanently rendered incompetent. If the humanity in the person has been permanently lost, then, barring previous promises to the person or other such commitments, we have neither a direct nor an indirect duty to continue medical treatment.

Of course, this opens up the larger and more difficult question of how competent someone would have to be in order to remain a person, and how we would tell. Between a normal, healthy adult and someone in PVS, there is a wide range of persons or almost-persons with varying degrees of rationality. As I will show in chapter 10, Kant has trouble handling a sliding scale of personhood. At this point, however, we can conclude that someone who could otherwise remain a rational being, even if they are decrepit, in pain, or otherwise physically impaired, should not purposely let themselves die, whereas the withdrawal of medical treatment is permissible when someone has been permanently rendered incapable of reasoning.

Organ Donation: Opt-in or Opt-out?

The dignity of humanity places obligations on us to respect it, both in ourselves and in others. We cannot commit suicide, we cannot refuse life-saving medical treatment as long as we remain rational, we cannot harm others, and, as we saw in chapter 3, we have a duty to promote others' well-being through publicly funded health care. Because we ought to help others to advance their ends by (among other things) supporting their health, one clear duty we seem to have is to donate our organs, when we die, to those who are in need of transplants. Every year, about 7,000 otherwise healthy people die in the United States while they are waiting for transplants, even though Americans bury or cremate about 22,000 transplantable organs during that same period.[23] There is a tragic disconnect between the obvious need for organs and the seeming unwillingness among potential donors. Healthy organs in a cadaver have no value for the cadaver; they have inestimable value for the living. Although we are free to determine what we will do, it would be irrational and wrong not to donate. Were I to universalize the maxim of not donating, then I would be thwarting my own capacity to set and pursue ends – indeed, my own life – were I to have an illness that causes organ failure. No one would donate, so there would be no organs to transplant into me. By willing such a world, I would undermine my own activity, a contradiction in the will.[24]

Although we are morally required to donate our organs when we die, the law is more restricted in what it can force us to do. The dead person is no longer a person, and thus it would seem that we could use the body merely as a resource. However, according to Kant, a law-governed society recognizes obligations to the dead as well as the living. Such obligations are a consequence of prior commitments to respect the living person's wishes.[25] Legally, a person is not required to give his organs to those with organ failure, any more than the money he leaves must be distributed to those with economic need. With regard to inheritance, the person can form a contract with someone such that his property is transferred upon his death. Kant says that this is possible only in the civil condition, because only the law can ensure that the property changes hands when the person, by dying, has relinquished all claim to it (MM 293–4, 365–6).

Similarly, a person has the legal right to choose not to donate his organs, provided that he commits others by contract to take possession of his body when he dies, intact and with all of its organs, and dispose of it. This is typically how it is done today. A person either consents to have his organs removed for transplantation, or in the absence of such clearly stated wishes, the person's family members make the decision – similar to an inheritance law. The organs are property that is dispensed by the original "owner" or by the person who takes ownership of the body under the law. In fact, according to the Revised Uniform Anatomical Gift Act (2006), which has been widely accepted in the United States, coroners have the authority to donate the organs of unclaimed bodies.[26] In the absence of an "inheritor," the organs can be used without the consent of the person or his family members. But this is only when the person has not made his wishes clear and there is no one to take charge of the body. Usually, a person's organs are not taken unless he has clearly expressed his desire to give them up.

An emphasis on personal autonomy and the right over one's own body leads many countries, including the United States, to have an "opt-in" or explicit consent rule under which people must volunteer their organs after death. That is, if the organs are to be removed for transplantation, the person must decide to do this and must convey his wishes to the state, usually by signing a donor consent form while applying for a driver's license. A person who signs no such form has not consented to the procedure. To be sure, in the absence of clear wishes that his organs not be harvested, family members may consent to the procedure in the person's stead. They would be consenting, however, on behalf of the patient. Explicit consent is necessary, either from the person himself, his family members, or the coroner (in the case of unclaimed bodies).

Morally, there is no comparison between the value of saving a living being threatened with organ failure and the value of maintaining the physical integrity of a corpse. Still, we ought to carry out the wishes of the deceased, insofar as we have contracted to do so in civil society. A clear indication that the person does not want to donate his organs would obligate us not to misuse his body, just as we are bound to respect the decisions of the person regarding the inheritance of his property. There is a difference between what we ought to do and what we can be required to do under the law, given the purpose of the law to protect our right to act freely so long as our actions can coexist with others' freedom (MM 237). We have the legal right to do some things that it would be morally wrong for us to do. In this case, we are legally allowed to refuse to donate our organs, and we are obligated to respect others' refusal, even though we are also morally obligated to act beneficently, to donate in order to advance others' capacity to set and pursue ends.

The law cannot force people to do the right thing, but it can shape their choices and thus can impact their ability to develop morally and to choose rightly. Kant is a great defender of personal freedoms, and in particular freedom of conscience and freedom of speech. However, as we saw at the end of chapter 3, Kant claims that certain restrictions on our freedom under the law can actually increase our ability to use our freedom rightly. Ethically, being constrained by the demands of reason is true autonomy. Doing otherwise would amount to being pulled around by whatever inclinations we happen to have. Similarly, under the law, true freedom is made possible by the right kinds of limitations on our freedom: "A greater degree of civil freedom seems advantageous to a people's freedom of *spirit* and nevertheless puts up insurmountable barriers to it; a lesser degree of the former, on the other hand, provides a space for the latter to expand to its full capacity" (WE 41). That is, properly constraining our actions makes us freer than we would be if our actions were completely unchecked. This conception of freedom is very different from that of someone such as Thomas Hobbes, who equates freedom with a lack of constraint and who sees our consent to the social contract as an exchange of freedom for security. According to Kant, a lack of constraint would make us capricious rather than free.[27] Legal restrictions ought to make us better people by bringing our actions at least in conformity with respect for others and thereby helping to habituate us to morally appropriate behavior.

With regard to organ donation, the question becomes: What sort of law would encourage respect for other rational end-setters while also honoring each individual's right over his or her own body? Authoritarian governments would simply force people to donate, and one could make a case that Kant would agree with such a policy. After all, we saw in chapter 3 that Kant believes the government is justified in forcing people to pay taxes in order to redistribute wealth to the poor. It seems that the government would also be justified in taking people's organs when they die so they could be redistributed to those who need them. However, there are key differences between these two policies that make the routine removal of organs a violation of people's autonomy. Supplying the poor with health care is justified because it helps perpetuate a state to which the citizen has consented. This is not a violation of autonomy because such a state is necessary to protect the very freedoms that the person values. Redistributing wealth keeps a whole class of people from being susceptible to an asymmetric power relationship with members of the richer classes of society. By contrast, organ failure affects members of all classes of society. The deaths of those people would not pose a threat to society as a whole, and the risks the people face do not engender possible class warfare. Kant would add that those with healthy organs do not benefit in any way from those with organ failure, and so the former people are not indebted to the latter – which, again, is different from the potential for injustice between rich and poor. Distributing cadavers' organs to those who need them is not necessary to maintain the state. Therefore, Kant would conclude that, unlike forced taxation, forced organ donation is an unjust policy.

On the other hand, the opt-in strategy that now exists in the United States is insufficiently constraining. A U.S. government survey in 2005 showed that only 52.7 percent of eligible adults have granted permission for organ donation, even though 78 percent of survey respondents said that they would be likely or very likely to donate their organs.[28] The disparity between the two figures demands a different policy, since thousands of lives are at stake. People are not doing what they know they ought to do and what they claim to be committed to doing.

The balancing act between personal freedom and our regard for one another as fellow citizens, as constituents of a society that we strive to maintain, would be better achieved by a so-called "opt-out" system, a system of presumed consent. Under this policy, the state assumes that citizens want to donate their organs unless they explicitly refuse to do so. Refusal to participate would not be punishable because the law cannot require us to help one another. As a society, we respect a person's right to dispose of his body and his property however he wishes, as long as it does not harm others. At the same time, a policy of presumed consent would encourage us to do the right thing. Some people who do not opt out will do so purposely, out of respect for others and a desire to save lives. These are the same people who choose to donate under an opt-in system. Others will fail to opt out because they are lazy or absentminded, and their actions would not be morally praiseworthy. Unintentionally donating is in accordance with duty but not for the sake of duty. Nonetheless, an opt-out system makes it more likely that people will perform the right action, whether or not it is done for the right reason.

Of course, there are risks to this arrangement, risks to which Kant would be particularly sensitive. We should not depend on people's ignorance about the system, for example, to gain their consent. If people do not know about the policy or it is not clear how they would opt out, then a policy of presumed consent may amount to coercion. Getting someone to do something by hiding information from him does not allow him to choose for himself and thus treats him merely as a means – in this case, merely as an organ bank. Indeed, some critics of presumed consent claim that a person who avoids making a decision regarding organ donation is being forced into donating, which undermines the person's autonomy.[29]

To evaluate this objection, we should consider how such people – that is, people who fail to decide – are treated under the usual policy, the opt-in model. In such a system, if a patient has not given his express consent by the time of death, the person who has been given durable power of attorney or the next of kin makes the decision to donate or not. After all, under the opt-in model, not indicating one's preference may mean either that the patient does not want to donate, that he has made no decision, or that he wants to donate but has not taken the appropriate steps to do so. The surviving family members interpret the patient's action – or rather inaction – postmortem. Ultimately, then, the decision is made not by the patient himself, but by people who, even if they attempt to act in good faith, may contradict the wishes of the decedent.

The opt-out model treats people differently. The American Medical Association insists that people must be made aware of their tacit consent under the law and that ways of opting out must be accessible and effective.[30] Similarly, Richard Thaler and Cass Sunstein claim that people must be able to opt out *easily* if their fundamental freedom is to be preserved.[31] If these safeguards are in place, then people are not being tricked or coerced, and conceivably people would be more aware of what they have consented to allow after their death than they are under an opt-in policy, where, if the deceased has never indicated his preference, the decision is left to other decision-makers. If an opt-out policy is clear and promulgated, a person can be presumed to have consented, and this is more likely to conform to the person's intentions than if his family members were to make the decision after his death. Indeed, studies show that when a patient's wishes are unknown to the family, the family is more likely not to consent to the donation.[32]

Under an opt-in system, a lack of express consent is typically equated with a refusal to donate. That is, patients who have not declared themselves to be organ donors are assumed to have decided not to participate. However, if 78 percent of people want to donate their organs (as the U.S. government survey indicates), then assuming their consent (unless they indicate otherwise) is more likely to accord with patients' actual wishes than assuming that they do not want to donate. In other words, if silence on the part of the decedent is taken to indicate acceptance rather than refusal, then the person's choice is more likely to be respected by doctors and by next of kin if organs are extracted as a matter of course, given the fact that a greater percentage of people want to donate rather than not.

There is evidence that an opt-out system would increase organ donation rates. A recent statistical analysis finds that, other things being equal, a country's donation rate increases by roughly 16 percent when it switches from an opt-in system to an opt-out system.[33] Nonetheless, support for presumed consent is far from unanimous, and some people have suggested other alternatives. For example, the AMA recommends mandated choice instead, where each person *must* decide whether or not to donate; no one can simply fail to choose one way or the other, so nothing needs to be "presumed." Thaler and Sunstein do not express a preference between mandated choice and presumed consent.[34] However, if our goal is to bring people's actions into accordance with a respect for others without thereby violating people's right to self-determination, then evidence suggests that presumed consent is a better policy. Although mandated choice respects the personal autonomy of the potential donor, it fails to advance the ends of those who are in need. Where this policy has been implemented, it has actually led to a decrease in the number of available organs.[35]

Still, people are concerned about the erosion of personal freedom under an opt-out policy. For example, Robert Veatch has objected to the policy of presumed consent by claiming that it fundamentally transforms the relationship between the individual and the society. Under an opt-out model, he says, a significant number of people would have their organs taken against their will, simply because they do not indicate their preference not to donate. These people cannot be presumed to have consented to donate, which is why Veatch rejects the language of consent. Instead, Veatch calls it a kind of routine salvaging whereby the state is taken to have a claim on a person's organs. In a liberal system, the presumption should be in favor of individual rights, not using the individual to advance the greater good.[36] As we saw in the Introduction, the prohibition against using people's bodies without their consent is an important implication of Kant's ethics, and it is a basic assumption of modern medical practice, as expressed in the Nuremberg Code and the Belmont Report.

Whether consent can be presumed depends on how transparent the process is and how easy it is for the person to opt out. The easier the process, the more a policy of presumed consent begins to resemble a policy of mandated choice – which, incidentally, is the position endorsed by Veatch. As examples, Veatch recommends requiring patients to indicate whether or not they agree to donate when they are given routine physicals, or having potential drivers check a box when they complete their license applications.[37] A similar model could be devised under an opt-out policy: a doctor or someone at the Department of Motor Vehicles would inform the person about the policy and give him a card to sign and return to the office if he wants to opt out. Such a minor policy shift – given ample opportunity to indicate no, as opposed to being pressured to answer yes or no – hardly amounts to a step down the slippery slope toward totalitarianism. If it is implemented correctly, an opt-out policy is no more coercive than an opt-in policy or a policy of mandated choice.

A clearly promulgated opt-out policy would also avoid the high number of "false positives" that Veatch anticipates. He claims that the state would be harvesting organs from unwilling donors about 30 percent of the time, since approximately 70 percent of people are "very likely" or "somewhat likely" to donate their organs.[38] In making this claim, however, he assumes that *none* of the people who do not want to donate would in fact opt out; they would all be the victims of routine harvesting. If all of these people are given the means to opt out, in a simple and straightforward way, then presumably the vast majority of them would refuse to donate. Their freedom to choose would be respected.

Of course, this does not imply that a person who says nothing has freely chosen to donate. Some people who end up donating under an opt-out system would not have volunteered under an opt-in system. Even people who say they want to or are likely to donate their organs ultimately may have decided not to donate; their intention may be a "mere wish" rather than "the summoning of all means insofar as they are in our control" (G 394). The question here, though, is not whether everyone who fails to opt out is choosing to donate. Rather, we must ask if, in the absence of a clear choice by the decedent, doctors can be legally allowed to extract the dead person's organs in order to save the lives of those in need. If the law is made clear to people and opting out is not a difficult process, then respect for the value of the living can better be coupled with a respect for personal autonomy with an opt-out system.

An opt-out system would best adhere to a Kantian conception of the law: people would have the option to choose what happens to their bodies after death, just as they can choose what happens to their (other) property, but the law would be devised such that it encourages us to act in a way that is consistent with the value of rational agency. It would respect the autonomy of the decedent while also respecting the autonomy of the still-living.

Autonomy and the Body

Kant argues that autonomy is strengthened when our choices are limited in the right ways. For those who reject or do not understand this claim, it sounds strange to say that there are moral restrictions on what a person can do with her own body and that the state ought to structure our choices in order to discourage morally impermissible actions. In the United States in particular, it is often thought that one's actions should only be limited if they harm others, and that we relinquish some of our freedom under the law to gain the security that we do not have in the state of nature. Like Hobbes, we tend to believe that any constraint amounts to a loss of freedom.

What Kant shows us is that freedom is not so simple. One of his great contributions to philosophy is his explanation of why acting freely is not the same thing as acting capriciously. The *Groundwork* sets out the constraints to which we must adhere in order for our maxims to be consistent with rational end-setting. We must act rightly, in a way that is determined by reason rather than our inclinations, if we are to act autonomously. The *Metaphysics of Morals* sets out the limits of our freedom when acting in a community of agents. By adhering to these limits, we give up our "wild, lawless freedom" and consent to the law that reason prescribes, thus maintaining our freedom "undiminished" (MM 316).

Valuing autonomy in the Kantian sense is not equivalent to the liberal claim that each person can do whatever she wants as long as she only affects herself. Onora O'Neill clearly explains this distinction: Kantian autonomy is not something that individuals possess in relation to other individuals, but is rather a property of principles that are shareable by all other agents. People tend to think of patient autonomy as choice without constraint, but Kant understands autonomy as being constrained in a particular way, by the formal conditions of rational end-setting. What O'Neill calls "*principled autonomy*" limits what we can do if we are to determine our actions freely.[39]

By applying Kant's practical philosophy to some important issues in bioethics, we have begun to trace the contours of what rational autonomy amounts to. We also have a clearer sense of how Kant thinks ethics and the law are related, an issue that will receive much more attention in chapters 5 and 6. Most importantly, however, we realize that a person's body is not like any other piece of property that she can discard on a whim. With physician-assisted suicide, the refusal of medical treatment, and presumed consent in organ donation, we see that Kant is deeply concerned with the treatment of the body. To be sure, the body is morally relevant because it is crucial to our being agents; it has no value in itself. Nonetheless, the body must be regulated by reason, just as citizens must be regulated by the law.

As the first section of the book concludes, it is clear that Kant has important contributions to make to a number of perennial issues in applied ethics. Kant's practical philosophy yields many of the principles governing ethical human experimentation. Kant is partly responsible for our ingrained anthropocentrism, so it makes sense that his commitment to the dignity of persons and the value of autonomy would resonate with us. However, as we continue to grapple with Kant's legacy, we must be careful not to assume that animals and nature are simply expendable resources and that personal freedom ought to be unrestricted. Kantian principles go a long way toward justifying environmental conservation and restoration, as well as giving us compelling arguments for why we should be concerned with animal welfare. Kant's ethics justifies government intervention to provide health care and reasonable limitations on our choices as patients at the end of life. In each case, Kant begins with foundational moral principles – we should not make exceptions of ourselves, we should not use people as mere instruments for our own purposes, etc. – and he reaches conclusions that are contrary to the caricature of Kant as a proto-libertarian and an "invidious humanist" who poses a threat to all nonhuman beings.[40] Even after two hundred years of scholarly activity, Kant's importance for applied ethics has yet to be fully realized.

Notes

1 John Locke explicitly makes this claim of self-ownership: "every Man has [through the law of nature] a Property in his own Person. This no Body has any Right to but himself" (*Second Treatise of Government*, ed. C. B. Macpherson [Indianapolis, Ind.: Hackett, 1980], §27).

2 Arthur J. Dyck, "An Alternative to the Ethic of Euthanasia," in *To Live and To Die: When, Why, and How*, ed. Robert H. Williams (New York: Springer, 1973), 98–112, esp. 106.

3 I include the caveat "barring strange circumstances" to cover extraordinary cases where one's suicide would drastically affect others' lives. For example, if

I see a kid drowning in a shallow pond and no one else is there, killing myself at that moment would also amount to shirking my moral obligation to save the kid. Also, Kant mentions that a pregnant woman who kills herself would be committing a crime not only against herself but "against another" (MM 422). I will discuss the tricky issue of pregnancy in chapter 10.

4   Jean-Jacques Rousseau, *On the Social Contract*, trans. Judith R. Masters, ed. Roger D. Masters (New York: St. Martin's, 1978), 50–2.

5   Locke, *Second Treatise*, §§23–4.

6   Kant says at one point that a slave should not risk death in trying to escape because death cuts off any possibility of being a self-determining person, while a slave still has the capacity for autonomy and may at some point regain his freedom (LE 603).

7   Barbara Herman, *The Practice of Moral Judgment* (Cambridge, Mass.: Harvard University Press, 1993), 228.

8   Michael J. Cholbi, "Suicide Intervention and Non-Ideal Kantian Theory," *Journal of Applied Philosophy* 19, no. 3 (Dec. 2002): 245–59 (p. 249).

9   Ibid., 253. Kant's analysis of what motivates suicide is not as one-dimensional as Cholbi makes it out to be. It is true that, in the *Moralphilosophie Collins* and the *Groundwork*, Kant conceives of suicide as an act of prudence in which the person decides to minimize his unhappiness by killing himself (LE 343, 369–75; G 422, 429). In the *Anthropology*, however, Kant recognizes different ways of being driven to suicide: by a sudden impulse or change of mood (*raptus*) (A 213); by despondency, anger, despair (either strong or weak), or by "a mental disorder stemming from anguish" (A 258–9). Elsewhere Kant says that being "in deep sadness . . . is . . . also a kind of insanity" (LM 28:255).

10 This is the intent of the law, at least. As Cholbi reminds us, the difficulty of determining if a suicidal person is mentally ill does complicate things. According to Oregon's and Washington's Death with Dignity Acts, patients who request PAS must be referred for counseling only if the attending physician or the consulting physician believes that the patient may be suffering from a mental disorder (ORS 127.825 s.3.03, RCW 70.245 s.6). It is possible, then, that in any given case medical doctors are the only physicians who are making judgments about a patient's competence, rather than psychiatrists or psychologists who are trained and qualified to recognize mental illness. This increases the possibility that some PAS patients are incompetent.

11 It could be worse. According to Kant, "willfully *killing* oneself can be called murdering oneself" (MM 422).

12 Dennis R. Cooley, "A Kantian Moral Duty for the Soon-to-be Demented to Commit Suicide," *American Journal of Bioethics* 7, no. 6 (June 2007): 37–44 (p. 41).

13 Ibid., 39.

14 Ibid., 43.

15 There is some tension among the various claims that Kant makes about slavery and death. At one point, he says that an honorable person should choose death over servitude, if given the choice (LE 376), but as I mentioned earlier, he also says that a slave should not risk his life in an escape, because the possibility that he may someday be freed is preferable to death (LE 603).

16 Constance Perry, "Suicide Fails to Pass the Categorical Imperative," *American Journal of Bioethics* 7, no. 6 (June 2007): 51–3 (p. 52).

17 Stephen R. Latham, "Kant Condemned All Suicide," *American Journal of Bioethics* 7, no. 6 (June 2007): 49–51 (p. 51).

18 Cooley, "A Kantian Moral Duty," 39.

19 American Medical Association, *Code of Medical Ethics*, Opinion 2.211: Physician-Assisted Suicide, www.ama-assn.org/ama/pub/physician-resources/medical-ethics/code-medical-ethics/opinion2211.shtml.

20 American Medical Association, *Code of Medical Ethics*, Opinion 2.20: Withholding or Withdrawing Life-Sustaining Medical Treatment, www.ama-assn.org/ama/pub/physician-resources/medical-ethics/code-medical-ethics/opinion220.shtml.

21 James Rachels, "Active and Passive Euthanasia," *New England Journal of Medicine* 292, no. 2 (9 Jan. 1975): 78–80. Rachels concludes that the AMA's endorsement of passive euthanasia (withholding treatment) is inconsistent with its condemnation of active euthanasia (taking direct action to end a patient's life).

22 The Catholic Church makes what is at bottom a slippery slope argument: "We are gravely concerned about current attitudes and policy trends in our society that would too easily dismiss patients without apparent mental faculties as nonpersons or as undeserving of human care and concern. In this climate, even legitimate moral arguments intended to have a careful and limited application can easily be misinterpreted, broadened and abused by others to erode respect for the lives of some of our society's most helpless members" (U.S. Bishops' Pro-Life Committee, "Nutrition and Hydration: Moral and Pastoral Reflections," in *Ethical Issues in Modern Medicine: Contemporary Readings in Bioethics*, ed. Bonnie Steinbock, John D. Arras, and Alex John London, 7th edn. [Boston: McGraw-Hill, 2009], 429–35 [p. 435]). As we will see in chapter 10, the Catholic Church and others have claimed that, like our treatment of PVS patients, our treatment of unborn children also affects our attitudes toward persons. Abortion shows a general disrespect for human life, and thus corrupts our moral character.

23 Organ Procurement and Transplantation Network, United States Department of Health and Human Services, "Removal Reasons by Year," optn.transplant.hrsa.gov/latestData/rptData.asp. In 2009, 7,107 people died while on the waiting list for transplants. That same year, 21,815 transplantable organs were supplied by 8,021 deceased organ donors. Organs are recovered from about 50 percent of medically eligible deceased donors, meaning that approximately 22,000 transplantable organs were buried or cremated (United States Department of Health and Human Services, Office of Inspector General, "Variation in Organ Donation among Transplant Centers," 2003, oig.hhs.gov/oei/reports/oei-01-02-00210.pdf).

24 David Steinberg has suggested that this appeal to fairness and reciprocity should be made real rather than merely being a hypothetical scenario to test maxims. A system based on "reciprocal altruism" would give people preference for receiving organs, should they need them, *if* they agree to donate their organs to others. The way that they treat others (donating or not donating) would

then affect how others treat them (prioritizing or not prioritizing their needs). See David Steinberg, "An 'Opting In' Paradigm for Kidney Transplantation," *American Journal of Bioethics* 4, no. 4 (fall 2004): 4–14.

25 The question of how a dead person can be harmed has been addressed by several philosophers. The so-called Pitcher–Feinberg thesis is the most compelling account. We have duties to the "antemortem person" to whom we made the promise. After he is dead, we cannot consider only his existing interests; a "postmortem person" has no interests. Breaking the promise at that point would amount to harming the person while he was alive. See George Pitcher, "The Misfortunes of the Dead," *American Philosophical Quarterly* 21, no. 2 (Apr. 1984): 183–8, and Joel Feinberg, *Harm to Others*, vol. 1 of *The Moral Limits of the Criminal Law* (New York: Oxford University Press, 1984), 79–95.

26 National Conference of Commissioners on Uniform State Laws, "Revised Uniform Anatomical Gift Act" (2006), www.law.upenn.edu/bll/archives/ulc/uaga/2009final.htm.

27 Kant's theory of freedom and his approach to the law in protecting our freedom differ significantly from the views of classic liberal political theorists, as we will see in chapter 6. For Kant, true freedom means being constrained in the right way, not being left alone to pursue whatever one wants.

28 Health Resources and Services Administration, Division of Transplantation, "2005 National Survey of Organ and Tissue Donation Attitudes and Behaviors" (Washington, D.C.: Gallup Organization, 2005), ftp://ftp.hrsa.gov/organdonor/survey2005.pdf. Similar results were found by E. Guadagnoli et al., "The Public's Willingness to Discuss Their Preference for Organ Donation with Family Members," *Clinical Transplantation* 13, no. 4 (Aug. 1999): 342–8.

29 This kind of charge was leveled against Cass Sunstein during his (ultimately successful) confirmation hearings to head the Office of Information and Regulatory Affairs in the Obama administration. Some of Sunstein's conservative detractors, especially Glenn Beck, claimed that presumed consent amounts to the forced removal of people's organs regardless of their personal preferences. These opponents of Sunstein confused presumed consent with routine removal, even though Sunstein explicitly rejects the latter policy because it does not allow people the freedom to decide what to do with their bodies. See Richard H. Thaler and Cass R. Sunstein, *Nudge: Improving Decisions about Health, Wealth, and Happiness* (New Haven, Conn.: Yale University Press, 2008), 177.

30 American Medical Association, Council on Ethical and Judicial Affairs, Report 7-A-05, http://www.ama-assn.org/ama1/pub/upload/mm/369/ceja_7a05.pdf.

31 Thaler and Sunstein, *Nudge*, 177–8.

32 Laura A. Siminoff and Renee H. Lawrence, "Knowing Patients' Preferences about Organ Donation: Does It Make a Difference?" *Journal of Trauma* 53, no. 4 (Oct. 2002): 754–60. In some countries, including New Zealand, families have a legal right to veto decisions to donate that were made by deceased family members during their lifetimes. In the United States, Australia, and Great Britain, the family has no legal right to refuse if the deceased has previously consented to donate, but in practice medical staff often defer to the family,

either because they worry about lawsuits or because they do not want to add to the stress of grieving family members. Studies show that, in the United States, families refuse consent up to 50 percent of the time (Ellen Sheehy et al., "Estimating the Number of Potential Organ Donors in the United States," *New England Journal of Medicine* 349, no. 7 [14 Aug. 2003]: 667–74). If the opt-out strategy is to result in increased organ donations, governments and hospitals must adopt consistent policies that properly balance respect for the wishes (or presumed wishes) of the deceased, the growing demand for transplantable organs, and consideration for the interests of the family. See especially T. M. Wilkinson, "Individual and Family Decisions about Organ Donation," *Journal of Applied Philosophy* 24, no. 1 (Feb. 2007): 26–40, and Jurgen De Wispelaere and Lindsay Stirton, "Advance Commitment: An Alternative Approach to the Family Veto Problem in Organ Procurement," *Journal of Medical Ethics* 36, no. 3 (March 2010): 180–3.

33　Alberto Abadie and Sebastian Gay, "The Impact of Presumed Consent Legislation on Cadaveric Organ Donation: A Cross Country Study," National Bureau of Economic Research (NBER) Working Paper no. W10604, July 2004, www.nber.org/papers/w10604. See also Arthur J. Mattas et al., "A Proposal for Cadaver Organ Procurement: Routine Removal with Right of Informed Refusal," *Journal of Health Politics, Policy and Law* 10, no. 2 (summer 1985): 231–44; Laurie G. Futterman, "Presumed Consent: The Solution to the Critical Organ Donor Shortage?" *American Journal of Respiratory and Critical Care Medicine* 4, no. 5 (1995): 383–8; Fady Moustarah, "Organ Procurement: Let's Presume Consent," *Canadian Medical Association Journal* 158, no. 2 (27 Jan. 1998): 231–4; and Eric J. Johnson and Daniel Goldstein, "Do Defaults Save Lives?" *Science* 302, no. 5649 (21 Nov. 2003): 1338–9.

34　Thaler and Sunstein, *Nudge*, 180–1.

35　Laura A. Siminoff and Mary Beth Mercer, "Public Policy, Public Opinion, and Consent for Organ Donation," *Cambridge Quarterly of Healthcare Ethics* 10, no. 4 (fall 2001): 377–86.

36　Robert M. Veatch, *Transplantation Ethics* (Washington, D.C.: Georgetown University Press, 2000), 167–74.

37　Ibid., 178–9.

38　Ibid., 170–1.

39　Onora O'Neill, *Autonomy and Trust in Bioethics* (Cambridge: Cambridge University Press, 2002), esp. 83–95. See also Onora O'Neill, "Autonomy: The Emperor's New Clothes, The Inaugural Address," *Proceedings of the Aristotelian Society* 77 (2003): 1–21.

40　Christina Hoff, "Kant's Invidious Humanism," *Environmental Ethics* 5, no. 1 (1983): 63–70.

Part II

Kantian Arguments against Kant's Conclusions

The first four chapters have shown that Kant's practical philosophy has important contributions to make to bioethics and environmental ethics. With its emphasis on the value of moral agency, Kantian ethics justifies a deep concern for public health, emphasizes the importance of patient autonomy in medical decisions, and enjoins us to develop a moral regard for animals and for nature. Kant stakes out positions that are consistent with our moral intuitions and, when they challenge those intuitions, he provides compelling reasons to revise our views – namely, by appealing to the dignity and worth of persons.

Surprisingly, in some cases Kant's insights regarding the value of humanity and our duties to others challenge even his own avowed positions. Our critical appraisal of Kant's philosophy begins in chapter 5, with an examination of his justification for capital punishment. Kant's support for the death penalty was not atypical at the time, and retributivist arguments like Kant's are still used to defend it. Nevertheless, I argue that we cannot be obligated by the law of retribution in capital cases because of the possibility of wrongful convictions. If we faithfully apply Kant's categorical imperative, we cannot commit ourselves to a system in which we may be put to death despite our actual innocence.

In chapter 6, I turn to the same-sex marriage debate. Kant strongly condemned homosexuality, claiming that it was unnatural, degrading, and dehumanizing (LE 391). However, Kant's condemnation of homosexuality does not stand up to scrutiny, nor is it consistent with Kant's own moral views. In fact, once we fully understand Kant's conception of the law and the function of marriage as a legal institution, it becomes clear that we ought to support same-sex marriage based entirely on Kantian principles. As we will see, Kant's moral philosophy is much more progressive than Kant himself seems to have been.

Kant and Applied Ethics: The Uses and Limits of Kant's Practical Philosophy, First Edition.
Matthew C. Altman.
© 2011 John Wiley & Sons Inc. Published 2011 by Blackwell Publishing Ltd.

5

Subjecting Ourselves to Capital Punishment

The idea that someone who has taken a life should in turn have his life taken appeals to some of our unreflective impulses, but Immanuel Kant, who is one of the strongest critics of using our inclinations as the basis of juridical legislation, concludes that the practice is also rationally required of us by the law of retribution: we must execute murderers because they deserve to die. Although retributivism is one of the theoretical approaches most often used to justify capital punishment, Kant's conclusion seems inconsistent with some of our considered moral intuitions – most notably, that no wrongly convicted person should be killed.

In this chapter, I argue that retribution cannot warrant the application of capital punishment in practice because its seeming plausibility rests on a fundamental confusion: granting the moral claim that a murderer deserves to die does not mean that we ought to kill someone who has been convicted of murder. The retributivist tends to see these as identical claims, but they cannot be conflated for two related reasons, both of which are grounded in Kantian principles. First, our inability to know a person's motives precludes the possibility of imputing guilt to the accused; second, the necessary fallibility of our justice system and the possibility of wrongly executing the innocent undermine the reasonableness of our consenting to the death penalty. Although this may seem to imply that punishments in general cannot be justified on retributivist grounds, the finality of the death penalty makes the execution of convicted killers morally problematic in a way that other coercive measures are not. In the end, a committed Kantian may continue to support the death penalty in principle, but must oppose it in practice.

Kant and Applied Ethics: The Uses and Limits of Kant's Practical Philosophy, First Edition.
Matthew C. Altman.
© 2011 John Wiley & Sons Inc. Published 2011 by Blackwell Publishing Ltd.

The Difference between Morality and Legality

To understand how retribution is supposed to be justified when we apply
the law in criminal cases, it helps to see how our legal responsibilities are
related to our moral obligations. In the *Groundwork of the Metaphysics of
Morals*, Kant argues that right and wrong must be determined by appealing
to a deontological moral principle. To be fully self-legislating, we must act
on the basis of reasons that are shareable by all rational end-setters *qua*
reasoners. Specifically, we must do what is right because it is right, not
because it satisfies our contingent desires. Conforming to the conditions
under which my reasons could serve for everyone (as universal) and could
bind everyone (as practically necessary) – as if I were a law-making member
of the kingdom of ends – is a necessary condition of the reasonableness of
my maxim (G 438).

This kind of pure moral philosophy abstracts from all empirical concepts
in considering the moral agent simply as a rational being with a will:
given the formal conditions that constrain the capacity to set ends, how
should the agent act? Of course, actual agents are situated in particular
social and material circumstances, so some of this must be considered when
establishing what is right under the law. But even when legality (rather than
morality) is at issue, agents still must be conceived in terms of what they
share with other agents. The law that constrains a person cannot depend
on her unique desires and physical capacities. Kant believes that applied
moral philosophy, like all philosophy, must be *a priori* – specifically, an *a
priori* investigation into the practical link between the moral law and
empirical concepts.[1] Applied moral philosophy conceives of us as finite
agents with physical needs and limited resources, who confront other agents
in a social setting. After Kant justifies the criterion of universalizability in
the *Groundwork*, the *Doctrine of Right* deals with how any finite rational
being ought to act among other rational beings. For example, our legal
obligations concern how we as property owners are restricted by pure,
rational principles in our relations with other property owners.

Although the legality of an action follows in part from our moral obligations to ourselves and other agents, the two must be strictly distinguished.
Legality has to do both with one's physical behavior, which (if free) follows
from the principles one chooses, and with how that behavior affects other
people. Morality is only concerned with the maxims that stand behind one's
actions and whether those maxims are universalizable. To use Kant's terminology, the *Doctrine of Right* concerns "outer freedom" rather than
"inner freedom" (MM 396). Only the former is subject to coercion by the
state: "The concept of right . . . has to do, *first*, only with the external and
indeed practical relation of one person to another, insofar as their actions,

as deeds, can have (direct or indirect) influence on each other" (MM 230). Inner freedom is our capacity to act on the basis of pure practical principles, and is the concern of pure moral philosophy. Outer freedom is our capacity to achieve ends that we set within a community of end-setters, and is the concern of applied moral philosophy. In other words, morality concerns the formal conditions of acting at all and demands that any subjective principle of action be adoptable by all rational beings (i.e., universalizable). The legality of what I do depends on whether my actions are consistent with the freedom of other rational beings who physically inhabit the same world that I do, a world with finite resources and in which our actions affect one another.

The distinction between legality and morality becomes clearer when we look at the reasons that particular actions are condemned. For example, stealing is morally impermissible because such a maxim would be impossible to adopt if it were universalized. My being able to steal depends on a general sense of trust, which I take advantage of in pilfering something from my unsuspecting victim. By contrast, it is illegal to steal because a person can achieve the purposes she sets for herself only if she has things to employ as instruments.[2] She must own property securely so that she can be secure in her ability to act. Therefore, my stealing from her is inconsistent with her freedom. This justifies private property laws.

Retribution and the Death Penalty

For Kant, we are morally obligated to leave the state of nature and subject ourselves to a social contract. By engaging other rational beings in a civil society, I agree to fix my freedom within limits so that my actions can be consistent with the freedom of others. My consenting to restrict my freedom under the law thus follows from my respect for their capacity to set ends. I will pursue what I value as long as it does not inhibit another person's ability to pursue what he values.

In civil society, the agent may be motivated to act lawfully wholly out of a sense of duty toward the law, but what the law requires of him can be fulfilled regardless of his disposition. A person may refrain from stealing others' property out of respect for them as rational beings or simply out of fear of punishment; the latter is perfectly legal, although it is not morally praiseworthy. For this, the agent would have to be motivated by duty. In principle, coercion cannot enforce this sort of obligation. As opposed to moral laws that constrain practical reasoning, juridical legislation deals only with the legality of actions: "The mere conformity or nonconformity of an action with law, irrespective of the incentive to it, is called its *legality* (lawfulness); but that conformity in which the idea of duty arising from the law is also the incentive to the action is called its *morality*" (MM 219). Legality has to do with the agent's action, while morality has to do with the agent's maxim. Someone who obeys the law out of self-interest is legally blameless but morally lacking.

Because legal concerns involve only outer freedom, they can be enforced through punishment and the threat of punishment. We consent to the law in accordance with the rational demand to respect others as free pursuers of ends, and we act rightly by constraining our actions through coercive measures. Only by agreeing to the enforcement of external laws do we fulfill our moral duty to further the ends of others – specifically, by thwarting those actions that are inconsistent with outer freedom: "if a certain use of freedom is itself a hindrance to freedom in accordance with universal laws (i.e., wrong), coercion that is opposed to this (as a *hindering of a hindrance to freedom*) is consistent with freedom in accordance with universal laws, that is, it is right" (MM 231). The threat of fines or a prison sentence discourages people from violating the freedom of others and thus promotes freedom in general.

In matters concerning virtue, conscience serves as an "*internal court*" that determines guilt or innocence based on whether the agent acts for the sake of duty (MM 438). When someone violates external law, however, the alleged criminal cannot serve as judge in his own case. If he has in fact committed the crime, then he has violated the law to which he has previously consented. He has acted contrary to what reason requires and what he has agreed to as a citizen. He is not fit to pronounce judgment and must instead be tried by an impartial court that has the authority, vested in it by the social contract, "to impute with rightful force" – that is, to judge an action under the law and to sentence the offender (MM 227).

To do this, the court must make two kinds of assessments: it must decide whether the deed can be properly imputed to the accused, and it must determine the kind and degree of punishment that is appropriate. To accomplish the latter task, the court must look to "the *law of retribution*," according to which a punishment is legitimate only when it is proportional to the crime (MM 332). According to Kant, other possible justifications violate the moral basis of the social contract. Only the principle of equality between crime and punishment holds categorically, as rationally necessary: "all other principles are fluctuating and unsuited for a sentence of pure and strict justice because extraneous considerations are mixed into them" (MM 332; see also LE 555). We cannot warrant punishment by appealing to its deterrent effects, for example, because this would amount to using the criminal to promote the larger social good, a mere means to an end. The general welfare is only conditionally good, and cannot be pursued at the expense of moral rightness – specifically, respect for others and ourselves as rational agents. However, if we give a person what he deserves for acting wrongly, then we treat him as a rational being who can be held responsible for what he does. As we saw in chapter 1, only those beings to whom we can impute responsibility are morally considerable. Punishing someone based on his guilt treats the person as a moral agent who chooses to act wrongly rather than merely an animal whose behavior must be corrected. We respect what Martin Perlmutter calls the person's "right to be punished."[3]

Because the severity of a crime varies according to both the kind of crime that is committed and the person's degree of responsibility, the appropriate punishment also varies. Whether a crime is premeditated affects the culpability of the accused: "the state of mind of the subject, whether he committed the deed in a state of agitation or with cool deliberation, makes a difference in imputation" (MM 228). Of course, all crimes violate the dignity of the victim: stealing from someone shows lack of respect for the private property that he needs to accomplish his ends, killing someone treats him as an expendable thing rather than a person with absolute worth, etc. Still, some crimes are more egregious than others, either because the criminal acted with malice or because he did something much more damaging to a person's humanity, and such crimes deserve harsher punishments.

In each case, the punishment ought to be appropriate for the crime that is committed: for example, a slanderer ought to apologize publicly, so that his vanity is similarly harmed; a thief ought to be deprived of property and made to work for the state to pay for his own incarceration; and a murderer ought to be put to death (LE 555–6; MM 332–3). Death is not comparable to any amount of hardship that would come with a loss of honor or a prison term, so murder can only be repaid in kind by executing the murderer. With any punishment, the state must take measures not to abuse the criminal in a way that demeans him and us – we should not rape rapists, torture torturers, or inflict the same pain on killers that they inflict on their victims. Still, in the case of murder, Kant maintains that only capital punishment fulfills the law of retribution:

> If . . . he has committed murder he must *die*. Here there is no substitute that will satisfy justice. There is no *similarity* between life, however wretched it may be, and death, hence no likeness between the crime and the retribution unless death is judicially carried out upon the wrongdoer, although it must still be freed from any mistreatment that could make the humanity in the person suffering it into something abominable. (MM 333)

The just response to a crime is to punish the offender in accordance with the law, and the law is justified by the *a priori* law of retribution. Because the murder of another person takes away the life of the victim, the death of the murderer is the only equivalent and appropriate punishment. Other violations are comparable to one another – those convicted of petty theft tend to get fewer years in prison than those convicted of battery, who tend to get fewer years in prison than those convicted of arson, etc. – but murder cannot be placed on the same spectrum of relative value as property damage or (reparable) harm to the body. Although all crimes undermine the dignity of rational end-setters, only murder undermines the victim's very capacity to set ends, as opposed to their ability to achieve the ends they set. A life brought to an abrupt end is not like money stolen, an arm broken, or a building burned. It is an offense against the very foundation of civil society: the capacity for rational consent.

Consenting to Capital Punishment

A person who is convicted of a crime is subject to the law because she is "a colegislator in dictating the *penal law*," and this (prior) rational consent demands that she be punished for her (subsequent) violations of the law (MM 335). This is not to say that, by participating in a civil society, the person is willing her own punishment. If she did, the agent would be undermining her own capacity to will, which would put the will in contradiction with itself. Rather, the person's pure reason dictates that, according to the law of retribution, *anyone* who commits a crime ought to be punished appropriately; and that, according to the principle of equality, *were* she to commit a crime, she also ought to be punished.[4]

In making this distinction, Kant is responding to an objection by Cesare Beccaria, an Italian philosopher and politician who argued that the contemporary penal codes were so cruel that they could not be thought to have received the consent of the people. Rationally consenting to the death penalty, in particular, would amount to killing oneself – an irrational act.[5] Kant rejects this interpretation. The criminal does not will her own punishment. Instead, she wills a punishable action that violates the law prescribed by reason. The agent as colegislator of the law acts rationally in setting punishments that should be handed down by the courts, but the agent as murderer does not act rationally in undermining her very ability to act – that is, by acting in a way that brings the death penalty upon her.[6] We must distinguish the purely rational legislator of the law from the imperfect agent who violates the law, just as we must distinguish the reason in the person that is bound to the moral law from the inclination to self-love. When I commit a crime, I am subject to the law to which I have consented, but this does not mean that my participation in the original social contract is problematic.

Although this is a fine distinction, the central question for the Kantian retributivist is not whether a person can rationally consent to the social contract, but whether the legislators of civil society ought to establish and enforce the death penalty in particular. A person who constrains herself according to the rational requirements of civil society and then murders someone does place her will into contradiction with itself, but the real question is whether we ought to adopt juridical legislation that has us execute those whom the state finds guilty of murder. In other words, can someone rationally consent to capital punishment with the understanding that a person's conviction in a court of law is sufficient to sanction the punishment?[7]

Determining the "Inner Wickedness" of the Accused

The law to which we consent must be consistent with its moral basis in respect for the dignity of others. And, according to Kant, because the law of retribution is rationally required of us, a person's murder conviction by an impartial judge justifies only one appropriate punishment:

> This fitting of punishment to the crime, which can occur only by a judge imposing the death sentence in accordance with the strict law of retribution, is shown by the fact that only by this is a sentence of death pronounced on every criminal in proportion to his *inner wickedness* . . . (MM 333)

In order to give the accused what he deserves, the judge must not only determine whether he actually killed someone, but must also assess his motivation in committing the crime. The act must be the result of the agent's free choice, not the result of "natural necessity." For example, the person must have chosen to push a drowning victim into the water (or been otherwise responsible, e.g., because he was drunk) rather than doing so because of a physical cause, such as a dizzy spell (LE 558–9). A person is a murderer only if he intentionally brings about a death, with malice afore-thought. Therefore, the killer's state of mind is crucial in justifying a death sentence.

The problem is that we can never accurately assess the criminal's intent, so it seems that we are unable ever to enforce the law of retribution. As Kant says, why a person acts in a certain way is necessarily unavailable both to the observation of others and to the inner sense of the person himself. Neither one's "inner wickedness" nor the actual extent of one's own responsibility can ever be known, so neither the "internal court" of conscience nor the state's criminal court can determine the appropriate punishment:

> The real morality of actions (their merit and guilt), even that of our own conduct, therefore remains entirely hidden from us. Our imputations can be

referred only to the empirical character. How much of it is to be ascribed to mere nature and innocent defects of temperament or to its happy constitution (*merito fortunae*) this no one can discover, and hence no one can judge it with complete justice. (CPR A551n/B579n; see also G 407, 419)

According to Kant's transcendental idealism, we can only know the world and ourselves as they appear to us, subject to the categories of the understanding, including the concept of causality. We cannot know things as they are in themselves. This allows Kant to distinguish causally determined phenomena from our uncaused capacity for self-determination. Only the former can be known. As moral agents, we are responsible for our actions only when we consider ourselves as free beings, apart from the categories, so self-knowledge does not extend to the principles upon which we have chosen to act. The idea that our motives are inscrutable does not depend on this particular epistemological thesis, however. Since Nietzsche and Freud, this conception of ourselves has become commonly accepted.

In any given case, we are necessarily ignorant of whether we are dealing with an action or merely an event. Murder ought to be punished, but whether a murder has taken place rather than merely the bringing about of a death – that is, a killing without "inner wickedness" – is unknown and unknowable, even to the accused. We believe that we can determine what is most probable given the circumstances of the crime – whether it was planned in advance, for example – but what is apparent to us still may be the result of "mere nature," what the law typically calls a mental defect. Kant holds a very high evidentiary standard for determining criminal guilt: judgments that the deed actually took place and that it was freely caused by the accused – that it was the result of choice rather than madness, for example (A 213–14) – "must have the utmost moral and logical certainty" (MM 566). Unfortunately, we can never be certain whether the crime was performed freely or with malice, yet we need to know these things in order to determine guilt and to set the appropriate punishment.

As we saw earlier, the *Doctrine of Right* is concerned with the application of *a priori* moral principles to the sort of rational beings we happen to be – finite agents whose actions may come into conflict – rather than the subjective principles upon which we act. Someone may obey the law for any number of reasons, many of which (such as self-interest) are less than praiseworthy. For example, a person may refrain from shoplifting because it is morally wrong or because he worries about being spotted by security cameras. As far as the law is concerned, the person's motive is irrelevant, because in each case the action is legal.

Because of this, Thomas Pogge has claimed that external legislation, which is the subject of the *Doctrine of Right*, can only be concerned with "possible conflicts among actions."[8] The law cannot concern itself with "inner states," whose regulation does not affect the compatibility of different people's external freedom. "Such laws" – laws that would regulate our intentions – "fall outside *Recht* as Kant defines it." According to Pogge, this is a problem for Kant's theory, since legal systems must consider intentions in defining crimes and determining appropriate punishments.[9]

The latter point is certainly true, but Kant's inability to explain or justify such a legal system results from a deeper problem having to do with Kant's theory of agency (rather than simply his definition of *Recht*). According to Kant, actions that seem blameless may involve hidden, baser motives ("secret impulsions" [G 407]); alternatively, an agent may not in fact be responsible for what seems like a blameworthy action – it may be "ascribed to mere nature" (CPR A551n/B579n). The problem is that, in the case of illegal actions, the judge must determine the culpability of the criminal in order to impose the appropriate punishment. For example, a case of involuntary manslaughter must be distinguished from premeditated murder. But neither the judge nor the criminal himself can tell whether his action is or is not imputable to him as a free agent, or what his true reasons are for committing the act. If this is so, then the first element in passing any judgment upon the accused – imputing guilt – is, for us, an impossible task.[10]

The Fallibility of Justice

Kant specifies that, in order justifiably to be punished, the person must have committed the crime as a free act; it must be "a certain use of freedom" that hinders the freedom of others (MM 231). And, as we have seen, Kant claims that we can never know whether this is the case. However, even if we grant that actions that seem to be free are actions for which the person can be held legally responsible – that is, even if the intent of the accused criminal is somehow made manifest in the deed itself – attributing guilt and justifying coercion against a supposed criminal faces an additional problem that parallels, but is not identical to, the necessarily uncertain determination of the person's "inner wickedness." According to the law of retribution, a murderer deserves to die. But even if we agree with this abstract claim, we cannot derive from it our duty to kill someone who has been convicted of murder, simply because we can never determine with certainty whether the convicted person is the one who committed the crime and deserves to be punished.

We can be obligated to act on a principle only if we are able to adopt it as our principle of action. 'Ought' implies 'can'; if you cannot do something, you cannot be obligated to do it. It is impossible for us to adopt the law of retribution, because the facts that we would need in order to fulfill that obligation are unknown to us. Therefore, we cannot have a duty to carry out the law of retribution. At least, we cannot enforce the death penalty on that basis.

Despite our best efforts, we cannot distinguish putting to death an innocent person who has been found guilty of murder from putting to death the actual murderer. Legal judgments are necessarily fallible: witnesses can be mistaken, juries can be prejudiced, and confessions can be coerced. Recent history is rife with examples of innocent people who narrowly averted lethal injections.[11] Between 1977 and 2000, thirteen men on death row in Illinois were exonerated. These cases are widely known because they prompted Illinois governor George Ryan, a supporter of capital punishment, to impose a moratorium on the death penalty. Such errors in judgment are not unusual, however; the threat that capital punishment poses to the innocent is a longstanding problem. Michael Radelet, Hugo Adam Bedau, and Constance Putnam researched the period between 1900 and 1992 in the United States. During that time, and excluding those cases in which the defendant was merely(!) denied due process of law or in which a killing in self-defense was wrongly judged to be murder, the authors discovered 416 capital convictions in which the person was later found to be innocent of any involvement in the crime. In twenty-three of those cases, the person was executed before he was exonerated.[12] These figures are supported by a recent subcommittee report in the U.S. House of Representatives, which found that seven people who were probably innocent were executed between 1973 and 1992.[13] The Death Penalty Information Center has counted a total of 138 people who have been released from death row between 1973 and 2009 – not because of work by police investigators or by the courts, but because of journalists and activists who have conducted DNA tests or discovered witnesses who recanted their testimony.[14] Even as staunch a defender of the death penalty as Ernest van den Haag concedes that the institution of capital punishment "lead[s] to the execution of some innocents."[15] The debate over the death penalty continues, but the fact that innocent people are sometimes put to death is not seriously disputed.

With the emergence of widespread and more sophisticated DNA testing over the past twenty-five years, some people believe that erroneous convictions are becoming nearly impossible. Scholars in the U.S. are currently debating whether DNA evidence alone is sufficient to justify a criminal conviction, given how compelling it is for many juries. It is true that DNA profiling is an important tool for ruling in or ruling out suspects, and it can be a damning piece of evidence at trial. However, to believe in the infallibility of DNA evidence, we would have to ignore several possibilities: that evidence was planted by investigators or the actual criminal (both of which have been done); that errors were made at the testing laboratory; that the DNA sample was contaminated at the crime scene; that there was a coincidental match, which is more likely with a partial or damaged genetic profile; that the bands of DNA shifted and distorted over time, changing the measurements for analysis; and that an innocent person's DNA was left at the crime scene through the process of secondary transfer (when the innocent person shook hands with the criminal, etc.).[16] In short, the accused may be innocent because her DNA was not actually at the scene or because it was at the scene even though she did not commit the crime. DNA profiling is trusted by many law enforcement agencies and the general public, and that helps prosecutors to sway jurors. However, numerous scientists and statisticians have raised serious doubts about the technology. Supposed DNA evidence cannot prove with certainty that the accused committed the act, and it obviously cannot establish the intent of the accused criminal – whether it was rape or consensual sex, kidnapping or voluntary departure, murder or self-defense. No element of the crime is definitively established by DNA evidence, even if it does, in conjunction with other evidence, justify reasonable belief in a person's guilt.

Despite the advance of forensic techniques and technology, we cannot definitively establish whether a person violated the law. Kant says that "the real morality of actions (their merit and guilt)" cannot be judged "with complete justice," but it is also the case that we can never know whether a convicted criminal has in fact murdered someone (CPR A551n/B579n). Therefore, no society can be duty-bound to put murderers to death. We are able to kill those who are convicted of murder, but to kill only murderers is beyond our limited epistemic capacities. We cannot be bound by the law of retribution.

Capital Punishment Cannot Be Categorically Demanded of Us

This is not to say that moral commitments in general do not apply to us simply because we are imperfectly rational. We are not divine beings for whom the objectively necessary moral law is also subjectively necessary – we can act wrongly – but the moral law nonetheless constrains us as an imperative (G 412–14). Similarly, it seems plausible that the law of retribution could constrain us even if we do not always fulfill its demands. That is, it seems that we could be obligated to give murderers the death they deserve, even though we sometimes fail to fulfill this obligation. After all, we are morally obligated not to lie, to develop our talents, and to help others, all of which we sometimes fail to do. The occasional failure to live up to our moral obligations does not mean that there are no such obligations.

Our supposed obligation to the law of retribution is not like our obligation to the moral law, however; the cases are not parallel. The fact that we are bound to the moral law despite our imperfection implies nothing about our commitment to the law of retribution in criminal cases. An example will illustrate how they differ. Morally, I ought to have as my maxim that I will refrain from lying. I must decide whether not to lie (because I ought not to) or whether to adopt a contrary maxim and willfully deceive in violation of the categorical imperative. In making such a decision, I choose a maxim that would fulfill my duty, or I choose the opposite. By contrast, in order to fulfill my supposed duty to enforce the law of retribution, I must agree to punish the criminal in proportion to the crime he has committed. But the necessarily limited scope of my knowledge makes such a maxim impossible; I cannot have this as my subjective principle of action. I can only punish the criminal in proportion to the crime that, either correctly or incorrectly, I *take* him to have committed. It is not that I sometimes fail to act rightly – as, indeed, I sometimes lie – but that I cannot even adopt the principle that the law of retribution requires of me, because I cannot know whether the accused is in fact guilty.

In attempting to adhere to the law of retribution, we may, with some measure of luck, administer a deserved punishment. The fact that the consequence of such an action would be in accordance with the law of retribution, however, does not validate the maxim under which we act. When we kill a person who may be innocent, we do so under the only retributive principle that is possible for us, but this may not accord with the actual law of retribution. A person chooses whether to fulfill his duty not to lie depending on the maxim that he adopts, but we cannot choose whether or not to punish rightly – that is, for the sake of retribution – because we cannot simply decide to punish the criminal in proportion to the crime he has in fact committed.[17]

Whether we assign the punishment that is deserved is not a matter of choice, but depends, for example, on whether the evidence is an accurate indicator of the person's guilt. To one extent or another, this is a matter of chance. That the person must be found guilty beyond a reasonable doubt only increases the likelihood that we are correct. For this reason, the law of retribution cannot constrain us, because in any given situation we do not have the means knowingly to fulfill such an obligation. As Kant reminds us, any candidate for moral obligation cannot be contingent on circumstances and luck. Qua law, the moral law universally binds all rational beings with strict necessity:

> Unless we want to deny to the concept of morality any truth and any relation to some possible object, we cannot dispute that its law is so extensive in its import that it must hold not only for human beings but for all *rational beings as such*, not merely under contingent conditions and with exceptions, but with *absolute necessity* . . . (G 408)

Although the categorical imperative necessitates that we act rationally, such that, for example, we always ought to refrain from lying, it cannot be the case that we always ought to administer the death penalty in accordance with the law of retribution, because our discovering who deserves to be killed is subject to "contingent conditions" – for example, whether the evidence we have points to the actual murderer. Despite Kant's claim to the contrary, the requirement that the "unlawful killing of another must be punished by death" cannot be "the categorical imperative of penal justice" (MM 336–7).

To say that we must enforce capital punishment even if we cannot tell (with certainty) who the murderers are is parallel to the claim that we ought to act for the sake of duty even if we are unfree. A person or animal whose actions take place "solely in accordance with laws of nature" cannot be subject to the moral law, because this requires the capacity to act on the basis of purely rational (formal) constraints (CPR A445/B473)'. And a person who cannot know whether someone is actually guilty cannot be constrained by the law of retribution, because the law requires punishing that person in proportion to the crime he has in fact committed, and in proportion to his guilt. Yet we are plagued by different kinds of ignorance: Did the person do it at all? Is he a moral agent? Was he responsible at the time? What is his degree of culpability? etc. As the divine arbiter of happiness in proportion to virtue, an omniscient god may carry out the law of retribution, but because we cannot answer these questions, the law cannot constrain us as an imperative.[18]

A Moral Assessment of the Supposed Duty to Kill

Because many innocent people have been sentenced to death and a number of those have actually been executed, we know that we can err in our judgment despite the precautions taken in criminal trials. Our inability to preclude the taking of an innocent life must therefore be incorporated into the principle under which we enforce the death penalty. Attempting to adhere to the law of retribution, I adopt the maxim that I will consent to the killing of someone who has been convicted of murder, disregarding his actual innocence as a reason to refrain from killing him. We know from experience that we cannot tell whether the person actually committed the crime. That is, we cannot know either of the conditions of criminal guilt: whether the person is the one who committed the crime and, if he did, whether he is responsible for doing so with an "inner wickedness." Therefore, by supporting the death penalty, I consent to the possible killing of some innocent people, because I as an impartial judge or jury member do not know which convicted murderers are innocent.

Such a maxim, however, is not in accordance with the categorical imperative. If, in attempting to fulfill the law of retribution, I were to will as a universal law that all convicted murderers be executed, I could just as easily be put to death – as an innocent person who is wrongly found guilty of a capital crime – despite my acting in accordance with the law. Yet, by willing the destruction of my own person, I have undermined the conditions of free agency – specifically, my continued existence. I cannot adopt a maxim that is inconsistent with another rational being's end-setting, because, were I to will such a maxim as a universal law, it would contradict my own capacity to adopt such a maxim. In short, I am morally prohibited from consenting to the death penalty.

Kant anticipated something like this objection when he answered Beccaria. The person who wills the law is, so to speak, not the same person as the one who breaks the law; the former is acting rationally as a colegislator of the law, and the latter is a subject under the law and acts unreasonably. However, given the fallibility of any criminal justice system that is administered by finite agents, Beccaria's objection reemerges in a stronger form: if capital punishment is part of the original contract, then everyone will have consented to lose his life if he is convicted of murder. On Kant's view, each person ought to accept the court as the decision-maker in whether he lives or dies. But this is problematic. The rational agent has consented to be killed even if he acts wholly in accordance with reason – that is, if he is in fact not guilty – yet, as Beccaria rightly notes, this is "impossible for anyone to consent to" (MM 335).[19]

Whether someone has willed a punishable action is not something that can be known, by others or by the accused. What is relevant to the state is whether that person has been found guilty in a court of law. But because a wrongly convicted person is only *believed* to have willed a punishable action, the pure reason with which he legislates and consents to the original contract is identical with his reasoning as an innocent subject under the law. In such a case, there is no resolve to will a punishable offense. Like Beccaria, Kant agrees that "it is impossible *to will* to be punished" (MM 335). However, in the case of a wrongful conviction, the convicted criminal has not willed a punishable action, so the person who wills the law is identical with the person who is put to death. Therefore, if he were to will that such a policy be made a universal law, it would be contrary to the formal conditions of his willing the original legislation. He *would* be willing to be punished. It would be unreasonable to commit himself to the institution of capital punishment, because he would thereby be willing his own death – that is, as a rational agent who is mistakenly convicted of murder.

This is not to say that capital punishment is problematic merely because of correctable flaws in the legal system, or that the *a priori* law of retribution cannot be justified in principle. Rather, *we* cannot be constrained by the law of retribution because our judgment is *necessarily* fallible.[20] If an innocent person may be convicted and executed despite our best attempts to establish the truth, those who consent to the execution cease to regard humanity as inviolable in general. By taking away a person's life and thus his ability to realize the ends that he has set for himself, we commit the very transgression that is taken to warrant the death penalty in the first place.

Do These Objections Rule Out *All* Punishments?

This line of reasoning may seem to have absurd implications. If punishment is justified only if it is "a *hindering of a hindrance to freedom*," and if there is always the potential of unjustly harming the innocent, then we can never know whether any instance of state-sponsored coercion is justified or not (MM 231). If this uncertainty makes it wrong to impose the death penalty, then the implication seems to be that every punishment is wrong, because we cannot know whether any punishment we inflict accords with the law of retribution. Indeed, by this reasoning, it seems that everything we do is wrong, since no matter what we do, we may unknowingly harm the innocent. When we intend to help someone, for example, we do it knowing that we may mistakenly harm: if I approach an old lady to help her cross the street, it is possible that I will startle her and cause her to stumble into traffic. Of course, the harm itself is not important. What is important is the maxim under which I act. But given our recognition that mistakes are possible, we must take this into account when we formulate even our most pedestrian maxims.

How, then, is the death penalty ruled out in a way that other actions, and specifically other punishments, are not? Certainly, my recognition that errors in judgment are possible places a special burden on me as a responsible agent. I must not only take measures to reduce the chance that mistakes will be made, but I must commit myself to correcting my mistakes. In fulfilling my imperfect duty to be beneficent, I ought to be careful not to harm the person in the process, and if I do cause harm, I ought to undo it or at least allow for its abolition: I should try not to startle the old lady, and I had better be ready to help her out of the street if things go awry.[21] With regard to punishment in general, rational agents recognize the first of these demands (to reduce the possibility of mistakes) with the presumption of innocence, the jury system, and the right to adequate counsel, among other things. And if a person's conviction is overturned, she may be released from prison or granted a new trial, so that constitutional violations or other mistakes made at trial can be corrected.

Although all of these safeguards are initially[22] available to those sentenced to death, the actual carrying out of the sentence is irrevocable. We may have a right intention and perform an action that turns out to be harmful; this by itself does not make us guilty of wrongdoing. In the case of capital punishment, however, the very real possibility that innocent people may be executed (and the fact that they have been executed) places us in conflict with the moral law. I cannot be at fault if my attempt to help someone fails, because a maxim of beneficence is rationally consistent. If, as a universal law, all agents were to act beneficently, my ability to act as such would not be undermined.[23] However, my maxim to enforce the death penalty cannot be rationally willed precisely because doing so subjects me, as a rational agent who may erroneously be put to death, to the same punishment. We are finite agents whose knowledge is limited, so the precautions we take against convicting the innocent are not enough to ensure the actual guilt of the accused. When universalized, my support for capital punishment undermines the very conditions of my reasoning.

Even though the death penalty is final in a way that other coercive measures are not, one may still wonder whether, given the possibility of wrongful conviction, the law of retribution can justify any form of punishment. Imprisonment takes away a person's outer freedom, and even though an innocent person's conviction may be overturned, it does not change the fact that the person was treated as a criminal – that is, as violating the law to which she has rationally consented – and in a way that is not proportional to what she has actually done. Neither the wrongful imposition of the death penalty nor the undeserved loss of outer freedom can be corrected with payments to the family, exoneration in the press, or some other form of compensation. A thief who is punished cannot undo the crime, but merely pays for it; the state is in the same position with regard to its own unjust punishments. The absolute value of one's capacity to act freely cannot be compared to any amount of money, which has merely relative value. The maxim under which we impose any punishment therefore must take into account our fallibility in determining the actual guilt of the accused, and the limits of our epistemic abilities seem to undermine the possibility of our being bound by the law of retribution in any case. My helping the old lady is best described as an act of beneficence, but when we consent to the punishment of those who are convicted of crimes, capital or otherwise, the intent is to harm.

Although every punishment restricts my rational agency, the finality of the death penalty distinguishes it from such punishments as fines or imprisonment. A fine or a prison sentence limits my range of ends and my ability to achieve those ends, but they do not undermine my very capacity to set ends. This is a crucial difference, because my existence as a rational being is maintained only when I am not executed. Analogously, Kant says that slaves cannot risk their lives in trying to escape, because doing so "frustrate[s] all attempts whereby they might be freed from their unhappy condition" (LE 603).[24] Slaves are deprived of their freedom to a greater extent than prisoners are, but the possibility of freedom remains as long as they are alive and capable of self-determination. No punishment can be annulled – the years in prison cannot be given back to me – but, as Kant says, "there is no *similarity* between life, however wretched it may be, and death" (MM 333). The finality of an execution means that the person can no longer choose at all, or act on the basis of reasons. When an innocent person is put to death, it strikes at the foundation of civil society by undermining her very capacity to consent. By contrast, other punishments, like enslavement, merely limit the choices that are available to her. A criminal's participation as a consenting member of the social contract can be restored if she is exonerated.

Ultimately, whether this line of argument successfully defends retributivism with regard to non-capital cases is irrelevant to what I am claiming here. I have argued only for the death penalty as a limiting case: the law of retribution cannot constrain us if it extends to the institution of capital punishment; or, to put it more succinctly, Kant cannot consistently justify the death penalty on retributivist grounds.

Of course, for every crime the retributivist must determine whether a person is guilty and must assess the extent of her guilt in order to discover the appropriate punishment. If Kant's larger project cannot be insulated from the implications of my criticism, then perhaps this chapter provides the means for a broader attack on *a priori* moral philosophy in general. When the formal morality of the *Groundwork* is extended to a *Metaphysics of Morals*, an account of our particular duties is given within a consideration of the contingent facts of human existence. In the case I have examined here, it may be true *a priori* that the state is authorized to punish and that the criminal deserves to be punished in a way that fits the crime. But whether we convict the right person is an empirical matter. Although ideally we must consent to a system in which the truly guilty are punished appropriately, we also confront the undeniable fact that, despite all precautions, we can fail to convict the person who commits the crime and, more disturbingly, that we sometimes execute the innocent.

In short, even if we accept Kant's *a priori* derivation of the law of retribution, it is unclear how the law applies to *us*. Considering empirical issues such as the fallibility of legal judgments may cast doubt not only on Kant's approach to capital punishment, but his justification of lesser punishments as well. The larger question, then, concerns the viability of *a priori* moral philosophy in general, or its applicability to imperfect beings like us – a topic that I will continue to explore in coming chapters.

Whose Dignity Is at Stake?

Although the law of retribution may apply to beings who are capable of acting rationally *and* of knowing with certainty who has freely engaged in criminal acts, this so-called "categorical imperative of penal justice" cannot have any purchase on those for whom such determinations are always questionable, and it cannot constrain us as an imperative (MM 337). We can never know whether a deed is rightfully imputed to the accused, so the very conditions of rational agency would be undermined were we to legislate capital punishment universally. In short, I cannot be subject to the law of retribution because I cannot rationally consent to it.

There is always the possibility of error, and although we can reduce this possibility by, among other things, exposing racial bias, requiring more appeals, and providing adequate legal counsel, we can never erase the risk that we may kill innocent people. The criticism of capital punishment that is advanced in this chapter thus brings together two of the traditional objections to the death penalty: objecting to the death penalty on pragmatic grounds warrants a principled opposition to the practice. Because it may be unfairly and mistakenly implemented, the formal principle on which it is based commits us to a general devaluation of the dignity of those who are executed. The most important insight here is that it also undermines the dignity of those who consent to it.

Notes

1   It is beyond the scope of this book to explain how such an inquiry can remain *a priori* despite Kant's consideration of empirical concepts – in this case, his consideration of the sort of finite beings we happen to be. For a thorough treatment of this issue, see Mary J. Gregor, *Laws of Freedom: A Study of Kant's Method of Applying the Categorical Imperative in the "Metaphysik der Sitten"* (Oxford: Basil Blackwell, 1963).

2   Along with ourselves and other persons, things are one of the true needs listed by Barbara Herman. See Herman, *The Practice of Moral Judgment* (Cambridge, Mass.: Harvard University Press, 1993), 53.

3   Martin Perlmutter, "Desert and Capital Punishment," in *Morality and Moral Controversies: Readings in Moral, Social, and Political Philosophy*, ed. John Arthur, 7th edn. (Upper Saddle River, N.J.: Pearson Prentice Hall, 2005), 124–31.

4   Jeffrie Murphy similarly interprets this element of Kant's philosophy of right: when we punish a criminal, we presume that she has agreed to a system of enforceable laws and thus has tacitly consented to be punished on the condition that she commit a punishable offense ("Marxism and Retribution," *Philosophy and Public Affairs* 2, no. 3 [spring 1973]: 217–43 [pp. 229–30]). This correctly

characterizes Kant's position. However, both Kant and Murphy misconstrue the actual content of the agreement. By participating in a social contract, the criminal does not consent to be punished if she commits a crime (as Kant and Murphy claim), but instead consents to be punished if she is *convicted of* committing a crime. As I will show, a person cannot rationally consent to this in the case of capital punishment.

5   Cesare Bonesana, Marchese di Beccaria, makes these points in *Dei delitti e della pene* (1764), which is translated in *On Crimes and Punishments, and Other Writings*, ed. Richard Bellamy, trans. Richard Davies, Virginia Cox, and Richard Bellamy (Cambridge: Cambridge University Press, 1995).

6   This distinction is missed by Steven Schwarzschild, who, following Beccaria, claims that a person's assent to capital punishment amounts to "a disguised form of suicide" ("Kantianism on the Death Penalty [and Related Social Problems]," *Archiv für Rechts- und Sozialphilosophie* 71, no. 3 [1985]: 343–72 [p. 360]).

7   In this chapter, I am addressing what the foundational laws of civil society should be. This is different from the question that Socrates considers in the *Crito*, which is about whether we should follow already existing laws. Socrates says that, because he has lived in Athens, even after he reached maturity, and because he has benefited from living there, he has tacitly consented to its laws. Therefore, he must accept his punishment, even though it is unjust. Kant agrees with this conclusion. He claims that we must follow the law even as we debate it in the public sphere. Famously, Kant summarizes the position of Friedrich the Great as follows: "*Argue* as much as you will and about whatever you will, *but obey!*" (WE 37; see also TP 299–300). Indeed, Socrates and Kant agree that we should follow a law to which we have consented. But this leaves aside the question of whether it would be reasonable for us to consent to capital punishment in the first place.

8   Thomas W. Pogge, "Is Kant's *Rechtslehre* a 'Comprehensive Liberalism'?" in *Kant's "Metaphysics of Morals": Interpretive Essays*, ed. Mark Timmons (Oxford: Oxford University Press, 2002), 133–58 (p. 139).

9   Ibid., 156.

10   This objection to Kant's position on the death penalty has been made by others, most notably by the neo-Kantian Hermann Cohen. See his "Vernichtung der sittlichen Person," in *Hermann Cohens Schriften zur Philosophie und Zeitgeschichte*, vol. 2, ed. Albert Görland and Ernst Cassirer (Berlin: Akademieverlag, 1928), 341. See also Friedrich Kaulbach, "Der Herrschaftsanspruch der Vernunft in Recht und Moral bei Kant," *Kant-Studien* 67 (1976): 390–408 (pp. 395–6), and Schwarzschild, "Kantianism on the Death Penalty," 344–5, 348–9.

11   In any given year, most executions are carried out in countries other than the United States. I will focus on the U.S. only because its lawmakers and courts have tried hardest to make capital punishment consistent with the basic rights and dignity of convicted criminals. If the death penalty cannot be justified under circumstances in which the accused is given a fair trial and modern technology is used to determine guilt or innocence, then presumably it would not be justified in China or Iran.

12   Michael L. Radelet, Hugo Adam Bedau, and Constance E. Putnam, *In Spite of Innocence: Erroneous Convictions in Capital Cases* (Boston: Northeastern University Press, 1992). See also Michael L. Radelet, William S. Lofquist, and Hugo Adam Bedau, "Prisoners Released from Death Rows since 1970 Because of Doubts about Their Guilt," *Thomas M. Cooley Law Review* 13, no. 3 (1996): 907–66.

13   Subcommittee on Civil and Constitutional Rights, *Innocence and the Death Penalty: Assessing the Danger of Mistaken Executions*, Staff Report, Committee on the Judiciary, 103rd Congress, 1st Session (1993).

14   The names of all 138 people who have been released are given at the Death Penalty Information Center, "The Innocence List," www.deathpenaltyinfo.org/innocence-list-those-freed-death-row.

15   Ernest van den Haag believes that these "miscarriages of justice" are "offset" by the moral and material benefits, such as appropriate retribution (in most cases) and deterrence, which only the death penalty can provide ("The Death Penalty Once More," in *The Death Penalty in America: Current Controversies*, ed. Hugo Adam Bedau [Oxford: Oxford University Press, 1997], 445–56 [p. 451]). See also Van den Haag, "The Ultimate Punishment: A Defense," *Harvard Law Review* 99, no. 7 (May 1986): 1662–9 (pp. 1664–5). Of course, using innocent people to deter other potential murderers is anathema to Kant.

16   There are many articles on problems with DNA profiling and the possibility of false convictions. The following sources provide a good overview: Gina Kolata, "Some Scientists Doubt the Value of 'Genetic Fingerprint' Evidence," *New York Times*, 29 Jan. 1990, late edition, A1; Richard Lempert, "Some Caveats Concerning DNA as Criminal Identification Evidence: With Thanks to the Reverend Bayes," *Cardozo Law Review* 13, no. 303 (1991): 303–41; William C. Thompson, "Tarnish on the 'Gold Standard': Understanding Recent Problems in Forensic DNA Testing," *The Champion* 30, no. 1 (Jan./Feb. 2006): 10–16; Jason Felch and Maura Dolan, "DNA: Genes as Evidence; FBI Resists Scrutiny of 'Matches'," *Los Angeles Times*, 20 July 2008, A1; William C. Thompson, "The Potential for Error in Forensic DNA Testing (and How That Complicates the Use of DNA Databases for Criminal Identification)" (paper presented at the national conference for the Council for Responsible Genetics, New York, June 2008), www.councilforresponsiblegenetics.org/pageDocuments/H4T5EOYUZI.pdf; and Andrew Pollack, "Scientists Show That It's Possible to Create Fake DNA Evidence," *New York Times*, 18 Aug. 2009, late edition, D3.

17   The limits on what we can know make it impossible for us to fulfill our supposed duty to the law of retribution, but they also have other implications for Kant's moral philosophy. Maxims must be formulated with our epistemic limits in mind. For example, I can never have as my maxim that I will tell the truth, given that I can be mistaken about what is in fact true. I can only adopt the maxim that roughly corresponds to it – that I will not knowingly lie. And even the latter maxim must be carefully defined: not that I will refrain from telling a falsehood, but that I will not knowingly tell someone what I take to be false, with the intent to deceive. This attempt to exclude contingency from the moral assessment of our actions ultimately has its limits. Whether our epistemic

standards are strong or weak, for example, will affect whether we mislead and indeed how our actions are judged, but what we take to be the truth may be affected by a number of antecedent circumstances. How this issue affects Kant's treatment of moral responsibility in general is discussed in Thomas Nagel, "Moral Luck," in *Mortal Questions* (Cambridge: Cambridge University Press, 1979), 24–38. This issue will also become very relevant in chapter 8, where I make the case that how we formulate a maxim or conceive of an action is dependent on social expectations.

18 On this basis, Jeffrie Murphy concludes that Kant's position (at least outside of the *Doctrine of Right*) is that punishment can only be justified in terms of deterrence: "To set any more morally ambitious goal for punishment would be to adopt an unacceptable theory of the role of the state and would represent an attempt to play God, revealing a lack of proper insight into our own short-comings, a lack of appreciation of the role of luck in our own achievements of virtue, and a lack of the posture of humility appropriate to creatures of our sort" ("Does Kant Have a Theory of Punishment?" *Columbia Law Review* 87, no. 3 [Apr. 1987], 509–32 [pp. 517–18]). As I show in this chapter, our limited knowledge makes it impossible for us to be bound by the law of retribution. Hence, I agree with what Murphy says here. However, Murphy's conclusion, that Kant can only appeal to deterrence to justify punishment, does not follow. This would treat criminals merely as means and possibly imply that their actual guilt is irrelevant, both of which are contrary to Kant's moral philosophy.

19 In this quote (MM 335), Kant is paraphrasing Beccaria: "Who has ever willingly given up to others the authority to kill him? How on earth can the minimum sacrifice of each individual's freedom involve handing over the greatest of all goods, life itself? And even if that were so, how can it be reconciled with the other principle which denies that a man is free to commit suicide, which he must be, if he is able to transfer that right to others or to society as a whole?" (Beccaria, *On Crimes and Punishments*, 66). Beccaria's objection is successful against Kant only if we take account of the possibility of wrongful conviction. Were we able to convict only actual murderers, there would be no contradiction.

20 Charles Black explains the problem clearly and forcefully: "We are not presently confronted, as a political society, with the question whether something called 'the state' has some abstract right to kill 'those who deserve to die.' We are confronted by the single unitary question posed by reality: 'Shall we kill those who are chosen to be killed by our legal process as it stands?'" (*Capital Punishment: The Inevitability of Caprice and Mistake*, 2nd edn. [New York: Norton, 1981], 166).

21 We are duty-bound to help, but we are also duty-bound not to harm and to correct the harms that we cause. Although this formulation of the problem is consistent with a strictly Kantian approach, it could also be formulated in terms of standing *prima facie* duties of beneficence, nonmaleficence, and reparation. See W. D. Ross, *The Right and the Good* (Indianapolis, Ind.: Hackett, 1988).

22 Although in the United States the review of trial errors and constitutional violations can be appealed as high as the Supreme Court, statutes in most states limit the period in which new evidence can be introduced that was not heard

at trial, either because of lawyers' mistakes or because the facts simply had not come to light. After this period, the U.S. Supreme Court held in *Herrera v. Collins* (506 U.S. 390 [1993]) that a claim of actual innocence based on newly discovered evidence cannot justify federal *habeas corpus* relief. After conviction, the defendant is no longer presumed innocent. The only business of a federal appeals court, then, is determine whether the trial took place according to constitutional provisions. The fact that a newly supported claim of actual innocence is not grounds for federal *habeas* relief helps to emphasize that what is relevant under the law (subsequent to trial) is whether the person has been convicted of committing a crime, not whether she has in fact done so.

23 Because the morality of an action is evaluated on the basis of its maxim, harming another person in self-defense does not run afoul of the criticisms to which institutionalized punishment is susceptible. A person whose life is threatened and who needs to harm or kill her attacker in order to protect herself has a duty to do so. If she were simply to allow herself to be killed, she would be contradicting the "principle of self-love . . . whose destination [*Bestimmung*] is to impel toward the furtherance of life"; it would be the moral equivalent of suicide (G 422). The morality of an action is evaluated on the basis of its maxim, and in this case the maxim is best conceived as one of self-protection. The means to that end may involve taking someone else's life. However, strictly speaking, the person's intent is not to kill, but to save herself. The Doctrine of Double Effect is relevant here: a legitimate act (self-defense) brings about an effect that is wrong under normal circumstances (killing someone).

24 See chapter 4, note 15.

6

Same-Sex Marriage as a Means to Mutual Respect

In the previous chapter, we saw that the law of retribution cannot obligate us to carry out capital punishment because of our limited knowledge of a person's motives and of reality – specifically, who committed the crime and under what circumstances. Kant makes a mistake in his derivation of our specific duties as they follow from a more general principle. In Kant's moral philosophy, the demand that we respect one another's humanity as an end in itself is an even more fundamental principle than the law of retribution. From the formula of humanity, Kant draws several conclusions about the institution of marriage, especially its importance for ensuring morally appropriate sexual relations. However, as with the death penalty, Kant's specific thoughts on marriage do not reflect the actual implications of his philosophy. Kant wrongly limits marriage to male–female pairings, when in fact his theoretical claims also justify marriage for same-sex couples. Kant's practical philosophy provides a strong argument for the moral and social value of same-sex marriage, and studying his approach will help us to understand why the issue has seemed so intractable.

The debate about same-sex marriage will never be resolved as long as the two sides conceive of the institution in fundamentally different ways. In the United States and elsewhere in the West, many people see it in religious (primarily Christian) terms.[1] Marriage is bound by the specific moral restrictions enumerated in the Bible and interpreted by church authority as a sacrament by which the two people receive divine grace. Traditionally, the law in the U.S. has reflected this viewpoint by only allowing heterosexual couples to marry.[2] Other people conceive of marriage as nothing more than a contract between consenting parties primarily for the sharing of property and health insurance, hospital visitation rights, and so on.

Kant and Applied Ethics: The Uses and Limits of Kant's Practical Philosophy, First Edition.
Matthew C. Altman.
© 2011 John Wiley & Sons Inc. Published 2011 by Blackwell Publishing Ltd.

According to this view, any adults with the proper legal standing ought to be able to get married. For both sides, the question is usually posed in terms of whether the government can legislate morality, and they take opposite positions on that issue.

Structuring the debate in this way overlooks a vast middle ground. When marriage is depicted as a moral issue, the term 'moral' is used uncritically, as if ethical claims were definitively established by gesturing at religious tradition. On the other hand, characterizing marriage wholly in terms of legal rights and responsibilities leaves aside the important moral dimensions that are absent in other social arrangements, and it ignores the special obligations that spouses have to one another beyond merely their contractual duties.

To decide whether the state should allow same-sex marriages, we must begin with the more basic questions of how the legal institution of marriage is justified and whether the justification also applies to homosexual couples. Kant addresses the former question in his moral and political philosophy. Surprisingly, he also provides us with the tools to mediate between the two dominant positions on same-sex marriage and to untangle their discordant intuitions. Kant explains the ethical rationale for marriage, but he does so without appealing to either religious tradition or legal precedent. Marriage grows out of mutual respect, as a requirement for having sexual relations in accordance with how we ought to treat one another. Framing the contemporary debate about same-sex marriage in such comprehensive terms bridges the gap between the two sides and provides a justifiable solution: because we cannot base morality on the Bible or what is "natural," heterosexual and homosexual sex are morally equivalent. Therefore, marriage ought to be available to both gay and straight couples so that they can pursue happiness in a way that respects their personhood.

To be sure, few people think of Kant when it comes to marriage, let alone same-sex marriage. Most queer theorists and feminist philosophers reject many of Kant's basic assumptions – for example, the strict distinction between reason and the inclinations, the derivation of legal constraints from moral constraints, the normative assumption that marriage is an institution toward which all people should aspire, and, most importantly, his blanket condemnation of homosexuality. Given their fundamentally different starting points, why should gay rights activists concern themselves with Kant at all?

It is true that those who disagree with Kant's foundational premises will find little common ground with him. Neither this chapter nor the book as a whole is an attempt to establish Kantian ethics and political theory incontrovertibly from the ground up. Instead, what I will show is that defenders of same-sex marriage can look to Kant for an effective argumentative strategy: they can concede to their opponents that marriage is an important moral institution and conclude on that basis that, given the importance of sexual activity for the purpose of pleasure (not only procreation), marriage ought to be available to homosexual partners as well. Only then will same-sex couples be able to act in accordance with their dignity as rational beings. By critically examining Kant's thoughts on marriage and sexuality, we can demonstrate why, on his own terms, it is morally required of us to endorse same-sex marriage.

Sex Is Morally Problematic

Kant believes that marriage is necessary as a legal institution in order to overcome the moral problems inherent in sexual relations. Kant contends that sexual desire is an "appetite" for what he calls a person's "sex" – that is, a desire to use the person's body (specifically, the sex organs) for the sake of gaining pleasure (LE 384–5). We wish to satisfy ourselves through physical, not intellectual or emotional, intercourse. However, a person is a rational animal; the body and the capacity to reason – the person's humanity – form a whole that together constitutes the person (LE 387; MM 278). By relating ourselves to the other essentially as a means to our own pleasure, then, we demean the person and make him or her into a sexualized object. We use the person as "a *consumable* thing" (MM 360), or "an instrument for satisfying desires and inclinations" (LE 385).

Of course, we can also love our sexual partners; we can respect them and try to promote their happiness. Kant recognizes that "true human affection" can be coupled with sexual desire, such that we care for a person whose body interests us (LE 384; see also MM 426). But one is not essential to the other. One is affection; the other is merely appetite. With sexual desire, there need not be any moral concern for the person as a person. We see the person as a thing to be used and discarded, "as one throws away a lemon after sucking the juice from it" (LE 384). In this way, the desire for sex is like the desire for food. When we are hungry, we want to eat. Even if we crave particular foods, our basic desire is to have our hunger satisfied. Similarly, our desire for sex is not immediately directed at any particular person. We desire *someone*. Using the person to satisfy a desire of ours is akin to cannibalism (MM 359).[3]

Obviously, for Kant this is morally problematic, because we should never treat someone merely as a means to an end. By using another person's sexual organs to satisfy his desires, the person fails to have the proper moral regard for someone who is not simply an object, but a rational being. Moreover, the person fails to respect himself in the proper way, given that he is allowing himself to be instrumentalized both by his sexual partner and by his own desires. He is treated simply as a body, or a possession that is used by another person to satisfy his or her appetite, and he gives himself over to what his body wants rather than adhering to what the moral law requires. In doing so, he consents to become a thing.

When someone has sex with another person, he succumbs to an animal impulse, allows himself to be used, and uses another person merely as a means to his own pleasure. In short, the person turns away from what he is capable of as a rational being: "the sexual impulse puts humanity in peril of being equated with animality" (LE 385). This violates the formula of humanity in how he treats himself and how he treats others. Morally, one should not degrade others or allow himself to be degraded.

Certainly, many people would object to this characterization of sexual attraction. This may seem like one more example of Kant's puritanism and disdain for the body. However, we should not dismiss Kant too quickly. We need to be careful not to confuse the feelings that usually accompany an attraction to someone with the desire for sex itself. Sigmund Freud conceives of our desire for sex as a fundamental drive to be satisfied that is disjoined from a concern for any particular person. Evolutionary theorists explain our desire for sex as a means to perpetuate the species, an instinct that we share with other animals. As Barbara Herman demonstrates, Kant's claim that we objectify one another through sexual desire also resonates in contemporary feminist philosophy, in the work of Catherine MacKinnon, Andrea Dworkin, and others.[4] This is not to say that Kant's understanding of sex is necessarily correct, but clearly sex confronts us as a moral problem that needs to be addressed. How can we treat each other with the dignity we deserve as rational persons when, in sexual terms, we are out to use each other for the sake of some end, be it our own pleasure or reproduction?

Sex Is (Conditionally) Good

The fact that sex involves the use of myself and another person as mere things is a problem because sex is not something that we ought simply to abandon. Sex is *prima facie* wrong because of how we treat others in the process, but Kant recognizes sexual desire as something that we ought to satisfy in accordance with our animal nature. As rational beings, or beings who are able to act for the sake of the moral law itself, we have certain duties, things that we should do simply because they are right. However, we also have obligations to ourselves as *embodied* rational beings. We should not completely deny our natural desires. Doing so would threaten our physical selves, and it is only as physical beings that we are able to act at all.

Our natural drives have particular purposes, and in general we ought to act in accordance with those purposes because doing so maintains the conditions of rational agency. So-called "*mechanical* self-love" is our predisposition to preserve ourselves, the community, and the species (Rel 26). These tendencies incline us to act rightly: they give us a natural aversion to suicide and a strong instinct to survive, a need for social intercourse, and the desire to engage one another in sexual relations. Of course, these natural drives may be misused. Vices can be "grafted" onto them, either when we indulge our natural drives unhealthily (gluttony, "*wild lawlessness*," or adultery) or when we contradict them (not nourishing our bodies, shunning human society, or engaging in sexual behavior that cannot lead to procreation) (Rel 27–8; see also MM 421–8). However, the drives themselves are directed toward purposes that have value, and we therefore ought to act in accordance with them when it is morally permissible to do so. With regard to sex in particular, Kant claims repeatedly that its natural end is to perpetuate the human species (LE 391, 639; MM 277, 424–6; A 303, 310). We are obligated to advance that purpose so that the kinds of beings with absolute value can continue to exist. Sex is important because it is the means through which rational agents reproduce themselves.[5]

Kant does not want us to deny our bodily impulses. In fact, he recognizes that the desire for (heterosexual) sex is perfectly natural and in accordance with who we are as rational animals: "a person who did not have this [sexual] impulse would be an imperfect individual, in that one would believe that he lacked the necessary organs, which would thus be an imperfection on his part, as a human being" (LE 385). Of course, any obligations we have to satisfy our natural inclinations are only conditionally good. If pursuing our natural ends ever conflicts with what is morally required of us, we ought to do what is right, not what is natural. For example, if the species could be perpetuated only by raping someone or committing adultery, the person should not do it because it would be using someone merely as a means. Only a good will has unconditional value, whether or not it promotes human life.

This poses a problem. Whether sex is consensual or takes place within a monogamous relationship is not crucial to Kant. Sex amounts to instrumentalizing ourselves and others, so indulging this inclination seems to be morally dangerous regardless of the context. Yet Kant concedes that we have a natural desire for sex. It serves a worthwhile purpose (perpetuation of the species), and fulfilling this desire is an important part of a full and happy life. How, then, can we satisfy this natural desire, one that Kant fully approves of, and still do what is morally required of us? Is there a way for us to be sexual beings and still treat each other in accordance with our humanity? In short, when it comes to sex, how do we reconcile what is natural with what is rational?

Exchanging Ourselves: Marriage in the *Moralphilosophie Collins*

Kant argues that only the institution of marriage can place two people in a context where they can use each other's bodies while still respecting one another as rational beings. Within marriage, spouses still use each other as means to satisfy the desire for sex, but they do not treat each other *merely* as means: "[sexual intercourse] can be done only under the condition of *marriage*. Since marriage is a reciprocal giving of one's very person into the possession of the other, it must *first* be concluded, so that neither is dehumanized through the bodily use that one makes of the other" (MM 359). The natural purpose of sex is procreation, but marriage is a relation of right established so that we can achieve this natural purpose in a way that is morally permissible.[6]

In the *Moralphilosophie Collins*, Kant uses the language of exchange to explain how marriage transforms the sexual relationship. When I give myself to another person as a thing, I become that person's possession. But if that person also gives herself to me as a thing, then my humanity is not lost, for I come to own myself again in being given the person to whom I gave myself in the first place. The reciprocity of the trade is crucial:

> if I hand over my whole person to the other, and thereby obtain the person of the other in place of it, I get myself back again, and have thereby regained possession of myself; for I have given myself to be the other's property, but am in turn taking the other as my property, and thereby regain myself, for I gain the person to whom I gave myself as property. (LE 388)

In entering a marriage contract, two people become one person in the eyes of the law. What this means is that, if someone owns me and I own that person, then I also own myself, since I have possession over what is owned by my possessions, including my spouse. Herman illustrates this relationship with an illuminating metaphor: if I give you all of my pencils on the condition that you give me all of your pencils, then the pencils I give you (and you own) become mine again.[7]

Kory Schaff has drawn on this conception of possession and exchange to claim that, on Kant's own terms, marriage as a legal institution is unnecessary. If two people have a mutually beneficial, consensual sexual relationship – with or without marriage vows, in heterosexual or homosexual unions – then an exchange (of pleasure) is made by which they take full possession of one another. Even though each person is objectified by the other, the exchange is reciprocal, so, Schaff says, they regain themselves simply by consenting to it.[8] This is consistent with Herman's pencil analogy. If two people agree to use each other's pencils, why is the law necessary at all?

Kant and Political Liberalism

The problem with this interpretation is that it fails to get at how the people and their relationship are fundamentally transformed by the social contract. Although the account of marriage in the early *Moralphilosophie Collins* is mostly consistent with the post-critical *Metaphysics of Morals*, in the later work Kant emphasizes more clearly how and why the state is necessary to maintain our humanity. And we see there that Kant's conception of private right differs fundamentally from the liberal model that Schaff describes.

Kant's political philosophy comes into focus more clearly when contrasted with the work of John Locke. For Locke, people have complete freedom to do as they please in the state of nature, but standards of justice exist nonetheless. What Locke calls the law of nature predates the political order, which is established to codify and enforce a law that already constrains us. For example, human beings' natural desire to couple and produce offspring brings up a number of concerns surrounding the rightful transfer of property. These natural relationships justify the formation of laws governing marriage and divorce, inheritance, and parental responsibilities, among other things. By engaging in a marital contract, people take on all kinds of rights and responsibilities that are enforced by the commonwealth.

Like Locke, Kant supports individual rights, and he defends several key elements of liberal political theories. However, Kant does not claim that the relationships standing outside of or prior to the state's jurisdiction are merely recognized and protected under the law. Rather, they are fundamentally transformed by the law. I relate to other people as beings who are worthy of respect only by agreeing to limit my freedom so that my actions can be consistent with the freedom of others. By consenting to the law, I constrain myself – at least outwardly – to act in ways that are morally permissible. Hence, only as part of civil society do I take on the responsibility I have as a rational being.

Here Kant rejects classical liberalism, with its emphasis on what Isaiah Berlin calls negative liberty.[9] For people such as Locke, Thomas Hobbes, and John Stuart Mill, freedom is defined as the absence of restrictions on our activity. The state is established to enforce a preexisting relation of right by protecting us from encroachments on our freedom (including our property) and enforcing binding agreements – in this case, a marriage contract. Mutual consent, under the law or not, is enough to establish the joint ownership involved in marriage, since relations of right predate legal relations. By contrast, Kant, Jean-Jacques Rousseau, and G. W. F. Hegel contend that we are truly free only when we consent to laws that constrain us to act rationally. That is how we become more than self-interested animals:

> One cannot say: the human being in a state has sacrificed a *part* of his innate outer freedom for the sake of an end, but rather, he has relinquished entirely his wild, lawless freedom in order to find his freedom as such undiminished, in a dependence upon laws, that is, in a rightful condition, since this dependence arises from his own lawgiving will. (MM 315–16; see also PP 357)[10]

According to Locke, people in a state of nature decide to restrict their freedom to do whatever they want because only then are they able to have private spheres that are protected by a sovereign power and within which they are free to enjoy what is rightfully theirs. They limit their natural freedom in order to gain a lesser but more secure freedom under the law. By contrast, Kant believes that people entering into a social contract do not have their freedom limited in not being allowed to act lawlessly. Instead, they become truly free for the first time. They are free in a positive sense because they agree to be bound by the laws that reason prescribes – that is, they agree (under threat of punishment) to act in ways that respect other people's freedom. Only by recognizing the limits that a respect for other people's right to self-determination places upon them, and by codifying these limits with enforceable restrictions on their behavior, are people bound to act rationally.

Kant's approach to property rights is instructive here. Locke claims that a person acquires property in a state of nature by mixing her labor with something that is held in common. She then has a right to that thing, and people have the corresponding duty not to steal it. Formal laws merely recognize and enforce what she already owns by natural right. By contrast, Kant claims that original acquisition does not establish rightful ownership but merely forms a presupposition of ownership, a *"provisional"* property right. *"Conclusive* possession" or "the *rational title* of acquisition" emerges within civil society (MM 257, 264). Property rights become possible only when there is a coercive system established under a law to which the members of civil society have rationally consented. Each person is legally obligated to respect others' property rights only on the condition that they agree to respect hers in turn (MM 255–6). There is no "natural" right to property apart from legal constraints. Rather, by entering into a commonwealth, people are transformed into the sort of beings who can engage one another in a relation of right and can thus have rightful ownership of things.

Transforming Ourselves into Husbands and Wives: Marriage in the *Metaphysics of Morals*

Sex without marriage is prohibited because that would amount to possessing someone immorally – that is, treating the person merely as a means to one's own pleasure. In a state of nature, the person would be giving in to her animal desires without regard for her or her partner's rational nature. Philosophers (such as Schaff) who appeal solely to consent between unmarried persons equate marriage with a typical contract. But a contract is an enforceable commitment that a person will do something for me; in a state of nature, it is merely a promise. Marriage goes beyond this. It grants a person "possession of an external object *as a thing* and use of it *as a person*," which is necessary because sex amounts to treating the person as a thing (MM 276). Although a woman's spouse remains a man, he also becomes *her* husband. Marriage does not merely enjoin someone to act in a particular way (as most contracts do), but changes how two people are related to one another. There is a parallel here with property ownership. Conclusive possession and marriage are possible only in civil society.

The problem is that a person cannot consent to have his humanity degraded by becoming a sexualized object. Here Kant agrees with Locke and Rousseau in claiming that one cannot enter into a contract by which he becomes a mere thing to be used: "a contract by which one party would completely renounce its freedom for the other's advantage would be self-contradictory, that is, null and void, since by it one party would cease to be a person and so would have no duty to keep the contract but would recognize only force" (MM 283). So, marriage cannot be an agreement to submit oneself entirely to the will of one's spouse. That would amount to slavery, which, as we saw in chapter 4, contradicts the conditions under which someone could freely consent to anything. Instead, in taking on the role of husband or wife, neither ceases to be a person. Marriage is a matter of possession, to be sure. Sex involves use of the other person as a thing; therefore, a marriage must be consummated for the person truly to be taken possession of (MM 280). But the constraints of civil society and the conditions of marriage establish them as equal partners under the law. This is crucial to transform the sexual relationship into a morally appropriate union between rational agents.

In marriage, a person binds him- or herself under the law to another person as a person, not a thing. A husband is not merely concerned with his wife's genitalia, but is given "the right to dispose over the other's whole person." Thus he is responsible for his spouse's "total state of happiness," not just the part that can be used for his own satisfaction (LE 388). The law constrains him such that he is bound to take on her ends as his own, including her own happiness. The wife has the same obligations to her husband.

We are all naturally inclined to be happy – indeed, happiness is "the satisfaction of all inclinations as a sum" – so we all value happiness as (conditionally) good (G 399). By taking on her happiness as one of his ends, then, the husband recognizes his wife as someone to whom he has a moral responsibility. Although he uses her for his own sexual gratification, she is not *merely* a thing to be used. By agreeing to be legally bound to treat her as a person, he respects her dignity in furthering the ends she sets for herself – by facilitating her ability to achieve those ends through financial support, among other things. This is not like owning a dog or a house, because a person can have no duties to these things. A person only has indirect duties to himself with regard to these things: being cruel to animals would make him callous to the suffering of others, and not having a home would jeopardize his health, which is a condition of acting. But within a marriage contract, the husband is made to act in accordance with his duty (of beneficence) to another person. He recognizes his wife's ability to set ends and he agrees to constraints that would force him to further those ends: "The two persons thus constitute a unity of will" (LE 388). Respecting the other person is not simply recognizing her power to consent. By becoming her husband, he acts in accordance with his own humanity by promoting the ends she sets for herself. In fact, they take on the same end: "to promote the common interest of the household" (MM 279).

The reciprocity of this commitment is also important. Not only is he given possession of his spouse, but he in turn gives the right over himself to her. This reinforces his regard for her as a person because he recognizes her as someone who is capable of consenting to the marriage, but it also ensures that he is not made into a mere thing. He has sex with her on the condition that she marries him – that is, on the condition that she respects his humanity by furthering his ends as well. In doing so, he conceives of himself not primarily as a sexualized object, but as a person with dignity. The equality and mutuality of the marriage contract are key, because only then does he respect the humanity of his spouse – being concerned with her overall happiness – and respect the humanity in himself – by having his spouse agree (under threat of coercion) to further his ends and not to treat him merely as a means.

Because laws of the state involve only external freedom, they can be enforced through punishment and the threat of punishment. We consent to the law in accordance with the rational demand to respect others as end-setters, and we act freely by constraining our actions through coercive measures. Only by agreeing to the enforcement of external laws do we fulfill our moral duty to further the ends of others – specifically, by thwarting those actions that are inconsistent with outer freedom. The threat of punishment discourages people from violating the freedom of others – in this case, by requiring someone to take responsibility for his spouse's well-being and forbidding any attempt to treat her merely as a means.

This is why a legal arrangement is so central to maintaining the humanity of the two parties. The threat of punishment constrains the husband and wife to act in ways that are consistent with respect for one another. Without such a threat, their humanity remains at risk. For Kant, as opposed to Locke, rightful possession depends on a system to enforce property rights. Otherwise, a person's provisional claim does not constitute rightful ownership. Similarly, mutual respect between sexual partners depends on a system of legally defined rights and responsibilities. Lara Denis puts it this way:

> If marriage were based merely on feelings, partners would lack security of possession. They would have no guarantee that their partners recognized them as anything other than objects of desire. Even if marriage were a morally binding relationship, based on duty rather than feeling, without legal sanction to back it up, partners would lack the security and the implicit recognition of equality that legal marriage provides.[11]

Being constrained by the state gives the sexual partners an assurance that mere consent cannot. Husbands and wives allow the state to restrict their freedom if they were to neglect their rational commitment. People honor their spouse's "total state of happiness" because they ought to or because they are threatened – either way, the humanity of their spouse is respected, at least outwardly (LE 388).

Kant has been criticized for having such an impoverished view of marriage, which lacks the morally beneficial characteristics of a good friendship.[12] It is true that Kant does not consider much of what makes marriage worthwhile, nor does he focus on what motivates people to get married. However, he does explain why marriage should be regulated under the law in a way that other relationships should not. Kant defines friendship as "the union of two persons through equal mutual love and respect" (MM 469). But sexual relations are morally problematic, so marriage is necessary as a legal institution in order to provide an environment in which our desires can be satisfied in a morally acceptable way. Friendships are founded on mutual concern, but we have no such concern when it comes to sexual desire. A woman may love someone as a person, but because she also has an appetite for him as a sexual object, the law is necessary to make her actions consistent with his and her dignity.

The importance of marriage as a legal arrangement enforceable through coercion is missed by Elizabeth Brake, who claims that "the moral feeling of respect" is the only relevant factor in whether we treat our partner virtuously. According to Brake, laws that enforce the just treatment of others may affect one's attitudes, but they do not directly bear on whether a person is treating someone merely as a means.[13] It is true that the law can only require us to show the outward signs of concern for the other person's welfare. It cannot force us to have moral regard for his or her well-being. Although we have a moral obligation to act beneficently, beneficence as a character trait cannot be commanded by the state. Getting married does not mean that the two people will in fact abide by the law and treat each other with respect, any more than a person's (prior) rational consent to the law means that he will never commit a crime. Marriage is necessary for sex to be morally permissible, but it is not sufficient. Brake is right to point out that being married is "compatible with lack of respect."[14] If a person committed marital rape, for example, he would be treating his spouse merely as a means. The person would fail the obligations of marriage to which he has previously consented and would place his will in contradiction with itself. The law to which he consented is consistent with its moral basis in respect for the dignity of others, but he acts immorally and illegally if he violates that law.

Although Brake correctly distinguishes the concerns of justice from the concerns of virtue and correctly notes that marriage is not sufficient to overcome sexual objectification, she overlooks the way in which the demands of justice are relevant to the moral evaluation of one's actions, and in doing so she fails to recognize why marriage is necessary for sex to be morally permissible. Although maxims are broadly defined as intentions – indeed, Brake repeats this equivalence[15] – maxims are not wholly separable from what one is doing. According to John Rawls's influential definition, maxims have the following form: "I am to do X in circumstances C in order to bring about Y. (Here X is an action and Y is a state of affairs.)."[16] Evaluating one's actions depends on the intentions – murder or manslaughter, for example – but the actions that one actually takes are also morally relevant. If a husband who is the sole provider supports his wife financially, he helps her to advance her ends. He may do so because he respects her as a person or simply because he does not want to be arrested – refusal to support one's spouse is a crime. Whatever his reason, getting married commits him to supporting her, and so, assuming that he abides by his commitment, what he does is at least morally permissible, whether or not it is morally praiseworthy. That one has bound oneself to be constrained by the law reflects a person's resolve to do what is rationally required of him as a moral agent. In short, his commitment to justice grows out of his moral obligations, which is exactly why the *Metaphysics of Morals* has as its foundation (*Grundlegung*) Kant's classic work in ethical theory.

Establishing a marital relationship provides the necessary condition under which spouses can satisfy their sexual impulses in a way that is consistent with the categorical imperative. Simply having some positive attitude (as Brake says we must) or engaging in a consensual relationship (as Schaff requires) is insufficient. Whether the spouses love and agree to share themselves with one another, they take on legal responsibility for one another's well-being only when they become husband and wife. Love cannot be legally enforced, but within the institution of marriage each person's actions are consistent with (not contrary to) the respect for persons that is required by the moral law. The spouses treat each other as means, certainly, but not merely as means. They may not be acting for the sake of the moral law, treating one another with respect because they deserve it, but their actions are made to accord with the moral law through coercion by the state. Sex within marriage is morally permissible.

Is Something Wrong Because It Is Unnatural?

Sex is morally problematic because having sex with another person threatens to undermine the dignity of both partners: they each use someone and allow themselves to be used. Yet sex is a natural drive with at least one purpose – procreation – and willing to achieve this purpose is conditionally good. Marriage allows this end to be achieved in a morally permissible way by motivating me, with the threat of coercion, to act in accordance with the respect I ought to have for my partner. Because sex between men or between women is unable to produce offspring, however, homosexuality contradicts the natural end of sexual desire: "[Homosexuality] runs counter to the ends of humanity, for the end of humanity in regard to this [sexual] impulse is to preserve the species without forfeiture of the person" (LE 391). Given the purposes of our natural drives and our obligation to act in accordance with those purposes (so that we do not undermine our capacity to will), Kant says that those who engage in sexual activity with members of the same sex contradict their humanity. Marriage could not legitimate such a union because gay or lesbian sex serves no positive end; it is purely desire-driven and is therefore morally impermissible. By indulging this unnatural desire, Kant says, "I . . . forfeit my person, and so degrade myself below the beasts" (LE 391). Apparently, homosexuals are even worse than animals, presumably because Kant (incorrectly) thinks that animals, in keeping with what is natural, are invariably heterosexual.[17]

Despite Kant's vehemence on this point, his position faces several problems that call into question his moral condemnation of homosexuality and the resulting prohibition on same-sex marriage. First and most generally, Kant merely assumes a close link between our natural ends and the categorical imperative without showing how or why contradicting our natural ends would necessarily amount to irrational action. In the *Metaphysics of Morals*,

Kant relates the formula of humanity to what he identifies as the natural end of sexual intercourse, the preservation of the species:

> What is now in question is whether a person's use of his sexual capacity is subject to a limiting law of duty with regard to the person himself or whether he is authorized to direct the use of his sexual attributes to mere animal pleasure, without having in view the preservation of the species, and would not *thereby* [*damit*] be acting contrary to a duty to himself. (MM 424, emphasis added)

Elsewhere, Kant makes a similarly fallacious appeal to nature. The unnaturalness of a given sex act alone makes it contrary to duty. Note the 'so' in the following passage:

> If . . . the wife is pregnant or sterile (because of age or sickness), or if she feels no desire for intercourse, is it not contrary to nature's end, and *so* [*hiemit*[18]] also contrary to one's duty to oneself, for one or the other of them, to make use of their sexual attributes – just as in unnatural lust? (MM 426, emphasis added)

Eventually, Kant concludes that recreational sex between married persons is not wrong – more on this later. What is most important in this passage is the connection Kant makes between natural ends and self-regarding duties. Kant simply asserts that contradicting the purpose of sexual desire (procreation) *amounts to* using oneself merely as a means, but he does not explain how or why. He says that these have something to do with one another – recreational sex may be wrong *because* it is unnatural – but gives no argument to support their connection.[19]

Kant seems to have admitted a bit of natural law theory into his ethics, an approach that he explicitly criticizes in the *Groundwork* (G 441–4). As he says there, an appeal to natural purposes alone cannot get us to moral duties. Being obligated by natural laws, whether given by our psychology, our biology, or by God, would contradict the rational autonomy that forms the basis of our obligation to the categorical imperative. Such laws would not be self-legislated, as the moral law must be.

Of course, misusing our desires could potentially violate the categorical imperative. Like any natural desire, the desire for sex could contradict a person's humanity if he became obsessed with it or overindulged, such that he was in a constant state of stupefaction. Only when hampering our well-being would also undermine our ability to deliberate and to achieve the ends that we set for ourselves would such a thing be morally wrong. The natural desire for food and drink, for example, subverts a person's capacity to act if it leads to gluttony: "When stuffed with food he is in a condition in which he is incapacitated, for a time, for actions that would require him to use his powers with skill and deliberation" (MM 427). An obsession with sex could lead a person to subjugate his reason to his desires. That would amount to using himself merely as a means to his own pleasure. However, homosexual sex itself is not any more "incapacitating" than heterosexual sex. The natural desire for sex is wrongly directed not in same-sex relations in particular, but in any sexual activity that violates a duty to oneself, and that includes all sex outside of marriage, whether homosexual or heterosexual.

The idea that the species must be perpetuated also has more limited implications for our behavior than to imply a blanket condemnation of homosexuality. Nature's end can be achieved even if some people engage in "unnatural" sexual practices. Again, contradicting some natural desires that we have may undermine our capacity to act. If someone consistently refuses to eat despite her hunger, it will have deleterious effects on her body and mind. She has a duty to maintain her health. However, unlike refusing to eat, which contradicts a person's drive to live and would (eventually) cause her death, simply not having procreation as her end does not undermine her capacity to procreate and it does not undermine human beings' ability to reproduce in general. The end of procreation is not being thwarted by homosexual sex. It is simply not being advanced by it. Even if an argument could be made that human beings *as a whole* have some obligation to perpetuate the species, that would not imply that everyone must procreate. I must try to save a child from drowning if I am able *and* if no one else is saving her. Similarly, given a regular growth in population, homosexuals need not fulfill a *prima facie* obligation to reproduce, even if there were such a thing.

There is no imperfect duty of heterosexuality. The imperfect duty of self-improvement implies that I must cultivate my talents at least some of the time, but everyone need not engage in procreational sex some of the time. The maxim to procreate is more like a coordination maxim. Even if we concede to Kant that perpetuating the species is a positive aim, homosexuals need not advance that aim if they can reasonably assume that the population is increasing well enough without them. A maxim must include the circumstances in which the action is taken. It is conceivable that, if the only two people left on earth were a gay man and a lesbian, they would be morally obligated to procreate. The desire for pleasure would not override the duty to create more rational agents. However, barring such extraordinary circumstances, such a duty does not apply to the homosexual minority of a population that is reproducing at a healthy rate.

Failing to contribute to the perpetuation of the species also does not contradict the formula of universal law. Some people implicitly draw on Kant by claiming that engaging in homosexual sex cannot be universalized: if everyone had same-sex partners exclusively, then no one would be born, including me. That would amount to a contradiction in the will, since it would undermine my ability to set and pursue ends. However, this misapplies the Kantian insight that I should not make an exception of myself. If my maxim were universalized – everyone has intercourse only with someone of the same sex – that would not undermine my capacity to act unless universalizing the maxim were retroactive to my parents. When Kant himself applies the categorical imperative, however, he considers whether the universalized maxim is consistent with the actions that I *will* take: whether not developing my talents *will* affect my pursuit of ends, whether a law of nonbeneficence *will* make it impossible for me to receive help when I need it, and so forth (G 422–3).[20] Even if we grant that I and everyone in the world would cease procreating if everyone were homosexual, there is nothing conceptually incoherent about my being a homosexual in a world of homosexuals, and my existing in such a world does not harm my moral agency.

Incidentally, we must remember that homosexuals can have intercourse and reproduce with members of the opposite sex, including surrogate parents, while still identifying as homosexuals and maintaining homosexual relationships. Modern technology also allows same-sex couples to become parents through *in vitro* fertilization. Cloning and genetic manipulation may one day make it possible for homosexual couples to have children using DNA from both partners. The fact that homosexual sex itself cannot produce a child does not imply that homosexuals cannot reproduce. It means only that they cannot reproduce through same-sex intercourse. Even if we grant that reproduction is one of nature's purposes, homosexuals are as capable of furthering that purpose as heterosexuals are. The fact that homosexuals want sexual relationships with members of the same sex does not make reproduction, including reproduction by them, impossible.

Kant places great emphasis on the importance of procreation. If not reproducing were impermissible, however, it would mean that everyone is morally obligated to procreate. Homosexual sex would be morally prohibited, but so would sexual abstinence and all forms of recreational sex within marriage. Yet according to Kant and our common intuitions, there is nothing wrong with either of these. In chapter 10, I will show how the permissibility of celibacy is important for understanding why abortion does not lead to a contradiction in the will. At this point, however, understanding why there is nothing wrong with celibacy or recreational sex within marriage will help to demonstrate that, in order to be consistent, Kant must also approve of same-sex marriage.

Pleasure as an End of Nature

What is most damaging to Kant's position on homosexuality is that the morally relevant distinction is between sex within marriage and sex outside of marriage, not between sex that does (potentially) or does not lead to procreation. Indeed, Kant does not object to heterosexual sex rooted entirely in the desire for pleasure. Whether a person wants to have sex with someone for the purpose of producing offspring or for the sake of "merely animal intercourse," in both cases he would be objectifying his potential partner – unless it takes place "under the condition of *marriage*" (MM 359). What matters is not the "naturalness" or "unnaturalness" of a given sex act, but whether the two partners have bound themselves to one another under a legal arrangement that ensures their mutual respect. That is why abstinence is not morally objectionable and also why sex within marriage is morally permissible even when procreation is impossible:

> The end of begetting and bringing up children may be an end of nature, for which it implanted the inclinations of the sexes for each other; but it is not *requisite* for human beings who marry to make this their end in order for their union to be compatible with rights, for otherwise marriage would be dissolved when procreation ceases.
>
> Even if it is supposed that their end is the pleasure of using each other's sexual attributes, the marriage contract is not up to their discretion but is a contract that is necessary by the law of humanity, that is, if a man and a woman want to enjoy each other's sexual attributes they *must* necessarily marry, and this is necessary in accordance with pure reason's laws of right. (MM 277–8; see also LE 639–40; MM 426)

Kant accepts that spouses may have recreational sex because their objectification of one another is overcome. Sex with an infertile (e.g., post-menopausal) woman or a sterile man is "unnatural" in the sense that procreation is impossible, but it is morally permissible if those involved respect each other's humanity by having entered into a marriage contract. On Kant's own terms, then, one cannot object to a sexual relationship because it fails to fulfill its supposedly natural function of reproduction. Instead, sex is prohibited only if it violates the formula of humanity by treating a person merely as a means – that is, if a person has sex with someone who is not his or her spouse.

If married people can engage in sexual intercourse simply for the purpose of pleasing themselves, even when procreation is impossible, why is *that* not unnatural? The reason is that Kant identifies another aim of the sexual impulse: "the natural use that one sex makes of the other's sexual organs is *enjoyment*, for which one gives itself up to the other" (MM 278; see also LE 637). Sex in general may be good because it helps to maintain the species, but it need not justify any particular sex act. Kant identifies at least three purposes for sexual intercourse, including mutual pleasure.[21] Although such teleological claims can only be regulative, one of the aims of nature in designing sex the way it did – as opposed to having us reproduce by budding or parthenogenesis – may have been simply for us to be able to please one another. Kant recognizes a natural desire for happiness. If a healthy sexual relationship is an important part of a happy life, then enjoyment is worthwhile, even apart from procreation. Of course, it is conditionally good, just as procreation is, but its goodness depends on thwarting the objectification of the other by entering into a marriage with that person.

In short, Kant allows for recreational sex within marriage despite its "unnaturalness" – that is, despite the fact that it does not aim at one of the ends set by nature. The rightness or wrongness of sex does not depend on whether it potentially leads to reproduction, but whether it takes place between spouses. Therefore, Kant's objection to homosexual sex cannot be that it fails to perpetuate the species. The question with regard to any sexual practice should be: Is the person treating herself and her partner merely as a means? *Any* sex act outside of marriage does this, whether it is heterosexual or homosexual. Kant's appeal to what is natural is not only unjustified but also irrelevant.

Marital Equality as a Criterion of Legitimacy

Sexual relations for the purpose of mutual pleasure are morally permissible as long as the people are married. And marriage is a legal institution whereby two people relinquish themselves to one another. Because each person in the couple takes on the other's ends as his or her own, the two of them enter into an arrangement in which they agree to respect one another's humanity, under threat of punishment. Marriage blocks the dehumanizing effects of sex and makes possible a morally permissible exchange of pleasure.

The question of whether such a legal arrangement should be available to same-sex couples can be answered by studying Kant's objections to other kinds of marriages, or other kinds of relationships that are not candidates for marriage. Kant prohibits a number of potential couplings, sometimes because of their unnaturalness. But when it comes to whether those involved can become legally married, Kant focuses entirely on whether the union would be between equals. For example, Kant prohibits a marriage "which takes advantage of the inequality of estate of the two parties to give one of them dominion over the other" (MM 279). In a morganatic marriage, in which the husband's possessions and rank do not transfer to the woman or their children, the husband fails to give himself entirely to his spouse. There is no equality of exchange, so the marriage fails to satisfy the legal requirements of a marriage. Similarly, a polygamous relationship in which a man marries several women dehumanizes the women, because they give themselves completely to the man while he gives himself only in part to each of them. So, there is no "unity of will" between the man and any of the women (LE 388). The women would not be "regaining themselves" through the marriage contract (LE 389; MM 278). Incest between parents and their children is also morally inappropriate because marriage cannot overcome their natural inequality: "in regard to these two a respect is necessary that also has to endure throughout life; but respect rules out equality. . . . Between parents and children the subordination is all on one side; the children are merely subordinated to the parents, and hence there is no true intercourse" (LE 389–90). Only a contract between equal partners accomplishes the purpose of marriage, because only when two people give possession of themselves completely to one another is sexual objectification overcome through a commitment to the spouse as a person. Marriage is only morally appropriate when husband and wife regain their personhood through the exchange (to use the language of the *Moralphilosophie Collins*) or when they take full possession of and thus assume complete and equal responsibility for one another (to use the language of the *Metaphysics of Morals*). A potential marriage between unequal partners could not fulfill the conditions of a morally appropriate union, so no law could ever validate it.

This does not rule out incest between siblings. Kant does say that we have a natural tendency to be sexually drawn to those outside of our family and a certain coldness toward our family members, "since where bonding and familiarity are all too excessive, the impulse produces indifference and disgust" (LE 389). However, there is no unconditional moral restriction on such unions (LE 389–90). Sibling incest is only wrong conditionally, if it takes place outside of the marriage contract. There are many good reasons not to allow siblings to marry – in addition to worries about reproduction, such a relationship would probably have roots in childhood sexuality and so may inhibit their social and psychological development – but the supposed unnaturalness of sibling incest carries no legal or moral weight, even for Kant.

Similarly, even if some people have an aversion to homosexuality, even if this feeling could be traced back to some natural desire for the species to be perpetuated (and scorn for those who do not advance the cause), this is not morally or legally relevant. What is necessary for marriage is two sexual partners who are able to give themselves to one another equally, such that they form a "unity of will" (LE 388). We ought to determine which marriages to allow not by looking at whether a particular relationship is "natural," but whether there is inequality that would lead to one person being used merely as a means.

People often argue that allowing for same-sex marriages would open the door to all kinds of things: polygamous unions, marriages between parents and their children, between people and animals, etc. This slippery slope argument does not get any traction against Kant. In all of these cases, there is no equality of exchange by which the parties take on full and equal responsibility for one another. Therefore, they are morally prohibited even if monogamous homosexual unions are permitted.

It should be noted that, according to Kant, a certain kind of inequality is necessary for "the unity and indissolubility of a union" (A 303). One person must have "dominance" over the other, so that they can contribute their "different gifts" to the preservation of the marriage and the family (LE 50). Kant claims that a heterosexual union is most likely to succeed as a marriage because of "the natural superiority of the husband to the wife": "he is the party to direct, she to obey" (MM 279). A homosexual relationship does not have this power differential. It is not a situation in which a man guides and a woman is guided. Whatever we think of Kant's opinions here, even if he is right that supposedly natural gender differences improve a marriage, it hardly constitutes an objection to same-sex marriage as a legal institution.[22]

If the purpose of sex in general is not only (or not necessarily) procreation but also enjoyment, and if a healthy, non-demeaning sexual relationship is an important part of the good life, then two consenting adults should be allowed to form a contract in order to express their sexuality in a way that preserves their dignity. This can only be done under the law. Once we view homosexuals as rational actors rather than placing them "below the beasts" (LE 391), Kant's conception of marriage as a morally necessary contract validates same-sex unions.

How the Same-Sex Marriage Debate Should Proceed

On Kant's own terms and despite his protestations to the contrary, the absence of any good argument for the moral impermissibility of homosexuality means that marriage must be construed broadly to include both heterosexuals and homosexuals. But again, why should we listen to Kant on this? As I mentioned earlier, there are sharp divisions between Kant and contemporary defenders of gay rights.

Kant is important because tensions in his own position reflect current tensions in the debate over same-sex marriage. Some people believe that homosexuality is immoral, either because of its unnaturalness or because of biblical injunction. But neither of these can provide us with reasons to forbid a practice. We can only know what is right by appealing to our own moral concepts; we only know that God is good and that we ought to follow the Bible because (or when) they correspond to what we determine to be right (LE 342–3; G 443; CPrR 128–30; Rel 3–6; MM 443–4, 487–8; Ak 19:148 [R 6753], 19:150 [R 6759]). Therefore, gesturing at the Bible or at nature does not amount to a moral argument. We need independent ethical criteria.

Kant shows us that there is a moral argument to be made for marriage, even apart from its religious history. He preserves the moral and social value of marriage while justifying it as a legal institution. Studying Kant's approach to marriage can thus help us to recast the debate. We ought to look beyond legal precedent and constitutional mandate to explore what we ought to do given the foundational principles of civil society. Preserving our mutual freedom depends on respecting one another's personhood, and that personhood is under threat when we engage each other sexually. The law gives us the tools to overcome this moral problem, so that we do not treat others and ourselves merely as means to an end.

Of course, many people would dismiss Kant's contention that all sex outside of marriage is immoral and, in doing so, would reject the very basis of his claims about marriage. Advocates for same-sex marriage in particular do not typically restrict proper, morally acceptable sexual relations in that way, whether it is homosexual or heterosexual. This is hardly surprising given that marriage has not been an option for homosexuals and that their sexuality could be expressed only outside of marriage. To accept Kant's key claim would be to admit that all practicing homosexuals have heretofore been acting immorally. Whether Kant is right on this matter is an open question. However, even those who would reject Kant's blanket prohibition on extramarital sex concede that the institution of marriage involves a different kind of commitment than a purely sexual relationship: it asks for mutual support, sharing of property, and many other special legal responsibilities. In this way, when two people formally bind their lives together, they commit themselves to respect one another, at least outwardly, enforced by the threat of punishment.

Sexual relationships that are outside of marriage can be fulfilling and emotionally satisfying for both partners, but many couples, even those who have lived together for years, see marriage as an important step because it binds them together in a way that less formal arrangements do not. That is why the debate is so personal to so many people on both sides of the issue, more than if it were simply a matter of equal treatment under the law. A recent sociological study found that same-sex couples tend to see marriage as a kind of commitment that entails special obligations for the two of them: to remain together permanently, to work through interpersonal problems, to support one another's growth, and so on.[23] Legal benefits that are available only to married couples are certainly desired by many homosexual partners, but typically they are not *reasons* why they want to marry. This is characteristic, for example, of the broader attitude toward marriage in America. In the U.S. Supreme Court decision *Turner v. Safley* (482 U.S. 78 [1987]), the justices list the "important attributes" of marriage: marriage is a way for couples to commit to one another publicly and to be recognized by others, it has religious significance for many people, and it provides a healthy context for sexual relations – a Kantian idea. Only after these attributes do the justices note that marriage is also a "precondi-tion" for a number of legal and economic benefits. Opponents of same-sex marriage tend to be bothered less by the prospect of homosexual couples filing joint tax returns than by the mark of legitimacy that this and other legal changes would give them.

As a compromise, some governments have sanctioned the legal recogni-tion of same-sex couples while refusing to call it marriage, instead opting for "civil unions" or "domestic partnerships." Whether any of these alter-natives are adequate depends on whether there is a complete giving of the two people to one another and a transformation of their status under the law. In some places, civil unions are equivalent to marriage, different in name only. Washington state's domestic partnership law (SB 5688/HB 1727), for example, is often called the "everything-but-marriage" bill. However, when such legal arrangements are not equivalent and homosexual couples are denied benefits that are given to married couples, it should prompt us to reflect on how the two institutions should be made equal – whether heterosexual couples should be denied the same benefits, or whether homosexuals' benefits should be enlarged.[24] If we set aside the groundless appeal to what is natural, there is no reason for homosexual couples to be treated differently under the law.

A lot of ink has been spilled over this seemingly insignificant but highly emotional semantic question. For the Kantian defender of same-sex mar-riage, what we call same-sex marriage is irrelevant, provided that the two institutions (marriage and civil unions) are equal. However, given the moral imperative that we allow same-sex marriage, the justificatory burden shifts to those who would deny homosexuals the term "marriage." If the only reasons not to call it marriage have to do with its historical connotations or cultural custom, these should carry little weight in a moral argument. Kant's approach to the ethics of marriage justifies equality only. Separate but equal is inherently unequal.[25]

Kant addresses the moral dimensions of marriage in a way that those who appeal merely to economic and legal rights do not. He concedes the institution's moral significance to the defenders of traditional marriage, but he also gives us a way to discuss the value of marriage without reference to reproductive purposes or divine sanction. We can adapt his position to show why heterosexual and homosexual marriages are morally equivalent. This is exactly what many advocates of same-sex marriage have been claiming.

The debate should not be about the historical roots of marriage, but whether people ought to be able to express their desire for members of the same sex in a morally appropriate way. Without being able to sustain objec-tions based on the unnaturalness of homosexuality, there is no legally or morally relevant objection to same-sex marriage. Heterosexual sex and homosexual sex are morally equivalent outside of marriage, and they are morally equivalent within marriage. In both, people are using each other as a means to satisfy a basic human purpose, be it procreation or pleasure. Only a marriage contract transforms the morality of this behavior, gay or straight. What is important is the quality of the union, the mutual respect that is enforceable under a legal arrangement, not the gender of the people involved.

The irony, then, is that it is not the immorality of homosexuality that precludes marriage; rather, not having marriage available to homosexuals makes homosexual unions immoral. To be more precise, it does not allow them to pursue their own sexual fulfillment, which is an important element of a good life, in a morally appropriate way. Opponents of same-sex marriage worry that legalizing it would amount to condoning homosexual activity. It would. But it would condone it only within an institution based on mutual respect, one that overcomes the inherent moral risks of sexual intercourse. It would have us understand marriage as a morally transformative institution and would emphasize the power of marriage to make us better people.

Notes

1   It is interesting to note that same-sex marriage is not a modern invention. Marriages between men were accepted among the ancient Romans. The emperor Nero (37–68 CE) married two different men in addition to his three wives. Same-sex weddings became increasingly common in Rome in the first and second centuries CE, although they were outlawed in 342 – between the time that Constantine converted to Christianity and the time that Christianity became the official state religion. See Marilyn Yalom, *A History of the Wife* (New York: HarperCollins, 2001), 40–2.

2   Although this interpretation, in which the significance of marriage is essentially spiritual, has grown out of religious tradition, restricting marriage to heterosexual couples has functioned at a social and political level as a way to regulate reproduction. This dimension of marriage enters into the same-sex marriage controversy, of course: the claim that homosexual sex (and, by extension, same-sex marriage) is unnatural derives from the judgment that only reproductively oriented sex is legitimate. In fact, Kant repeats this association which, as we will see, does not stand up to critical scrutiny. The linkage between heterosexual marriage and reproduction also spawns the related controversy of same-sex couples, married or not, having children through adoption or *in vitro* fertilization and raising those children in a "non-nuclear" household. This issue lies outside the scope of this chapter. The real incommensurability in the same-sex marriage debate is between the spiritual conception of marriage and its purely legal counterpart, not a difference in identifying the practical functions of marriage.

3   Talk of sex as cannibalism is not just a metaphor for Kant. He says that sexual intercourse may literally consume the person. Pregnancy places a great demand on the woman's body and may even result in death, and frequent sex may "exhaust" the man's "sexual capacity" (MM 359–60; see also LE 638).

4   Barbara Herman, "Could It Be Worth Thinking about Kant on Sex and Marriage?" in *A Mind of One's Own: Feminist Essays on Reason and Objectivity*, ed. Louise M. Antony and Charlotte Witt (Boulder, Colo.: Westview, 1993), 49–67. See also Lina Papadaki, "Sexual Objectification: From Kant to Contemporary Feminism," *Contemporary Political Theory* 6, no. 3 (Aug. 2007): 330–48. Allen Wood traces the Kantian influence on Dworkin's views through Simone de Beauvoir to Jean-Paul Sartre, "who took over Kant's view of sex with mainly terminological and stylistic modifications" (*Kant's Ethical Thought* [Cambridge: Cambridge University Press, 1999], 396–7n11). Elizabeth Brake has taken issue with Herman's comparison and has instead emphasized the differences between Kant and MacKinnon. See Brake, "Justice and Virtue in Kant's Account of Marriage," *Kantian Review* 9 (May 2005): 58–94 (pp. 83–8).

5   As we saw in chapter 2, this appeal to natural purposes depends on a particular understanding of teleological judgment. In the *Critique of Judgment*, Kant argues that such judgments are reflective and regulative rather than determinative and constitutive. They concern how we must subjectively understand natural organisms (as organic wholes) rather than the very conditions of making objective claims at all. For a general explanation of how Kant's doctrine of teleology shapes his practical philosophy, see Vincent M. Cooke, "Kant, Teleology, and Sexual Ethics," *International Philosophical Quarterly* 31, no. 1 (March 1991): 3–13. Holly L. Wilson discusses what Kant identifies as the natural purposes of sex, sexual differentiation, and marriage. See Wilson, "Kant's Evolutionary Theory of Marriage," in *Autonomy and Community: Readings in Contemporary Kantian Social Philosophy*, ed. Jane Kneller and Sidney Axinn (Albany: State University of New York Press, 1998), 283–306.

6   Kory Schaff misinterprets Kant on this point. He takes Kant to be claiming that marriage is necessary for procreation in a natural or physical sense: "if the natural purpose of human sexual activity is procreation, then the ethical requirement that it take place within marriage has an extranatural premise. Procreating as a result of intercourse between men and women has no biological precondition in matrimony. In short, one's reproductive capacities are not suddenly 'turned on' when the marriage ceremony is over" ("Kant, Political Liberalism, and the Ethics of Same-Sex Relations," *Journal of Social Philosophy* 32 [fall 2001]: 446–62 [p. 454]). This objection has nothing to do with Kant's position. According to Kant, procreation is the natural purpose of sex, not marriage. Marriage has no natural purpose, but is a relation of right under the law. It provides the context in which we can have sex without violating the formula of humanity.

7   Barbara Herman, *The Practice of Moral Judgment* (Cambridge, Mass.: Harvard University Press, 1993), 60.

8   Schaff, "Kant, Political Liberalism, and the Ethics of Same-Sex Relations," esp. 455–7.

9 Isaiah Berlin, "Two Concepts of Liberty," in *Four Essays on Liberty* (Oxford: Oxford University Press, 1969), 118–72.

10 Although Kant rejects what he takes to be Rousseau's glorification of our natural state and needs (MM 318, 445), Kant's political philosophy owes a great deal to the work of his predecessor. Like Kant, Rousseau claims that we truly become moral beings only in civil society: "This passage from the state of nature to the civil state produces a remarkable change in man by substituting justice for instinct in his behavior and giving his actions the morality they previously lacked. Only then, when the voice of duty replaces physical impulse and right replaces appetite, does man, who until that time only considered himself, find himself forced to act upon other principles and to consult his reason before heeding his inclinations. . . . For the impulse of appetite alone is slavery, and obedience to the law one has prescribed for oneself is freedom" (Jean-Jacques Rousseau, *On the Social Contract*, trans. Judith R. Masters, ed. Roger D. Masters [New York: St. Martin's, 1978], 55–6). Rather than just being pulled around by whatever we happen to want (our inclinations), we can reflect on our actions and decide what we ought to do. In forming a body politic, there is some rational standard to which we aspire. A citizen becomes capable of concern for the common good rather than whatever he wants as a particular individual.

11 Lara Denis, "From Friendship to Marriage: Revising Kant," *Philosophy and Phenomenological Research* 63, no. 1 (July 2001): 1–28 (p. 12). See also Denis, "Kant on the Wrongness of 'Unnatural' Sex," *History of Philosophy Quarterly* 16, no. 2 (Apr. 1999): 225–48 (p. 231).

12 See especially Denis, "From Friendship to Marriage."

13 Brake, "Justice and Virtue in Kant's Account of Marriage."

14 Ibid., 86.

15 Ibid., 80.

16 John Rawls, "Themes in Kant's Moral Philosophy," in *Kant's Transcendental Deductions: The Three "Critiques" and the "Opus Postumum"*, ed. Eckart Förster (Stanford, Calif.: Stanford University Press, 1989), 81–113 (p. 83).

17 We now know that homosexuality is not limited to human beings. There are many nonhuman animals that have intercourse and stable pairing relationships with members of the same sex. See Bruce Bagemihl, *Biological Exuberance: Animal Homosexuality and Natural Diversity* (New York: Stonewall Inn, 2000).

18 *Hiemit* is the antiquated spelling of *hiermit* in modern German, meaning "with this," "herewith," or "hereby."

19 Alan Soble, "Kant and Sexual Perversion," *The Monist* 86, no. 1 (Jan. 2003): 55–89 (pp. 57–8, 67).

20 This methodological claim for how we ought to test maxims will also be relevant in chapter 10, when I discuss abortion. If the universalized maxim of having an abortion is retroactive, then my parents would abort me and end my own life. Some people conclude that there would be a contradiction in the will were I to will abortion as a universal law of nature.

21 In addition to reproduction and pleasure, Kant specifies a third purpose of the sexual impulse: it encourages human beings to become more "refined."

Specifically, Kant thinks that men behave more sociably and are made more amenable to acting morally because "nature . . . made this [female] sex man's ruler," and women are more capable of such refinements (A 306). Allen Wood contends that there is yet another purpose of sexual desire, which he finds in Kant's *Conjectural Beginning of Human History*: sex helps us to develop intimate, respectful relationships with other persons by drawing us toward one another. Specifically, Wood says, "the essence of human sexual desire is that it is desire directed at another human being, regarded as a rational or self-conscious agent" (*Kantian Ethics* [Cambridge: Cambridge University Press, 2008], 231). The Kant passage that Wood quotes is cryptic and says nothing as clearly as this. What it says is that "the power of the imagination" keeps us interested in possible partners, even after merely physical satisfaction (CB 112). Animals are incapable of this kind of persisting interest. Given that Wood's interpretation – his claim that we take sexual interest in others *as* rational beings – is at odds with most of what Kant says about sex elsewhere (as an objectifying impulse), I hesitate to follow Wood here.

22 Kant states his opinion on the differences between men and women most clearly in the section "On the Character of the Sexes" in the *Anthropology* (303–11). The less said about this, the better. However, his negative view of women also emerges in ways that cannot be so easily overlooked. On the supposedly rational basis of the political inequality between men and women in Kant's philosophy of right, see Susan Mendus, "Kant: 'An Honest but Narrow-Minded Bourgeois'?" in *Women in Western Political Philosophy: Kant to Nietzsche*, ed. Ellen Kennedy and Susan Mendus (New York: Palgrave Macmillan, 1987), 21–43, and Hannelore Schröder, "Kant's Patriarchal Order," trans. Rita Gircour, in *Feminist Interpretations of Immanuel Kant*, ed. Robin May Schott (University Park: Pennsylvania State University Press, 1997), 275–96.

23 Gretchen A. Stiers, *From This Day Forward: Commitment, Marriage, and Family in Lesbian and Gay Relationships* (New York: St. Martin's, 1999), 45–68.

24 Most gay rights advocates argue that same-sex couples should be able to get married in order to achieve legal equality. However, Richard Thaler and Cass Sunstein take the opposite route. They argue that all couples, gay and straight, should only be allowed to engage in civil unions under the law, although marriage could continue to be granted by religious and other private organizations. The state would thus not be endorsing a particular kind of relationship, because any two people could engage in such a domestic partnership. See Thaler and Sunstein, *Nudge: Improving Decisions about Health, Wealth, and Happiness* (New Haven, Conn.: Yale University Press, 2008), 215–26.

25 Of course, this is a reference to the U.S. Supreme Court's landmark decision *Brown v. Board of Education* (347 U.S. 483 [1954]). Some gay rights activists have identified parallels between the treatment of African Americans during the Jim Crow era and the current treatment of homosexuals.

Part III

Limitations of Kant's Theory

Despite its anthropocentric and supposedly radical libertarian principles, Kant's ethics was and still is very progressive. Its implications contradict some of the views that were typical during Kant's time, including some that were held by Kant himself. His theory challenges even some of our own assumptions. Many people continue to believe that animals (especially the ones we eat) deserve little or no moral consideration, that the government has no business in providing health care for its citizens, that the death penalty is a morally appropriate punishment, and that defending traditional marriage is necessary as a bulwark against a corrupt moral relativism. By bringing Kant into the conversation, these socially conservative positions are shown to be unreasonable once we commit ourselves to the absolute value of humanity and individual autonomy.

As we will see in the next four chapters, however, Kant's theory faces challenges of its own. Kant largely neglects the social conditions within which we determine our moral duties. Therefore, he cannot adequately address coercive conditions that undermine personal responsibility. He cannot define our maxims except in the context of social expectations. Kant's understanding of moral agency hardly allows business ethics to get off the ground, because he rejects the idea of corporate responsibility. And since Kant limits direct moral consideration to rational beings, he cannot resolve the abortion debate.

All of these problems reveal the limitations of Kant's philosophy. Autonomy, dignity, and universalizability are important ethical concepts, but reasoning in an applied context requires that we incorporate theoretical elements that go beyond strict Kantian doctrine – elements that, I will suggest, can be found in the Hegelian and communitarian emphasis on the social conditions of subjectivity and moral judgment.

Kant and Applied Ethics: The Uses and Limits of Kant's Practical Philosophy, First Edition.
Matthew C. Altman.
© 2011 John Wiley & Sons Inc. Published 2011 by Blackwell Publishing Ltd.

7

Consent, Mail-Order Brides, and the Marriage Contract

Kant's ethics has remained philosophically relevant for a number of reasons, not the least of which is his insistence on the absolute worth of persons and the resulting demand that we respect their capacity to consent. These ideas are particularly important in Kant's account of marriage, a legal arrangement that is designed to protect the spouses against the dehumanizing effects of sexual gratification. However, looking at a test case, so-called "mail-order brides," reveals a series of tensions in Kant's account of marriage and, in doing so, exposes some of the limits of his practical philosophy. In many ways, mail-order marriages seem like Kant's ideal, yet such arrangements actually serve the social function of reinforcing the subjugation of women. Furthermore, the social and economic conditions that pressure women into these marriages erode their freedom to choose. Kant's approach to consent cannot adequately account for this.

Ultimately, Kant's contention that spouses must be equal under the law (in that both must consent to the marriage) *and* his simultaneous defense of the doctrine of coverture reveal a deeper problem with Kantian moral theory: Kant's theory of agency is flawed because it is shaped by prejudices that are both factually dubious and morally troubling. We should not wholly reject Kant, of course. His emphasis on the value of humanity is extraordinarily compelling. But the question of who is to be included in the moral community and how we ought to understand humanity, I will suggest, can better be addressed through a different methodological approach to ethics – one that is not *a priori*, but is informed by the empirical social sciences.

Kant and Applied Ethics: The Uses and Limits of Kant's Practical Philosophy, First Edition.
Matthew C. Altman.
© 2011 John Wiley & Sons Inc. Published 2011 by Blackwell Publishing Ltd.

The Purpose of Marriage

The history of marriage in the West is largely characterized by the exploitation of women for economic purposes – to control reproduction, create a workforce, and maintain personal estates through primogeniture. While men had economic and political power, women were treated merely as means, subservient to the demands of their husbands and society in general. According to Friedrich Engels, the emergence of private property introduces the desire to control the inheritance of that property in bourgeois marriage, and the biological fact that paternity can be ambiguous (whereas maternity generally cannot be) leads to the glorification of the monogamous family. Reproduction had to be regulated, and women were subordinated to the economic interests of the bourgeois class: as Engels puts it, "the overthrow of mother right was the *world historical defeat of the female sex*."[1] In other words, women are no longer empowered by their ability to reproduce, as they were in ancient matriarchies. This ability is co-opted within capitalist relations of production as the capacity to produce heirs (among the bourgeoisie) and additional workers (among the proletariat). Within a capitalist system, women become reproductive laborers who not only physically give birth to children, but who also provide all the services necessary to sustain those who labor in the public sphere by feeding and clothing them, cleaning, nursing the sick, and maintaining emotional relationships. Women's responsibilities are associated with private life, and they have no independent purposes. Ideally, their actions and desires ought to support the purposes and goals of others.

Kant's view of marriage marks a historical advance in the conception of marriage, in that the whole reason behind marriage as a legal institution is to protect the woman (and the man) from merely being used to accomplish some end. We saw in chapter 6 that Kant focuses on the sexual relationship in particular, and the worry that when two people have sex they are concerned only with one another as bodies rather than as persons. Using someone for sexual release risks violating the categorical imperative, specifically the formula of humanity.

Marriage transforms the relationship in two ways. First, by forming a contract with his partner, the husband is explicitly recognizing that his spouse is the sort of being who must consent to be used, whereas packhorses and bricks do not. Although the spouse is being treated as a means, then, she is not being treated *merely* as a means. As we saw in chapter 6, the relationship is also crucially transformed by the fact that the spouses commit themselves to each other under the law. Specifically, the husband and wife take responsibility for one another's "total state of happiness," and thus agree, under threat of punishment, to act in ways that are consistent with respecting one another as rational beings (LE 388). Under this theory, marriage rules out treating a woman merely as a means in any number of senses – a sex object, a producer of heirs, a homemaker, etc. In any case, the requirements that the woman consent to the union and that the husband take on his spouse's ends as his own overcome the objectification of women sexually and economically.

All of this hinges on consent – the spouses' consent to further one another's ends, and the fact that their agreement to a contract distinguishes them as rational beings who are worthy of moral consideration. In this sense, Kant situates himself in the liberal tradition, in which someone can only be bound by the law if he or she has consented to it, and in which individuals confront one another as beings who have the freedom to choose without coercion.

Like modern feminist philosophers, Engels and Kant share the worry that women (and men) are objectified. Engels believes that, within capitalism, women are used merely as reproductive laborers and that they lack even the small degree of freedom that male laborers have. For Kant, sexual desire is inherently objectifying; exploitation does not depend on social circumstances but inclinations that are natural to human beings. Although they both confront the issue of dehumanization, their approaches to marriage reveal very different responses to this problem. Engels conceives of marriage as monogamous prostitution, in that the woman is taken care of in exchange for producing heirs or wage-earners. By contrast, for Kant the fact that spouses consent to a contract negates this danger of objectification. Engels and Kant thus typify the classic divide between the liberal emphasis on free choice as a particular, transformative act and the Marxist idea that desire has a history, that social conditions matter for understanding what the person is doing. Seemingly free acts may in fact reinforce a system of unwitting exploitation.

Consent and Coercion

For Kant, sex outside of marriage instrumentalizes the woman, treating her merely as a means for the sake of satisfying the man's desires.[2] By marrying the woman, however, the man recognizes her ability to decide what she does, and in this sense he treats her as a person. Drawing on this connection between freedom and personhood, Onora O'Neill has interpreted the formula of humanity in terms of consent: "to use someone as a *mere means* is to involve them in a scheme of action *to which they could not in principle consent.*"[3] In disregarding a person's capacity to consent, we do not respect her ability to set her own ends. For example, if I lie to someone, I am not giving her the information she needs to make her own decision.[4] To take

Kant's example, promising a person that you will repay a loan when you have no intention of doing so manipulates her. You are shaping her choices through false information, such that she is doing something contrary to what she intends to do. One cannot in principle consent to be lied to, because in consenting to it, one would know that it is a lie and would dismiss it as a "vain pretense" (G 422). Similarly, coercion treats someone merely as a tool; the person is being physically controlled to accomplish a given end. An armed robber who threatens a bank teller at gunpoint may get the money, but the teller is not choosing to cooperate. The coercive conditions of her decision are such that the choice is not really hers, so she cannot be blamed for it.

The moral prohibition on treating a person in a way to which he or she could not in principle consent has its legal correlate in the protection of individual rights. As I mentioned in chapter 4, Kant claims that *"there is only one innate right,"* the right to determine one's own actions: *"Freedom* (independence from being constrained by another's choice), insofar as it can coexist with the freedom of every other in accordance with a universal law, is the only original right belonging to every man by virtue of his humanity" (MM 237). Any acquired right is justified by tracing its basis to this one innate right. For example, we have property rights so that we can have the means to act freely – that is, so we can accomplish the ends that we set for ourselves. The state is justified in limiting my actions when they threaten my or other people's rights. State coercion and the threat of punishment are thus "a *hindering of a hindrance to freedom*" (MM 231).

Mail-Order Marriages as the Kantian Ideal

Kant's conception of marriage largely neglects the conditions under which people consent to be married, even though this is crucial for determining whether someone is in fact treated as a person. In other words, because coercion violates a person's dignity by manipulating her, the decision to get married must not be coerced if it is to overcome the objectification of the potential spouse. Sexual desire risks instrumentalizing the person, but so does coercion, and Kant fails to appreciate the latter when it comes to the social conditions that erode personal choice.

As a test case, consider international marriage agencies, what are often called "mail-order bride" services. These companies now operate mostly online, where their clients (who are typically male) search for potential mates by using a set of criteria: age is the most common search term, but clients may also specify a particular height or weight range, as well as eye and hair color. This is precisely the sort of thing that Kant criticizes. At least initially, the woman is chosen based wholly on her physical characteristics. For Kant, however, a person consists of a rational part and a nonrational part, a unified whole that cannot be separated, so sexual desire risks treating the humanity in her merely as a means (LE 387; MM 278). The woman is perceived as a body; the humanity in her person is at risk of being used.

Women who advertise with such agencies usually have as their goal marrying men in more developed or more prosperous countries so they can gain citizenship and live safer and more comfortable lives. Typically, Russian, Ukrainian, Filipino, and Columbian women seek husbands in the United States, Canada, Australia, and Great Britain. After a woman is selected, the potential mates interact with each other via letters or internet chat rooms. Then they must meet in person at least once before she can be granted a fiancée visa to enter the country for the purpose of marriage.

There are a few things to note here. First, what motivates people to get married does not matter for Kant. The woman may want a comfortable life without being interested in the man himself, and the man may be interested in having a beautiful woman who is half his age as a mere sex object. Whether they love each other is irrelevant to fulfilling the purpose of marriage: to guard against their using one another merely as means. In the case of mail-order marriages, they are using each other, but Kant thinks that this is common to all sexual relationships. What is important is that they are engaging in the contract as consenting adults. Therefore, they are not being treated *merely* as means, and the fact that they agree to be bound by the law to support one another means that, at least outwardly, they will respect one another's personhood.

The second thing to note is that Kant's emphasis on marriage as a legal arrangement is consistent with the perception on both sides that this is a business deal made possible by marriage brokers. For Kant, a contract is defined primarily in terms of possession, in the sense that it determines people's rights regarding certain property: "An act of the united choice of two persons by which anything at all that belongs to one passes to the other is a *contract*" (MM 271). In marriage, what is transferred to the spouse is the use of one's body for sexual enjoyment ("equality . . . in their possession of each other as persons"), and the property that they bring to the marriage becomes jointly owned ("equality in their possession of material goods") (MM 278). In the case of mail-order brides, the focus is on the husband's possession of the woman's body in exchange for the wife's becoming a citizen and gaining increased economic security. The husband's citizenship and his wealth are the "possessions" that are given. With little talk of marriage as a divine sacrament or as a confirmation of two people's love, these kinds of marriages are more explicitly Kantian than many others.[5] Love is neither necessary nor sufficient for marriage. All that is required is consent and the threat of legal punishment if the commitment to support one's spouse is not fulfilled.

Third, in mail-order marriages the contract is between two consenting adults. Kant prohibits polygamous and incestuous (parent–child) unions because of the inequality of exchange (LE 389–90; MM 278). Such inequality does not allow for the spouses fully to take on one another's ends; someone is being exploited. Mail-order marriages do not have this problem. There is no such inequality between, for example, a 20-year-old Russian woman and a 50-year-old American man. They are both rational adults who are held responsible for their actions and who agree to a contract in which they possess one another equally. To be sure, there are inequalities of power, which I will discuss later in the chapter, but from a Kantian perspective what is important is that there are two adults involved and they have the opportunity either to give or withhold consent.

The final point is that, although the two are responsible for their actions and are capable of consenting to such a contract, the inequality that Kant does recommend between husbands and wives is typical of mail-order marriages. As I mentioned in chapter 6, Kant claims that a certain kind of inequality is necessary "for the unity and indissolubility of a union" (A 303). The man must have "dominance" over the woman, so that they can contribute their "different gifts" to the preservation of the marriage and the family (LE 50). In accordance with this, most men who turn to international marriage agencies want an asymmetrical power relationship between them and their wives. Many of these men blame modern feminism for transforming gender roles and making Western women unfit for marriage as the men envision it. The mutually beneficial exchange is not only about sex and citizenship, but power: "On one side of the Pacific, there's a limitless supply of desperately poor females who'll do anything to become U.S. citizens. On the other, there's an increasing demand for their services from men who'll do anything to retain their power advantage within family life."[6] One of the reasons why women from non-Western countries are so popular as mail-order brides is the perception among Westerners that such women are more deferential to their husbands, that they will not want to work outside of the home, and that they will concentrate on maintaining their husbands and families, occupying themselves primarily with cooking and cleaning.[7]

International marriage agencies recognize this resistance to women's liberation in their male clients, and they tailor their messages accordingly. On one popular website, "hot Russian Brides" are described in the following terms:

A sexy Russian girl doesn't have a choice to stay home and take care of her husband, house, children and marriage[.] [F]or her, it is a dream. . . . For Russian women, the attitude about her self is feminine. She expects to be treated as a lady; she is the weaker gender and knows it. Russian girls have not been exposed to the world of rampant feminism that asserts its rights in America. She remains sweet and tender with a softness that is absolutely desirable.[8]

A number of things are notable even in this brief description. Apart from the obvious characterization of them as soft and weak, the women are infantilized ("girls"), stripped of their agency ("doesn't have a choice"), and (thankfully) ignorant of their "rights." In the past, agencies such as Cherry Blossoms and Anastasia International – specializing in Asian and Russian women, respectively – have been especially adept at exploiting stereotypes about non-Western women, who are characterized as "feminine" and "delicate," as opposed to the career-driven Western women who want to supplant the man's place in the workforce and at home.[9] According to Kant, such women are ideal for marriage, because spouses ought to be unequal. Critics have debated how Kant's position relates to modern feminism,[10] but his attitude toward marital gender relations is clear: "he is the party to direct, she to obey" (MM 279).

Treating Mail-Order Brides Merely as Means

In many ways, then, mail-order marriages are paradigms of the Kantian marriage. But that should give us pause. Kant's characterization of marriage as a contract for the spouses' mutual use of one another's bodies is particularly pronounced here. In addition to the fact that men select the women based primarily on their appearance, potential mail-order brides are screened by marriage agencies with a series of personal questions that make it clear what will appeal to Western suitors: "What size breasts do you have? Do you believe in women's liberation? Are you sexually active? Which underwear do you like to wear?"[11] Although potential spouses typically exchange letters and phone calls, the basis of such a marriage is the exchange of citizenship in a Western country for a woman who is young, attractive, and submissive (or at least is thought to be submissive). Critics have pointed out that Kant ignores the emotional bond that seems to be crucial for a good marriage.[12] This is particularly problematic in mail-order marriages, where the lack of such feeling often leads to abuse.

Regardless of whether the woman actually comes from a culture that promotes deference to the husband – this stereotype has been challenged[13] – the social and legal circumstances of a mail-order marriage make power differences almost inevitable. Mail-order brides often face sexism in their own countries, including inheritance and property laws that undermine any chance at financial independence. They are not allowed to pursue higher education and thus are less employable at home and do not qualify for visas that would allow them to emigrate to the West. Because they tend to have fewer job skills than their male counterparts, they are less likely to find work in economies with high unemployment. Their poor families may pressure them to live abroad and send money home; many Third World families depend on an influx of foreign currency to survive. Because many Western countries base their immigration admission criteria on educational and financial qualifications, marriage is the only way available to many non-Western women to acquire residence and citizenship in the West and to escape enduring poverty at home.[14]

In mail-order marriages, the difference in power is compounded by the fact that the man has invested a lot of money in the union – subscribing to the matchmaking service, making overseas phone calls, sending gifts, flying to the woman's native country, paying for the wedding, and submitting the filing fees to secure the woman's legal residency. Mail-order brides, then, are not only objectified, but commodified. Lou Florence, the husband of a mail-order bride and co-founder of American-Asian World Wide Services, which specializes in Asian mail-order brides, puts it this way: "Asian countries make fine superior products. And I prefer a fine superior lady for my wife."[15] All of this leads to the perception that mail-order brides are "women for sale."[16]

Once a mail-order bride arrives in her husband's country, she is subject to him in ways that non-immigrant spouses are not subject to their husbands. A woman with dependent immigrant status cannot legally seek employment, which means that she relies on her husband to support her economically. Without fluency in English, many mail-order brides cannot get along in their new culture without the husband's assistance. The citizen husband is even responsible for his wife's status under the law. In the United States, according to the Immigration Marriage Fraud Amendments of 1986 (Pub. L. 99–639, 100 Stat. 3537), the spouses must jointly petition for the immigrant spouse to obtain "conditional resident status" for two years, during which time they must remain married and after which the woman can obtain permanent residency only when the man and the woman jointly petition the Immigration and Naturalization Service. The woman cannot submit her own petition, which means that her husband determines whether she is deportable.[17]

The mandatory two-year waiting period gives the man a tool to pressure the woman to do what he wants and to keep her from reporting domestic abuse.[18] Although it is hard to determine how rampant abuse is among the class of mail-order brides – abuse often goes unreported, there are language barriers, and agencies that assist abused women do not record data on mail-order brides in particular (as opposed to other immigrants) – one study reports that 77 percent of women with dependent immigrant status are battered.[19] Recognizing the risk of domestic violence and abuse, the U.S.

Congress passed a law in 1990 (Pub. L. 101–649, 104 Stat. 4978) that allows the woman to apply for a waiver of the waiting period if abuse can be proven, but the Immigration and Naturalization Service and its current incarnation, the U.S. Citizenship and Immigration Services, have interpreted the law so strictly, with such a high evidentiary bar, that they have largely prevented the legislation from having any impact.[20] The objectification and commodification of the woman, the near-total power that the man has over her, and his initial desire to marry a woman who embraces a subservient, domestic role all have the combined effect of promoting a lack of respect for her as a person.

Kant would condemn domestic violence. He may respond to such widespread abuse by saying that, under the current law, husbands are not being forced to act in accordance with the demands of mutual respect, so the law ought to be changed and/or enforced. However, this misses the point. Kant is ignoring the social and cultural factors that, in this case, make abuse a common phenomenon. Punishing abuse does not address the patriarchal conditions that tend to give rise to abuse. Because mail-order brides depend on their new husbands economically, linguistically, and politically, the men have a lot of power over them. And this kind of arrangement is consistent with what Kant says is "the natural superiority of the husband to the wife" (MM 279).

Kant claims that "anyone whose preservation in existence . . . depends not on his management of his own business but on arrangements made by another" is prohibited from active participation as a member of the commonwealth (MM 314). Such people must be legally represented by others, cannot go to court, cannot vote, and in general lack the rights that full citizens have. Examples of such "*passive* citizens" include domestic servants, children, and women. Women and children must be ruled by men because, unlike men, they are incapable of the kind of independence that is needed to be an active citizen, a moral capacity to be bound to the law as a matter of right (MM 314–15; see also TP 295; A 209). Indeed, Kant says that women are unable to think much at all: "in matters of understanding women are pretty much children" (Ak 20:115; see also Ak 15:530, 558). It seems that Kant, like the men who participate in mail-order marriages, would insist that modern feminism is doing something unnatural in trying to support women's independence and self-sufficiency.

Kant believes that the mere fact that two people are married is necessary to overcome the morally problematic features of sexual desire. Although the husband may not in fact respect his spouse, by engaging in the marriage contract – that is, by agreeing to be forced by the government to take on her ends as his own – he is bound to act in a way that is in accordance with, but not necessarily for the sake of, the respect he ought to have for her as a person. As I noted in chapter 6, Elizabeth Brake has objected to this idea, claiming that the only relevant factor is "the moral feeling of respect" for one another, not the legal arrangement. The law cannot affect our intentions with regard to our spouses, so whether two people are married is morally unimportant.[21]

I argued in chapter 6 that Brake overlooks the purpose of marriage as a legal institution, and the fact that the spouses agree to be bound to what they rationally ought to agree to, under threat of punishment. The law forces spouses to act in a way that is consistent with respect for one another, but they may still adopt the wrong maxims. For example, they may assist one another only to avoid punishment. Therefore, marriage for Kant is necessary for mutual respect, but not sufficient. It ensures that people do not treat one another wrongly, but it cannot force them to have good wills.

This is the extent of Kant's theory of marriage, and this is where we see the limits of his practical philosophy when it comes to this issue: by focusing entirely on marriage as a legal institution, Kant fails to consider what would sufficiently motivate someone to respect his spouse. Brake's objection reemerges in a revised, Hegelian form. Hegel criticizes Kant's definition of marriage as a contract under which two people agree to use each other's bodies. Hegel calls this "disgraceful" and instead claims that marriage is an "*immediate ethical relationship*" in which each spouse discovers his or her consciousness in the other. Although marriage begins with a contract in which they confront one another as two rights-bearers, that standpoint is overcome when they "consent to *constitute a single person*."[22] Only such an ethical union can accomplish the mutual respect that Kant hopes to achieve under the law.

Kant only considers the fact that rational beings have agreed to the union and the fact that it is legally enforced. He ignores the extent to which the circumstances of a marriage may undermine mutual respect. Mail-order marriages are in many ways the Kantian ideal of what a marriage should be, and yet the circumstances of such marriages are inimical to the moral consideration that would overcome the two parties' objectification of one another. Ironically, the mail-order marriage itself serves as an instrument for the treatment of the woman as a nurse, a maid, or a concubine, because the woman is supported by the man economically and, under U.S. law for example, she depends on him for her legal status. Engels claims that wives in capitalist systems have no independent purpose, but are used merely to support male wage-laborers. Most mail-order brides are prohibited from having an economic function in the public sphere because, among other reasons, this would mean that they are asserting their independence – that is, that they have been corrupted by modern feminism.

Attempts to Criticize Mail-Order Marriages from a Kantian Perspective

A mail-order marriage is not a forced marriage, where parents compel their (sometimes underage and usually female) child to marry someone of the parents' own choosing, without the child's consent. Most Western nations and international organizations agree that forced marriages are coercive and a rights violation, and they have adopted appropriate laws and principles opposing the practice.[23] By contrast, mail-order marriages are still legal in most countries because they are thought to be consensual arrangements between adults with the freedom to decide for themselves.

Still, the distinction between forced marriages and mail-order marriages may not be as sharp as it seems. O'Neill explains that treating someone as an end means not treating the person as just another abstract agent, but focusing on the specific circumstances in which the person is choosing.[24] For example, prostitutes cannot be understood simply as engaging in a free exchange, given the violence of pimps, the coercive atmosphere at brothels, and the women's lack of economic independence. The fact that mail-order brides choose to marry First World husbands does not mean that they do so voluntarily. Marriage may be seen as the only way out of a bad situation, such as poverty or political instability. As O'Neill reminds us, "a choice between marriage partners does not show that the married life has been chosen."[25] By extending O'Neill's account of coercion, we may be able to explain the moral qualms we have about mail-order marriages, drawing only on the resources given to us by Kant.

Sharon Anderson-Gold takes a different approach. She looks to Kant's conception of cosmopolitan right and his claim that we ought to prohibit the exploitation of the people of other, less developed nations.[26] Kant enjoins Europeans not to take land from pastoral and nomadic societies by force, but instead to establish treaties with them in a way that "does not take advantage of the ignorance of those inhabitants with respect to ceding their lands" (MM 353). Kant also claims that China and Japan were justified in restricting their peoples' freedom to trade with the Europeans in order to protect them from unfair outcomes (PP 359). There are contemporary versions of these kinds of laws. For example, the Philippines passed a law in 1990, the Prohibition against Mail-Order Brides (Republic Act No. 6955), with the stated aim of protecting Filipino women from exploitation by foreign nationals. Perhaps we can infer from Kant's all-too-brief discussion of the principle of hospitality that mail-order brides are being manipulated and mistreated, that Westerners are playing on their ignorance in order to take advantage of them.

Both O'Neill and Anderson-Gold are right to condemn coercion, but they are appealing to a philosophy that is ill equipped to handle more diffuse coercive conditions, as opposed to coercive acts on behalf of individuals. First of all, Kant has a very high standard of what counts as coercion. Typically, these women do not come from violent, war-torn regions where they fear for their lives. Some face economic hardship and social ostracism, to be sure, but the fact that such women desire a better life does not necessarily imply that they are being coerced. If this were coercion, then I would be coerced any time that I have a strong desire to be safer or more financially stable, and I could never be blamed for following my inclinations at the expense of my duty. Mail-order brides marry Western men because they want more comfortable lives. Some people go to work every day for the same reason, but that alone does not imply that their freedom is compromised. With regard to mail-order marriages, a Kantian is hard pressed to identify the specific elements that would make this kind of marriage coercive rather than a mutually beneficial exchange of citizenship for sex. At the end of her essay on coercion, O'Neill leaves us with the vague assertion that relations must not be impersonal, but there is no reason to believe that mail-order marriages are any less personal than garden-variety sexual desire, at least as Kant understands it. If Kant believes that the moral problems inherent in sexual desire can be overcome through marriage, any impersonality in the mail-order bride business can similarly be overcome.

Furthermore, claiming that mail-order marriages are inherently exploitative rests on a key assumption: that mail-order brides are ignorant bumpkins who are taken advantage of by crafty Westerners. Concern for exploited peoples is often laudable, but in this case it masks a kind of Eurocentrism according to which non-Westerners are less capable of making intelligent and informed decisions. Wanting to have a better life, and being willing to marry someone in order to achieve that, could be construed as a wise, prudential decision rather than the desperate move of a woman with no other option. Indeed, the characterization of mail-order brides as uneducated and ripe for exploitation is unsupported by the facts. In her recent book on Russian mail-order brides, Ericka Johnson stresses that the women come from a variety of backgrounds: "To imagine Russian mail-order brides only as economically desperate, delicate young things is to overlook the diversity among them."[27] Although it is not universally the case, some mail-order brides are gainfully employed and well educated. They advertise through international matchmaking agencies for a variety of reasons. To be sure, some mail-order brides are deceived or ignorant of what they are doing, and many, perhaps most, mail-order brides are driven to their decision out of economic necessity. However, all prudential actions are motivated by circumstances of one kind or another. In this context, the Kantian theorist has to address some important questions: Can Kant's practical philosophy explain the important differences between mail-order marriages and the more common kind of union in the West? And can Kant's theory make moral distinctions among mail-order marriages themselves, with their wide variety of background assumptions, social pressures, and personal motivations?

There is some question as to whether Kant can make sense of coercive social conditions at all, as opposed to specific acts of coercion. It is wrong for a moral agent to force another person to do something, because that manipulates the person and thus treats her merely as a means. That is simple enough. However, for Kant the fact that the person is coerced does not necessarily mitigate her moral responsibility. Kant gives several examples in which a person is supposed to do the right thing even at the risk of life and limb. Famously, Kant says that a person who is hiding a friend cannot lie to a murderer who asks for his whereabouts. Kant even says that someone who lies in this situation must be held responsible if the lie is part of a chain of events leading to the victim's murder (SRL 425–30). Kant also says that a woman who is being raped ought to fight her attacker to the death, lest the rape proceed and her honor be tarnished (LE 371; see also LE 377). It sounds strange to our ears that, were she to live through the ordeal, the victim's dignity would be tainted by the forceful act of another. I mentioned in chapter 3 that the body is not irrelevant to our humanity, and in chapter 6 that Kant conceives of us as unified beings, both physical and rational. However, in these two cases, the murderer at the door and the rapist, Kant all too strictly distinguishes physical well-being from moral agency. Physical threats should not sway us from our absolute moral duties. Apparently, the bank teller with the gun to her head would be guilty of stealing were she to give in to the robber's demands.[28] Kant can make sense of what the robber does wrong, but he cannot make sense of how being coerced at least qualifies the teller's moral responsibility.

Setting aside this larger issue, we cannot draw on Kant's philosophy in order criticize mail-order marriages because what goes on in such relationships is not radically different from what goes on in normal sexual relationships, at least as Kant understands them. Mail-order marriages are mutually beneficial exchanges, no better or worse than Kant's typical marriage, where the spouses engage in a contract by which they use one another's bodies on the condition that they agree to advance one another's interests. We must not forget that objectifying sexual attraction characterizes nearly all relationships that culminate in marriage. Although people may be motivated to marry each other for different reasons, the ethical significance of marriage has to do with an exchange of desire-satisfaction within a system that ensures that the partners act in accordance with mutual concern. Kant would not object to mail-order marriages simply because the transaction is made more explicit. If we strictly apply Kant's theory, there is no reason to believe that such marriages are immoral forms of exploitation.

Are Mail-Order Brides Coerced?

For Kant, consent and equality of exchange are necessary for a marriage to accomplish its task. Part of respecting a potential spouse as a person is allowing her to agree to the contract of her own volition. O'Neill reminds us that the woman is treated merely as a means if she is not given a choice in the matter. The practice of forced marriage, in which at least one of the parties refuses to consent to the union, clearly violates the person's fundamental right to freedom. A person who is made to marry someone is not bound to the contract because she has not agreed to be bound to it. The spouses must give themselves to each other reciprocally.

But here is where Kant faces problems and where his dismissive attitude toward women cannot be so easily overlooked. Kant intimates that women are not only less rational than men, but that they are in fact incapable of acting rationally at all: "Women will avoid evil not because it is unjust but because it is ugly. . . . Nothing of ought, nothing of must, nothing of obligation. . . . It is difficult for me to believe that the fair sex is capable of principles" (OBS 231–2). To be sure, Kant says that few men choose to act rightly, but that is very different from not being "capable [*fähig*]" of moral reasoning. Since it is this capacity – "to act *in accordance with the representation* of laws, that is, in accordance with principles" – that makes a person worthy of respect, Kant calls into question women's humanity and whether rational beings have any direct duties to them (G 412). He later adds that women are moved by sentiment, and so must be trained (like dogs?) to love what is good, because reason is not sufficiently motivating (OBS 232). Given Kant's claims in the *Groundwork*, that would mean that nothing a woman does has moral worth. Although her actions may be in accordance with what is right, she is incapable of doing something for the sake of duty.

Of course, if Kant actually believes that women are incapable of rational self-determination, then he could not claim that they are able to consent at all. Like children and animals, they could not be held responsible for what they do and would not be bound by contracts or other legal commitments. Kant clearly believes that women can consent to the marriage contract, and he believes that objectifying them sexually is problematic because they are persons. If we eliminate this contradiction by assuming that women are rational beings – that is, if we disregard Kant's claims that they are "pretty much children" – then he faces a second problem (Ak 20:115). Saying that women are rational and that their choices are attributable to them neglects the social conditions that shape the choices that are available to them. And these social conditions affect personal responsibility in a way that Kant's philosophy cannot make sense of. There seem to be degrees of responsibility, in which choices are limited and undermined to a greater or lesser extent.

Kant wants to make a strict distinction between treating someone merely as a means and not treating someone merely as a means. Someone either is or is not coerced; someone is or is not deceived. However, when we concentrate on the circumstances that affect someone's choices, there seems to be a spectrum of external constraint. On the far end, we have cases that are clearly coercion, such as kidnapping or threats of extreme physical harm. But there are lesser kinds of pressure: pressure from parents to relocate and send money home, bad economic circumstances that make life in the West seem attractive, and political upheaval that may threaten one's very existence. For Kant, these either are or are not forms of coercion. Because one must freely consent to the marriage contract, the line must be drawn if Kant's ethics is to tell us whether it is permissible to select and marry a mail-order bride.

Remember that, typically, mail-order brides participate out of desperation, in an attempt to escape bad situations in their home countries: "For many women, the main reason for leaving is the poverty-stricken nature or the political unrest in their homelands. Finding a foreign national for a husband is a ticket out of a life of poverty and oppression."[29] If a woman were forced to marry someone in response to physical intimidation or if she were threatened with financial ruin and malnutrition, that would be grounds for a legal annulment. Kant would accept this. But does a climate of fear and destitution constitute coercion, especially if it is not the result of an act of coercion by particular agents? If someone is not under financial pressure to marry, the choice is freer (barring other factors) than a choice made under desperate economic circumstances. Someone who decides to escape a life of poverty by marrying a foreigner is freer than someone who is forced to marry someone at gunpoint. For Kant, however, one's choice is either free or not free. The second scenario, in which the woman faces various social pressures, is most typical for mail-order brides. For the purposes of assigning responsibility within the Kantian system, however, this would have to be roughly equivalent either to the first case (being threatened or forced) or to the third case (freely choosing to better oneself). But this seems like an oversimplification.

Kant's moral philosophy tells us that coercion is wrong. However, apart from obvious cases such as lying to or threatening someone, it is hard to tell what constitutes treating someone merely as a means. In this case, the woman faces great hardships at home that motivate her to advertise herself as a submissive mate to Western men. Is she being forced into this by her circumstances, or is she making a prudent decision based on the circumstances? The former amounts to a kind of coercion, but in the latter case she is solely responsible for what she does. How Kant answers this question is crucial to determining the usefulness of his theory, yet Kant gives us little guidance here. He cannot seem to tell us whether mail-order marriages are morally permissible.

One of the reasons for his silence is his general neglect of the conditions under which choices are made. To be sure, the *Metaphysics of Morals* applies the formal moral constraints developed in the *Groundwork* to us as embodied beings. But for Kant applied moral philosophy must remain *a priori*, and so it considers us in very abstract terms, as finite rational beings whose actions affect other finite rational beings. A common complaint against Kant is that he fails to consider the context in which the categorical imperative is applied. This objection is misguided because, in the *Groundwork*, Kant is only trying to establish that morality is justified *a priori* and cannot be overridden by inclinations. Beyond this important distinction, the morally relevant features of a given situation cannot be discovered *a priori*, but must be picked out through judgment. We cannot expect Kant to spell out the complex implications of his theory for lives as they are lived throughout human history and in different parts of the world.

This is certainly true, but the objection here is not about testing maxims. Instead, it is that Kant's abstract view of agency – specifically, the relation between rational beings and their circumstances – oversimplifies responsibility and misconstrues the nature of choice. Consider prostitution. In cases where prostitutes are forced by pimps or tricked by people they trust, O'Neill claims that this mitigates their responsibility, because they are being coerced.[30] Their maxim has been chosen for them. What Kant himself would say is less clear. In the *Lectures on Ethics*, Kant says that "if somebody . . . can preserve life no longer save by surrendering their person to the will of another, they are bound rather to sacrifice their life, than to dishonour the dignity of humanity in their person, which is what they do by giving themselves up as a thing to the will of someone else" (LE 377). Kant cites the case of Lucretia, who he says should have fought Sextus to the death when he raped her, "in defense of her honour" (LE 371). Of course, Kant would condemn the attacker. However, if Kant goes so far as to claim that a raped woman is guilty of violating a moral obligation to herself – he says that fighting to the death "observe[s] the duty to oneself" – then it hardly seems likely that he would leniently judge a prostitute who is pressed for money or pressured by other people. If you do something or even let something happen to you, on pain of death, Kant seems to say that you are partly responsible if it compromises your moral integrity. You violate a duty to yourself. Lucretia has somehow consented to the rape by not "choosing" to die instead. One wonders whether Kant can understand coercion at all.

Unfortunately, we have largely inherited Kant's conception of agency. We tend to believe that consent and coercion are mutually exclusive: either someone consented or she did not. Among other things, such a binary model has led to contemporary legal paroxysms around sexual assault. Although the majority of sexual assaults are committed by someone the victim knows,[31] sexual assaults are most likely to be reported and prosecuted successfully when they are committed by a stranger.[32] A prior relationship with the rapist opens up the question of consent, a question that has been used to dismiss the accusation of rape in both formal and informal settings. The fact that marital rape was not recognized as a crime in the United States until 1975 reflects this conceptual blind spot.[33] If marriage is a contract in which two people consent to the use of one another's bodies, as Kant says it is, then it is hard to make sense of the idea that consent can be withheld within the marriage. Legally and morally, it is easier to conceive of consent and coercion as sharply separated alternatives, but the situations of women who choose to have sex in order to placate a violent husband or boyfriend, who marry out of economic necessity, or who pursue foreign men based on cultural stereotypes muddy these waters. Our current confusion about what counts as consent is attributable at least in part to Kant's inability to account for the non-innocent history of choice.

This element of Kant's practical philosophy resonates in modern liberal political theory. We tend to believe that a person is free to do something if she is not restricted from acting in a certain way; being able to choose means that there are no impediments to the exercise of freedom. In believing this, however, we de-emphasize the conditions that are necessary such that the person can actually accomplish what she is free to accomplish. So, for example, the United States legislates against overt racial discrimination but tends not to address the cycles of poverty and substandard inner-city public schools that give African American children less of a chance to succeed. In chapter 3, I explained that Kant's theory justifies more equitable health-care allocation in order to facilitate free activity. However, Kant and modern liberalism ignore the vaguer and more diffuse conditions that shape what seem to be real options for the agent. Engels's critique of the modern family continues to challenge us, specifically the Marxist emphasis on how material relations transform sexual and gender relations, social expectations, and marriage as a legal institution.

Interestingly enough, O'Neill claims that such social considerations could figure into Kant's analysis of consent and coercion. A factory worker in nineteenth-century England faces different pressures than a college professor in twenty-first-century America, so the Kantian must consider their social situations when evaluating the worker's actions and determining whether the choice to work was truly free. The problem is that neither Kant nor O'Neill gives us the tools to decide how to interpret the various social situations. When do social pressures go beyond merely affecting or influencing the person and become coercion? Marx claims that employment within a capitalist system amounts to a veiled form of slavery, because one must either work or starve to death. Liberal theorists see the relationship between employer and employee as a free exchange: the conditions of employment are clearly stated up front and a contract proposed, so the person's free and informed consent is given. Kant cannot give us any guidance as to which social theory is correct, but we need this to determine whether the factory worker or the professor – or both, or neither – is consenting. O'Neill can only gesture at possibilities: "*If*, for example, we take an idealized Marxist account of capitalist employment, the Kantian approach would generate clear ethical results."[34] But *should* we accept Marx's account? The Kantian cannot say, and O'Neill does not say. We are left without "clear ethical results."

Questioning the *a priori* Basis of Kant's Ethics

In addition to the question of when free consent is undermined, there is also the issue of whether one can rationally consent to be a mail-order bride even if one is not pressured to do so. As Kant envisions it, the law should prohibit some relationships, even though they are consensual, to protect the dignity of human beings. Kant condemns concubinage, saying that the woman would be allowing herself to become merely a thing that is subject to the whim of another (MM 278–9). It would be a kind of sexual slavery, and Kant prohibits other kinds of slavery for the same reason. A person cannot consent to be enslaved because, by giving up her personhood, she would not be bound by the commitment she made as a person – a self-contradiction (MM 283). Because the man is drawn to a mail-order bride primarily (or initially) as a subservient sex object, and because he depends on her being in such dire straits that the marriage seems like the best way out, marriage to a mail-order bride resembles concubinage. In fact, the Coalition against Trafficking in Women has proposed a United Nations Convention against Sexual Exploitation that includes mail-order marriages as similar to prostitution and pornography, in that all three involve someone's financial or sexual advancement at the expense of someone else's dignity and autonomy.[35]

Of course, mail-order marriages are distinguished from concubinage and prostitution by the fact that mail-order brides actually marry their First World suitors. This is crucial for Kant. The prostitute or the concubine engages in a contract "to *let* and *hire* (*location-conductio*) a member for another's use," so the contract is unenforceable. Either person can cancel the contract without violating the other person's rights, since the person is treated only as a thing (MM 278–9). By contrast, marriage is not a contract to enslave oneself, but rather ensures under the law that the husband will take on his wife's ends as his own. He thus treats her as a person to whom he owes the duty of beneficence, even if he does not in fact have that as his motive.

With regard to mail-order marriages, however, Kant faces a problem: How do we reconcile this commitment to advance the woman's ends with the fact that men who look for mail-order brides are typically looking for someone simply to control, who see the marriage as a "quick means of re-acquiring a sock-sorter or a live-in nurse"?[36] The marriage contract is supposed to force people, through coercive measures by the state, to treat one another in a way that is morally permissible. Nonetheless, the conditions under which some women consent lead to their being treated merely as means.

Kant claims that, if someone consents to be a slave, the contract would be void, because that would amount to a complete renunciation of the person's rights. Ironically, Kant also claims that a married woman *does* renounce her rights, only to regain them by giving them over to her husband. The classic description of this arrangement, known as "coverture," is given in William Blackstone's *Commentaries on the Laws of England*: "By marriage, the husband and wife are one person in law: that is, the very being or legal existence of the woman is suspended during the marriage, or at least is incorporated and consolidated into that of the husband: under whose wing, protection, and *cover*, she performs every thing."[37] Although the woman's "very being" is "suspended" in a marriage contract, she does not completely renounce her rights; rather, her rights are taken on, or "covered," by the man. As we saw earlier, Kant accepts the concept of coverture, in which the male head of household is the active citizen who enters the social contract, while all other members of the household lie under his protection and are only capable of passive citizenship – that is, they are represented under the law by the man (MM 314–15; A 209).

Again we see the tensions in Kant's position on marriage. He claims both that there must be equality of exchange in a marriage contract – husband and wife must give themselves completely to one another so that they can regain themselves through the marriage contract (LE 389; MM 278) – *and* that the woman's rights are taken on by the man, such that they are not regained except to the extent that the man serves as the woman's "protector." To be sure, marriage and coverture are separate doctrines under the law; Kant is not simply equating them. However, because marriage must take place under the law, and because the state views women in lesser terms, the supposedly equal possession of marriage takes place within a system of legally enforced gender inequality that threatens the legitimacy of the marriage.[38] When a woman and a man get married, it is essential to Kant that they confront one another as equal beings – that is, as rational adults who are both capable of consenting to the marriage contract. However, once they are actually married, the man becomes the woman's representative in all things political, and she is relegated to the home (A 209). The seeming reciprocity of the marriage contract is undermined by the public/private split.

Carole Pateman has made much of this tension in *The Sexual Contract*, where she claims that the exclusion of women from the social contract has wide-ranging legal implications, including coverture. According to Pateman, Kant is guilty of "the simultaneous denial and affirmation that women are 'individuals'" because he claims both that a woman is like any other rational being in consenting to the marriage *and* that she is and must remain subordinate to the man. She is a citizen, but not an active citizen. She is subject to the "sexual contract" under which only the man has full standing under the law, so she can only have rights through him.[39]

This is particularly important when it comes to mail-order brides. Historically, the doctrine of coverture has applied particularly to property rights, and although it was overturned by nineteenth-century laws in both Europe and the United States, it continues to affect immigration law. The citizen spouse must petition for his wife's legal residence, which gives him the power to determine whether she is deportable, whether she can work, and whether she can remain with her citizen children (if there are any).[40] For Kant, this is justifiable not necessarily because the woman is an immigrant, but because, as a woman, her husband must represent her interests in the public sphere. He is the active citizen.

Some defenders of Kant have sought to separate his views on women, which are colored by his cultural and historical circumstances, from his moral philosophy, and particularly his theory of agency. They defend the value of autonomy while claiming that women are equally capable of such a rational ideal. Others, most notably Jean Rumsey, have countered this, claiming that Kant's account of agency is based on what are traditionally identified as masculine traits. According to Rumsey, the male ideal (as Kant understands it) is Kant's template for normal agency.[41] The moral demand that we be autonomous obligates us not only to resist our inclinations, but to free ourselves from dependence on others – Kant says that receiving help from others places us in their debt in a way that can never be overcome (MM 454) – and even to gain power over them: "The human being's self-will is always ready to break out in aversion toward his neighbor, and he always presses his claim to unconditional freedom; freedom not merely to be independent of others, but even to be master over other beings who by nature are equal to him" (A 327). The characteristics that are traditionally identified with women – sociability, emotion, the body in general – are rejected in favor of what are traditionally considered masculine qualities, such as independence, rationality, and the intellect.[42] Hence, women are excluded, for example, from the political sphere not because they depend on the man – this is not always the case, and it was not always the case in Kant's time – but because they are thought to pose a threat to the rational order. Being associated with the body and emotions, women are the victims of a xenophobia that excludes them from full agency and full citizenship.[43]

The idea that we are distinguished as "rational animals" or that the body ought to be purified in favor of the mind is a very old understanding of what it is to be human. But we cannot forget that this has gendered associations. Just as Descartes attempts to extricate himself from the contingent prejudices that cloud his judgment, Kant attempts to ground philosophy in *a priori* propositions. But this very aim, to free ourselves from contingency, is the result of a system of prejudices that inform the Western philosophical tradition. The belief that reason can be free from prejudice is itself a prejudice.[44] As much as Kant tries to extract himself from his history, the idealization of reason and the association of rationality with masculinity are the contingent result of historical processes.

Kant's moral philosophy is not *a priori* reasoning based purely on the conception of what it is to be a rational being (*Groundwork*), or what it is to be one embodied rational being among others (*Metaphysics of Morals*). It is not pure philosophy onto which Kant's personal and cultural prejudices have been uneasily grafted. Instead, Kant's ethics itself is a social artifact whose seeming veracity depends in many ways on constructed dichotomies and the prioritization of what are traditionally considered to be masculine traits. To be sure, we still tend to value reason over emotion, the mind over the body, independence over dependence, and thinking over feeling. And we associate men, white men in particular, much more with the valued halves of these dichotomies.[45] But the historical formation of such a system of value calls into question the basis of Kant's ethics. It becomes a cultural artifact rather than an ahistorical reflection on the nature of duty.

Notes toward a Genealogy of Kantianism

Kant approaches the ethics of marriage in a way that undermines its moral function: he conceives of marriage simply as a contract and leaves out respect as a basis of a virtuous relationship, he fails to recognize the cultural biases that would dehumanize people and make them merely objects of desire, and he conceives of women in general as children who are incapable of understanding. These are not isolated missteps. Kant's conception of marriage as a contract to protect the dignity and worth of the individual is part of a larger pattern in which he eschews ethics as a social phenomenon. In other words, Kant's focus on the individual as he or she attempts to act rationally misconstrues the ways in which we are embedded in a cultural system of relating to one another through particular social norms.

The irony is that, as we have seen, the Kantian moral apparatus depends on Kant's own social circumstances. Once we expose the cultural and historical biases that inform the Kantian project, we can approach Kant's ethics through a genealogy of his conceptual framework, in the Nietzschean sense, in which the absolute value of rational autonomy is called into question. Much of feminist philosophy has been doing just this. Carol Gilligan questions the rule-based ethics that privileges autonomy over relationships and claims that Kantian ethics puts forward masculine values as a moral ideal in a way that wrongly neglects relational or care-based approaches.[46] Susan Bordo explores various distinctions – mind and body, reason and the emotions, culture and nature – and reveals how they affect our lives in unhealthy ways. In her view, the Cartesian/Kantian conception of the body motivates anorexia as well as much broader anxieties about how we relate to the mortal, messy part of ourselves.[47] Naomi Scheman understands the ideal of rational autonomy as a psychologically unhealthy response to the external world. Traditionally, Western philosophers, including Kant, repress the inclinations, emotions, and dependence on others only to project these things onto people who are thought to be incapable of pure intellectual labor. Women, minorities, and non-Westerners are then oppressed in a paranoid attempt by the privileged to do away with their own corporeality.[48] All three of these philosophers attempt to expose the contingency and the morally significant, real-world consequences of Kant's practical philosophy.

There are many other critics of the Kantian view of reason and autonomy, of course, and not only among feminist philosophers. We must recognize that Kant's focus on consent, rational self-sufficiency, and the importance of enforceable contracts obscures the very real social conditions that promote degradation and exploitation. As an example, I have focused on the coercive conditions of mail-order marriages and Kant's difficulty in making sense of them. But this analysis has broader implications. Once we see that Kant's neglect of context and culture masks an implicit dependence on the patriarchal attitudes of his time, the way becomes clear to critique Kant's moral theory from a historical, sociological, and psychological perspective.

Notes

1   Friedrich Engels, *The Origin of the Family, Private Property and the State, in the Light of the Researches of Lewis H. Morgan*, trans. Alec West (New York: International, 1972), 120.

2   Although both men and women are objectified in sexual relationships, I focus on men's treatment of women in this chapter because that is more relevant when it comes to mail-order marriages, the majority of which involve foreign brides rather than foreign grooms.

3   Onora O'Neill, "The Moral Perplexities of Famine Relief," in *Matters of Life and Death*, ed. Tom Regan (Philadelphia: Temple University Press, 1980), 260–98 (p. 286).

4   As we saw in the Introduction, scientists respect the autonomy of research subjects by getting their consent after they have been fully informed about the experiment's methodology, risks, and benefits.

5   In many cases, the people who are involved in a mail-order marriage claim to love one another. In her *Romance on a Global Stage: Pen Pals, Virtual Ethnography, and "Mail-Order" Marriages* (Berkeley: University of California Press, 2003), Nicole Constable takes issue with the way people's motivations are often characterized when they select mates through international matchmaking agencies. She claims that the couples often develop deep feelings for one another and that the resulting marriages are usually not merely crass exchanges of goods. Despite her protestations, it is no coincidence that the women involved come from relatively poor social and economic circumstances and that agencies target men in prosperous Western democracies. The people may fall in love with one another, but what is crucial for the woman is the fact that they will be married and that this will result in citizenship in her husband's country. That is why the women are advertising for marriage rather than permanent pen pals, and why they are not searching for men, say, in Africa. It is not because African men are less capable of love, but because such a union would probably not substantially improve the women's economic and political circumstances.

6   John Krich, "Here Come the Brides: The Blossoming Business of Imported Love," *Mother Jones* 11, no. 2 (Feb./Mar. 1986): 34–7 (p. 36).

7   Raymond A. Joseph, "American Men Find Asian Brides Fill the Unliberated Bill: Mail-Order Firms Help Them Look for the Ideal Woman They Didn't Find at Home," *Wall Street Journal*, 25 Jan. 1984, 1; Carol Agus, "Fed Up with U.S. Women, Single Men Turning to Asia for Docile Mail-Order Brides," *Oakland Tribune*, 24 May 1984, D1, D3; Michael Small and Dirk Mathison, "For Men Who Want an Old-Fashioned Girl, the Latest Wedding March Is Here Comes the Asian Mail-Order Bride," *People Weekly*, 16 Sept. 1985, 127–9; Venny Villipando, "The Business of Selling Mail-Order Brides," in *Making Waves: An Anthology of Writing by and about Asian-American Women*, ed. Asian Women United of California (Boston: Beacon, 1989), 318–26; and Melissa Fletcher Stoeltje, "Customers Look to Russia for Love; Local Firm Puts Women on Web," *San Antonio Express-News*, 24 Dec. 2000, metro edition, 1A.

8   www.russiansoulmates.com.au. The text has been slightly revised for the website's current incarnation, www.russianladies.permian.ru.

9   Villipando, "The Business of Selling Mail-Order Brides." The Japanese American Citizens League has concluded that, typically, the men who participate in mail-order marriages are "white, much older than the brides they choose, are socially alienated, experience a feeling of personal inadequacy, are politically conservative, frustrated by the women's movement, and find the traditional Asian value of deference to men reassuring" (quoted in Mila Glodava and Richard Onizuka, *Mail-Order Brides: Women for Sale* [Fort Collins, Colo.: Alaken, 1994], 27). Ericka Johnson notes that men often criticize American women in letters to mail-order brides and that they "universally" blame the feminist movement (*Dreaming of a Mail-Order Husband: Russian–American Internet Romance* [Durham, N.C.: Duke University Press, 2007], 27). She also claims that this antipathy toward feminism is "well received" by Russian women, who seem to believe "that the appropriate, ideal type of womanhood is tightly coupled with domesticity and the appearance of subservience" (29). The most cited research on these men is Davor Jedlicka, *American Men in Search of Oriental Brides: A Preliminary Study Released as a Courtesy to the Survey Participants* (Austin: University of Texas, 1988).

10 See especially Robin May Schott, ed., *Feminist Interpretations of Immanuel Kant* (University Park: Pennsylvania State University Press, 1997), and Robin May Schott, "Feminism and Kant: Antipathy or Sympathy?" in *Autonomy and Community: Readings in Contemporary Kantian Social Philosophy*, ed. Jane Kneller and Sidney Axinn (Albany: State University of New York Press, 1998), 87–100.

11 Small and Mathison, "For Men Who Want an Old-Fashioned Girl," 128. See also Glodava and Onizuka, *Mail-Order Brides*, 20.

12 Lara Denis, "From Friendship to Marriage: Revising Kant," *Philosophy and Phenomenological Research* 63, no. 1 (July 2001): 1–28, and Elizabeth Brake, "Justice and Virtue in Kant's Account of Marriage," *Kantian Review* 9 (May 2005): 58–94.

13 Constable, *Romance on a Global Stage*, 63–90.

14 Marie-Claire Belleau, "Mail-Order Brides in a Global World," *Albany Law Review* 67, no. 2 (winter 2003): 595–607 (pp. 603–7). See also Michelle J. Anderson, "License to Abuse: The Impact of Conditional Status on Female Immigrants," *Yale Law Journal* 102, no. 6 (1993): 1041–30 (pp. 1407–11), and Villipando, "Business of Selling Mail-Order Brides," 322–3.

15 Small and Mathison, "For Men Who Want an Old-Fashioned Girl," 129. It is interesting how often the idea of the Asian's manufacturing prowess comes up when clients are talking about their mail-order brides. One man is quoted as saying: "American women put themselves on a pedestal and are neglecting U.S. men. It's the same thing as when Ford and General Motors keep turning out bad products. You turn to the Japanese" (Joseph, "American Men Find Asian Brides," 1).

16 This is the subtitle of Glodava and Onizuka's *Mail-Order Brides*.

17 Janet M. Calvo, "Spouse-Based Immigration Laws: The Legacies of Coverture," *San Diego Law Review* 28, no. 3 (Aug.–Sept. 1991): 590–628 (pp. 613–14).

18   On the coercive effect of the two-year conditional status, see especially Eddy Meng, "Mail-Order Brides: Gilded Prostitution and the Legal Response," *University of Michigan Journal of Law Reform* 28, no. 1 (fall 1994): 197–248.

19   This is from a sample taken of Latina women in the Washington, D.C. area. See Anderson, "License to Abuse," 1403n9.

20   Calvo, "Spouse-Based Immigration Laws," 631–41; Anderson, "License to Abuse"; and Uma Narayan, "'Male-Order' Brides: Immigrant Women, Domestic Violence and Immigration Law," *Hypatia* 10, no. 1 (winter 1995): 104–20.

21   Brake, "Justice and Virtue in Kant's Account of Marriage."

22   G. W. F. Hegel, *Elements of the Philosophy of Right*, ed. Allen W. Wood, trans. H. B. Nisbet (Cambridge: Cambridge University Press, 1991), §§75, 161–3.

23   For example, the Universal Declaration of Human Rights states: "Marriage shall be entered into only with the free and full consent of the intending spouses" (Article 16.2). The Catholic Church considers forcing someone to marry sufficient grounds for an annulment (*Catechism of the Catholic Church*, 1625–32, www.vatican.va/archive/catechism/p2s2c3a7.htm#I). And in 2007 the British government passed the Forced Marriage (Civil Protection) Act, which provides legal protections and remedies for those involved in forced marriages.

24   Onora O'Neill, "Between Consenting Adults," *Philosophy and Public Affairs* 14, no. 3 (summer 1985): 252–77.

25   Ibid., 255.

26   Sharon Anderson-Gold, "Cosmopolitanism and Democracy: Global Governance without a Global State" (paper presented at the International Social Philosophy Conference, Portland, Oregon, July 2008).

27   Johnson, *Dreaming of a Mail-Order Husband*, 19.

28   In this and the case of the murderer at the door, Kant seems to commit himself to a very un-Kantian idea: what Bernard Williams calls "negative responsibility" ("A Critique of Utilitarianism," in *Utilitarianism: For and Against*, by J. J. C. Smart and Bernard Williams [Cambridge: Cambridge University Press, 1973], 75–150 [pp. 94–5]). This doctrine is usually attributed to consequentialism, and it holds that I am responsible for whatever is a consequence of what I do, whether I actually perform the wrong action or merely allow it to happen. Of course, we can be guilty of inaction in some cases. However, we are not morally responsible *in the same way* as the person who actually performs the action, even if we were part of the causal chain leading to it. The murderer's maxim is not the friend's maxim; there is a distinction between my agency and another person's agency.

29   Glodava and Onizuka, *Mail-Order Brides*, 47.

30   O'Neill, "Between Consenting Adults," 268–9.

31   Almost eight out of ten victims of sexual assault and rape report that the offender was an acquaintance or relative (Bureau of Justice Statistics, United States Department of Justice, "Violence against Women: Estimates from the Redesigned National Crime Victimization Survey," 1995, bjs.ojp.usdoj.gov/index.cfm?ty=pbdetail&iid=805).

32   A recent well-publicized study found that non-stranger rapes are more likely to be reported, but that 80 percent of prosecuted sexual assault cases involve stranger rapes. In other words, stranger rapes are prosecuted more often, despite the fact that more complaints are made against men whom the women know. See Rebecca Campbell et al., "Preventing the 'Second Rape': Rape Survivors' Experiences with Community Service Providers," *Journal of Interpersonal Violence* 16, no. 12 (Dec. 2001): 1239–59.

33   Before 1975, laws in the United States explicitly excluded spouses from being prosecuted for rape. Between 1975 and 1993, all fifty states gradually removed this exemption. Nonetheless, in thirty-three states spousal rape is still a lesser crime than other forms of rape, and there are some exceptions given to the husband, when his wife's consent is not necessary – for example, if the wife is mentally or physically impaired or unconscious, or if she is legally unable to consent due to age or disability. It is relevant to our study of Kant that one of the risk factors for marital rape is when the husband views his wife as property. See Raquel Kennedy Bergen, "Marital Rape: New Research and Directions," National Online Resource Center on Violence against Women, 2006, www.wcsap.org/MaritalRapeRevised.pdf.

34   O'Neill, "Between Consenting Adults," 274; emphasis added.

35   Coalition against Trafficking in Women, *Coalition Report* (Philadelphia: Coalition against Trafficking in Women, 1992).

36   Krich, "Here Come the Brides," 37.

37   William Blackstone, *Blackstone's Commentaries*, ed. St. George Tucker (South Hackensack, N.J.: Rothman Reprints, 1969), 2:442.

38   Kant recognized the tension here, but he claimed to resolve it by attributing the man's exalted position to his "natural superiority" (MM 279).

39   Carole Pateman, *The Sexual Contract* (Stanford, Calif.: Stanford University Press, 1988), 168–73.

40   Calvo, "Spouse-Based Immigration Laws."

41   Jean P. Rumsey, "Re-Visions of Agency in Kant's Moral Theory," in *Feminist Interpretations of Immanuel Kant*, 125–44. I focus on the feminist critique of Kant in this chapter, but Emmanuel Chukwudi Eze, Robert Bernasconi, and Susan Shell make similar claims regarding race. Eze argues that Kant's anthropological writings on race are integrally related to the transcendental philosophy, including Kant's moral theory and his conception of reason. Bernasconi traces Kant's views on teleological judgment back to his views on the distinction and hierarchy of the races. And Shell explains how race serves an important function in Kant's conception of historical progress and the achievement of a cosmopolitan society. See Eze, "The Color of Reason: The Idea of 'Race' in Kant's Anthropology," in *Postcolonial African Philosophy: A Critical Reader*, ed. Emmanuel Chukwudi Eze (Oxford: Blackwell, 1997), 103–40; Bernasconi, "Who Invented the Concept of Race? Kant's Role in the Enlightenment Construction of Race," in *Race*, ed. Robert Bernasconi (Oxford: Blackwell, 2001), 11–36; and Shell, "Kant's Conception of a Human Race," in *The German Invention of Race*, ed. Sara Eigen and Mark Larrimore (Albany: State University of New York Press, 2006), 55–72.

42   Rumsey, "Re-Visions of Agency in Kant's Moral Theory," 132.

43 Adrian Piper claims that this attitude toward women and non-whites is a kind of xenophobia, which is the result of Kant's rejection of anything that cannot be rationally incorporated into a conceptual system. See Piper, "Xenophobia and Kantian Rationalism," in *African-American Perspectives and Philosophical Traditions*, ed. John P. Pittman (New York: Routledge, 1997), 188–232.

44 Hans-Georg Gadamer, *Truth and Method*, trans. Joel Weinsheimer and Donald G. Marshall, 2nd edn. (New York: Continuum, 2004), 272–3.

45 Within the conceptual framework of dualism, the body becomes the defining feature of those persons designated as inherently heteronomous, including men of non-European origin. These associations can either be feminized, as in the caricature of Asian men as manipulative and weak, or hyper-masculinized, as in the portrayal of African men as primitive and bestial. Defining other people by the weakness or strength of their bodies, their indulgence in sensual pleasures, or their closeness to nature is a form of degradation and dehumanization. See Frantz Fanon, *Black Skin, White Masks*, trans. Richard Philcox (New York: Grove, 2008), and Edward W. Said, *Orientalism* (New York: Pantheon, 1978). Kant is particularly guilty of this. Kant believes that the different races are the result of what he calls germs or natural predispositions unfolding differently in different climates, and he says this of blacks: "humid warmth is beneficial to the robust growth of animals in general and, in short, this results in the Negro, who is well suited to his climate, namely strong, fleshy, supple, but who, given the abundant provision of his mother land, is lazy, soft and trifling" (DR 434–8). I will discuss Kant's views on race in more detail in chapter 8.

46 Carol Gilligan, *In a Different Voice: Psychological Theory and Women's Development* (Cambridge, Mass.: Harvard University Press, 1982). See also Annette C. Baier, *Moral Prejudices: Essays on Ethics* (Cambridge, Mass.: Harvard University Press, 1994), 18–32, and Sally Sedgwick, "Can Kant's Ethics Survive the Feminist Critique?" in *Feminist Interpretations of Immanuel Kant*, 77–100 (pp. 93–5).

47 Susan Bordo, *Unbearable Weight: Feminism, Western Culture, and the Body* (Berkeley: University of California Press, 1993).

48 Naomi Scheman, *Engenderings: Constructions of Knowledge, Authority, and Privilege* (New York: Routledge, 1993). See also Piper, "Xenophobia and Kantian Rationalism."

8

Individual Maxims and Social Justice

From its first appearance, a number of philosophers have questioned whether the categorical imperative can properly guide us in our most complex moral decisions. The social context, personal convictions, and even the consequences of potential actions seem to overtax the simple demand for rational consistency. We saw this is the previous chapter, with Kant's inability to conceptualize degrees of coercion and autonomy. But Kant also has trouble making sense of the scope of our moral duties, the objects of our moral attention, and what we can reasonably be held accountable for.

This is especially true when it comes to larger issues, where our obligations extend beyond individual, clearly identifiable subjects to social problems such as poverty and world hunger. Because one can best fulfill these kinds of duties by working through institutions such as governments and charities, the agent is morally obligated to determine their effectiveness so that she can truly will the maxim of beneficence. Yet what constitutes justified expectations or negligence can only be defined against social standards of reasonableness. Furthermore, even though the agent affects other persons only indirectly, she must respect the humanity in those who deserve her assistance. Here too Kant fails adequately to consider the contingent conditions that obstruct our recognition of others as persons. In some cases, social conditions make it unreasonable to expect that one would acknowledge duties to the poor, for example. Therefore, Kant's deontological ethics is incapable of handling the promotion of social goods without considering the context in which the maxim is formulated. In considering that context, however, Kant must abandon *a priori* moral theory and its exclusive concern with the formal character of maxims.

Kant and Applied Ethics: The Uses and Limits of Kant's Practical Philosophy, First Edition.
Matthew C. Altman.
© 2011 John Wiley & Sons Inc. Published 2011 by Blackwell Publishing Ltd.

How Kant Answers Hegel's Formalism Charge

Hegel was an early critic of Kant's moral philosophy, claiming that its formal character made it useless on its own. Famously, Hegel said that the categorical imperative yields only empty tautologies, because any maxim could be universalized, depending on our particular social assumptions and expectations.[1] Furthermore, whether a maxim is permissible depends on the background against which we interpret its key terms. For example, one can conclude that it is morally wrong to "deny a deposit which no one can prove has been made" only if personal ownership is presupposed. In other words, a maxim to steal money that has been entrusted to me "annihilates itself" when universalized only if there is the institution of private property (CPrR 27). But if all things are owned in common or there is no such thing as ownership at all, situations that Hegel claims are rationally consistent,[2] then the proposed maxim would be universalizable.[3] Whether it is right or wrong depends on contingent social institutions and expectations. Therefore, Hegel concludes, the categorical imperative by itself can give us no moral guidance. Kant's ethics of duty is empty.

Although Kant would concede that the consistency of some maxims depends on particular background conditions, he would also claim that those conditions are presupposed in the maxim itself. My being able to keep the deposit depends on my willing a world in which the depositor believes that the money is his and has certain expectations that it will be returned, and in which this expectation is generally enforced. This is why it is a deposit rather than simply a transfer of funds, and why it is relevant that the deposit is unrecorded. Were I to universalize my maxim, the person would never have made what is properly called a deposit in the first place. As Kant says, "there would be no deposits at all" (CPrR 27). Hence, the maxim of stealing a deposit is self-contradictory. Just as the very concept of lying depends on its relation to a general expectation of honest dealings and stealing makes sense only if the item belongs to someone else, the very idea of an unrecorded deposit would not make sense unless there is private property. To apply the categorical imperative, we need not import a social background that is extraneous to the person's motive. The concepts in a properly formulated maxim already include the morally relevant expectations.

Basic Principles versus Particular Duties: Kant and Rawls

Although social conventions are presupposed in some maxims, there is another way in which Kant's practical philosophy seems to ignore a larger context – not because of its formal character, but because of its focus on particular end-setters with particular ends. Typically, Kantian theorists deal with individual actions that affect the agent himself or other individuals: lying to a friend, stealing a deposit, killing someone. Group actions that shape social policies have often been overlooked, even though these broader issues are important for making sense of our duty to promote social justice.

Some philosophers have charged Kant with conceiving of agents as essentially individualistic, rational end-setters who exist prior to and independent of social relations. That is not the focus of my argument in this chapter. Here I am considering the scope of our obligations and the fact that Kant seems best equipped to assess how individual persons treat one another. The problem is that, in our practical lives, we are concerned with more than relations among rational individuals. When we are concerned with social justice, we are addressing a community's obligations to correct conditions that are detrimental to some group of persons or persons in general: not whether I have a responsibility to help a poor person who confronts me on the street – to give him what he deserves, or not to treat him as a mere thing – but whether we as a community, and I as a member of that community, have a duty to reduce poverty. Such duties would be general in a different sense than sweeping moral judgments – for example, that we should not lie to or steal from *anyone*. Instead, the promotion of social justice would only indirectly affect particular persons by addressing the overall conditions under which those persons develop and exercise their capacity for rational agency.

John Rawls would seem to be an obvious resource in setting out how we can use Kantian principles to promote social justice. Rawls claims that deontological ethics is deeply concerned with justice, which he opposes to utility. Social decisions should not be made by weighing advantages and disadvantages for overall happiness, but should follow from a social contract under which each person is treated "in virtue of his nature as a free and equal rational being."[4] Given our highest-order interest in exercising our capacity for justice, Rawls claims, we would choose two principles that would best provide us with what he calls primary goods: the liberty principle, which would give us the opportunity freely to pursue what we value, and the distribution principle, which would provide us with the means to pursue it. According to the latter principle, we would agree to the unequal distribution of wealth, property, jobs, and other goods only if the situation of the worst off were improved. Although this would not (necessarily) equalize the fortunes of rich and poor, the gap would be acceptable if it was agreed to from a fair starting point. Social justice would be achieved despite the existence of relative poverty.

Rawls's concern for justice, however, extends only to the basic principles that govern the structure of social institutions, as opposed to particular policies or the actions of individual citizens within those institutions. In other words, the law protects people's freedom to pursue what they take to be good, ensuring equality of opportunity, but it does not mean that people will not be needy or that people are not obligated to assist others on their own. If the basic structure governing the pursuit of goods is fair, then the results for those who act under that structure are also fair.[5] But agreeing to a fair starting point does not mean that we will have discharged our moral obligations to one another given the outcome of that arrangement – namely, given the persistence of poverty and the income gap between rich and poor. The work of social institutions does not substitute for the actions of particular agents. Regardless of how we structure those institutions, we still have a personal duty to help those who are on the losing end of systematic inequalities, even if they result from a fair starting point.

For Kant, social institutions do not enforce morality. Under the law, I am justifiably punished if I violate someone's basic liberties because I rationally consent to respect others' freedoms, but regulating the effects of my actions cannot dictate what motivates me. As I have noted in previous chapters, the scope and effectiveness of the law are limited; moral obligations are separate concerns.

Of course, citizens may use the government as an instrument to fulfill their duties. The established bureaucracy of the United States government is more capable than I am of combating poverty, within my own country and globally. I could work to elect those who will advance that aim by reallocating tax revenue, for example. Because taxes are collected under threat of fines and a prison sentence, however, paying one's taxes may not constitute a beneficent act. That depends on the person's motive, specifically whether the individual citizen pays his taxes with the intention of helping those in need, simply because it is right.

This is a key difference between Kantianism and utilitarianism. For Jeremy Bentham and John Stuart Mill, institutions and public policies can themselves be moral if they promote utility more than the alternatives. As we will see in chapter 9, Kant cannot make sense of collective responsibility, and therefore cannot make sense of the morality of such group actions. For Kant, the state and its laws are not moral agents even if particular agents bring about their purposes by means of the state. The obligation rests with the individuals who govern, elected representatives and the voters, rather than the government and the law themselves. The same can be said of charities, businesses, and churches. I, not they, am personally responsible for the demands of social justice, if Kant can make sense of such a thing. But that leaves open the question of whether the individual can be obligated to promote something as broad as social justice. If Kant cannot make sense of collective agents, can he make sense of general aims?

What Is My Obligation to Reduce Poverty?

A number of theorists have drawn on Kant's moral philosophy to explain our personal obligation to address large-scale problems. Most notably, Onora O'Neill argues that the requirement that we respect the personhood of others implies that we have a moral duty to help alleviate world hunger and not to take advantage of people who are helpless in times of famine. However, when it comes to enumerating the specific duties we have, O'Neill usually focuses on individual actions as they affect other individuals: for example, profiteering or cheating others out of their fair share. Taking advantage of a person's helplessness amounts to coercion; it does not respect her capacity freely to consent.[6] The rightness of any maxim depends on whether it aims to "increase anybody's possibility for autonomous action" or to "*transform* the possibilities of action for some."[7] We must specify how our actions affect an "anybody" or "some" people. The supposed obligation to end world hunger, then, is not a moral obligation unless fulfilling it would sustain some agent's rational activity.

Like O'Neill, who attempts to apply the formula of humanity specifically to times of scarcity, Hegel also rejects overly broad moral precepts. He claims that the duty of beneficence must be given specificity in a historical and social context, lest the duty amount to an empty platitude:

> The Bible is more rational when it commands, Love your neighbor as yourself, that is, love the human beings with whom you are in relation or with whom you come to be in relation. "All" is merely empty bombast. The universal formal aspect of good "cannot be fulfilled as an abstraction; it must first acquire the further determination of particularity."[8]

A beneficent action must be related somehow to personal autonomy, so our duty can never be to address social problems instead of helping individual people, and particularly the individuals near me whose well-being I am most able to affect. Our duties must be given determinacy. I can be morally obligated to alleviate *someone's* hunger, but not to alleviate *world* hunger.

This is not splitting hairs. For the utilitarian, secondary principles that do not directly appeal to happiness are obligatory as long as they ultimately maximize utility.[9] In other words, under utilitarianism, the command to "reduce poverty" makes sense as a moral imperative. Social goods can be the immediate goal of my actions, even if I do not consider whether actual persons would benefit. For Kant, however, "I will reduce poverty" is not an appropriate maxim because the proposed policy is too general actually to describe my actions. Reducing poverty may be the eventual goal of my efforts, but *what* am I doing to reduce poverty? A maxim must include the means to achieve the end. Furthermore, reducing poverty is not clearly an instance of beneficence. It does not, at least directly, help to further the ends that a particular poor person sets for himself. In short, reducing poverty is not an appropriate end because it does not do what a morally obligatory action ought to do – namely, it does not protect or advance others' autonomy in any clear way – and it is not an appropriate means because of its vagueness.

Of course, whether people are actually helped is not crucial for Kant. Rather, the agent must be rightly motivated. But how we properly conceive of the person's motive does not only depend on what the agent sincerely believes. Because a maxim's rightness depends on its attempt to further the rational pursuit of ends, we cannot judge actions by whether they advance social programs or improve circumstances. For the agent truly to adopt a maxim of beneficence, he must have as his object respecting the personhood of other agents. His action may have the effect of strengthening a charity or even reducing poverty in general, but the *reason* for the action must be to treat the humanity in himself and others as ends in themselves.

Social Contexts Specify the Content of Maxims

In order to assess what someone is doing, a maxim must reflect the agent's true motives – an impossible task, as we saw in chapter 5. Setting aside this problem for the time being, the maxim must also be "rational given the agent's situation and the alternatives," to use Rawls's phrasing.[10] Whether a maxim is rationally formulated is vague, of course, but one would at least have to consider other options, recognize unintended consequences, and make a rough calculation concerning the likelihood of accomplishing the end. Whether a maxim is right thus depends on whether the agent is reasonable in assuming that his actions will further the ends of those whose lack of resources limits their attempts to achieve them. But the reasonableness of an agent's expectations – whether an agent is negligent, among other things – depends in large part on the network of social expectations within which he sets his maxims. As Hegel insists, we can understand the maxim and assess its rightness only with reference to external circumstances.

An example will help to illustrate this point. Imagine that Joe gives $50 to a local charity whose stated purpose is to feed the hungry. Obviously, being properly nourished is a condition of moral agency. Food is one of our "true needs," so people who are starving have a moral claim on us to help them (MM 393, 432).[11] Joe is obligated to help others because he cannot universalize a maxim of nonmaleficence; beneficence is obligatory (G 423). Imagine also that Joe is rightly motivated. He feels a sense of satisfaction for having given, but he gives because he ought to help the less fortunate.

Therefore, assuming that Joe can afford it, giving to charity in this case seems like a morally praiseworthy act.

Imagine, however, that the charity is so poorly run (or even corrupt) that all of Joe's money goes toward overhead costs, especially the salaries of the people who are managing the charity. None of it helps the less fortunate. According to utilitarianism, the poor obviously need the resources more than either Joe or the administrators, so giving to a better charity or giving directly to the poor (if that is an effective option) would have been the right thing to do. Still, because Joe was only negligibly harmed – he can afford it, after all – and the administrators were negligibly helped, and most importantly, because it made Joe happy, the utilitarian may conclude that giving was better than not giving, even if none of the intended recipients are helped.

Kant, however, could legitimately question whether giving the money was better than keeping it, because it does not seem to be an act of beneficence at all. Joe's maxim is not "When I can afford it, I will help those in need," but the less laudatory "When I can afford it, I will give to an organization that professes to help those in need." By acting under the latter maxim, Joe is not clearly willing to advance the ends of anyone who actually needs his help, as opposed to merely hoping that they are helped indirectly through his actions, in conjunction with the work that is done directly by the charity.

As noted earlier, consequences are not important for assessing the moral worth of an action. However, the effectiveness of what we are trying to accomplish through our actions is not completely disregarded by Kant. In the *Groundwork*, he makes an important distinction between willing something to be the case and merely wishing it to be so:

> Even if, by a special disfavor of fortune or by the niggardly provision of a stepmotherly nature, this will should wholly lack the capacity to carry out its purpose – if with its greatest efforts it should yet achieve nothing and only the good will were left (not, of course, as a mere wish but as the summoning of all means insofar as they are in our control) – then, like a jewel, it would still shine by itself, as something that has its full worth in itself. (G 394)

Almost every reader of Kant focuses on the fact that Kant is not a consequentialist. The value of an action depends on the agent's maxim rather than the state of affairs brought about by the action. Whether the poor are in fact helped does not affect whether the agent acts beneficently. But this overlooks an important qualification. According to Kant, an agent cannot be unconcerned with whether the intended end is achieved. Determining what a person's maxim is depends on what he can reasonably expect to accomplish. Joe certainly wants to help the poor, but he gives to the charity without having any idea whether it is effective. Because numerous resources are available to discover this information – various websites, organizations such as the American Institute of Philanthropy, even friends' opinions – we can legitimately question whether Joe is in fact willing to help the poor at all. Is he "summoning . . . all means insofar as they are in [his] control"? Is he in fact willing the beneficent act or merely wishing that the poor are better off? It depends on which resources are available to him and how much research it is reasonable to expect of him in attempting to fulfill his duty.

These kinds of questions are seldom asked because Kant's focus on the maxim rather than the consequences is often taken to endorse "good intentions," broadly construed. In their first encounter with Kant, students in particular often misinterpret deontological ethics as a kind of moral subjectivism. If a police officer chases an armed robber into a bunch of innocent bystanders, she is justified in shooting recklessly into the crowd as long as she is trying to stop the criminal and she does not intend to kill innocent people. Because she sincerely believes that she is doing the right thing, it must in fact be right.

Maxims, however, must accurately describe what the person is doing, and what we take ourselves to be doing does not necessarily reflect our actual motivations. There are two reasons for this. First, as I discussed in chapter 5 and as Kant himself recognizes, our maxims are in principle unknowable, since they are the result of transcendentally free choices that are unavailable to inner sense (CPR A551n/B579n; G 407, 419). Joe may think that he is giving to charity because it is the right thing to do, when in fact he is driven by pathological motives – to avoid guilt or to atone for some transgression, real or imagined. Perhaps the cop is satisfying a general feeling of aggression that she cannot recognize in herself. The fact that she thinks she is acting for the sake of duty does not make it so. We may be mistaken about even our own motives.

In addition to this insuperable barrier between inner sense and noumenal freedom, maxims may also be misconstrued because of the agent's ignorance of the facts. Such ignorance is not always blameless. This is especially evident in cases of gross negligence, when one disregards or is simply oblivious to what is relevant in making a moral decision. The officer's failure properly to assess the risk involved in shooting into a crowd makes her morally responsible for any deaths she causes, because she *should* have considered this. An agent is obligated not only to act on maxims that are morally permissible or obligatory, but to assess accurately what she is in fact doing – who is helped and harmed, and who is potentially helped and harmed. This is not just a question of strategy, but is integral to judging the value of the person's maxim. The consequences of the action do not determine whether the action is right. However, correctly formulating the maxim is necessary to determine whether it is universalizable – a fact first noted by Hegel.

Whether Joe has fulfilled his duty of beneficence depends on whether his ignorance of the charity's ineffectiveness is blameworthy or not. If Joe gave the money to a ne'er-do-well skulking in a dark alley who swears he will give it to the poor, that is not a charity, but a con (and not a very good one). Joe should have realized that if he was serious about helping others. To advance his aim, Joe ought to research the various possible outlets for his charity and give to those that are most efficient at helping the poor, or those that also advance some larger agenda that promotes their agency – for example, a soup kitchen operated in conjunction with a drug rehabilitation program. If Joe gives to the Red Cross knowing that its efficiency rating is very high,[12] then even if, for some reason, the organization does not spend his money appropriately in this particular case, even if the executives were corrupt – if the CEO embezzled the money and fled to Argentina – Joe's expectation that people would be helped by the Red Cross is reasonable, and he is acting under a maxim of beneficence even if no one is in fact helped. This would amount to "the summoning of all means" to accomplish his end, even though nothing comes of it (G 394). Again, the consequences of the act – the fact that the poor receive no assistance in this case – are not relevant. What is relevant is that Joe was reasonable in expecting that they would be helped. Unfortunately, the reasonableness of Joe's expectation also depends on whether he is reasonable in assuming that his research accurately reflects the efficiency of the agency. There is a regress of conditions that we must consider in order for the maxim to be properly understood.

In everyday moral thinking, of course, we make the distinction between negligence and reasonable thoroughness all the time. Some people claim that we make these kinds of judgments intuitively. However, Kant cannot define what is reasonable and unreasonable by appealing to common sense. Kant dismisses such appeals in the preface to the *Prolegomena*. Saying that "everyone knows" what is reasonable is not any kind of explanation or justification. Rather, it is an attempt to stop the inquiry into how we ought properly to describe the person's action, or how her maxim is to be formulated. There must be some ground to decide what is reasonable and what is unreasonable. This is not self-evident to everyone, given how imperfectly rational beings are constituted (P 258–9).

Pure reason, not common sense, is the arbiter of morality. Kant cannot terminate the regress of justification – determining whether one's expectations are reasonable, whether one's evidence for reasonableness ought to be trusted, etc. – by appealing to some fixed, universal standard that applies to all rational beings as such. There is no way to formalize what counts as reasonable expectations. But if we appeal to social expectations, as we often do, then that leads to a kind of cultural variability that Kant rejects. We will return to this later.

That one could be morally blamed for ignorance also implies that a seemingly right action may not be praiseworthy if it results from ignorance. If Joe gave to the Red Cross without the slightest idea that it is an efficient distributor of charitable contributions, then that may not be an act of beneficence. Perhaps he gave to the Red Cross instead of the ne'er-do-well only because the Red Cross got to Joe first. Even though Joe was right in assuming it is a reliable organization, he was not justified in believing that. That he did the right thing is a matter of luck rather than a result of any effort on his part.

The rightness of an action depends on what the agent knows and what he can reasonably be expected to know. And, like world hunger, the problem of poverty in general is not easily addressed, which makes it difficult to determine what a person is obligated to do.[13] First, it is unclear when one's moral obligations to the poor have been fulfilled. Aside from the problem of how to measure pleasures and pains, for utilitarianism this is easily settled: one must give to the point of marginal utility. If the needy can benefit from Joe's money more than he can, then he ought to give until an additional amount would harm Joe more than it would help others. For Kant, however, it is difficult to understand even what a good answer would amount to. Kant does try to specify how much we ought to give: "How far should one expend one's resources in practicing beneficence? Surely not to the extent that he himself would finally come to need the beneficence of others" (MM 454). This is true enough, but it only pushes the question back: When do I *need* beneficence? How effective must my willing be in order for me not to be in need? This is difficult to answer, especially because, for Kant, what I accomplish through my willing is morally irrelevant, provided that I strive to fulfill my duty.

With the formula of humanity, Kant conceives of moral obligation in relational terms: as a rational being, I ought to further the ends of other rational beings. This is beneficence. It is easy to see how this plays out in personal confrontations with those in need. When Joe encounters a starving person, he has a duty to help her, just as he would have a duty to save a person from drowning if he came upon her in a shallow pond.[14] When it comes to larger social issues such as poverty or world hunger, however, the obligation becomes vaguer and much more diffuse. Joe's $50 may help to make one or more people less hungry overall, but does it help to "advance their purposes" in any appreciable sense?

This is not a question of whether Joe should help. We can grant that everyone, including Joe, ought to be beneficent. The fact that beneficence is an imperfect duty, however, gives us a certain amount of leeway in determining how and when to help others. When Joe gives, the answers to "how much?" and "to whom?" depend on the circumstances: how destitute those in need are, how much is given by others, how effective the charity is, etc. Kant can handle that, since relevant circumstances are included in the maxim. Nonetheless, even if Kant is right that we should test maxims on grounds of formal consistency, we need to introduce some independent standard of reasonableness into order to formulate the maxim that is being tested. An *a priori* metaphysics of morals cannot make sense of what someone can be reasonably expected to know in performing a given action. What Joe can reasonably be expected to understand about the circumstances, or what is morally relevant in a given case, varies depending on his psychology and our social expectations. Determining whether the maxim he adopts is in fact a maxim of beneficence depends on a number of factors that are external to the agent's will.

Herman's Rules of Moral Salience

In defending the practical value of Kant's ethics, Barbara Herman tries to explain the role of social factors in an agent's conception of what is morally relevant. What she calls "rules of moral salience" (RMS) are acquired during a person's moral education, and they help the person to judge when the categorical imperative ought to be used and how it ought to be used in different cases. Such rules make it possible for us to know what ought to be considered and who is morally considerable. Herman's approach is decidedly Kantian; she contends that this is consistent with Kant's general moral framework. Furthermore, she says that such rules are necessary for Kant's moral theory to get off the ground. Yet Herman recognizes that such rules are "a function of a community's particular circumstances."[15] The categorical imperative constrains all rational beings necessarily, but how different agents are constrained varies according to their upbringing.

In a later work, Herman develops a related concept called "moral literacy," which she describes as a basic competence to recognize and respond to morally salient facts. Herman compares this kind of competence to the background knowledge that is necessary in order to drive a car. To drive well, we must understand traffic laws, be familiar with the mechanical operation of the vehicle, and be able to follow the law even when we are tempted to break it.[16] Similarly, in order to be capable of morality, we must have an understanding of our place in a given society, a familiarity with what is morally relevant in making a decision, and an ability to resist inclination and act for the sake of duty. In short, we must be morally literate.

This is a compelling approach to moral decision-making, and it rightly recognizes the importance Kant places on education in the development of a person's character. However, Herman admits that it lends itself to relativism, since what is morally relevant in making a decision is a function of contingent factors such as our upbringing. Herman claims that Kant avoids the pitfalls of relativism because both the rules of moral salience and those of moral literacy are constrained by the categorical imperative: "the ordered set of principles of practical rationality constrain the whole [of our deliberative field],"[17] and the rules of moral salience are ultimately grounded in the moral law that commands us to recognize and respond to the dignity of others.[18] Herman realizes that the validity of any practical principles depends on their compatibility with the moral law. Allowing just any rules of moral salience would commit Kant to a kind of subjectivism, according to which I need only consider those things that I take to be morally relevant. As we have already noted, Kant's ethics does not validate anything we do as long as we think we are doing the right thing. Intentions matter, but having "good intentions" does not give us license to disregard the dignity of rational beings. The same is true for Herman's rules of moral salience. If I fail to recognize that another person's distress makes a moral claim on me, then I have an obligation to try to overcome my insensitivity so that I can fulfill the moral duties I have to others.

Herman is assuming here that there are two separate issues involved: what we ought to do and what we can recognize that we ought to do. The categorical imperative procedure tells us which maxims are morally permissible. This is a question of fact: which maxims are in fact consistently adoptable by rational agents. By contrast, the rules of moral salience form the conceptual background that we bring to the procedure. This is an epistemological question: whether we know what is morally relevant when assessing a given maxim. If we do not know, we should know – the fact of reason urges us to know – because some rules are more correct than others: "We will want to distinguish cultures with defective RMS from those whose rules of moral practice are deviant or blatantly invalid."[19] Herman identifies Nazis as holders of blatantly invalid rules, because those rules exclude a large class of human beings from moral consideration.

The problem with Herman's approach is that cultural variation is not merely a matter of discovering acceptable alternatives within what the categorical imperative deems to be morally permissible. Herman talks about how moral literacy is necessary as a practical capacity that makes moral judgment possible. But it is more than that. Our moral obligations only make sense with reference to cultural expectations through which we develop and interpret our maxims. In other words, the question of what is morally permissible is not settled by appealing to the categorical imperative alone. For example, what constitutes helping or harming, and how much help is appropriate, cannot in principle be determined simply by attempting to universalize a maxim.

Nor is social training merely a matter of getting people to recognize what is already clear to a reasoning being. Robert Louden's defense of Kant tries to fill out what he takes to be a misreading of Kant's ethics by considering how Kant's work in education, anthropology, and history is a necessary supplement to the formalism of the *Groundwork*. But Louden too says that ultimately our social education only helps to recognize what is clearly dictated by the moral law: "the aim of [Kant's] impure ethics is not to think ethically without principles but rather to find ways (ways based on objective empirical research into human nature) to make these principles efficacious in human life."[20] There is a set goal of education. Our moral understanding is shaped by our education only in the sense that we get a clearer or less clear vision of what we ought to do. What Louden misses is that our moral education shapes what it is that we ought to do by, among other things, determining what we can reasonably be expected to do in discharging our duties to the poor.

For Herman, the moral law is the ultimate rule of moral salience, and all other rules get their authority from their compatibility with the moral law. For Louden, a moral education is necessary in order for us to understand what the moral law requires and to act accordingly. However, by considering as a test case the duty to reduce poverty, we can see that what the moral law means for us is itself dependent on contextual interpretation. To be sure, beneficence is required of us, but what beneficence *is* varies. To say that beneficence is required is only true and only makes sense relative to particular circumstances. Knowing that we are finite agents with limited resources is not enough. We must also know what we mean by the term, and that is a result of both how we understand beneficence and our recognition of who is in need within a given community. There is not variability simply in the application of what the moral law requires of everyone. Rather, what the moral law means for different agents varies depending on the agent and the circumstances.

The Humanity of Others Is Not Simply Given

It is often hard to determine what it is reasonable to expect in fulfilling our moral obligations, but it is particularly difficult to evaluate our response to poverty. Among other things, it is unclear what qualifies someone as poor: the lack of essential goods and services such as health care, exclusion from social benefits such as education, or a low level of income and wealth. Poverty in the latter sense is defined differently by different organizations. For example, the World Bank defines extreme poverty as living on less than US$1 a day, and moderate poverty as less than $2 a day. This is an international standard. By contrast, the U.S. government defines poverty relative to its own high standard of living. In 2010, a two-person household earning less than $14,634 per year (about $40 a day) was considered poor.[21] Furthermore, the diverse causes and effects of poverty make it difficult for whole governments, let alone individuals, to address. The poor do not lack one resource such as food, but rather have an interlaced set of needs, and poverty in general is a complex social problem with no clear corrective. It certainly is not alleviated merely by monetary contributions to non-governmental organizations.

Just as "reducing poverty" is not a coherent maxim, the ignorance with which we necessarily approach the problem makes any effort potentially in vain. How would we determine in any given circumstances whether the person is "summoning all means" to accomplish the goal of furthering others' ends? With such limited understanding of how to address the problem of poverty and whom to help, it is difficult to distinguish a truly charitable action from one that seems charitable but is merely tilting at windmills.

Among the many effects of poverty are hunger and homelessness, a lessening of people's sense of self-worth, an increase in illegal behavior and social unrest, and a growing class divide that threatens our recognition of one another as persons. That social and economic relationships influence our understanding of one another is especially relevant when it comes to morality, because acting rightly amounts to treating others (and ourselves) in accordance with their dignity. As we have already seen, Kant's approach neglects the social conditions that must be considered in order to determine a person's motive. But Kant also overlooks how these conditions affect our perception of others, and how they affect what we can reasonably be expected to do in fulfilling our moral obligations to them.

Primarily in the formula of humanity and the formula of the kingdom of ends, Kant conceives of moral responsibility in terms of a relation between persons: one rational being recognizes that other rational beings deserve respect. This is one of the theory's strengths and one of the things that distinguishes it from utilitarianism. Bernard Williams criticizes utilitarianism because it reduces the agent to a mere conduit for the production of happiness,[22] but utilitarianism also reduces the recipients of beneficence to merely sensing beings. Even if we are capable of higher pleasures or complex preferences, the existence of the other is valued only because of the actual or potential experiences the person can have and not because of her inherent worth. By contrast, Kant places the dignity of the person at the center of his ethics. Some critics have objected to Kant's anthropocentrism, but a distinct advantage of his position is that all people deserve respect – the poor and the diseased, both genders, as well as members of other religions, races, and countries. I identify myself as a complex, thinking being who decides what to do and why. To conceive of others as mere pleasure centers is demeaning to them and seems not to capture what is distinctive about the moral attitude.

The recognition of the other as a person, however, depends in large part on one's social, economic, and educational background. Capitalist economic relationships, for example, color our perception of others, and especially our consideration of the poor. In Marxist terms, with the commodification of wage-labor, the bourgeoisie sees the proletariat as an undifferentiated source of labor power. "The poor" as a class is merely a resource with a "*market price*" rather than a number of individual persons, each with "*dignity*" (G 434–5). Of course, the personhood of real and potential wage-laborers is not entirely disregarded, but there is an ambivalence to the poor, as people who are at once like the rich and not like them. The poor are responsible beings because they are said to be at fault for their condition. They could "pull themselves up by their own bootstraps," if only they would work hard enough. They also have rights, including the right to sell their labor for a wage. However, they are not equal to those who can afford to help them because they have not used their freedom rightly, to earn money and gain social status. Their property rights are limited to not much more than their own capacity to labor. Their humanity is qualified in a way that the humanity of business owners is not.

Of course, Kant would insist that we are morally obligated to overcome this prejudice. Herman considers bigotry to be a kind of moral illiteracy, and Louden would call for a change in our moral education. As I said, Kant is not a subjectivist who believes that one has a good will as long as one thinks that one is doing the right thing. We have duties to those who have dignity, not only those whom we think have dignity. However, a person's culpability in failing to consider all persons equally is mitigated by the cultural training he has received. We saw earlier how ignorance regarding the relevant moral considerations (such as the effectiveness of a charity) may amount to negligence. What one thinks he intends may not be what he actually intends, and in some cases he should know the difference, as when Joe gives his money to the ne'er-do-well. But ignorance is excusable when the person could not reasonably be expected to make what is (objectively) the right choice under the circumstances.

If someone is systematically taught that the poor lack dignity and do not deserve our moral consideration, then he would rightly be praised for overcoming this prejudice. Failing to consider them as persons is a sign of ignorance. But the social conditions under which his moral sensibility developed makes it unreasonable to expect him to overcome it purely through strength of will. Society may have a duty to correct this prejudice in its citizens, but the person cannot have a duty to do something that social conditions make him (nearly?) incapable of doing. This is where Kantian ethics comes closest to subjectivism, or perhaps cultural relativism: what makes a particular maxim morally permissible depends a great deal on what one can reasonably be expected to understand given his upbringing.

I have focused on majority attitudes toward a cultural minority, but the reverse is true as well: a historically grounded distrust of the majority may qualify a minority person's obligations, regardless of what a supposedly objective, rational agent ought to do. For example, in chapter 4 I claimed that it would be morally impermissible not to donate one's organs when one dies. However, members of some disadvantaged minority groups have good reason not to volunteer, given a history of unfair health-care distribution and inferior treatment by the medical establishment, including but not limited to the Tuskegee syphilis study.[23] In justifying our duty to give, I presupposed a system that would not needlessly endanger the lives of organ donors. But, arguably, it is reasonable for minorities to worry that they would be allowed to die so that their organs can be harvested for affluent, white patients. If this is in fact a reasonable belief – and it may be given the long history of racism in the West – then it undermines the claim that everyone is equally obligated to become an organ donor. The duty of beneficence applies differently to the minority population than it does to the idealized (white?) rational agent.

Systematic discrimination against a group of people in a given society can shape a person's moral attitudes, but that often reflects the community's moral shortcomings rather than some individual choice. If those sometimes oppressive conditions are assumed when formulating maxims, then the demand for formal consistency does not provide us with the tools to reflect on and criticize those foundational assumptions, as opposed to criticizing a person's particular maxim. According to Jeffrey Gauthier, this is what Hegel's criticism of Kant amounts to:

> Where oppressive relations come to form part of the accepted background assumptions for applying a formal criterion of right, it will be impossible within the purely formal mechanisms of the criterion to come to an awareness of the objectionable relation. No matter how conscientiously an agent attempts to apply the test, no matter how searching her introspection may be, unless the system of social relations that informs her judgment comes to light, she may remain blind to the oppression her agency embodies.[24]

Gauthier focuses on the ways in which Hegel's moral theory, as opposed to Kant's, provides the tools for a feminist critique of oppressive gender norms. For Hegel, the individual is mediating between her particular desires and the universal norms that are embodied in social institutions, and she tries to unite both in a self-conscious and rational unity. By contrast, Kant's moral agent repeatedly confronts the clash between reason and her personal inclinations, and thus remains in what Hegel calls the realm of particularity, unconnected to universality as it relates to the life of the community. And within this particular point of view, the social norms that inform one's maxims do not become an object of moral scrutiny.

This is not to say that Kant is unconcerned with political and social philosophy, but that his approach to society as a whole is merely an extension of his individualistic ethics. Kant conceives of the community as a collection of individuals rather than seeing the larger whole as being foundational to moral agency and constitutive of what Hegel calls the "ethical life" (*Sittlichkeit*).[25] Kant's emphasis on formal consistency thus allows the specific agent's maxim to be shaped by unscrutinized and morally weighty assumptions about other agents. In short, Kant overlooks the extent to which we are not purely autonomous beings in the formation of moral judgments. We may deliberate and be bound by the formal conditions of rational willing, but we cannot abstract entirely from our social training in deciding to whom we have obligations, what features of a situation are morally relevant, and when we are negligent.

Kant's practical philosophy considers who we are as rational and sensible beings. We have inclinations but can also act for the sake of the moral law. Moral duties, of course, are not conditional upon a certain psychological propensity to recognize other persons as persons. However, the effectiveness of the moral law actually to motivate us depends in large part on whom we acknowledge to be deserving of respect. We have a duty to recognize those who need assistance as people who deserve our help, but our ability to recognize them as such depends on a number of social factors for which we are not individually responsible. This recognition of other people does not amount to sympathy – that would be a heteronomous action, not purely motivated – but rather is a phenomenological condition for us to have a sense of duty to them in the first place.

Developing Moral Judgment: The Case of Kant Himself

Because of our humanity, I have duties to myself and to others who are sufficiently like me to warrant the same kind of respect. Given this anthropocentric basis of Kant's deontological ethics, Kantians must give an account of how a group comes to be recognized as a collection of particular persons with absolute worth. If I am socially conditioned to regard others as faceless competitors or simply as useful resources on the open market, how can I come to see the poor or any other marginalized group as persons whose value equals my own?

When Kant describes moral education in the *Doctrine of Virtue*, he is talking primarily about the process by which individuals become rational rather than the ways in which we come to recognize others' humanity. Kant attempts to address such heuristic questions in *Anthropology from a Pragmatic Point of View*, where he deals with the empirical or impure part of ethics – namely, the cultural and historical factors, as well as the personal abilities, that advance or hinder the attempt actually to be moral in practice. This is done, of course, to show how we can encourage the moral attitude toward ourselves and others.

To judge Kant's success in explaining the basis of interpersonal moral engagement, let us examine whether the resolve to follow the categorical imperative is sufficient (as Herman claims it is) to overcome exclusionary moral prejudices. Kant's own treatment of the other, specifically his attitude toward women and nonwhites (or non-Europeans), serves as an instructive case study. The previous chapter covered Kant's attitudes toward women. In *Observations on the Feeling of the Beautiful and Sublime*, Kant claims that woman's "philosophical wisdom [*Weltweisheit*] is not reasoning but sentiment" (OBS 230). And in the *Anthropology*, he says that women have two natural purposes: to perpetuate the species and to encourage men (through pressure, enticement, and other manipulation) to act more rationally (A 303–11). Women have the natural function of reproducing human beings while men have the moral responsibility of advancing the culture.

Kant has similarly strong views regarding nonwhites. Kant explains racial differences in terms of natural purposes – in this case, that human beings populate the entire globe. Humans have preformed "germs [*Keime*]," or natural tendencies within the organism, such that, when humans confront different climates, germs express themselves differently. Because of this, members of the species *Homo sapiens* develop a variety of skin types. Beyond merely a variation in pigmentation, however, what develops are different races (*Rasse*): a stable, biologically defined differentiation within the species, with accompanying variations in mental capabilities and the capacity for virtue (DR 434–6). For example, Kant says that tropical climates stifle human activity, so humans who inhabit those places develop corresponding character traits. Blacks are less energetic, less suited to hard labor, and less capable of self-improvement than white Europeans (DR 438). In the *Observations*, Kant repeats David Hume's allegation that, contrary to the achievements of many whites who begin from poor circumstances, no black person "has accomplished something great in art or science or shown any other praiseworthy quality" (OBS 253). Kant also makes an unfortunate remark in which he dismisses the comments of a Caribbean man simply because he is black, which Kant takes to be a reflection of a lack of reason: "There might be something here worth considering, except for the fact that this scoundrel was completely black from head to foot, a distinct proof that what he said was stupid" (OBS 254–5). In fact, all nonwhites are similarly ill suited to the progress of civilization: Native Americans "will not become more perfect," black Africans "are also not capable of further civilization," and the Indians and Chinese "appear to be at a standstill in their perfection" (Ak 25:843). Although Kant believes that the entire species of human beings is developing toward moral perfection, which is nature's final goal, "humanity achieves its greatest perfection in the white race" (Ak 9:316).[26] The upshot of all of this is that white men are better at using their rational capacities, so they are primarily responsible for advancing the species.

Kant claims that all rational beings ought to be respected because of their dignity, meaning that differences in race and sex affect the kinds of duties we have toward one another, but not the bare fact that we have duties to one another. Kant never claims that women or nonwhites are not rational beings, or that we have no duties to them. In fact, Kant says just the opposite. In the *Anthropology*, he says that both men and women are rational beings (A 303). And because all of the races are derived from a common ancestor, the races are not different in kind, only in degree of perfection. Still, we should not minimize the morally significant distinctions that Kant does make based on race and gender. At the very least, Kant claims that women and nonwhites inherently lack rational development and cannot use their reason as well as white men.

There are two things to note here. First, Kant recognizes the impact that one's cultural circumstances, and even one's physical environment, have on one's capacity to do what is right. Even though we are equally subject to the moral law as a formal condition of practical reasoning, the moral law does not place the same demands on all of us because of contingent differences. That is, given the same duty (such as beneficence) and the same circumstances, different people may have different obligations given their different capacities for moral judgment. Second and more importantly, we can step back and focus not on the implications of Kant's philosophy, but rather on Kant himself. For a philosophy that is predicated on an equal concern for all persons, Kant's own devaluing of women and nonwhites demonstrates the difficulties in arriving at this position, even if we are committed to racial and gender equality in theory. What Kant or anyone else can reasonably be expected to consider in their moral judgment depends in large part on the social background that shapes their thinking.

Kant bases morality on the power of reason to transcend our egoistic and even altruistic feelings – that is, to establish the autonomy of the rational subject with regard to inclinations or hypothetical imperatives. However, what we mean when we use the formula of humanity is vulnerable to conventional and highly contingent definitions of who counts as a person. Kant's own racism and sexism are significant here. Reason can function as rationalization, justifying the irrational beliefs that we become committed to by being immersed in a particular cultural context – appealing to the "natural purposes" of women and nonwhites, for example. Regarding the poor, the perpetuation of inequality is likely to happen both through rationalizations about individuals earning what they deserve and through the invisibility of the poor as human beings, by physical means (ghettoization or suburbanization) and by ideological ones (whereby the poor become an indistinct mass, lacking individuality). A morality based on our individual obligations to other individuals thus sustains the non-personhood of poor persons (or women, or nonwhites), because it reinforces a culturally contingent conception of who is fully rational. In other words, Kant's ethics is predicated on recognizing others *as* persons, but this is where social training is most likely to be influential. Our supposed rational autonomy is conditioned by the irrationality that pervades human relations and that shapes my understanding of what I am and should be doing. As we have seen, Kant's neglect of this irrational dimension of moral decision-making limits his ability to speak to issues of social justice.

None of this is meant to be a criticism of Kant personally, let alone an *ad hominem* dismissal of Kantian ethics. The assumptions that were common in eighteenth-century Prussia make it unreasonable for us to expect Kant to be a champion of equal rights. And Allen Wood rightly claims that, as wrong as Kant's views are regarding women and nonwhites, that does not imply that Kantian ethics should be rejected, simply because it could not keep Kant himself from wrongheaded opinions. According to Wood, Kant's moral theory is committed to the equal dignity of all rational beings even though Kant himself was bound to the prejudices of his own time, and these two points can be separated.[27] I agree. The hypocrisy of a given philosopher does not imply that his or her philosophy is wrong. In fact, I am conceding that there are social conditions that (arguably) excuse Kant's failure to recognize the full, equal personhood of women and nonwhites.

But that is precisely my point. Given the social conditions under which agents form their conceptions of others, in what sense can we say that Kant himself was constrained by the categorical imperative to acknowledge the humanity of all people? Moral judgment depends on historical circumstances, and not just because the same categorical imperative must be applied differently in different situations. Kant himself cannot be held responsible for mistakes in applying the concept of personhood because his culpability depends on social expectations and norms rather than how he fares when judged against a categorical imperative. At the very least, then, we must qualify what we mean when we say that the moral law constrains rational beings universally and necessarily. At most, we must question the very possibility of an *a priori* moral philosophy.

Kant would readily grant that our moral judgment depends on knowing something of the empirical structure of the world and detecting within it (the phenomenal character of) other rational end-setters. He would say that culture makes it easier or harder to act rightly, but that a thing's moral considerability is a matter of fact – namely, whether it has the right properties. This factual issue is not a matter of cultural variation, but a matter of the being's rational capacity. This is all well within the letter and the spirit of Kant's ethics.

The problem lies in what it means for a categorical imperative to be categorical if there are excusing conditions that depend on one's cultural circumstances. If, for all practical purposes, Kant could not have recognized that women and nonwhites are equally capable of rational autonomy, then we cannot say that he ought to have done so. This seems problematic for a moral philosophy that is supposed to constrain all rational beings as such, necessarily and universally, rather than as, say, twenty-first-century Americans with a particular attitude toward racial and gender equality – an attitude that is, after all, also a result of contingent historical processes.

The Return of Hegel

The myriad conditions enumerated above reveal how complicated the duty to help the poor actually is. To adopt the maxim of beneficence toward the poor as a general class of people, the agent must have reasonable expectations regarding the effectiveness of his actions, who will be impacted by his decisions (both positively and negatively), and when his obligation to them has been fulfilled. However, what we can reasonably expect the agent to know depends on the resources available to him, whether he is aware or should be aware of those resources, and the extent to which he recognizes the poor as rational beings. These depend on a number of contingent circumstances. For example, we now have much more information with which to assess charitable organizations than we did two hundred years ago. This generates a stronger obligation to give to the most effective organization. On the other hand, the persistence of class biases, if they are strong enough, may actually excuse someone who fails to recognize the poor as deserving of help. It is only the case that he ought to recognize them as persons if he is able to do so, given his upbringing, his education, or his social training in general. And whether the agent is negligent in his behavior depends a great deal on what we expect a person to consider in making a decision.

This brings us back to Hegel. Whether someone accurately conceives of what he is doing depends not only on whether he is sincere, but also on whether he is reasonable in including some things and excluding others from moral consideration. The latter judgment can only be made within contextual standards of reasonableness that have been internalized – what Hegel calls absolute universality, as opposed to Kant's abstract universality, that characterizes the ethical life.[28] Although Hegel's formalism charge can be answered, its basic sentiment reemerges in a stronger form: the need to transform ethics from a timeless meditation on the formal conditions of reason to a consideration of the historical and social conditions for the possibility of moral judgment. Understanding how Kantian principles relate to human existence, with its uncertainty and prejudices, is necessary from the beginning.

Notes

1 G. W. F. Hegel, *Phenomenology of Spirit*, trans. A. V. Miller (Oxford: Oxford University Press, 1977), §431.
2 Kant disagrees with Hegel here. In the *Doctrine of Right*, Kant argues that there is a moral imperative to enforce the institution of private property. Not having private property would contradict my agency because I would not securely own the means to achieve anything. Willing a situation in which private property rights are not enforced would undermine my own "*rightful* power" to use something – "freedom would be depriving itself of the use of its choice with regard to an object of choice" – so I must consent to a law that protects private ownership (MM 250). Although property is originally held in common, a civil society must enforce private property rights that derive from provisional acquisition and the rightful transfer of property. See MM 245–76.
3 Hegel, *Phenomenology*, §430.
4 John Rawls, *A Theory of Justice*, rev. edn. (Cambridge, Mass.: Belknap, 1999), 222.
5 Ibid., 73–8.
6 As we saw in chapter 7, explaining when an action is coercive is very difficult for Kant.
7 Onora O'Neill, "Ending World Hunger," in *Matters of Life and Death: New Introductory Essays in Moral Philosophy*, ed. Tom Regan, 3rd edn. (New York: McGraw-Hill, 1993), 235–79 (p. 265).
8 G. W. F. Hegel, *Elements of the Philosophy of Right*, trans. H. B. Nisbet (Cambridge: Cambridge University Press, 1991), §134.
9 John Stuart Mill, *Utilitarianism*, ed. George Sher (Indianapolis, Ind.: Hackett, 1979), 24–5.
10 John Rawls, "Themes in Kant's Moral Philosophy," in *Kant's Transcendental Deductions: The Three "Critiques" and the "Opus postumum"*, ed. Eckart Förster (Stanford, Calif.: Stanford University Press, 1989), 81–113 (p. 83).
11 See also Rawls, "Themes," 85–6, and Barbara Herman, *The Practice of Moral Judgment* (Cambridge, Mass.: Harvard University Press, 1993), 55.
12 A charity's efficiency is determined by how much of its spending goes toward the services it provides rather than overhead costs. The Red Cross is quite efficient, but of course it is not perfect. According to Charity Navigator, which evaluates the efficiency of nonprofits, about 92 percent of the Red Cross's revenue goes to program expenses, while the other 8 percent is used for

fundraising and administration (www.charitynavigator.org/index.cfm?bay= search.summary&orgid=3277).

13 John Kekes claims that our ignorance about what to do, especially when it comes to alleviating people's suffering in distant parts of the world, constitutes a practical argument against the duty of generalized benevolence. See Kekes, "Benevolence: A Minor Virtue," *Social Philosophy and Policy* 4, no. 2 (spring 1987): 21–36 (p. 27).

14 The child-in-a-drowning-pond scenario is taken from Peter Singer, "Famine, Affluence, and Morality," *Philosophy and Public Affairs* 1, no. 3 (spring 1972): 229–43 (p. 231).

15 Herman, *Practice of Moral Judgment*, 83.

16 Barbara Herman, *Moral Literacy* (Cambridge, Mass.: Harvard University Press, 2007), 99.

17 Ibid., 41.

18 Herman, *Practice of Moral Judgment*, 85.

19 Ibid., 91.

20 Robert B. Louden, *Kant's Impure Ethics: From Rational Beings to Human Beings* (New York: Oxford University Press, 2000), 170.

21 United States Census Bureau, "Poverty Thresholds 2010," www.census.gov/ hhes/www/poverty/data/threshld/thresh10.html.

22 Bernard Williams, "A Critique of Utilitarianism," in *Utilitarianism: For and Against*, by J. J. C. Smart and Bernard Williams (Cambridge: Cambridge University Press, 1973), 75–150 (pp. 108–18).

23 See Annette Dula, "African American Suspicion of the Healthcare System Is Justified: What Do We Do about It?" *Cambridge Quarterly of Healthcare Ethics* 3, no. 3 (1994): 47–57, and Sara Goering and Annette Dula, "Reasonable People, Double Jeopardy, and Justice," *American Journal of Bioethics* 4, no. 4 (fall 2004): 37–9.

24 Jeffrey A. Gauthier, *Hegel and Feminist Social Criticism: Justice, Recognition, and the Feminine* (Albany: State University of New York Press, 1997), 22.

25 See especially Hegel, *Elements of the Philosophy of Right*, §§142–57.

26 Kant contends that there are only four races – white, yellow, black, and red – and in his hierarchy, Europeans are at the top, then "Orientals," Africans, and Native Americans.

27 Allen W. Wood, *Kant's Ethical Thought* (Cambridge: Cambridge University Press, 1999), 6–12.

28 Hegel, *Elements of the Philosophy of Right*, §7.

9

The Decomposition of the Corporate Body

Chapters 7 and 8 revealed the limitations of Kant's practical philosophy for understanding actions in their broader contexts. As we saw, Kant has trouble accounting for social conditions that may or may not be coercive as well as standards of reasonableness that are individually and culturally variable. Diffuse social conditions, as opposed to actions by particular agents, may undermine our capacity to consent, and our contingent backgrounds affect the moral duties we have, even as we say that the categorical imperative is necessarily and universally constraining. In the remainder of the book, I turn to Kant's theory of agency, and specifically who or what can be held to account in moral judgment and directly considered in moral deliberation. I begin by examining corporate agency. Whether Kant can handle cases where responsibility cannot be assigned to any particular agents will be crucial in evaluating the usefulness of his theory for addressing a host of ethical issues in business.

Such an analysis of Kant's relevance is important given the current state of business ethics. In part because business ethics has emerged relatively recently as a distinct subdiscipline, its theoretical bearings are still very much defined by the classic moral philosophies. Kant's ethics in particular seems to be swiftly gaining popularity for addressing issues that are specific to business, even though Kant himself hardly mentions such issues in his own work. Kant scholars such as Barbara Herman and Onora O'Neill have applied his theory to nontraditional subjects such as targeted advertising and coercive employment practices,[1] and business ethicists such as William Evan and Edward Freeman have shown how Kantian ethics could guide

Kant and Applied Ethics: The Uses and Limits of Kant's Practical Philosophy, First Edition.
Matthew C. Altman.
© 2011 John Wiley & Sons Inc. Published 2011 by Blackwell Publishing Ltd.

businesses toward policies that respect the humanity of stakeholders rather than simply maximizing profits for shareholders.[2] Most notably, Norman Bowie has written extensively on business ethics, taking "a Kantian perspective" on any number of issues: why corporations ought to deal honestly with suppliers and customers, provide meaningful work for employees, and contribute to the good of society in general.[3]

Despite the number of recent Kantian approaches to these issues, philosophers who apply Kant's ethics to business often use the theory in a way that is contrary to its own foundational assumptions. Kant's account of how we are bound by the categorical imperative depends on a particular conception of moral agency that precludes collective responsibility and, more specifically, corporate responsibility.[4] A business can act, but its actions can only be judged morally with reference to the reasons held by particular businesspeople. Because of the need to assess corporate actions (and not just the actions of individuals), and because Kant cannot make sense of the moral obligations that constrain corporations as a whole, Kant's theory has limited application in business ethics.

Decision-Making Procedures and Maxims in Corporate Settings

Kant's practical philosophy does have a number of implications for how we ought to behave in a business setting. Among other things, we can draw on his insights into the conditions of rational activity to counter some classic objections to the very idea of business ethics. Some people have argued that placing ethical constraints on business decisions is completely misguided, that business is a game with its own rules, where deception is not only useful but expected,[5] or that a properly functioning corporation has no "social responsibility" other than to maximize profits for its shareholders.[6] The latter position, advanced by Milton Friedman, and similar thoughts from John Boatright have been roundly criticized by business ethicists, primarily because they so strictly separate the executive's obligations as a businessperson from her other obligations, her "role responsibility" from her "individual responsibility."[7] Although Friedman and Boatright recognize that an individual has other (personal) duties, they claim that the person's position in the company requires that she have only one motive in her professional capacity – the profit motive. The person ought to be guided by the demands of the market rather than her moral convictions. This may involve compliance with the law, and it may even mean that the company should do the right thing when it incurs a cost – for example, by adopting environmentally friendly policies. But the motive behind these actions must always be to maximize profits for investors: adhering to the law avoids hefty fines from regulators, and reducing environmental damage may be a good marketing strategy, among other things.

Many authors claim that social obligations should in certain cases restrict the profit motive – for example, minimizing the public health effects of industrial waste, even beyond what is legally required. The duty not to harm should, they insist, override executives' duties to shareholders. Kantian ethics has been used to support this view: wealth is conditionally good, but a good will is the only thing that is good without qualification (G 393). The actions of particular businesspeople can be judged against moral principles, which is unsurprising, since business decisions are a kind of human action and all (free) human actions are constrained by the categorical imperative.

Businesses ethicists have also objected to Friedman because he conceives of the business itself as nothing but an artificial entity whose sole purpose is to make money for its investors. Although Friedman concedes that the businessperson has other responsibilities as a husband/wife, father/mother, or community member, the corporation itself is not a moral agent, so it cannot be responsible for its effects on the larger group of stakeholders. In contrast to Friedman's approach, many theoretical orientations in business ethics, including supposedly Kantian approaches, depend on the assumption that we can assess the morality of corporate actions apart from the decisions of particular businesspeople – praising Johnson & Johnson or condemning Philip Morris rather than the members of their ever-changing boards of directors. Being able to do this depends on a robust notion of corporate agency, something that Friedman rejects.

The argument for assigning moral responsibility (rather than merely legal responsibility) to businesses is fairly straightforward: People can be held morally responsible because they have certain characteristics. Businesses have those same characteristics, so businesses can also be held morally responsible. The relevant characteristics are understood differently by different authors, but usually they are related to the fact that corporations engage in analogous decision-making procedures. For example, Kenneth Goodpaster and John Matthews argue that moral agents exhibit two traits: they make decisions on the basis of reasons rather than merely acting on impulse, and they consider how their actions will affect others.[8] We do not judge animals' behavior in a moral sense because they do not weigh options and decide the best way to act, but rational agents recognize that their actions may help or harm others, and they act in accordance with the decisions they make. Businesses do the same thing. They go through rational processes to decide on corporate behavior, and because they consider the effects of their behavior on others (even if they eventually disregard the interests of consumers and community members), businesses have the same kind of moral responsibility that people have.

This sounds a lot like Kant's account of moral agency. According to Kant, nonrational things are moved by natural laws, but we *decide* how to act. We can choose whether to act as we ought to act given the constraints of the moral law, and we sometimes do so by overcoming desires that tempt us to act wrongly. Therefore, a person's actions can be understood not only in terms of the prior events that give rise to them. From a practical perspective, she is subject to moral judgment because of the maxims that she sets for herself. For example, we need to know a person's maxim to figure out whether she purposely tripped someone or merely caused someone to fall without being morally blameworthy. The person who falls may be harmed either way, but whether a blameworthy act has been committed depends on whether the other person meant to trip him. The person's ability to make such a choice distinguishes her from nonrational things. Such things do not freely adopt maxims, so they cannot be held morally responsible for what they do. A rock or a dog does nothing wrong in tripping a person. Only moral agents have what are properly called intentions.

According to many business ethicists, some group actions can also be assessed morally because they are the result of what those theorists consider to be collectively adopted maxims. Peter French, for example, notes that the actions of employees are often organized by a corporate internal decision (CID) structure, which guides employees' actions much like a maxim determines the will of an individual.[9] The CID structure "in effect absorbs the intentions and acts of individual persons into a 'corporate decision'."[10] Similarly, O'Neill attributes intentions to "agencies that (like corporations and governments and student unions) have decision-making procedures."[11] This allows us to determine whether a given corporate arrangement is just. Certainly, if a business chooses maxims on which to act – it has policies and goals that govern the actions of employees – a business would seem to be capable of moral agency just as human beings are, and so it would be bound by the moral law.

The Need for Collective Responsibility in Business Ethics

Because a business has its own characteristic decision-making procedures and because it acts in ways that are morally significant (that is, because it affects stakeholders), it seems that the business itself is subject to ethical scrutiny. Of course, this does not preclude individual responsibility. Although one could blame only the corporation and not the people in it, one could also hold each person involved in the decision fully responsible or could assign proportional blame depending on how involved each person was.[12] For example, if an individual worker sexually harasses a coworker *and* there is a corporate culture that tolerates that kind of behavior, both the individual and the company may be morally and legally responsible for the harm.

Still, there are some cases in which we cannot attribute responsibility to any particular agent(s) and *only* the corporation is responsible. This is true primarily because, in a bureaucratic setting, responsibility is diffused across a number of different corporate positions. Consider this example: if each person in the company contributed to the making of a defective and harmful product, and if none of them could be expected to anticipate the danger, then no one person would be held responsible for the resulting injuries to consumers. But the harm may have resulted from a corporate policy that led to cuts in safety inspectors and the purchase of inferior materials. Managers who fired the inspectors or purchasers who bought the material may not be responsible, because their actions taken in isolation may not be harmful at all. By itself, there may be nothing wrong with having fewer inspectors or using cheaper materials. In a bureaucratic environment, many decisions are made without an awareness of what is happening in other corporate divisions, so the managers and purchasers may not know the cumulative effect of their actions. But these actions, along with the design and production process, as well as marketing and sales – all of which are necessary to bring the product to consumers – collectively result in regrettable harm. All of these workers are contributing to the creation and distribution of the harmful product, and none of them may be entirely responsible for it. But because the product actually harms people, a wrong seems to have been committed. If none of these individuals are responsible, however, then it seems that no one is responsible – unless we attribute responsibility to the workers and executives as a group. Corporate responsibility is necessary because sometimes no identifiable agents are individually responsible, but the corporation as a whole, the collection of individuals, does something wrong that harms innocent people.

This is only one example, but there are many other cases where businesses as a whole can be held responsible for what they do: when they subject employees to unsafe working conditions, fail to provide fair and adequate compensation, or pollute the environment, among other things. When a business contaminates drinking water, it is the result of what is produced, how it is produced, and corporate policies regarding the disposal of chemical waste – as well as all the workers, administrators, and investors who contribute to this lengthy process. There are many causes that give rise to the eventual effect.

If no one person decided to cause the harm or could foresee the danger posed by the company's activity, then the harm would be attributable to the company itself or to the employees as a group. But if the harm is a direct result of corporate policy, then it is not simply an accident. The company, not the individuals, holds the maxim-like CID structure that produces the wrong action. Therefore, the corporation is responsible. Collective responsibility is crucial in business ethics, because at least some business decisions are not the responsibility of particular agents.

Applying the Categorical Imperative to Businesses

If businesses act in the morally relevant sense, we can apply the different versions of the categorical imperative to determine the moral permissibility or impermissibility of corporate policies. The formula of universal law rules out deceptive business practices, for example. In Kantian terms, filing a false earnings report is wrong because the maxim cannot be universalized: If every corporation submitted false reports, stockbrokers and potential investors would be unable to determine their value. However, the functioning of the stock market depends on certain background conditions, including the honest assessment of a business's revenue. If every company lies, the market could not set an accurate price for any stock, so there would be no public trading. No one would invest in a company on the basis of what is known to be a false report. The whole purpose of the deception – generating more revenue for the company – could not be achieved if every corporation did the same thing. When universalized, such a policy is self-undermining, so it is morally wrong.

According to the formula of humanity, we ought never to treat someone merely as a means but ought to respect the person's humanity as an end in itself. This too has implications for business activities. To take an obvious example, it is impermissible to work illegal immigrants in near-slave conditions – threatening them with deportation unless they work sixteen-hour days for little pay – because such coercion does not respect their capacity freely to consent, and the failure to provide adequate pay and working conditions amounts to treating them like expendable machines or pack-horses rather than persons. Laws are in place to discourage such behavior, by threatening harsh penalties for the owners and managers of sweatshops. Also, some corporations have policies that expressly forbid this and threaten divestment if a supplier is found guilty.

But here is where we begin to see the problems with a Kantian approach to business ethics. Corporate policies can encourage people to act in certain ways or discourage them from doing something, but the morality of a given action cannot be determined by such policies. Policies that govern a corporation are similar to laws that govern a state. As opposed to moral laws that constrain the principles we choose in deciding how to act, juridical legislation deals only with the actions we take rather than the reasons behind them (MM 219). In civil society, a person may obey the law wholly out of a sense of duty to the state and her fellow citizens, but what the law requires of her can be fulfilled regardless of her disposition.

Just as laws of the state cannot determine what motivates its citizens to obey, CID structures cannot determine an employee's maxim. A person who follows a corporate policy that encourages the fair treatment of others may do it simply out of self-interest (to be promoted, to avoid being fired, etc.), or she may do it because that is the right thing to do. An employee always has her own reasons for following or not following a corporate policy. Yet for Kant, whether a morally permissible action is praiseworthy depends on whether it was done for the sake of duty. In other words, it depends on what motivated the person to act that way. Kant gives an example of a shopkeeper who does not overcharge his customers. Treating people fairly and honestly is consistent with the demands of the moral law, but we cannot tell whether it was motivated by duty, since such a policy also helps to maintain a loyal customer base and is therefore in the shopkeeper's self-interest (G 397).

A business cannot act through its workers and cannot be judged morally by means of its workers' actions because, for Kant, motives are the proper object of moral evaluation, and the corporation cannot determine what motivates its employees. In short, a CID structure, even if it does shape a worker's behavior, does not determine the one thing that is essential for moral evaluation: the worker's maxim. If the business itself is to be held morally accountable, then the business itself must have motives. The question then becomes: Even though a business acts, is it possible for it to have motives, as particular businesspeople do? I believe that the answer is no.

Kant's Account of Moral Agency and the Categorical Imperative

Characterizing a business as motivated would fundamentally misconstrue what a corporation is and would transgress the limited scope of Kantian moral theory. For Kant, the whole is never greater than the sum of its parts; in a moral sense, we can only judge businesspeople, not businesses. We are constrained by the moral law not because we act, but because we choose whether to set our maxims in accordance with reason or the inclinations, neither of which is possessed by a business. It is certainly true that a business does things. However, there is no corporate maxim distinct from the maxims of the individuals who comprise the organization.

Over the course of this book we have returned again and again to the key principles of Kant's ethics: we ought to do what is right because it is right; the moral law constrains us as an imperative because we are not only rational beings but are also pathologically affected by our inclinations; we have dignity because of our capacity to set ends, and so we ought never to be treated merely as a means, etc. This approach to practical philosophy depends on a complex picture of the moral agent that Kant develops in a number of his writings. The distinction between appearances and things in themselves in the *Critique of Pure Reason* allows rational beings to be sensibly affected but not sensibly determined. Under transcendental idealism, any natural predispositions we have are governed by the category of causality, but we can act independently of such desires when we consider ourselves from a practical standpoint, as intelligible rather than sensible beings. In the *Groundwork* and the second *Critique*, Kant conceptualizes this self-constraint as an adherence to a law that is rationally self-legislated. The inclinations that are given to us as a result of prior (contingent) causes are distinct from the moral law that we necessarily impose on ourselves in choosing to act at all. In the *Religion*, Kant says that we are able to be motivated by inclinations or by the moral law because of our "human nature": we have a "predisposition to animality" (desires for self- and species-preservation, which are neither good nor bad in themselves) *and* a "predisposition to personality" (the capacity to act purely for the sake of duty, or to have moral feeling as an incentive). We are "*responsible [zurech-nungsfähig]*" beings because we are capable of rational self-determination (Rel 26–8).

Because of these characteristics and the tensions between them – sensible and intelligible, desirous and rational, with competing predispositions – human beings are distinct from other things that live and act, and human beings have a unique relationship to the moral law. Animals cannot act rightly or wrongly because they are incapable of rational self-determination. God necessarily acts rightly, so God cannot be constrained by the categorical imperative. Human beings are rational animals, or imperfect gods. We are necessitated to act for the sake of duty because we can act rightly but are also tempted (and able) to do otherwise (G 412–14). This is the basis of moral constraint and the reason why we confront the moral law as an imperative.

To be sure, Kant does not derive the moral law from human nature. That would make it contingent on the kind of beings we are, when in fact it holds necessarily for all rational beings as such (G 425). In the *Groundwork*, Kant proceeds by an analysis of what morality must be like, and in the *Critique of Practical Reason*, he demonstrates through our immediate consciousness of moral constraint (the fact of reason) that the moral law must apply to us. However, this does not mean that who we are is irrelevant for determining whether we are bound by and how we relate to the moral law.

Must We Never Treat a Business Merely as a Means?

Businesses certainly do things, such as sponsoring race cars and manufacturing products, but they do not have the "predispositions" that would make them subject to the categorical imperative. First, an artificial, nonmaterial entity is not pathologically affected by natural desires, so it cannot be tempted to act wrongly. Despite its seeming similarity to our desire for happiness, a company cannot be said to have the profit motive any more than the state can crave tax revenues. Members of the U.S. Congress may want the money to spend, and the majority of American citizens may support a tax increase, but the state itself cannot want anything. Similarly, employees may be motivated to increase profits, even at the expense of their moral obligations, but to say that the business desires profits is imprecise. For states and corporations, there is no self-interest to tempt them away from the demands of duty. These are artificial constructs within which people organize their individual actions. They are not the sorts of things that have inclinations.

Second, a business cannot be said to reason and to legislate the moral law for itself, because it has no rational nature. It certainly has no "faculty [*Vermögen*]" of freedom in the relevant sense of the term (CPrR 47). According to Kant, the fact of reason provides practical proof that I am a responsible agent who is necessitated by the moral law. But a business, a merely legal entity, has no consciousness of moral constraint and thus no humanity in the sense that Kant understands it. Members of the corporation may reason on the basis of corporate policies, but the policies are not set by the corporation itself. They are established by its directors and its shareholders. We cannot attribute moral personhood to a business without illegitimately anthropomorphizing it. In short, businesses are not pathologically affected, imperfectly rational beings, so they cannot be constrained by moral law as an imperative. It is a category mistake to apply the categorical imperative to businesses.

It is one thing to say that a business is *like* a moral agent, that it performs actions on the basis of strategic plans that *resemble* maxims. It is quite another thing to say that businesses *are* agents, or that CID structures *are* maxims. Just as we often say that a dog decides to go outside or a computer wants to be rebooted, a business can have desires and formulate maxims only in a metaphorical sense. A business cannot literally set its own ends, or else we would have to treat it with respect, in accordance with the dignity that all rational beings have.

Strange as it sounds, Bowie does assert that a business has special moral standing; it must be treated as an end in itself and never simply as a means. This follows directly from Bowie's Kantianism, coupled with his claim that a business is a moral agent. If businesses can be responsible, then we in turn have moral obligations to businesses, since moral agents are worthy of respect. However, Bowie does not argue in this way. Instead, he says that by using the business merely as an instrument, we would be undermining the dignity of the people who comprise it:

> When an organization is viewed as an instrument for the achievement of one's own ends, then it appears that a person is simply using the organization, *and thus using the people in the organization* for their own ends. This would violate the second formulation of the categorical imperative.[13]

This illustrates one of the problems with applying Kant to business ethics. For Kant, anyone who is capable of acting morally cannot be treated merely as a thing. Yet a business *is* a thing, the result of a legal arrangement to incorporate, or a group of people considered as a class. Here Bowie is in a bind. If the business is a moral agent, then it cannot be treated merely as a means. Yet it seems counterintuitive for an artificial entity to have dignity, so Bowie says that the business cannot be used merely as a means *because* doing so would disregard the dignity of the employees.

There are two problems with this approach. First, Bowie does not have an argument for why using the business would necessarily amount to using the people who work for the business. The "thus" in the passage is not an argument; it merely introduces an assumption. Second, if a business is capable of responsibility, then it would be wrong to use it merely as a means regardless of whether the people in the business were also used. If the business as an agent worthy of respect can only be understood in terms of or through particular agents, that weakens the claim of corporate responsibility.

Instead of treating the business as an instrument, Bowie insists that we must view the corporation as a moral community, a Kantian kingdom of ends. But this is a false dichotomy. The choice is not between using a business in ways that are morally impermissible or treating the business itself as a moral agent. There is a third option: a business is an artificial entity by which people work toward the achievement of some mutually beneficial end – namely, maximizing profits. And there is nothing wrong with doing so *as long as stakeholders are treated morally*. Employees cannot be used merely as means – they must consent to work without being coerced and perhaps (as Bowie contends) they must be given meaningful work – and people in the community cannot be purposely harmed, knowingly or unknowingly, by the corporation's industrial waste. However, for Kant there can be no duty to the business that is distinct from the duties to people who are affected by it. If, for example, all employees would benefit by selling the business to a competitor and sharing the profits, and if this could be done without breaking the contracts of employment and without harming other stakeholders (for example, by creating a monopoly), then there is no moral reason not to do so. Or if I enjoyed nothing better than filling out the paperwork and paying the fees to form a corporation, only to dissolve it the next day, this is not obviously immoral (although it may be imprudent).[14] Both of these actions would be wrong if the business itself were a moral agent, because we can never sacrifice one person for the well-being of others. However, we can sacrifice a business provided that the stakeholders are respected in the process.

To act as if one is both legislator and subject in a kingdom of ends simply means that one must act on those maxims which could be universally adopted and which would actualize a community in which people respect one another's humanity. As Bowie says, modeling a business on the kingdom of ends would amount to a cooperative enterprise. But it would not mean that the kingdom or the business has duties, or that we have duties to it. Members of the kingdom of ends can pursue happiness as long as they fulfill their moral duties to one another. Businesspeople pursue profit under the same conditions. In fact, Kant's ideal situation is one in which we do what is right *and* achieve happiness. That is what he calls the highest good.[15]

Corporate Policies and Individual Agents

Of course, corporate policies can be structured in ways that tend, on the whole, to produce actions that are either contrary to or in accordance with duty. There are better and worse CID structures, just as there are better and worse laws. However, the law itself is not moral or immoral. Rather, it encourages or discourages certain individual behaviors. The same thing is true with regard to businesses, and to that extent, Kant would encourage businesspeople to develop corporate cultures that, as far as possible, constrain them to do the right thing. But that does not imply that the business is a moral agent. Even though a mission statement is like a maxim in that it is a kind of practical principle, people must still decide whether to carry out the actions it prescribes. Employees are not instruments that are causally determined by the corporation. They are autonomous beings who decide on the basis of their own subjective principles whether or not to follow the CID structure. This places the responsibility on them. There is no analogous intermediary when it comes to the actions of individual persons. The corporation *influences* people's actions, but moral agents *cause* their actions by virtue of the maxims they adopt. As Manuel Velasquez says, the corporation and its employees are not related in the same way that a person is related to her body. Only in the latter case does the intention of the agent directly bring about the action.[16]

Actions taken by companies may be inconsistent or may undermine the conditions for their own possibility, as in the case of false earnings reports. What we are judging in this case is not the corporation itself, but a particular agent or a number of individual agents who performed these actions under the auspices of the corporation. For Kant, what matters morally is why the agent performs the action. A business may act, but given its lack of inclinations and lack of reason, it is not the sort of thing that is motivated either by desire or by respect for the moral law. As Michael Keeley puts it, there is a difference between goals *of* an organization and goals *for* an organization, between what the corporation intends and what people intend to achieve by means of the corporation.[17] Under Kant's conception of moral agency, any corporate strategy simply states the most general aims of its workers. It does not make sense to try to find out what motivated WorldCom to falsify its financial reports, but it does make sense to ask what motivated CFO Scott Sullivan. The action itself may be inconsistent given the background conditions necessary for businesses to function at all, but it is not immoral unless it is attributable to a responsible agent who chooses to reject the moral law in favor of self-interest.[18]

This is a fine distinction, but one that a Kantian must make. The pharmaceutical company Johnson & Johnson is often commended for ordering a full recall when, in 1982, seven people died after taking Tylenol capsules spiked with cyanide. Initially, the recall cost the company a lot of money and hurt its market value, so it is usually considered a case where public safety trumped the desire for profit. According to Kant, however, not only could the company's motives never be determined, but Johnson & Johnson itself could not be said to have motives at all, even though the executives did. They may have had genuine concern for others, or they may have been trying to minimize the long-term damage to their reputation. Like those of Kant's shopkeeper, the executives' motives are unknowable, yet they nonetheless have motives that could in principle be evaluated. By contrast, Johnson & Johnson itself has no motives to discover, any more than the shopkeeper's shop does. Only the members of the business are moral agents, not the business itself.

Bowie's Defense of Collective Responsibility, and the Need for an Alternative

The fact that, for Kant, only fully autonomous reasoning is morally praiseworthy highlights his focus on the individual person. Nonetheless, Bowie argues that both Kant's practical philosophy and our common word usage justify attributing moral responsibility to corporations. First Bowie tries to explicate Kant's kingdom of ends with reference to Rawls's conception of a social union, thereby emphasizing the moral community, and hence the business as a collection of rational beings, over individual end-setters.[19] However, this appeal to Rawls is misleading, because both Rawls and Kant see this social order as an outgrowth of moral self-regulation. Rawls is concerned with establishing a fair system of social cooperation, but it is predicated on the idea that human beings have a "social nature" and that they have a highest-order interest in exercising their capacity for justice.[20] The principles of justice arise out of a desire for primary goods, mutual disinterest, and a rational commitment to what is right: "By acting from these principles persons express their nature as free and equal rational beings subject to the general conditions of human life."[21] Similarly, Kant envisions an ethical commonwealth in which a community of people collectively pursues the ends of virtue, but the kingdom of ends expresses and symbolically represents individuals' attempts at self-perfection (Rel 91– 147). For Kant and Rawls, a just society is a group of particular agents whose social principles reflect what it means to be reasonable – an individualistic view of how people relate to one another.[22] No collection of individuals, a social union or a kingdom of ends, has a social nature, highest-order interests, or the ability to apply the moral law to its actions. Bowie finds something in the formula of the kingdom of ends that is not there: a community that acts toward a moral end and that can be said to be responsible for achieving or not achieving it.

Bowie also tries to argue for corporate agency within Kantianism by pointing out that we conventionally refer to corporations as moral and legal entities. For example, we often say that a business has obligations to its employees and its customers, and we blame a company for previous bad acts even if its entire board of directors has changed in the interim. Hence, Bowie believes that there is a "linguistic warrant" for conceiving of the business as an agent rather than simply an instrument.[23]

It is true that we often speak of the actions of corporations, and employees are said merely to carry out the corporate strategy. Corporations are also considered to be agents under the law: They own property. They can be sued (and this does not necessarily involve suing the employees personally). They have rights, including, in the United States, First Amendment rights to engage in corporate-funded political speech.[24] They can be held legally responsible for having certain policies (such as discriminatory hiring practices) or for acting in certain ways (such as engaging in false advertising). Because businesses do act, they can harm stakeholders by not respecting their capacity freely to consent to a given action, among other things.

Attempts to infer a corporation's moral responsibility on the basis of its legal standing are very common, as are attempts to judge the morality of actions as opposed to their maxims. Richard De George is typical:

> We can take a clue here from legal responsibility. [The corporation] can be sued, fined, forced to make reparations, desist from certain activities, undertake others, and so on. If the corporation is to take affirmative action, then the corporation as a whole is evaluated as to whether such action has been taken. All this views the corporation as an entity from the outside. The actions can be viewed from a moral point of view as well. . . . [I]t seems perfectly plausible to ascribe moral responsibility to corporations even if they do not have moral feelings. This is because it is proper and useful to speak of the actions of corporations, and since they affect society and its members, to evaluate those actions from a moral point of view.[25]

De George seems to be assuming a consequentialist moral position, which judges actions (rather than maxims) based on their effects on others. Furthermore, he blurs the distinction between legality and morality, a distinction that is fundamental for Kant. Although Kant can make sense of legal constraint based on how given actions affect people's ability to set and pursue ends, the actions themselves cannot be assessed morally when viewed "from the outside." As we saw earlier, legality only limits a person's actions, not their motives (MM 396). A corporation is legally constrained because it acts and affects people's lives, but if it cannot be said to act on the basis of reasons, then it has no moral obligations. Therefore, there is no appropriate analogy between a corporation's legal responsibility and moral responsibility, and the former does not imply the latter. A corporation is subject to the law because it acts, but it cannot be judged morally because it has no intentions. There is no such thing as a virtuous company.

For Kant, something must have the requisite characteristics – the capacity to reason and the ability to act purely for the sake of duty – in order to be the subject of praise and blame. Kant denies that commonly attributing agency to something constitutes it as a rational agent. Indeed, the idea that agency is a matter of being held to account by others reflects a larger trend away from Kant's singular focus on the capacities and predispositions of the autonomous individual. Early on, Hegel recognized how Kant's ethics excludes the social nature of moral obligations, resulting in a kind of moral atomism in which the basic unit of agency is the reasoning individual. By contrast, for Hegel an intention is not simply present subjectively to the agent; rather, a subject is responsible for what she and her community *take* her to be responsible for. This goes well beyond Kant's focus on what the individual agent intended or what is metaphysically true about the source of the action, to a consideration of how the action is conceived by others.[26] We saw in chapter 8 that a social standard of reasonableness is necessary to understand what someone is doing. Here we see that Hegel's philosophy is also pertinent when it comes to corporate responsibility. Entities, including corporate entities, become capable of agency by being situated in a particular social system that holds them morally accountable.

In fact, the attempt to hold businesses responsible goes beyond Hegel and draws on a Marxist criticism of Kant that most business ethicists fail to recognize. As we saw in chapter 7, by looking only at the choices of individual agents, Kant fails to see the larger social and economic conditions that structure those choices and determine the extent to which people are able to take advantage of them. But if we accept the notion of collective responsibility, then employees are absorbed into this larger intention, and their actions are guided by it (because their maxims are governed by its maxims). If a CID structure shapes the actions of employees, it becomes difficult to tell where the individual ends and the company begins.

From a Kantian perspective, the corporate culture acts as a pathological influence that threatens rational freedom. For Marx, however, making responsibility into a purely individual matter furthers the ends of capitalism by ignoring how the material conditions of production shape the kinds of subjects we are. Corporate responsibility is the culmination of freedom under capitalism: the corporation takes over the human function of decision-making and self-determination – the result of workers' alienating themselves to empower capital. Of course, business ethicists tend not to embrace all of Marx, but in many ways the field depends on relinquishing Kant's picture of autonomous self-determination in favor of Marx's materialist model of collective agency, including his understanding of group identity, class consciousness, and class action. In short, what underlies our linguistic assumptions about corporate agency is a philosophical orientation that is fundamentally at odds with the Kantian approach to subjectivity.

The derivation of the categorical imperative and its constraint on our actions depends on strict criteria for what counts as a moral agent. How we refer to a business cannot constitute it as a responsible entity. Because we do conceive of the organization itself as having rights and responsibilities, however, that should give us pause in drawing on Kant, precisely because his moral philosophy cannot make sense of collective responsibility. At the end of the chapter, I will come back to our current conception of subjectivity and how it is much more amenable to the notion of corporate responsibility. For now it suffices to say that if our common usage assigns agency to artificial entities such as corporations, then so much the worse for those who appeal to Kant in business ethics.

Personal Responsibility within the Corporation

Although Kant's ethics precludes corporate moral responsibility, it does not imply that people can never be blamed when they act on behalf of a company. However, this can happen only under certain conditions. For example, a shareholder or employee is morally culpable only if they knowingly further an immoral act or if they should know that they are doing so – that is, if they are negligent. Therefore, a low-level employee at Enron shares no responsibility for the pensions that were lost because she did not know and could not have known the deceptive business practices that were being conducted at the top. Even though financial support from shareholders made it possible for swindles to take place, they are not at fault as long as they were unaware that reports were being falsified. However, individual executives such as Kenneth Lay, Jeffrey Skilling, Andrew Fastow, and others are guilty of using immoral and illegal practices to maximize profits. They went about maximizing profits in the wrong way.

From a Kantian perspective, a corporation can have no responsibility at all. Insofar as it is a tool, and a good tool performs its designated function well, a good corporation maximizes profits for its shareholders. Friedman and Boatright are correct in that sense, but they go too far. They claim that, in their corporate roles, people are *only* obligated to maximize profits. Even though businesspeople have other, personal responsibilities, as agents of a company they have only one purpose. By contrast, Kant would claim that even the person's pursuit of corporate profit depends on its moral permissibility. In other words, there is only one duty in any given situation, not competing duties to the company and the community. In taking on their professions, businesspeople not only have obligations to shareholders, but also must give moral consideration to the larger group of stakeholders.

This is where Kant can give us guidance. Workers' moral duties to stakeholders can fruitfully be understood in terms of the categorical imperative, especially the formula of humanity. The categorical imperative specifies the parameters of morally appropriate relationships in a business setting, because it constrains the maxims we adopt in our attempts to increase corporate profits: "to use someone as a *mere means* is to involve them in a scheme of action *to which they could not in principle consent.*"[27] This has implications for the relationships between buyers and suppliers, employers and employees, executives and shareholders, businesspeople and stakeholders.[28]

Kant does not believe in conflicting duties (MM 224), but we can see the continuity between personal and professional obligations by drawing on the work of another deontological theorist, W. D. Ross.[29] Employees in a given corporation have an obligation to maximize profits for shareholders. In being hired by the company, they implicitly agree to advance the company's aim and thus are bound by what Ross calls the duty of fidelity.[30] But they also have a number of other duties, including the duties of beneficence and nonmaleficence. As a professor, I agree to meet with my classes every day; having classes is necessary to generate revenue for the university. However, if I am on my way to class and I see a child drowning in a shallow pond, I should save her even if doing so will make me miss my class.

Although I ought to fulfill my employment contract *and* save the child, the right thing to do in this situation is to save her from drowning. Businesspeople are in similar positions. They should maximize profits unless there is a more pressing moral duty to family, friends, other employees, or anyone else who is affected by their actions. Even their corporate behavior is morally constrained.

Only by adhering to what is demanded by pure reason does a businessperson act in accordance with her humanity. For Kant, a person's value depends on her autonomy, her capacity to set ends and to do what is right because it is right. The person does not have incomparable worth because of some contingent fact about her situation or because of some role she plays in advancing ends that are simply given to her. Ironically, this basic Kantian idea is contradicted *both* by those who think that a worker ought to be guided only by her particular corporate role *and* by those who argue for a robust sense of collective responsibility to stakeholders. According to each position, a person's actions are structured not by her own reasoning, but by the part she plays in some larger organization. Friedman sees the individual as a cog in the corporate machine. Although she can quit at any time, remaining in the organization requires that she pursue a particular goal that is set for her by the very nature of business and its function in the free market. The views of Goodpaster and others, however, similarly reflect a "profound disrespect" for individual agency, because for them, too, the employee is assigned a certain role – albeit a morally positive one – by paternalistic managers who have the social good as their aim.[31] Corporate values replace individual reasoning, and the business becomes the moral agent. The appeal to either collective agency or capitalist self-interest is therefore inimical to Kantian morality because both of them encourage heteronomous actions. That is, they conceive of our actions as determined either by the demands of the free market or by the company's CID structure. The worker becomes merely an instrument for carrying out the aims of the larger group, much like, under utilitarianism, the agent becomes merely a conduit for producing happiness.[32]

The Choice Facing Business Ethicists: Kant or Collective Responsibility?

Not treating people merely as means precludes such practices as lying on earnings reports, sexual harassment, and poisoning drinking water. The fact that Kant rules out such things makes his philosophy attractive to business ethicists. However, the actions themselves can only be evaluated with reference to an agent's intentions. A false earnings report is not itself morally wrong; it is merely incorrect. Only the person who wrote the report can be morally praised or blamed, depending on the maxim. And a maxim could never be adopted by a corporation because it does not engage in practical reasoning, even though the people in the corporation do. To say that the company is an agent because it is composed of agents is, from Kant's perspective, to commit the fallacy of composition. Appealing to Kant in business ethics comes at the cost of jettisoning the notion of collective responsibility and accepting his individualistic conception of moral agency.

Some business ethicists may be willing to do this. If the company produces a defective and harmful product, one or more people within the company ought to have made sure that the product meets appropriate standards of design. If no one had this responsibility, then the directors are responsible for not having created such a position – basically, they were negligent in not foreseeing the risk. If a responsibly designed product turns out to be defective, then no one is morally culpable, even though the corporation as a whole may be responsible in the eyes of the law.

For Kant, moral responsibility can only rest with the rational individual. The problem is that, as noted above, responsibility tends to be diffused in a corporate setting. If employees are only involved in isolated aspects of a larger project, they can fail to see that there is a moral dilemma at hand. They may not understand when a decision needs to be made, because they do not know when the corporation has come close to crossing a line, or they may not have information about how what they are doing will be used. Of course, recognizing this deficiency in their knowledge places a special burden on employees to be as informed as they can. But given "the bureaucratic pattern of organization that fragments the knowledge required for moral decisionmaking," this deficiency cannot always be overcome.[33]

One practical implication of adopting Kant's approach, then, is that some corporate actions will occur that cannot be judged because they cannot be attributed to anyone. Bureaucratization undermines the extent to which a person is aware of the consequences of his actions, or even what kind of action he is performing, whether it is innocuous or morally suspect. Think back to my earlier examples of manufacturing a harmful product or contaminating drinking water. Under common corporate conditions, a number of actions that we would normally consider to be morally wrong are involuntary and morally blameless.

If such business decisions are not completely outside the realm of morality, then philosophers have a choice to make: either apply the categorical imperative to the actions of particular businesspeople and surrender the notion of collective responsibility, or apply a different moral theory to the actions of businesses themselves. Kant judges people's actions with reference to their motives. Because businesses are not the sorts of things that choose maxims upon which to act (even though businesspeople do), Kant's applicability to business ethics is limited in a way that, say, utilitarianism is not.

Utilitarianism can evaluate an action in terms of its consequences, apart from what the subject takes himself to be doing.[34] In addition, laws, corporate codes, and social norms can be judged as either conducive or not conducive to maximizing utility.

It is ironic that utilitarianism would seem to be a more useful theory for passing moral judgment on businesses, because utilitarianism is often compared to the kinds of cost-benefit analyses that are characteristic of classical economic theory. Business ethics is usually thought to constrain businesses and hold them to moral ideals that are separate from profit maximization, but utilitarianism often justifies the profit motive under capitalism as morally appropriate, on the assumption that, when individuals work to advance their own interests, society as a whole will benefit. It is precisely this kind of end-state reasoning that Kantian theorists and many other business ethicists seek to challenge. Of course, utilitarianism is not the only alternative, but other options face similar problems: like Kant's ethics, virtue ethics focuses on an agent's character rather than a corporate environment, and attempts to make corporate culture conducive to the development of virtuous characters – so-called "system development ethics" – similarly privilege individualism in ethics as opposed to collective responsibility.[35]

The explanatory value of collective responsibility may motivate us to reevaluate what Kant can contribute to business ethics. Indeed, many philosophers after Kant have gradually moved away from this kind of moral atomism. As we saw earlier, beginning with Hegel there is an insistence on the necessarily intersubjective constitution of the individual as a subject. To the extent that we become capable of responsibility at all, we are conditioned by forces outside the self. A communitarian approach, according to which personal choices are understood against a social background of routines and expectations, is better able to account for corporate responsibility. We must focus our moral attention on whole communities, not just the supposedly isolated, liberal individual. For Hegel, the recognition of a business socially and legally is relevant to its moral status as a responsible agent. Holding it to account for its actions is relevant to determining whether it is the sort of thing that can act on the basis of principles.

After Hegel, our understanding of what sort of responsibility we are capable of becomes considerably more complicated. Friedrich Nietzsche denies the existence of the self apart from its actions and claims that the very idea of a responsible subject is a historical artifact.[36] Louis Althusser locates the inauguration of the subject in "rituals of ideological recognition," by which someone is "interpellated" as a subject through the process of being addressed by others *as* a subject.[37] Michel Foucault identifies the appeal to the authoritative subject as an echo of the desire for an absolutely free creator, with whose death we have not yet come to terms.[38] What it means to be a subject is thoroughly historical, and requires subjection to social and political forces. In all of these approaches, subjectivity is conditioned by the "outside," such that the subject is a porous entity. It is never isolated, but is always related to others – other subjects, political and economic ideologies, and the past, among other things.

The history of post-Kantian philosophy is in many ways an extended attempt to overcome the Enlightenment picture of the moral agent that Kant presupposes. Business ethicists continue this resistance to Kant by insisting that only collective responsibility can make sense of at least some corporate decisions. Kant's ethics has important implications for our moral lives, but when applying his theory to business, philosophers must either surrender the very basis of Kantian ethics or relinquish one of their own fundamental assumptions.

Notes

1   Barbara Herman, *The Practice of Moral Judgment* (Cambridge, Mass.: Harvard University Press, 1993), 206, and Onora O'Neill, *Constructions of Reason: Explorations of Kant's Practical Philosophy* (Cambridge: Cambridge University Press, 1989), 122–5.

2   William M. Evan and R. Edward Freeman, "A Stakeholder Theory of the Modern Corporation: Kantian Capitalism," in *Ethical Theory and Business*, ed. Tom L. Beauchamp and Norman E. Bowie, 4th edn. (Englewood Cliffs, N.J.: Prentice Hall, 1993), 75–84. The distinction between stakeholders and shareholders is commonplace in business ethics. Shareholders own part or all of a given company, and they are certainly affected by the performance of the business. However, there are many other people who are impacted by corporate behavior: employees, members of the community, suppliers, customers, the government, etc. These people have a stake in the company's actions, even though they may not own any part of it. And, so the argument goes, if they are affected by the actions of the company, then the company has moral obligations to them.

3   Norman E. Bowie is almost singlehandedly making up for the fact that Kant's philosophy was overlooked for so long in business ethics. Recent writings in which he explicitly references Kant include *Business Ethics: A Kantian Perspective* (Oxford: Blackwell, 1999); "A Kantian Theory of Leadership," *Leadership and Organization Development Journal* 21, no. 4 (2000): 185–93; (with Denis G. Arnold) "Sweatshops and Respect for Persons," *Business Ethics Quarterly* 13, no. 2 (Apr. 2003): 221–42; and "Kantian Capitalism," in *The Blackwell Encyclopedia of Management*, vol. 2, *Business Ethics*, ed. Patricia H. Werhane and R. Edward Freeman, 2nd edn. (Oxford: Blackwell, 2005), 285–8.

4   Corporate responsibility is one kind of collective responsibility. Some people also attribute group intentions and collective responsibility to such loose groups

of people as crowds and unaffiliated members of a particular profession. However, in general collective responsibility is only attributed to a group whose members' behavior is governed by established rules and which has a particular body to carry out the group action, such as an elected government or a board of directors. In any event, the claims made in this chapter apply both to the broader category of collective agency and to corporate agency. Kant cannot make sense of collective agency generally and thus cannot accommodate corporate agency in particular.

5　Albert Carr, "Is Business Bluffing Ethical?" *Harvard Business Review* 46, no. 1 (Jan.–Feb. 1968): 143–53.

6　Milton Friedman, "The Social Responsibility of Business Is to Increase Its Profits," *New York Times Magazine*, 13 Sept. 1970, 32–3, 122–6.

7　John R. Boatright, "Does Business Ethics Rest on a Mistake?" *Business Ethics Quarterly* 9, no. 4 (Oct. 1999): 583–91 (pp. 586–7).

8　Kenneth E. Goodpaster and John B. Matthews, Jr., "Can a Corporation Have a Conscience?" *Harvard Business Review* 60 (Jan./Feb. 1982): 132–41.

9　Peter French, "The Corporation as a Moral Person," *American Philosophical Quarterly* 16, no. 3 (July 1979): 207–15. See also French, *Collective and Corporate Responsibility* (New York: Columbia University Press, 1984), and Thomas Donaldson, *Corporations and Morality* (Englewood Cliffs, N.J.: Prentice Hall, 1982), 30–2. Kevin Gibson makes a slightly weaker claim: corporations are not moral agents, but because of their decision-making procedures – the fact that there is a corporate culture (a "continuing 'spirit'") that persists despite employee turnover – they are enough like agents ("quasi-persons") to have moral responsibilities. Thus the corporation can be held to account, but without "assigning intentionality to a nonhuman entity" ("The Moral Basis of Stakeholder Theory," *Journal of Business Ethics* 26, no. 3 [Aug. 2000]: 245–57 [pp. 251–2, 254]). For the purposes of this chapter, the distinction between French's stronger claim and Gibson's weaker claim is not important. As I will show, under Kant's deontological theory, a corporation is neither an agent nor enough like an agent to be held morally responsible for its actions.

10　William H. Shaw and Vincent Barry, *Moral Issues in Business*, 8th edn. (Belmont, Calif.: Wadsworth, 2001), 202.

11　Onora O'Neill, "The Moral Perplexities of Famine Relief," in *Matters of Life and Death*, ed. Tom Regan (Philadelphia: Temple University Press, 1980), 260–98 (p. 293). Similarly, David T. Ozar compares businesses to clubs and nations, which have rules that govern their actions. See his "The Moral Responsibility of Corporations," in *Ethical Issues in Business: A Philosophical Approach*, ed. Thomas Donaldson and Patricia H. Werhane (Englewood Cliffs, N.J.: Prentice-Hall, 1979), 294–300.

12　Richard T. De George, "Can Corporations Have Moral Responsibility?" in *Ethical Theory and Business*, ed. Tom L. Beauchamp and Norman E. Bowie, 2nd edn. (Englewood Cliffs, N.J.: Prentice Hall, 1983), 57–67 (pp. 63–5).

13　Bowie, *Business Ethics*, 83–4; emphasis added. By Bowie's count, the second formulation of the categorical imperative is the formula of humanity.

14　If a person wasted enough time and money doing this, we could conceivably criticize him for not developing his talents or for misdirecting resources that could help others. However, it would not be wrong because of how he is treating the business, which is what is important here.

15   For Kant, the condition of all other goods is simply adherence to the moral law. This is the supreme good. But for morality to make sense to us, for it to be complete, happiness and virtue must be united somehow. This is the highest good, which is only achievable if freedom, the immortal soul, and God are not just possible but actual. See CPrR 110–11.

16   Manuel G. Velasquez, "Why Corporations Are Not Morally Responsible for Anything They Do," *Business and Professional Ethics Journal* 2, no. 3 (fall 1983): 1–18.

17   Michael Keeley, "Organizations as Non-Persons," *Journal of Value Inquiry* 15, no. 2 (June 1981): 149–55.

18   This is where Velasquez and I seem to overlap. He does not look at the setting of maxims, however. Instead, he focuses on the physical act of bringing about a particular end as one of the conditions of moral responsibility. He claims that a business cannot actually do anything, and thus any intentions it does have cannot be actualized: "The intentions [Peter] French attributes to corporations, then, do not mark out corporate acts as intentional because the intentions are attributed to one entity (the corporation) whereas the acts are carried out by another entity (the corporate members)" ("Why Corporations Are Not Morally Responsible," 8). Businesspeople are agents of the corporation, but they are the ones who act. That is why the intentions of the corporation are irrelevant.

Unfortunately, Velasquez also notes that "corporations 'as a whole' may legitimately be held *causally* responsible for an act or an effect," which (he says) is a sense of responsibility distinct from moral responsibility (14). Yet agreeing with French that corporations can have intentions *and* conceding that they can be causally responsible for a given action seems to imply that they meet the two conditions Velasquez sets out for moral responsibility: that the agent "personally brought about the wrongful act" and that "he did so intentionally" (2). If he defines "personally" in a non-question-begging way, Velasquez must concede that, according to his criteria, corporations can be morally responsible.

By looking at responsibility through a Kantian lens, we can see that what seems to be an intention is actually just an artificial constraint that employees may or may not follow. Therefore, corporate responsibility is more effectively criticized by first explaining what is required for moral culpability, then by showing that businesses do not meet these conditions. That is the approach I take in this chapter.

19   Bowie, *Business Ethics*, 83–4.

20   John Rawls, *A Theory of Justice*, rev. edn. (Cambridge, Mass: Harvard University Press, 1999), 458.

21   Ibid., 222.

22   See Charles Taylor, "Atomism," in *Philosophy and the Human Sciences*, vol. 2 of *Philosophical Papers* (Cambridge: Cambridge University Press, 1982), 187–210.

23   Bowie, *Business Ethics*, 93.

24   *Citizens United v. Federal Election Commission*, 558 U.S. 50 [2010].

25 De George, "Can Corporations Have Moral Responsibility?" 61–2.
26 This theory of freedom is explained and developed in Robert B. Pippin, *Hegel's Practical Philosophy: Rational Agency as Ethical Life* (Cambridge: Cambridge University Press, 2008).
27 O'Neill, "The Moral Perplexities of Famine Relief," 286.
28 It would go beyond the scope of this chapter to talk more specifically about the obligations that agents of the corporation have. However, without collective agency, Kant's theory also cannot make sense of obligations to groups of people such as unions, which are not themselves deserving of respect, even though their members are. If, as Gibson argues, stakeholder theory depends on collective responsibility – that is, it depends on groups having moral obligations to other groups – then deontological ethics may undermine stakeholder theory in general ("The Moral Basis of Stakeholder Theory," 245–57). Unfortunately, many stakeholder theorists claim to be drawing on the formula of humanity to make their case. For example, R. Edward Freeman writes: "Each of these stakeholder *groups* has a right not to be treated as a means to some end, and therefore must participate in determining the future direction of the firm in which they have a stake" (*Strategic Management: A Stakeholder Approach* [Boston: Ballinger, 1984], xx; emphasis added). See also Evan and Freeman, "A Stakeholder Theory of the Modern Corporation," 76. Gibson's claim fails to convince me, however. Businesspeople are obligated to take into account the personhood of everyone who is affected by the business, even if they are not obligated to them as groups. If that is so, then Kant's individualistic view does not undermine stakeholder theory, but merely refocuses it on individual stakeholders.
29 W. D. Ross's clearest statement of his moral philosophy is *The Right and the Good* (Indianapolis, Ind.: Hackett, 1988), 16–47.
30 William Shaw and Vincent Barry claim that there is no "promissory relationship" between investors and employees. Instead, shareholders simply buy stock that they expect to increase. They do not make an arrangement with management to increase profits, and managers are not given a choice (as, for example, financial advisors are) to refuse the offer (*Moral Issues in Business*, 207). This interpretation assumes a rather one-dimensional notion of consent. Employees are hired on the assumption that they will advance the interests of the company, and that includes (at least) the commitment to attract and reward investors by increasing profits. They tacitly consent to such a relationship by taking a position in a publicly traded company. That is not their only obligation, but it is certainly one of them.
31 Daniel R. Gilbert, Jr., "Respect for Persons, Management Theory, and Business Ethics," in *Business Ethics: The State of the Art*, ed. R. Edward Freeman (Oxford: Oxford University Press, 1991), 111–21 (p. 116).
32 Bernard Williams, "A Critique of Utilitarianism," in *Utilitarianism: For and Against*, by J. J. C. Smart and Bernard Williams (Cambridge: Cambridge University Press, 1973), 75–150 (pp. 108–18).
33 David Luban, Alan Strudler, and David Wasserman, "Moral Responsibility in the Age of Bureaucracy," *Michigan Law Review* 90, no. 8 (Aug. 1992): 2348–92 (p. 2359). See also Donaldson, *Corporations and Morality*, 109–28, and

Robert Jackall, "Looking Up and Looking Around," in *Moral Mazes: The World of Corporate Managers* (Oxford: Oxford University Press, 1988), 75–100.

34   John Stuart Mill distinguishes how we judge the action from how we judge the person who performed the action, whether she has a character that (on the whole) tends to aim at maximizing utility. See Mill, *Utilitarianism*, ed. George Sher (Indianapolis, Ind.: Hackett, 1979), 19–20. Bad actions can issue from people whose character is good, so sometimes an action would be wrong even though the person is not blameworthy. When we are talking about the actions of a business, we can say that the action is wrong without attributing the action to some bad character. In such cases, there is no character to consider. When we talk about the "character" of the institution, we are referring to whether its policies encourage its employees to act rightly or not.

35   Joseph A. Petrick and John F. Quinn, *Management Ethics: Integrity at Work* (Thousand Oaks, Calif.: Sage, 1997), 53–5.

36   Friedrich Nietzsche, *On the Genealogy of Morals*, trans. Walter Kaufmann and R. J. Hollingdale, ed. Walter Kaufmann (New York: Vintage, 1967).

37   Louis Althusser, "Ideology and Ideological State Apparatuses (Notes towards an Investigation)," in *Lenin and Philosophy and Other Essays*, trans. Ben Brewster (New York: Monthly Review, 1971), 172.

38   Michel Foucault, "What Is an Author?" in *The Foucault Reader*, ed. Paul Rabinow (New York: Pantheon Books, 1984), 101–20.

10

Becoming a Person

What it means to be a moral agent is a complicated issue, as is the question of who should be considered in our moral deliberations. These two questions – who is responsible, and to whom – have run throughout the various chapters of this book. The different topics in applied ethics have prompted us to examine the moral status of nature, animals, businesses, patients with dementia, and even women and the poor, all through a Kantian lens. We began the book by examining the value of rational agency, which gives human beings incomparable worth. In more recent chapters, however, we have begun to see that Kant's approach to autonomy and subjectivity cannot adequately address issues around gender and equality, social justice, and collective responsibility.

It is fitting, then, to close the book by returning to the original question of who or what is morally considerable, which for Kant is equivalent to the question of who or what counts as a moral agent, or at least has an effect on moral agents. In this chapter, I consider perhaps the most heated contemporary debate about personhood: abortion. Any adequate moral theory must give us the tools, if not to make a moral judgment about abortion, at least to clarify the morally relevant facts involved in deliberating about it. As we will see, however, Kant's ethics cannot adequately consider the fetus, given its status as a potential person, so the theory has limited usefulness for addressing this important topic in applied ethics.

The Ancient Practice of Abortion, and Continuing Controversies

Abortion is not a recent phenomenon. The practice of inducing abortion can be traced back at least to the ancient Egyptians and has involved a

Kant and Applied Ethics: The Uses and Limits of Kant's Practical Philosophy, First Edition.
Matthew C. Altman.
© 2011 John Wiley & Sons Inc. Published 2011 by Blackwell Publishing Ltd.

number of different techniques, including the use of poisonous herbs, sharpened implements, and abdominal pressure.[1] Although abortion was not considered a moral or a legal offense for hundreds of years, by the thirteenth century English common law equated abortion with homicide, but only after the fetus was "formed or animated."[2] In the sixteenth and seventeenth centuries several European nations, including Germany, established laws that made abortion a crime punishable by death. The Catholic Church similarly condemned the practice but, like Germany and England, only did so after the fetus was said to be "ensouled."[3] There was great disagreement about when this took place – at conception, when the child was born, or, most commonly, after "quickening" (when the mother first feels the child move, after about 16–20 weeks of fetal development) – and this confusion over when the child has a "rational soul" has continued to the present day. In *Roe v. Wade* (410 U.S. 113 [1973]), the U.S. Supreme Court refused to take a position on when life begins, noting the lack of consensus among physicians, philosophers, and theologians.[4]

Some historians believe that the various European states first implemented abortion laws in order to assert their control over fertility, because of the population decline during the Thirty Years War.[5] Others suggest that the laws were a response to what had become a much more common procedure.[6] There is no way of telling how many abortions took place during Kant's time, since abortions were largely performed privately, in the home. What evidence we have suggests that the use of abortifacients was fairly widespread in seventeenth- and eighteenth-century Europe, although they were mostly used prior to quickening.[7] It is surprising, then, that Kant never expressed an opinion about the morality of abortion, especially since he wrote about such minutiae as whether it is morally permissible to cut your hair (yes, but you cannot sell it), to kneel before religious icons (no), or to accept an invitation to a banquet (it depends) (MM 423, 436–7, and 428, respectively). One of the reasons for this omission is certainly that abortion was then not the major moral issue that it is now. It was largely a family matter rather than a matter of public debate.

But this may not be the only reason that abortion is absent from Kant's writings. In this chapter, we will see that Kant's conception of the person has problematic implications that are clearly exposed in an analysis of abortion. Kant's philosophy cannot accommodate a continuum of mental maturity. For Kant, determining the ethics of abortion requires first that we determine the personhood of the fetus, yet an analysis of Kant's approach to personhood shows that the class of morally considerable agents is very limited. Kant's moral theory excludes not only fetuses but also young children. Alternative forms of reasoning that Kant uses to include children – the appeal to divine and natural purposes – are problematic and contrary to the basic claims of Kantian ethics. When it comes to borderline cases such as the unborn, Kant's philosophy faces insurmountable limitations.

Universalized Maxims Are Not Retroactive

Some philosophers claim that the categorical imperative has clear implications for the abortion debate. Appealing to the first formulation, R. M. Hare and Harry Gensler argue that the maxim one holds in having an abortion cannot be universalized, so abortion is morally impermissible.[8] Although Hare and Gensler each appeal to considerations that Kant would reject – my "preference" not to have been killed, or the fact that my having been aborted would conflict with the rest of my life, including my "desires"[9] – the spirit of their comments can be interpreted in strictly Kantian terms: If my maxim to abort a fetus were universalized, then everyone would abort fetuses, and the human race would be extinguished. Of course, this fact alone cannot rule out abortion; it is morally irrelevant that bad consequences would result. What is relevant is that I developed from a fetus, and making abortion a universal law would mean that my parents abort me and my own capacity to will would be thwarted. I could not will the maxim were it universalized – I would be willing my own nonexistence – so it must be wrong.

Although this reasoning seems Kantian, it actually misapplies the categorical imperative. I explained why in chapter 6 with regard to homosexuality. According to John Rawls's classic interpretation, I formulate and universalize the maxim, transform it into a law of nature that everyone follows, and then figure out what things would be like if the law were added to the existing laws of nature and the world had a chance to reach equilibrium – that is, everyone acts on the maxim and realizes that everyone is acting on the maxim. Only if I could act on my maxim or rationally choose to inhabit such a world is the initial maxim permissible.[10] Note that this is forward-looking in the sense that the world in which I would act *in the future* is (hypothetically) being transformed through my willing. Christine Korsgaard, Barbara Herman, and Kant himself similarly apply the categorical imperative to the future rather than the past. For example, Kant says that it is irrational to will a maxim of nonmaleficence because "many cases *could* occur in which one *would* need the love and sympathy of others" (G 423, emphasis added).[11] Kant does not say that I must act beneficently because I needed help last week or because I could not feed myself when I was a baby. I am a finite rational being, so I will need others' assistance to achieve my goals in the future.

Of course, Korsgaard, Herman, and even Kant may be wrong about not applying the categorical imperative to the past. A poll of philosophers does not settle a theoretical issue. However, there are separate reasons to believe that the universalization of a maxim must be forward-looking only. As Susan Feldman points out, a retroactive application of the categorical imperative would lead to absurd consequences. Even though a person cannot will her own nonexistence, that does not imply that she must will every previous action, including wrong actions, that made her birth possible – the slave master's rape of her great-great-grandmother, for example.[12] Universalizing a refusal to rape would seem to have the same effect, were it applied retroactively: the woman would never have been born. The rape was just as necessary for her existence as her having once been a fetus, yet Kant would condemn rape as a clear case of using someone merely as a means.

The fact that we are happy to be alive or that we cannot rationally commit suicide does not mean that we have to consent to situations that made our existence possible in the first place, including the sex act itself. According to Hare's application of the categorical imperative, even celibacy would be morally impermissible – we are products of sexual reproduction, after all – but Kant never claims such a thing. Kant mentions clerical celibacy in passing and without comment (MM 368). Indeed, Kant himself never married or had children, and he did not express any moral qualms about it. That each one of us is morally obligated to procreate would have seemed as absurd to Kant's ears as it does to ours. Yet a celibacy maxim would turn out to be morally impermissible if universalizing it meant making it a law of nature for my parents.

The Formula of Humanity: Appealing to Personhood

The fact that I, a rational being, was once a fetus seems relevant in determining whether abortion is morally acceptable, but the universalizability test fails to explain *why* this is relevant. Although the formula of universal law and the formula of humanity are equivalent and should come to the same conclusion, the latter formulation dictates more clearly how we ought to treat others, so it seems like a more promising avenue when it comes to the question of abortion. As we saw in chapter 1, Kant's ethics begins with a logocentric starting point that, according to Allen Wood, "grounds ethical theory neither in a principle to be obeyed nor in an end to be pursued, but in a value to be esteemed, honoured or respected."[13] Our duties to the fetus, if there are such duties, depend on whether the fetus has the right kind of value, such that we ought to respect it in any decision we make.

Some people have claimed that this approach comes at the issue from the wrong direction. For example, the Warnock Report says that we ought to determine what our moral obligations to the fetus are rather than debating whether the fetus is a person, because the latter is not a question of fact.[14] Both Judith Jarvis Thomson and Don Marquis, although they are on opposite sides of the abortion debate, set aside a consideration of whether the fetus is a person, claiming that this approach either is irrelevant or leads to an argumentative stalemate.[15] Jane English claims that those who participate in the abortion debate wrongly construe personhood as a thing with necessary and sufficient conditions, and that "a fetus lies in the penumbra region where our concept of a person is not so simple."[16] Still, many philosophers and most non-philosophers confront abortion by talking about what the fetus is like: it has certain genes but lacks certain brain waves, it has the capacity for pain but lacks the capacity to care about its future, or whatever.[17]

Kant cannot remain neutral in this debate. It is crucial to determine whether the fetus is a person, because, Kant says, we can have direct moral obligations only to those who have humanity. That we are dealing with a person puts absolute restrictions on how we can treat him. For example, we can never kill someone in order to maximize happiness, for doing so uses him merely as a means. We would be violating our duty to respect the absolute worth of the person, treating him as if he had merely a *"market price"* that could be outweighed by the greater good produced (G 434). However, if something is not a person, we can have no direct moral obligations to it. Any indirect moral obligations would come from what I owe to myself or to other people by means of the thing. As we saw in chapter 1, I should not abuse my dog because doing so would make me insensitive to others' suffering. And if I do not like an old chair I can throw it away, unless it is owned by or I have promised it to someone else. I have obligations to the people involved, but not to the dog or the chair.

So, is a fetus a person whom we ought to respect, or a thing whose well-being matters only insofar as it affects persons, such as the pregnant woman? Again, Kant must settle this question. If a fetus is a person, then aborting it for any reason other than (perhaps) to protect the life of the mother would be murder. Even in cases of rape and incest, the fetus could not be destroyed to protect the mother's psychological health or to remove an obligation to which she had not consented. She has a duty to maintain the person's life even if she would be greatly inconvenienced or harmed, because no amount of unhappiness on her part could outweigh the absolute value of the fetus. On the other hand, if fetuses are not persons, ending the pregnancy would be just as permissible as removing an abnormal growth in the body. Assuming no other moral obligations are involved, such as a promise by a surrogate mother to a childless couple or a duty to respect the rights of the father, then the pregnancy could be terminated for almost any reason.[18]

The importance of determining the personhood of the fetus is not accepted by all Kant scholars. Feldman attempts a Kantian analysis of abortion, but she pushes aside the status of the fetus and focuses on the personhood of the woman. Because the pregnant woman is a rational agent, Feldman claims, it is morally permissible – or even obligatory? – to abort a fetus that conflicts with her "life plans or independence," both of which are involved in the imperfect duty to develop her talents (self-improve-ment).[19] However, Feldman's conclusion is true *only if* the fetus is not a person. She assumes that it is not, which is why she says that there is no conflict between the woman's imperfect duty to herself and her perfect duty to the fetus. There is no duty to the fetus.[20]

As we will see, the question is more complicated than that. Feldman seems to acknowledge this when she addresses the same situation "even if fetuses were considered to be moral persons." Feldman says that the fetus would then be using the mother merely as a means, analogous to forcing someone to donate a kidney.[21] However, Feldman is assuming that some-thing that is directly morally considerable must also be morally responsible, a proposition that may not be true – more on this later. Furthermore, even if the fetus were using the woman's body, that would not necessarily justify aborting it. Someone who picks my pocket is using me merely as a means too, but that does not mean I can kill him. Assuming that the woman's life is not at stake, killing the fetus is not a justifiable act of self-defense. My duty to develop my talents or to protect myself is limited by the respect that I must show other persons. Under Kant's theory, the personhood of the fetus must be settled in order to assess the moral permissibility of abortion.

Thomson and Boonin: The Personhood of the Fetus Does Not Matter

A more formidable position has been advanced by Judith Jarvis Thomson and David Boonin, both of whom argue that, even if the fetus is a person, its right to life would not necessarily imply that the pregnant woman has a corresponding duty to carry the fetus to term. Thomson gives several well-known analogies to explain and justify her position. If I were kid-napped and surgically connected to a famous violinist, such that my kidneys were keeping him alive by filtering his blood, I would not be obligated to stay attached to him for nine months (at which point he would recover), even if severing him from me earlier than that meant that he would die. The violinist is a person with a right to life, but I would not be murdering him by disconnecting him. Analogously, it is morally permissible for a woman to terminate a pregnancy that is the result of rape. The same is true for a pregnancy that threatens the woman's life, or that results from the failure of contraceptives.[22] Thomson's conclusion is that, even if the fetus is a person, there is no conflict between the fetus's right to life and the woman's right to control her body, because the fetus has no justifiable claim on the woman's body that derives from its right to life.

Thomson's arguments have been endlessly debated in the secondary literature, but their relevance for a Kantian approach to abortion is limited because of their very different foundational assumptions. Thomson and Boonin claim that a person's rights largely determine the extent of other people's obligations to them, and thus they overemphasize the importance of only one kind of moral relation. To return to a useful hypothetical, imagine that I am on my way to an appointment when I notice a child drowning in a shallow pond. I can easily wade into the pond and save her, but doing so will make me late for my appointment, perhaps a very important appointment, and it will ruin my new, expensive shoes. What should I do? According to Kant, I have a moral duty to save the child, because my interest in my own happiness cannot outweigh the duty I have to save another person's life. This duty is based on the respect I ought to have for the person's humanity, which has intrinsic worth, as opposed to my own happiness, which is only conditionally good (G 434–5). Of course, the child has no right to my help, any more than the violinist has a right to my kidneys. But as we saw in chapter 3 (with regard to health care), the fact that they are in need obligates me to help them because I have a duty to further their ends. Whether they have a right to my help is irrelevant.

Thomson would grant that I have an obligation to save the drowning child. She makes an important distinction: it would not be unjust to let the child drown, since she has no right to my help, but it would nonetheless be "indecent" not to help. We are all obligated to be what Thomson calls "Minimally Decent Samaritans," but not "Good Samaritans." If the violinist had to be attached to me only for an hour, or if pregnancy lasted only for an hour, she says, then detaching the violinist or aborting the fetus would be morally wrong.[23] Getting my shoes wet and being late for an appointment are not important enough to justify my refusal to save the child. But the burden of carrying a child to term, especially if the woman did not consent to the pregnancy or the pregnancy threatens her life, cannot be morally demanded of her. According to Thomson, one cannot be obligated to sustain the fetus or the violinist for nine months, even if they are both persons – that is, even if the fetus has a right to life. Doing so would be supererogatory.

Thomson and Boonin presuppose a model of interpersonal relationships according to which we are essentially defined as individual, rights-bearing subjects.[24] If I consent to do something, or if someone has a claim on me because of some right that the person has, only then must I sacrifice a significant amount of my happiness. In the absence of a rights-based claim, the amount of happiness I can be obligated to forgo is relatively insignificant – say, one hour helping the violinist.

Critics of Thomson often accept her basic assumptions about the source of moral responsibility, and they condemn abortion by arguing that the woman has in fact consented to or is responsible for the pregnancy in a way that commits her to carrying the child to term. In response, Thomson and Boonin spend many pages explaining why a woman who willingly engages in sex has not consented and is not responsible for the fetus in a way that would make abortion wrong. Thomson says that even a rape victim is partly "responsible" for the chain of events that leads to her pregnancy – after all, she could have had a hysterectomy, etc. – and yet she has not willingly taken on responsibility for the fetus's well-being.[25] If abortion is permissible in cases of rape, it is also permissible in at least some cases where intercourse is voluntary – for example, in cases where a woman uses birth control (unsuccessfully) to prevent pregnancy. And Boonin says that engaging in a voluntary action that has a foreseeable result does not entail that the person consents to the result. Even if she does consent to the pregnancy, it does not imply that she has consented to carry it to term.[26] Without the requisite consent, the woman is under no obligation to make the sacrifices necessary to sustain the fetus, even if it is a person. As a Minimally Decent Samaritan, the woman is required to make only minimal sacrifices in the absence of her consent and in the absence of rights-based claims to her body. She cannot be morally required to take on the burdens of pregnancy for nine months. It is permissible to abort the fetus.

Thomson does not go into much detail about what distinguishes a Minimally Decent Samaritan from a Good Samaritan, or where the line should be drawn between what is required and what is supererogatory. She says only that "these things are a matter of degree."[27] For Kant, however, the line is drawn fairly easily: we are obligated to advance the humanity of others even when doing so is inconvenient to us, lessens our happiness, or forces us to adjust our life plans. Thomson's claim that, in the absence of a fetus's right to the woman's body, she is under no obligation to carry the fetus to term (even if it is a person), assumes that the woman's obligation to the fetus/person is less pressing than her own well-being – and that is at least in part because, according to Thomson, only the fetus's right to the woman's body would definitively trump her self-interest.

For Kant, however, our moral obligations to other persons do not depend on their having a right to our help or our having consented to help them. *If* the fetus is a person, then Kant would not recognize a morally significant difference between our obligations to the child in the shallow pond and our obligations to an unborn fetus. In both cases, the choice is between satisfying the inclinations (wanting to go the meeting on time and with clean shoes, not wanting to endure a full-term pregnancy and birth) or preserving the incomparable worth of a being with humanity. Thomson and Boonin are claiming that, if the fetus has no right to the woman's body, then it is permissible for the woman to value her own self-interest over the life of a person (the fetus), as long as it is not a very minimal inconvenience (a one-hour pregnancy, for example). However, this privileging of happiness over dignity amounts to a tacit refusal of the categorical imperative: "*So act that you use humanity, whether in your own person or in the person of any other, always at the same time as an end, never merely as a means*" (G 429). For Thomson, the person's life has a "market price" that is equal to a certain amount of happiness. For Kant, a person's dignity cannot be outweighed by any amount of happiness (G 434–5). A nine-month pregnancy is much more burdensome then wet shoes, to be sure. However, if the fetus is a person, it has incomparable moral worth and is more important than the woman's nonmoral interests, regardless of whether the fetus has a right to the woman's body.

As I wrote in the Introduction, we have internalized many of Kant's most important philosophical insights, including his claim that humanity has a different kind of value than desire-satisfaction. The debate over abortion tends to focus on whether the fetus is a person because many people assume, with Kant, that a fetus has a justifiable claim to a woman's body if it is a person. The value of a person's life places a burden on us to respect it, regardless of what we happen to want or regardless of our consent. From a Kantian perspective, Thomson and Boonin misconstrue the nature of moral obligation, and determining the personhood of the fetus is crucial for determining whether abortion is morally permissible.

The Elements of Personhood: Self-Consciousness, Humanity, Responsibility

If the permissibility of abortion depends entirely on whether the fetus is a person, the question seems easily settled because, according to Kant, personhood involves three conditions, none of which are possessed by the unborn. First, Kant defines a person as "that which is conscious of the numerical identity of itself at different times" (CPR A361). He reiterates this point in the *Anthropology*, where he notes its moral implications: "The fact that the human being can have the 'I' in his representations raises him infinitely above all other living beings on earth. Because of this he is a *person* . . . " (A 127). The activity of self-consciousness distinguishes us from things such as animals, which have no conception of themselves as identical over time and to which we have no direct duties.[28]

Insisting that all persons must be conscious of their experiences and self-aware is fairly common in the literature on abortion, most notably in the work of Mary Anne Warren.[29] However, Kant's account of self-consciousness is particularly instructive, since he relates it to the possibility of having experiences at all. In the *Critique of Pure Reason*, Kant demonstrates that synthesizing various perceptions is only possible if they are brought together under transcendental apperception, or the "I think" that accompanies all of my representations. I am justified in conceiving of myself as a numerically identical subject because a unified self-consciousness is a formal condition for the possibility of experience, both objective representations of the world (outer sense) and consciousness of my thoughts (inner sense) (CPR A106–7, B131–6). Of course, the apperceptive subject is only a transcendental concept of personality and not a transcendent substance (or soul) – Kant reveals this to be a dialectical inference in the Paralogisms of Pure Reason (CPR A341–405, B399–432) – but the activity of self-consciousness warrants a commitment to personhood, at least in its "practical use" (CPR A365). In other words, self-consciousness is a condition for the possibility of experience – the existence of self-consciousness is warranted by the critique of theoretical reason – and a singular consciousness gives credibility to our belief that we are moral agents. Something that lacks self-consciousness is not a candidate for personhood.

Second, persons are distinguished by what Kant calls their humanity. In the *Groundwork*, Kant differentiates humanity from animality by virtue of the ability to reason. Animals are moved to act purely by instinct, but human beings decide how they ought to act, whether to do what morality requires or what they want to do on the basis of their inclinations: "Everything in nature works in accordance with laws. Only a rational being has the capacity to act *in accordance with the representation* of laws, that is, in accordance with principles, or has a *will*" (G 412; see also MM 392). We may not always decide rightly, but we nonetheless choose the maxims upon which we act. Something becomes valuable for me only by my setting it as an end. The capacity to decide things and determine what is good thus has absolute value, because it is a condition of all other goods. This capacity gives rational beings absolute worth and leads to the third version of the categorical imperative, the formula of humanity.[30]

Finally, persons have, in addition to their reasoning, the ability to act on the basis of what they decide. Establishing this is one of the primary tasks of the *Critique of Practical Reason*, where Kant shows that we can be motivated purely by respect for the moral law. In addition to the lower faculty of desire (*Begehrungsvermögen*) that we share with animals, we also have a higher faculty of desire by which "respect for the moral law [serves] *as of itself a sufficient incentive to the power of choice*" (Rel 27). Because we can act on the basis of what we determine to be rationally required of us, we are not only rational but "*responsible [zurech-nungsfähig]* being[s]" (Rel 26). Kant claims that a person is distinguished from mere things because a person can act autonomously, on the basis of moral principles, and thus that he can be held accountable for what he does:

"A *person* is a subject whose actions can be *imputed* to him" (MM 223). Therefore, responsible beings are persons for the sake of moral evaluation.

As Kant understands it, each person has a unitary self-consciousness, the capacity to set their ends, and responsibility for what they do. From this it follows that fetuses at every stage of their development are not persons, because fetuses have none of these three characteristics: there is no unitary subject behind experiences (indeed, fetuses have no experiences, at least in the sense that Kant uses the term[31]); they have no capacity to decide anything; and any "actions" they engage in are a matter of reflex or random movements. At certain points, fetuses may attempt to avoid pain or satisfy needs that are characteristic of all animal behavior, but at no point are they moral agents who are responsible for their behavior.

Because fetuses are not persons according to Kant's criteria, we can have no direct moral obligations to them. Any duties that we have to fetuses would have to be indirect. As we saw in chapter 1, being cruel to animals tends to make a person callous. Conceivably, aborting fetuses may engender a similar disrespect for human life. I will address this possibility later in the chapter. However, at this point nothing in principle precludes the killing of fetuses, just as nothing in principle precludes using animals for work or food – that is, treating them merely as means. The disturbing implication of all of this seems to be that abortion is not a moral issue at all for Kant, that aborting a fetus at any stage in the pregnancy is as morally insignificant as whether you clip your fingernails. In neither case does it amount to the mother's harming herself, the only being who is worthy of any consideration in this case. Whether or not we think abortion is morally permissible, the issue is certainly more complicated than that.

An Attempt to Bring Fetuses into Kant's Moral Community: The Appeal to Kind

Exclusion from the moral community applies not only to fetuses, but also to others who lack at least some of Kant's characteristics: people with congenital and severe mental defects, the elderly at various stages of dementia, newborn infants, and others. If Kant's ethics cannot properly address difficult cases involving those at the margins of life, however, then its application is very limited. It cannot do what an adequate moral theory must do, because it can only cover actions taken by and affecting typical adults. Understandably, a number of Kantian philosophers are eager to show that Kant's ethical theory does not have this conceptual blind spot, that people who are not rational or not fully rational have the relevant characteristics to be included in Kant's moral universe. With regard to fetuses in particular, usually these philosophers make one of two arguments: fetuses are morally considerable either because they are members of the *class* of beings who typically have the capacity to reason, or because fetuses themselves are beings who have the *potential* to become persons.

Let us deal first with the claim that the unborn have moral worth because they are human beings, and as a rule human beings tend to be rational. Christine Korsgaard insists that, although children lack the rational capacity of adult moral agents, children are not nonpersons. Instead, they are persons at a particular stage of development. This argument could be extended to include fetuses: they are persons who have not yet become responsible, conscious beings. The "moral force" of this redescription implies that children and (perhaps) fetuses ought to be respected just as persons are, because children and fetuses *are* persons.[32] This is similar to Korsgaard's claim regarding animals that they are not simply like us, but that animals *are* valuers in the morally relevant sense of the term. Fetuses are valuers at an early stage of development, before they actually become capable of valuing.

Holly Wilson makes a similar argument, but one that relates fetuses and rational adults in terms of their species:

> Human beings are the animals who have the capacity for reason. Each human being, as a member of the species, has the potential for rationality even if she never exhibits it. This potential entails that we must still treat humans who do not exhibit rationality as ends-in-themselves.[33]

According to Wilson, a particular being need not be rational in order to be worthy of respect. Instead, it only needs to be part of a group whose members typically are rational. This argument has been echoed by Stephen Schwarz, who claims that being a *homo sapiens* is morally significant because all human beings have "the basic inherent capacity to function as a person, regardless of how developed this capacity is, or whether or not it is blocked, as in severe senility."[34] The capacity to think is a characteristic that only human beings have, so membership in the species is morally relevant whether or not a particular being, including a fetus, actually has that capacity.

Fuat Oduncu takes this line of reasoning to its logical conclusion. He eliminates the appeal to reason entirely, claiming that fetuses have dignity because they are humans. He simply equates being human with being a person:

> The human embryo is looked upon as a human being from the moment of its conception and thus attributed the fundamental principle of human dignity that guarantees the right to life of the embryo. According to Kant, human

dignity forbids and even condemns instrumentalization and reduction of a human being to a mere means and object. Human beings are persons and as such they are ends in themselves. . . . [T]he bioethical debate should be conducted on the grounds of a biological and anthropological concept of the human being. The concept of the human being and the inherent value of human dignity related to it may find a wider acceptance, as it refers to the biological species of the Homo sapiens sapiens.[35]

If successful, this argument would put to rest the debate about the moral permissibility of abortion and, indeed, stem cell research, at least from a Kantian perspective. In both cases, the fetus is used merely as a means: it is treated as expendable in abortions and as a useful source of stem cells in research. No one denies that fetuses (and the mentally handicapped, the comatose, etc.) are genetically in the class of *homo sapiens*. If this is sufficient justification for us to treat them as persons, as Wilson, Schwarz, and Oduncu claim, then Kant would prohibit abortion out of respect for fetuses, just as he prohibits murder out of respect for adult persons.

For both Korsgaard and Wilson, what matters is that the fetus (or the child) is a kind of thing, a human being, that usually has the capacity to reason – although not in the case of the fetus as a particular instance of a human being. This argument is unconvincing for several reasons, and it cannot ultimately justify moral respect for fetuses (or children for that matter). First, *kinds* do not engage in reasoning, although *members of a kind* can. When determining whether a thing has dignity, Kant would look to the individual rather than the group of which it is a member, because the group is not a morally relevant category. If someday we develop a robot with the capacity to reason, communicate, and act responsibly, Kant would not exclude it from moral consideration simply because it is not the kind of thing that typically has the capacity to reason, or because it is not the kind of thing that gradually (through stages) becomes more rational. What is important is that this particular robot is a person, morally speaking. Correlatively, for Kant what matters in the abortion debate is that the fetus is not a person.

Second, Wilson and Schwarz arbitrarily pick out the species *homo sapiens* as the relevant kind, but there is no independent reason to do that. If the focus is on membership in a group, then we should recognize that rational beings are also kinds of material things, kinds of carbon-based life, and kinds of animals. Since most members of these groups are not moral agents, can we conclude that rational human beings are not of the right kind, and therefore ought not to be given direct moral consideration? Obviously this is unacceptable, precisely because this would imply that individuals who are rational may be treated merely as means. Persons are morally distinct because of particular capacities, not because they are related to other members of an arbitrarily specified group.

Ironically, the capacity to reason is atypical even when we consider the class of *homo sapiens*. Only a small number of fertilized ova actually give rise to live infants – 60 to 80 percent of fertilized eggs fail to implant or are otherwise lost after conception[36] – so even the majority of human beings, if we define humans genetically, are nonrational. If we include embryos and fetuses in the class of human beings, membership in the human species is not decisive in establishing a thing's value. The only class that is morally relevant for Kant is the class of rational end-setters, all of whom are morally considerable because they are rational persons, not because they are members of a particular group. A person's moral status depends on whether she has the characteristics that make her worthy of respect, regardless of the class she is in and whether or not members of the class tend to be rational. The reverse is also true: even if a fetus is related to rational beings, even if it is related to the particular rational being that it may become someday, that does not make it worthy of consideration as a rational being. Its membership in a class of things that includes some rational beings is morally irrelevant.

Third, Oduncu simply equates humans with persons, even though the two classes are distinct. As Warren reminds us, many anti-abortion arguments play on the ambiguity of "human being," saying that the embryo is a human being from the moment of conception and that it is wrong to kill human beings (because they have dignity and a right to life). While embryos have the genetic material of *homo sapiens* from the very beginning, that does not settle the question of whether they are members of the moral community. We have duties to members of the moral community, but the genetic sense of "human" is different from what we mean when we say something is morally considerable.[37] Oduncu claims that "the bioethical debate should be conducted on the grounds of a biological and anthropological concept of the human being," but the physical makeup of embryos has no obvious moral implications.[38] There are plenty of things that have human DNA without having dignity, such as cadavers or human cancer-cell cultures in a petri dish.[39] The fact/value distinction is relevant here. It is a crucial element of Kant's ethics that we have dignity and deserve respect because of our autonomous activity and the activity of consciousness, not because of some physical or zoological fact.

Ultimately, it becomes apparent that Korsgaard, Oduncu, Schwarz, and Wilson beg the question. Wilson says that a child is a kind of thing that deserves respect, but she does not justify the focus on species rather than some other kind, and she does not explain why a thing's membership in a group is morally relevant. Oduncu says that embryos' genetic material makes them directly morally considerable without explaining why that natural fact should carry moral weight. Schwarz references the "capacity to function as a person" that all humans have, but he does not explain what it means for humans to have a capacity, especially when it is never developed in the majority of human beings. Korsgaard says that children will grow into rational adults, but she does not explain why a person's future moral status is relevant to its moral status *now*. Wood explicitly makes the connection between other kinds of prejudice and the speciesism at work in these sorts of arguments:

> To regard all humans as persons because they are members of our species seems no better than regarding as persons only those who share our nationality or religion or skin color. To argue that certain entities are persons because they are members of a rational species, when they are not in fact rational beings, is no better than arguing that children are already human adults because they belong to a species whose mature members are human adults.[40]

For Kant especially, having certain genes or being part of a taxonomic unit seems out of place. What is relevant is the humanity *in* the person, which is a characteristic that only some human beings have (G 429).

Before I continue, it is important to note that abandoning the biological standard of what counts as a person, as Kant does, makes the philosophical discussion of who has dignity much more complicated and much more charged. Defining the moral community becomes a political issue rather than what seems to be a more easily settled factual issue. The history of racism, colonialism, and sexism has made clear the moral dangers of separating persons from nonpersons. But the feminist movement has also challenged the entire strategy of appealing to biological facts as the foundation for political status. Noting the genetic differences between men and women implies nothing about the ways that their gender roles are defined in particular social and historical circumstances. Gender often preoccupies people in a way that one's biological characteristics do not. Similarly, when we distinguish humanity from humanness, we begin the crucial struggle for who is directly morally considerable. Kant appeals to rational end-setting, but as we are seeing, there are reasons to question whether his approach captures what it means when we as a community take someone to be a subject.

Another Common Strategy: The Argument from Potential

The appeal to natural kinds or natural development is perhaps most powerful when it is formulated as an appeal to potential. Opponents of abortion often emphasize that the fetus is a potential person in a way that, say, a rock or a dog is not. Rocks and dogs do not have the capacity for eventual personhood, but a fetus who is properly cared for will likely become a person one day, so (they claim) we ought to give it a special kind of moral consideration.

Sometimes Kant himself seems to hold this position. Kant says that all living things have species-specific "predispositions [*Anlage*]" that express themselves differently in different circumstances, much like the "germs" that give rise to different races (Ak 8:178–9). In the *Religion*, Kant defines the human being by its predispositions to animality, humanity, and personality (Rel 26–8). And he asserts that all human beings are persons (and have souls [LM 29:918]) from the moment of conception (MM 280; Ak 23:357), presumably because they have the psychological predispositions that will make them capable (eventually) of acting autonomously. Even though a person remains in a state of immaturity well into childhood, because "he has not yet mastered the use of his members or of his understanding," the child has been "endowed with freedom" and, assuming he is raised correctly, will become a moral agent (MM 280–1). This generates duties to the child and (it seems) to the fetus, not because the child and the fetus are rational agents, but because of their potential to achieve rational agency (because of their predispositions).

Before addressing the merits of this argument, it is important to recognize at the outset that potentiality is an ambiguous concept. It is true that a fetus eventually may become a person, but of course, not all fetuses will become persons. Complications during pregnancy, catastrophic interventions from without, medical malpractice, or defects in the organism itself – all of these things may upset the fetus's trajectory. Does a fetus that is less likely to survive the pregnancy have less potential than a "normal" fetus? Does it make sense to talk about degrees of potentiality? Since the rate of miscarriage among African American women is twice that of white women, is the fetus of an African American couple less of a potential person than the fetus of a white couple? This sounds absurd – and racist. But someone who appeals to a fetus's potential for personhood needs to specify what it means to have potential, a concept that is not as simple as it seems, if the argument is to get off the ground.

Those who appeal to potential seem to claim that all fetuses have potential, period. A rock does not have any potential, but every human fetus does. Speaking like this, though, misconstrues what we mean by potential, which seems to be a matter of degree rather than an all-or-nothing thing. In some sense, we all may become major league baseball players, but a person with more talent or better vision has more potential to become a major leaguer than I do. Is the bare possibility of becoming a person the same thing as having the potential to become a person? A dog could miraculously gain consciousness, but it is so unlikely that no one would say it has the potential for personhood. Or perhaps it has this potential, but it does not have any "real" or "natural" potential. Of course that just pushes the question back. When does something have real potential, as opposed to unreal potential (whatever that means)? Does a fetus still have natural potential if medical technology, an unnatural intervention, has to help it survive at some point? We may be able to give some specificity to the concept of potential personhood, but the prospects are not good.

Setting aside this problem, the appeal to a fetus's potential is probably the most common strategy for defending the fetus's moral worth. Although they are often conflated, there are two ways to understand the argument from potential: either the fetus ought to be respected because a particular outcome will be produced by means of it, an outcome that itself is valuable – this is a focus on future consequences – or the fetus itself is worthy of respect because it is the same being who will one day become a person, and thus has value because it is identical with that (future) subject.[41]

Wood takes the latter approach. As we saw in chapter 1, he rejects the idea that we can only have duties to persons. Some animals deserve direct moral consideration because, like us, they have preferences and satisfy their own desires. Although they are not rational, their capacities are related to rational nature in a way that distinguishes them from things that can be treated merely as a means. Fetuses do not engage in preference-satisfaction, but they are related to rational nature through their potential. Therefore, Wood says, they deserve respect:

> Honouring rational nature as an end in itself sometimes requires us to behave with respect toward nonrational beings if they bear the right relations to rational nature. Such relations . . . include having rational nature only potentially, or virtually, or having had it in the past, or having parts of it or necessary conditions of it.[42]

Once we reject the personification principle, Wood claims that Kantian ethics can justify direct moral duties to nonrational things that are enough like us to warrant our respect. This includes fetuses, children, and others who are the margins of moral considerability.[43]

The analysis of Wood's argument in chapter 1 revealed the shortcomings of this argumentative strategy. The fragments of rational nature are morally significant for Kant only when they in fact support moral agency. When they do not, as in the case of the fetus, then the thing is not directly considerable. The fetus is incapable of free activity, and thus is not a person, but only a potential person.

What is most relevant for this chapter is that, for Kant, the fetus's identity with the person it will become is not the kind of identity that is morally relevant – namely, self-consciousness over time. To be sure, the fetus will develop into a baby who will develop into a child who will develop into a person who is rational. The beings at different stages along this developmental pathway share DNA and have some of the same cells, but they do not have the same self-consciousness, because self-consciousness does not extend into the womb. In other words, the adult and the fetus may be genetically identical, but the two of them are not two points on one continuing self-consciousness. If, as Kant claims, a person is defined in an important way by having a unitary self-consciousness, then as the child develops self-consciousness, the child actually *becomes* a person, which it was not previously.

Furthermore, self-consciousness and moral responsibility constitute personhood, not the *capacity* to become a person with self-consciousness and moral responsibility. We cannot say that the fetus ought to be treated with respect because it will eventually become a person who is worthy of respect. This would be like saying that an acorn should be treated like an oak tree because it will grow into one, or that my son can command the armed forces because he is a potential president.[44] A thing's potential to become a person does not give it the dignity that persons have, so it does not have the humanity that we are obligated to respect by the categorical imperative. In short, having some relation to rational nature is not the same thing as having a rational nature, and it is the latter that makes someone worthy of direct moral consideration.

The second kind of appeal to a fetus's potential trades on what will happen if the fetus is allowed to develop. It is not that the fetus has worth now because it is a potential person, but it will have worth in the future, when it becomes a person. We ought to respect it now so that it will develop into a thing with absolute worth. Even on a cursory examination, however, this approach does not seem promising from a Kantian perspective. Appealing to the positive outcome of allowing a fetus to develop is consequentialist, whereas the formula of universal law demands rational consistency. Kant never appeals to what a thing may become, but only considers how an action affects existing rational beings. His position on masturbation is instructive here. A sperm could also be considered a potential person, in the sense that it may constitute (part of) a future person. Yet Kant never alludes to the loss of potential persons in his moral criticism of masturbation. Instead, he follows Thomas Aquinas and the Catholic Church in saying that masturbation contradicts the natural purpose of sexual desire, which is reproduction (MM 424–5).[45] We saw in chapter 6 that there are flaws in this argument. Masturbation is wrong only if someone becomes so obsessed with it that it thwarts the person's capacity to deliberate. In any event, neither the appeal to natural purposes nor the risk of stupefaction makes any reference to the potential life that is lost with wasted sperm. Masturbation violates a duty to oneself, not a duty to others – that is, the potential lives lost (MM 425).

This has clear implications for abortion. Having repeated abortions or having the procedure performed under unsafe conditions may endanger the health of the pregnant woman. In those cases, having an unnecessary abortion would amount to maiming oneself and thus undermining the woman's capacity to act (MM 422–3). Barring that, aborting a fetus neither contradicts the mother's natural impulse to self-preservation nor her own personhood. It does, of course, thwart the fetus's drive to preserve itself, which all living things have. But this by itself does not justify any moral obligations. If killing trees or cows is wrong, it is not because doing so disrupts their natural development. Similarly, there is nothing intrinsically immoral about thwarting the natural end of a fetus, which is also a nonrational being. The duty here is to the mother.

Someone may respond that abortion is wrong because there is a duty to future generations, which include conceived embryos. As noted in chapter 1, Kant does not require that an action's impact be specified by designating particular rational beings. Kant is not susceptible to Parfit's non-identity problem, where future generations are a kind of moving target and thus cannot be directly considered, because a maxim of environmental destruction is formulated as a lack of concern for an action's effect on others, whoever those others happen to be. This is why future generations are morally considerable for Kant: we can assume that some future people will be affected, even if we do not know the particular beings who are affected.

This reasoning does not imply anything about our treatment of fetuses because the choice to get an abortion is the choice to make it the case that there is no rational being to harm. With environmental damage, the harm is not done to potential beings. People who do not yet exist are harmed when they do exist, and it is that for which we would be morally culpable, even though the harm occurs many years after we damage the environment. By contrast, abortion ends the life of a living thing that is never a rational being but only a potential person. There is no future person to be harmed if the embryo is aborted. There is no moving target (so to speak), because there is no morally significant target at all.

The argument from potential gets us nowhere, and Kant himself does not appeal to potential in his defense of persons. Still, David Oderberg claims that, if we adopt personhood as the criterion of moral considerability, then our duties to a sleeping or temporarily comatose adult also depend on an appeal to potential – that is, to what he has the potential to become once he wakes up. Oderberg concludes that the appeal to personhood, including (presumably) Kant's approach, is susceptible to the same problems as the appeal to potential.[46]

Oderberg's objection fails, however, because he misconstrues what it means to be a person. Personhood need not be a genetic category in order to be relatively constant. Consciousness persists through waking and sleeping states, as does the capacity to choose rightly and to act dutifully. The capacity to choose rightly means that the person may potentially choose rightly, but the capacity itself is not mere potential (as it is with a fetus). The ability to reason does not turn off and on as we sleep and wake, get drunk and sober up, act stupidly and regain our composure. An adult who is sleeping is a rational being who is momentarily incapacitated, but a fetus is not a rational being at all. The fetus is a human being who may become rational – that is, the fetus may one day develop the ability to set ends – which hinges on an appeal to potential. A sleeping adult has that ability, actually rather than potentially, even though he is not using it while he is sleeping.[47]

Do We Have Indirect Duties to Fetuses?

Even though the potential personhood of fetuses does not warrant direct duties to them, it would be too hasty to conclude that their potentiality is completely irrelevant in deciding how we ought to treat them. It is conceivable that our actions toward potential persons could affect our moral attitude toward actual persons – indirectly, because of how abortion affects our character. Former President George W. Bush opposed abortion and stem cell research in order to foster what he called a "culture of life," the implication being that, were abortion to be permissible, we would become more callous, develop less respect for one another, and become a less "hospitable society."[48] This claim has been made explicitly by anti-abortion groups, the Catholic Church, and philosopher Carl Wellman, who says that disregarding the potential or hypothetical desires of the unborn reflects an underlying hard-heartedness that undermines the essential conditions of sociability.[49] Fetuses are vulnerable members of society that deserve our protection, lest we devalue human life in general.[50]

Were it true that abortion erodes our moral virtue, then we would have an indirect duty to protect fetuses, just as we have indirect duties not to be unnecessarily cruel toward animals or destructive of nature. A last man who decimates the natural world manifests a sick personality. The same would seem to be true of someone who thoughtlessly destroys a growing thing that will, if left alone, become a person. We ought to be caring and respectful people, so the injunction against abortion would be derived from the duty to ourselves.

The problem is that, although we have ample evidence that cruelty toward animals negatively affects our character,[51] there is no evidence to support the claim that accepting the legality or moral permissibility of abortion, having an abortion, or performing an abortion hardens one to the suffering and death of actual persons. In fact, there is evidence to the contrary. According to the Centers for Disease Control and Prevention, the number of legal abortions performed in the United States doubled in the six years following *Roe v. Wade*, from 615,831 in 1973 to 1,251,921 in 1979.[52] There was no concomitant rise in violence by women, no rash of abortion doctors turning into maniacs. There is no correlation between the rate of violent crime in a given country and the number of abortions carried out there, at least not the kind of correlation that would be relevant for Kant.[53] Furthermore, the American Psychological Association has found no evidence to support the claim that having an abortion causes mental health problems.[54] If abortion does not affect our character or our attitude toward persons, then we do not have indirect duties to fetuses. Abortion does not hamper our attempts to develop a virtuous character, so Kant cannot condemn abortion on those grounds.

There is a related Kantian argument to be made against abortion, however. In chapter 2 I talked about the need to live in harmony with natural purposes, and in chapter 6 I remarked that procreation is, according to Kant, one of the natural purposes of sex. Getting an abortion seems contrary to the natural purpose of reproduction, and therefore seems wrong – not simply because it is unnatural, but because it thwarts nature's purpose of producing rational beings with absolute worth. An abortion does not allow this "ultimate end" to be achieved (CJ 426).

The demand that we must reproduce does not imply that every person must reproduce, however, and it does not imply that every fetus must be born. Drawing on the environmental analogy, a healthy ecosystem probably is not affected by cutting down one tree. Similarly, the continuing community of rational beings is not affected by even thousands of abortions. In chapter 6, I claimed that there is no moral obligation for any one person to reproduce, given that the human race is growing at a healthy rate. To be sure, my maxim must be universalizable, but the maxim must consider the circumstances. A maxim to abort a fetus as the human race risks extinction may be morally problematic, but a maxim to abort a fetus under normal circumstances, when we are more at risk of overpopulation than mass extinction, is permissible.

Of course, it is possible that aborting a fetus may amount to wronging a person. For example, if a woman plans to have the baby but someone induces a miscarriage against her will – say, in a violent attack – then that person does something wrong. Or perhaps a woman has an abortion out of spite, in order to lash out at the would-be father. In both cases aborting the fetus is morally impermissible, but in neither case is someone violating a duty to the fetus. There is no such duty. Instead, because the fetus is not a person, the wrongdoers have harmed the only people involved here: the would-be mother or the would-be father. Killing a fetus under these circumstances is like breaking a chair that someone else owns, a chair for which the person really has a lot of affection.

There is neither a direct duty to the fetus nor an indirect duty to ourselves through the fetus. Any indirect duty we have to protect the fetus applies only in unusual circumstances, when we have a special commitment to other persons who would be harmed by an abortion. In normal cases when a woman chooses to terminate the pregnancy, there is no moral issue at all. According to Kant's practical philosophy, what the woman does is as morally insignificant as her choice of what to wear in the morning or what to have for lunch.

No Fetuses, No Children

As I noted earlier, the same criteria that exclude fetuses from moral consideration also exclude human beings who are, so to speak, at the margins of personhood – those with developmental disorders, those whose cognitive abilities are in decline due to dementia, or anyone else who is intellectually immature in the sense that he or she is not a responsible agent.[55] Newborn infants are a paradigm case of people to whom, it seems, we should have direct moral obligations, but whose capacities are not substantially beyond what they were just prior to birth. There is a lot of continuity between the late-term fetus and the newborn, so the two cannot be strictly distinguished for the purposes of moral evaluation. A number of philosophers have recognized this: when we limit the class of persons in a way that excludes fetuses, it seems that we also cease to have duties to young children.

According to Kant, rational and nonrational beings are different in kind, yet becoming a rational being is a process, and children become persons over time. First of all, a newborn has no ego-boundaries that would make a unitary consciousness possible. Kant says that children have no self-consciousness and thus are incapable of experience, "but merely . . . scattered perceptions not yet united under the concept of an object" (A 128). Furthermore, no one would claim that a 1-month-old baby is morally responsible for what she does; she does not suddenly become a moral agent the moment she exits the birth canal. Kant explicitly excludes children from the class of moral agents, comparing them to other people who are incapable of acting on the basis of reasons: "in some cases . . . [a human being has] no power of free choice, e.g., in the most tender childhood, or when he is insane, and in deep sadness, which is however also a kind of insanity" (LM 28:255; see also LM 29:917, where he says that "children, idiots, and the wholly stupid" are "neither morally worthy nor unworthy"). Young children are more like animals than human beings, in that their power of choice is necessitated by stimuli rather than self-determined on the basis of principles – *arbitrium brutum* as opposed to *arbitrium liberum* (CPR

A534/B562; LM 28:254–6). Therefore, like fetuses, young children lack the qualities requisite for personhood.

Kant himself recognizes that personhood is a gradual achievement rather than a state of being. The ability to determine our maxims and act on the ends we set for ourselves, especially our ability to act purely for the sake of duty, is something that we become capable of through the process of education. Unlike Locke, who says that education helps us to develop a preexisting capacity to reason,[56] Kant claims that our animal nature becomes human nature through the educational process. Discipline teaches the child to deny his inclinations when necessary, and instruction with moral examples teaches him how he should act (MM 477–85; Ak 9:437–99). Of course, Kant confronts an important paradox here: How can a child be educated to be free? The child cannot be taught to do the right thing with punishments or rewards. The resulting actions would not be done for the sake of duty. Regardless of how Kant resolves this, it is clear that a child has to learn to act autonomously. The child becomes a person gradually and thus acquires dignity over time. Does that mean that, like fetuses, young children who have not yet been properly educated can be used merely as means?

The Need for a Pragmatic Concept of Personhood

In another context (a criticism of Henry Sidgwick), Korsgaard cautions against taking a pragmatic concept to be metaphysically precise, and she mentions how this mistake has been made often in the abortion debate. "Rationality, intelligence, and self-control are themselves matters of degree," she claims, so any attempt to distinguish adults from children is bound to be culturally specific and largely pragmatic: "any setting of a certain amount of independence as a criterion of personhood will be arbitrary."[57] Based on the inexactness of the distinction between persons and nonpersons, some people have concluded that abortion must be morally condemned. Because we have no metaphysically precise definition of personhood, we are faced with a choice: *either* we protect only fully functioning adults and allow the killing of children and the mentally disabled, *or* we protect beings across the full spectrum of personhood, including those with only the potential for personhood. According to Korsgaard, however, recognizing that pragmatic concepts are often necessary, even in moral debates, may help us to avoid a line-drawing fallacy and to examine these issues without some self-evident, metaphysically precise concept.

Kant does say that a child is not merely an animal being – that is, "not merely a worldly being but a citizen of the world" (MM 280). The child is not a citizen of the state, of course, since he cannot consent to the law by which he agrees to respect others' freedom. Still, he is someone for whom we ought "to cultivate a disposition of reciprocity" (MM 473).[58] This is Kant's explanation of what is wrong with infanticide.

The problem is that Kant's argument is circular: we have reciprocal duties to someone if and only if he is a person, yet Kant seems to be saying that the child is a person because we have a duty to respect him. What is at issue is whether the child *is* in fact a person, someone to whom we *can* have duties. The child is clearly human, but his species is morally irrelevant. *Why*, then, can he never be used merely as a means? To answer this, Kant would have to demonstrate that the child is a person. But the child lacks at least some of the morally relevant characteristics of personhood, so asserting that he is "a citizen of the world" begs the question.

This seems to encourage a slide down the slippery slope. Korsgaard recognizes that the capacity to set ends is not a natural attribute for which we could ever have theoretical evidence. I am practically justified in believing that I am free, since my freedom follows from the fact of reason, but the personhood of others is especially problematic because I cannot sense their feeling of moral constraint. This is where Korsgaard makes her own fallacious inference:

> we ascribe [freedom] to other persons not because we have theoretical evidence that they have it but because it is a duty to do so. Respect for humanity in the persons of others demands that we attribute to them the capacity for free choice and action, regardless of how they are acting.[59]

Korsgaard says that I am justified in believing the person is free because I have moral obligations to him – even though I have (direct) obligations to someone if and only if that person is free. The question of his humanity is primary here and cannot be derived from a moral duty.[60] However, as Kant's philosophy of education demonstrates and Korsgaard insists, "what we find in the world is a continuum of more or less imperfectly rational beings."[61] There is not some specific moment when the light of the moral law breaks upon us and we become responsible. The question then becomes: Can Kant handle a pragmatic concept of personhood?

The answer to this question seems to be no. Kant does not have the philosophical tools to talk about degrees of personhood as, for example, the utilitarian can talk about degrees of sentience. Even though we can act in ways that are more or less rational, closer to or farther from the ideal of a holy will, someone cannot have a *fraction* of self-consciousness or *somewhat* of an ability to set ends. Someone either is or is not autonomous, and either can or cannot be used merely as a means. It does not make sense that something could *sort of* set its own ends or *mostly* be treated as an end in itself. When Korsgaard says that there is "a continuum of more or less imperfectly rational beings," she is confusing two senses of "rational": there is a difference between choosing to act rightly much of the time and being capable of responsible action at all. Kant can certainly accommodate a continuum of moral saintliness, but he cannot make sense of beings who are partially responsible for what they do.

Korsgaard is right that we should always err on the side of respect, treating people who are not fully rational as if they are.[62] On what basis, though, would Kant consider them to be persons in the first place? How do we know when to hedge our bets? That they share our genes or look like us is morally irrelevant for Kant. What is relevant is their humanity, their capacity to decide what their purposes will be. Kant has to conclude not only that we cannot know where our duties actually lie, but that, if the line between person and nonperson cannot be drawn, then our moral duties are in principle unable to be determined. Because personhood is an all-or-nothing proposition, a metaphysical concept would have to be established. When it comes to personhood, however, this is impossible. And it is impossible for the very reasons that Kant himself gives: children become rational agents only through the process of education, over time.

At this point in the book, we can understand that Wood's and Korsgaard's approaches to animals are attempts to make sense of a continuum of beings with rationality and fragments of rationality, or beings with different degrees of consciousness. Wood and Korsgaard are trying to transform Kant's metaphysically precise concept of humanity into a pragmatic concept. Wood talks about two different kinds of person: persons in the strict sense and persons in the extended sense, the latter of which are directly morally considerable, but have a *"lesser* status."[63] In fact, Wood's taxonomy of morally considerable beings includes at least four classes: full persons (rational adults), lesser persons (children), potential persons (fetuses), and those with the infrastructure of humanity (animals).[64]

It seems that some higher animals have the capacity to be self-aware, to evaluate their actions, to feel shame, and to express (second-order) preferences about their immediate inclinations.[65] They are not fully autonomous, in the sense that they probably have no conception of the moral law, but they do seem to have the roots of moral agency, beyond the mere awareness of and pursuit of first-order preferences that Wood and Korsgaard emphasize. Even if only persons are morally considerable, some animals would be part of the moral community, and we would have direct duties to them, were we to have a compelling pragmatic concept of personhood.

It makes sense that Wood and Korsgaard would try to develop a more complex picture of those to whom we have direct moral obligations, since our discussion of abortion has begun to reveal the problems with Kant's less sophisticated approach. However, using Kant's philosophical vocabulary and metaphysical assumptions to construct a pragmatic concept of personhood is misguided. As we saw in chapter 1, for Kant the infrastructure of rationality is valuable only when it does support a fully rational being; and as we saw earlier in this chapter, Wood's claim that potential persons have "the right relation to rational nature" fails because it is not the *relation* to rational nature that gives one dignity, but the *having* of rational nature.[66] Wood is resisting the implications of Kant's theoretical assumptions while continuing to assert that rationality is the criterion of moral worth, and that turns out to be an unsustainable position. One cannot derive a pragmatic concept of personhood from a metaphysically precise concept of rational nature, the latter of which is central to Kant's practical philosophy.

If Kant's approach fails to give us a broad enough definition of moral community and also fails to provide us with a continuum of personhood, how do we affirm the direct moral considerability of animals, fetuses, children, women(!), and those who are losing their mental faculties? Korsgaard herself recognizes that the distinction between fully functioning adults and less capable beings such as children and the disabled "depend[s] on features external to the persons in question – such as the kinds of work and the kinds of care that are available in the societies and cultures in which the distinctions are employed."[67] The introduction of cultural variability lends credence to the idea that moral considerability depends on being cared for and recognized as such by others, a conclusion that we also reached at the end of the previous chapter, and one that is more consistent with a theory such as communitarianism than with Kant's practical philosophy.

The Specter of Infanticide

If we hold fast to Kant's conception of personhood, both fetuses and children seem not to be morally considerable. Some authors have accepted this conclusion, that the permissibility of abortion would imply that infanticide is also permissible. For example, Jeffrey Reiman claims that neither fetuses nor very young children consciously value the continuation of their lives, so they lack the capacity that would make them directly morally considerable.[68] Michael Tooley and Joel Feinberg say that fetuses and newborn infants lack an interest in their continuing existence.[69] Mary Anne Warren admits that, like fetuses, young children do not have the essential traits of personhood, such as reasoning and the capacity for complex communication.[70] None of them say that children deserve direct moral consideration. Instead, we have indirect obligations to children because of our obligations to people who are related to children in the appropriate way. Reiman says that we ought to respect children out of the respect we have for those who love them, and Warren says that killing infants would deprive others who want to raise the children, or that it would violate our desire to keep them alive.[71] Infanticide wrongs adults who take an interest in the children, but the children themselves cannot be wronged.

This is a strange conclusion, and its strangeness should be recognized: if I break an infant's arm, I am hurting the parents; if I kill a child, I violate the interests of the parents and society. We may concede to Kant that we only have indirect duties to animals, but human infants seem to occupy a place in the moral community that animals do not. As the fetus grows inside the woman, she develops a relationship with it that continues after its birth, even if there is no rational communication or morally weighty kind of mutual recognition. Outside of philosophy journals, the idea that children are not directly morally considerable would seem absurd, even among those who staunchly support reproductive rights. Of course, parents are harmed when their child is harmed, but the idea that *only* they (and not the child) are harmed ignores whose life has been cut short. If infanticide wrongs the child as well – and again, this seems like something that an adequate moral theory must explain – then Kant must show how children are directly morally considerable even though they lack self-consciousness, humanity, and responsibility.

Kant's Appeal to God

Kant does claim that children cannot be treated merely as things and that we owe to children most of the duties that we owe to fully rational beings. Because children are not rational in the requisite sense, however, Kant cannot appeal to their dignity as the basis of our moral obligations to them. Instead, he appeals to divine purposes. The parents' duty to the child derives from the fact that the physical production of an autonomous being is inexplicable: "it is impossible to form a concept of the production of a being endowed with freedom through a physical operation" (MM 280). When I produce an object such as a chair, I can destroy it because it is merely a thing that belongs to me. But Kant says that a free being must be at once attributable to the parents – since they are the ones who, without the child's consent, brought her into the world – *and* attributable to God. The parents made the physical being, but God made the child capable of rationality. Because God is a supersensible being who is not subject to the category of causality, a child's creation as a free being by God is at least possible, since the child's actions would not follow necessarily from that initial act of creation (MM 280n). Therefore, the child has an "innate" right to be cared for by her parents because she has been entrusted to them by God. The child's capacity to obligate us is not "acquired" through the process of maturation that would seem to make her a person in the sense that Kant earlier defined it (MM 280).

Here it becomes even clearer why abortion is a particularly problematic issue for Kant, and why relatively little has been written on Kant and abortion in the secondary literature. Kantian ethics is well equipped to consider such things as suicide, false promising, self-improvement, and nonbeneficence – cases where some rational agent has duties to himself or other rational agents. However, Kant is unprepared to deal with the abortion issue because it involves something that gradually *becomes* a person over time. Possible objects of moral consideration either have absolute worth or they do not; there is no continuum of worth when we are dealing with dignity. Dignity is absolute and incomparable, as opposed to price, which is on a scale of relative value (G 434–5). The fact that Kant cannot handle the human being as a changing entity leads him to appeal to God as a kind of moral *deus ex machina*, bailing him out of the uncomfortable implications of his strict distinction between rational beings who warrant moral consideration and nonrational beings who warrant none (or at best, indirect duties).

If a child's potential for personhood cannot be attributed to the biological processes involved in human reproduction, then we are obligated to respect it as something that has been entrusted to us. If this is true, then the same can be said of the fetus. Kant claims as much: the unborn child is also a person for the purpose of assessing blame for its death. Specifically, Kant says that when a pregnant woman kills herself, she not only commits a crime against her own person, but against another person, her fetus, as well (MM 422).[72] The fetus meets none of the conditions that would make it an appropriate subject of moral obligation, yet we have an obligation not to kill it because its status as a potential person depends on God.

This appeal to God gives us a sense of how Kant is using *"Personen"* when he says that children are persons and that, when a pregnant woman kills herself, she commits a crime against the fetus. In his analysis of suicide in the *Metaphysics of Morals*, Kant iterates the claim made in the *Groundwork* that suicide amounts to using oneself merely as a means (G 429; MM 422–3). Killing oneself is wrong because the person is a moral agent and would be undermining her capacity to act merely for the sake of promoting happiness (by ending her pain). Kant also says that suicide violates the person's duty to others, because she has obligations to her spouse, her children, and her fellow citizens (MM 422). But how can killing a fetus be a moral crime if the fetus is not a person? Kant adds that killing oneself is also a violation of one's duty to God: a person's suicide can be regarded "finally even as a violation of duty to God, as his abandoning the post assigned him in the world without having been called away from it" (MM 422; see also LE 375). Kant's only rationale for claiming that a pregnant woman's suicide constitutes two murders rather than one thus seems to be that the creation of a rational or potentially rational being is attributable not to us but to God, and that we have a duty to God not to kill the fetus. We have no direct obligation to the fetus itself, only an indirect duty to God through the fetus.

Kant's approach is not anachronistic. In the early modern period, motherhood had become infused with religious significance. Pregnant women were described as being "of blessed body (*gesegneten Leibes*)," and "work metaphors (labour pains as *weibliche Arbeit* or the *zum Kind schaffen*) turned the process of giving birth into a kind of special female mission she was expected to fulfill."[73] Bearing children was the woman's natural purpose, given to her by the creator of all things. Kant makes the obvious moral inference: ending a life that will eventually become a rational being amounts to a violation of our duty to God, who has given the mother a "mission" and assigned the fetus a certain "post."

Kant's appeal to God prefigures the contemporary pro-life argument that an abortion is morally different from a miscarriage because only God has the authority over life and death. Miscarriages (spontaneous abortions) are acceptable because they are naturally caused, not deliberately induced. Like Kant's blanket condemnation of masturbation, however, this relies on a particular understanding of natural or divine purposes that cannot be frustrated. It is true that the value of the fetus depends on its eventually becoming a rational being, but we only have obligations to it now, when it is not a rational being, because God has created it with that purpose in mind. We saw earlier why its potential personhood is morally irrelevant. What is relevant is that the fetus's trajectory is divinely ordained.

Such an appeal to natural law is subject to a series of well-known objections, most notably that gesturing at natural or divine purposes does not by itself have any normative weight for us. The fact/value distinction is important here: even if we could identify some purpose that is given to us by God, we can still meaningfully ask whether we ought to have that purpose. This is one of Kant's primary advances over other moral philosophies. Attempts to derive moral duties from the principle of happiness (Epicurus, Francis Hutcheson, and John Stuart Mill) or from the principle of perfection (the Stoics and Christian Wolff) are heteronomous (G 441–3; CPrR 39–41). They depend on some object of the will that the agent is obligated to promote, yet promoting perfection or happiness cannot constrain rational beings universally and with absolute necessity. Instead, they can form only hypothetical imperatives: *If* you will perfection or happiness, *then* you ought to do certain things (G 444). While the categorical imperative is self-legislated – this explains why we are necessarily bound by it, because it is a condition of rational willing itself – an appeal to natural or moral feeling, or even our rational determination of perfection, would constrain the will on the basis of something that is legislated from without, by our inclinations or by God: "a foreign impulse would give the law to [the will] by means of the subject's nature" (G 444). Referring to God's purposes to condemn suicide or abortion is very un-Kantian.

In addition, Kant repeats Socrates' argument in the *Euthyphro* that there can be no explanation or justification for something being wrong if it is wrong only because God says so. In his discussion of suicide, Kant says:

> what, then, does the abominable nature of this act consist in? With all such duties, one must not look for the ground in any prohibition on the part of God, for suicide is not abominable because God has forbidden it; on the contrary, God has forbidden it because it is abominable. If it were otherwise, suicide would be abominable only by God's prohibition, and then I would not know why He should have forbidden it, if it were not abominable in itself. (LE 342; see also CPrR 128–30; Rel 3–6; MM 443–4, 487–8; Ak 19:148 [R 6753], 19:150 [R 6759])

In the context of abortion, we can always ask whether it is right for the fetus to remain at the "post" to which it has been assigned by God. Aside from the important question of how we know what God wants, responding that "God commands it" is not a compelling reason, because we can always ask why God has deemed something to be wrong, or why we should do what God wants us to do anyway. Kant's ethics answers both questions by deriving the categorical imperative as a formal constraint on rational willing itself – that is, by showing that in acting at all we are bound to act on universalizable maxims. We do our duty not because God says so, but because, rationally, we ought to.

God's purposes are not proper moral constraints unless they are independently required of us by the moral law. And the moral law dictates only that we respect humanity in ourselves and others. But that means that we can have no direct moral obligations to a number of beings whom we typically consider to be deserving of respect. Even if no metaphysically precise line can be drawn, it is clear that fetuses certainly, newborns probably, and young children possibly have no self-consciousness as Kant understands it – that is, they have no ability to attribute any experience to themselves as unitary subjects. They also have no capacity for rational choice and no responsibility for their actions. And if they have none of these characteristics, then we have neither a perfect duty not to kill them nor an imperfect duty of beneficence to keep them alive.

Problematic Implications of the Appeal to Personhood

Consequently, Kant is faced with a dilemma regarding abortion that confronts many other liberal philosophers: *either* his approach to personhood allows for abortion but also fails to rule out intuitively wrong actions such as infanticide, *or* it condemns abortion with an appeal to natural law that even Kant himself rejects. This impasse does not face a position such as utilitarianism, where what is morally relevant is a being's interests and preferences, or its capacity for pain and pleasure. The fetus's ability to have a life of potential pleasures after the point of viability may justify the restriction of abortion to the first and second trimesters, when respecting the right of the woman over her own body could (arguably) produce more good than protecting fetuses whose ability to feel pain is at least questionable. In any event, whether a fetus is sentient at various points during gestation could in principle be settled by medical science in a way that a being's rational capacity could not. We can examine how developed the fetus's nervous system is or how it behaves in response to stimuli at various points in its maturation, and this will determine how much weight to assign its pleasures and pains in a utilitarian calculus. Utilitarians also take into account the pleasure that will be experienced by a potential person if it is brought to term. If we assume that the child would become a person whose life on the whole would have more pleasure than pain, and if that life would not adversely affect the general population, then its potential personhood also enters into the calculus. Hare and other utilitarians can consider the potential interests of fetuses, but Kant, who appeals to a thing's capacity to reason rather than its interests, cannot.[74]

Given the problematic assumptions of Kant's moral philosophy, there are many other casuistical questions that it seems unable to settle. To return to an example from chapter 2, imagine that a woman uses harmful drugs recreationally while she is pregnant and that her behavior has a long-term impact on the child's capacity to reason after he is born. By undermining her own health, she is guilty of using herself merely as a means for pleasure. Is she also guilty of harming the child – the drugs have an effect on him eventually – or is she responsible only for damaging a fetus, which is a nonperson? Like long-term environmental damage and the hypothetical bomb in Times Square that I mentioned in chapter 2, this seems wrong because it harms a person, even though there is a time lag between the act and the effect. However, if the woman aborted the fetus after it was harmed by the drugs but before its birth, would that erase the moral guilt? Is there such a thing as potential moral guilt for a maxim that has already been chosen and an action that has already been taken? Would aborting the unborn victim (if there is such a thing) change how we formulate the woman's maxim and evaluate her drug use? If the fetus were so mentally disabled that it remains nonrational throughout its postnatal life, would the mother effectively make it such that she has no obligations either to the fetus or to the person it becomes, or would she be guilty of debilitating a rational being, even though such a being never comes to exist? These are important moral questions and are generally perplexing, but Kant's approach generates conflicting answers.

Our Kantian Heritage: Trouble with Those at the Margins of Personhood

Revising Kant's conception of personhood is not an option, since applying the categorical imperative depends on strictly distinguishing rational end-setters from those who are moved merely by impulse. Any moral concern for nonrational beings such as animals, fetuses, PVS patients, or even the severely mentally handicapped can, for Kant, only be understood indirectly, in terms of how our mistreatment of them affects rational beings. Kantians may be willing to accept that implication generally, especially when it comes to animals. But if such an approach leads to a general devaluation of human life, including the lives of fetuses, children, and perhaps even women, who have traditionally been considered less rational (including by Kant himself), then Kant's philosophy itself seems morally degenerative.

More importantly, how Kant frames the issue is emblematic of a larger failure within contemporary debates about abortion. We have not progressed much since the early modern period, when the question was still when the fetus was said to have a "rational soul," and even whether women are rational beings or merely the producers of rational beings. Opponents of abortion claim that, if we condone abortions, we conceive of fetuses as mere things, even though they are rights-bearers like other persons. Supporters of abortion rights say that, if we prohibit abortions, we instrumentalize women, conceiving of them as nothing but vessels for the production of children. Both sides presuppose that personhood is an either/or proposition – fetuses either are or are not persons – and that the woman and the fetus ought to be treated in ways that are appropriate given the facts of the matter. All of us are assuming a metaphysically precise concept of personhood. Even utilitarianism, which allows for a continuum of sentience or preference-satisfaction, and thus seems to have a pragmatic concept, does so at the cost of personhood generally. It considers a developed fetus as it does other people: as a thing, merely a locus of pains and pleasures. None of these approaches can account for the central fact of abortion: pregnancy highlights the permeability of the boundary between subjects and non-subjects. That is, the abortion issue frustrates our habit of reasoning in terms of being rather than becoming.

Abortion is such a difficult issue because we seem unable to make sense of a pragmatic concept of personhood. We tend to glorify a kind of static maturity – the rational, fully functioning adult – in contrast to forms of impairment and degeneration that handicap the very young and the very old. Aging persons and emerging persons lack what we consider to be full personhood, so they prompt a number of moral dilemmas for us about proper medical treatment, physician-assisted suicide, and abortion.

Perhaps in part because of Kant's legacy, we cannot extricate ourselves from the binary opposition that has no room for fetuses. Fetuses seem to be the limiting case, the place at which personhood and thinghood blur together. In many ways, how we understand fetuses is symbolic of how we understand humanity in general. Part of why the abortion issue is so fraught for us, while it was not for Kant, is that the scientific theory and cultural evolution of the last two hundred years have made us profoundly uneasy about whether we are naturally or divinely imbued with personhood. If we are merely more complex animals, then it is difficult to understand what makes us distinctive. Given this anxiety, our inclination is to claim that persons are defined by their nonnatural or nonobjective traits – and the two sides of the debate tend to emphasize the subjectivity of either the woman or the fetus. But this gets us nowhere.

A more productive attempt at resolving the abortion issue would reject this binarism. In order to make any progress, we first must recognize the fundamental continuity between persons and nonpersons, humans and animals, adults and children. Within this more complex taxonomy, determining the kind of thing something is would not be the starting point for determining our moral obligations. There are a number of promising alternatives. For example, Emmanuel Levinas explains how we become obligated simply by encountering the face of the other. My extreme passivity is already an ethical responding and precludes my domestication of the other as simply another being (like me).[75] Care ethicists such as Carol Gilligan and Nel Noddings conceive of the moral agent as embedded in relationships with others that shape my most basic reasoning about moral issues. Because I identify my own good with the good of others and I take on their ends as my own, I do not conceive of myself as one rights-bearer among many, but as part of a web of humanity.[76] Finally, communitarians such as Michael Sandel and Charles Taylor claim that personal identity is essentially defined by our relationships with others. Moral reasoning depends on a community that provides us with a range of options and a way of deciding among them that make individual freedom possible in the first place.[77] All three of these approaches face problems of their own: how specific moral obligations are ultimately justified is problematic for Levinas, and care ethicists and communitarians risk an unsustainable ethical relativism. However, these perspectives enrich our moral attunement to dimensions of reproductive issues that are neglected or distorted by traditional ethical accounts, by claiming that the primary object of moral consideration is not the rational individual.

And so we return to Hegel and the idea that ethics is about engaging others in a social context. We become persons by recognizing one another as persons, and we participate in an ethical life (*Sittlichkeit*) rather than merely confronting one another as particular subjects who hold ourselves to what reason requires of us individually. Like Kant, Hegel himself never wrote about abortion, but Loren Lomasky has taken up the rights of newborns with reference to social relationships, a method that is much more promising than the endless debates over personhood and potential personhood. According to Lomasky, personhood does not matter, either for the fetus or the child. What matters is the child's inclusion in the moral community by virtue of its recognition by others, its social position as "an identifiable and reidentifiable individual that can thereby elicit responses as a unique object of concern."[78] The ultrasound when the child's sex is determined is one way in which the fetus begins to develop a kind of particularity in the minds of its parents. As the fetus develops, the woman attributes characteristics to it: it is a restless child, a night owl, or a music lover. The parents name the child and call the newborn by that name – all of these events are important landmarks in his or her gradual entrance into the moral community. While Kant focuses on a person's self-identification over time through consciousness, Lomasky talks instead about something's identification by others.

This is different from the approaches of Reiman, Tooley, Feinberg, and Warren, who argue that we have indirect duties to children because of other people's attachment to them or that we ought to respect children because of the fact that they will someday develop actual interests.[79] Lomasky's claim is much more fundamental. According to Lomasky, the child herself *is* a rights-bearer, in the present, because of her relation to others. Lomasky is not continuing the atomistic conception of personhood that evaluates the qualities of each individual – rationality, sentience, self-consciousness, or whatever – in isolation from other people. This is what forces those who condemn infanticide to find some agent, some conscious being, or some person with interests to whom we owe duties indirectly, through the child – be it the child's parents or the person whom the child will one day become. If it is true that a child who is harmed or killed is herself wronged, then we must devise a different way of approaching moral considerability. We have direct obligations to the child because she stands in morally significant relations to others. Breaking a child's arm wrongs the child, not only the parents and not God. Claiming that we have direct moral obligations to children because we recognize them as worthy of respect amounts to a repudiation of Kant's criteria for what counts as a morally considerable being.

Kant overlooks the ways in which subjectivity is a relational phenomenon. Kant is not attending to the immediate experience of many pregnant women: the emerging personhood of the fetus as it matures in the womb, and the woman's growing attachment to it as it develops. For Kant, the woman is valued primarily because she is a carrier of a potentially rational being – she is doing God's work – even though she is also, incidentally, a rational being herself. Seeing the woman as a person in relation to something that is gradually becoming a person is a more woman-centered approach. Again, Kant's cultural prejudices shape his moral theory, and they are not easily accommodated when we try to apply his practical philosophy to such a crucial issue in applied ethics.

Fully developing an alternative to Kantian ethics would go beyond the scope of this chapter. I mention Hegel, Lomasky, and others only to suggest that making any progress on the abortion issue requires us to move beyond the idea that personhood is some property that is either possessed or not possessed, a Kantian assumption that has led to the argumentative stalemate over abortion that continues to plague us. Instead, we must think about the broader context in which we engage with one another as persons. Hegel, not Kant, gives us the philosophical framework to do this.

Notes

1   For a thorough survey of abortion in ancient Greece and Rome, see Konstantinos Kapparis, *Abortion in the Ancient World* (London: Duckworth, 2002).

2   Jean Gray Platt et al., "Special Project: Survey of Abortion Law," *Arizona State Law Journal* 67 (1980): 67–216 (p. 87).

3   Following Aristotle, Thomas Aquinas distinguished between early- and late-term fetuses for the purposes of assessing blame for abortion. See Aquinas, *Summa Theologica*, trans. T. C. O'Brien (New York: McGraw-Hill, 1964–74), Q I, q118, a2, and Q II-II, q64, a8. The Catholic Church only changed its position in 1869, when Pope Pius IX removed this distinction from canon law and claimed that the embryo is ensouled at the moment of conception.

4   For a brief history of abortion in early modern Europe, see Londa Schiebinger, *Plants and Empire: Colonial Bioprospecting in the Atlantic World* (Cambridge, Mass.: Harvard University Press, 2004), 113–28. For a detailed history of abortion laws, see Platt, "Special Project: Survey of Abortion Law."

5   Ulinka Rublack, "The Public Body: Policing Abortion in Early Modern Germany," in *Gender Relations in German History: Power, Agency, and Experience from the Sixteenth to the Twentieth Century*, ed. Lynn Abrams and Elizabeth Harvey (London: University of London Press, 1996), 57–79 (p. 60).

6   Louis Lewin, *Die Fruchtabtreibung durch Gifte und Andere Mittel: Ein Handbuch für Ärzte, Juristen, Politiker, Nationalökonomen* (Berlin: Stilke,

1925), and Larissa Leibrick-Plehn, *Hexenkräuter oder Arznei: Die Abtreibungsmittel im 16. und 17. Jahrhundert* (Stuttgart: Wissenschaftliche Verlagsgesellschaft, 1992).

7   See Rublack, "Public Body."

8   R. M. Hare, "A Kantian Approach to Abortion," in *Essays on Bioethics* (Oxford: Oxford University Press, 1996), 168–84, and Harry J. Gensler, "A Kantian Argument against Abortion," *Philosophical Studies* 49, no. 1 (1986): 83–98.

9   Hare, "A Kantian Approach to Abortion," 173–4, 177–8, 181, and Gensler, "A Kantian Argument against Abortion," 90. Hare's interpretation is skewed by the fact that he believes deontological ethics and utilitarianism are compatible (172–3). He relies primarily on the fact that the person's interests (rather than his will) would be frustrated were he to be aborted: "I value my existence, not for its own sake, but for the sake of the good things that happen to me, which could not happen if I did not exist" (173–4). See also R. M. Hare, "Abortion and the Golden Rule," *Philosophy and Public Affairs* 4, no. 3 (spring 1975): 201–22. This passage, with Hare imagining that he is the fetus, seems to confirm Marilyn Frye's analysis that many philosophers condemn abortion because they sympathize with the (male) fetus rather than the woman who is carrying it. See Frye, "Some Reflections on Separatism and Power," in *The Politics of Reality: Essays in Feminist Theory* (Berkeley: Crossing, 1983), 95–109.

10   John Rawls, "Themes in Kant's Moral Philosophy," in *Kant's Transcendental Deductions: The Three "Critiques" and the "Opus Postumum"*, ed. Eckart Förster (Stanford, Calif.: Stanford University Press, 1989), 81–113.

11   According to Christine Korsgaard's "Practical Contradiction Interpretation" of the formula of universal law, a maxim is morally impermissible if, when universalized, I cannot achieve the intended purpose of my action (*Creating the Kingdom of Ends* [Cambridge: Cambridge University Press, 1996], 77–105). And, like Kant, Barbara Herman says that one cannot will universal nonmaleficence because "we cannot guarantee that we *shall* always be capable of realizing our ends unaided" (*The Practice of Moral Judgment* [Cambridge, Mass.: Harvard University Press, 1993], 55; emphasis added).

12   Susan Feldman, "From Occupied Bodies to Pregnant Persons: How Kantian Ethics Should Treat Pregnancy and Abortion," in *Autonomy and Community: Readings in Contemporary Kantian Social Philosophy*, ed. Jane Kneller and Sidney Axinn (Albany: State University of New York Press, 1998), 265–82 (p. 269).

13   Allen W. Wood, "Kant on Duties Regarding Nonrational Nature," *Proceedings of the Aristotelian Society for the Systematic Study of Philosophy*, supplement 72 (1998): 189–210 (p. 196).

14   Department of Health and Social Security, *Report of the Committee of Inquiry into Human Fertilisation and Embryology* (Chairperson: Mary Warnock) (London: HMSO, 1984). This report was commissioned by the British government so that it could address the ethics and legality of research on human embryos.

15   Judith Jarvis Thomson, "A Defense of Abortion," *Philosophy and Public Affairs* 1, no. 1 (autumn 1971): 47–66 (pp. 47–8), and Don Marquis, "Why

Abortion Is Immoral," *Journal of Philosophy* 86, no. 4 (Apr. 1989): 183–202 (pp. 183–8).

16 Jane English, "Abortion and the Concept of a Person," *Canadian Journal of Philosophy* 5, no. 2 (Oct. 1975): 233–43 (p. 235).

17 Respectively, I refer here to the positions of Paul Ramsey (genes), Baruch Brody (brain waves), L. W. Sumner (sentience), and Jeffrey Reiman (caring about living). See Ramsey, "The Morality of Abortion," in *Moral Problems*, ed. James Rachels (New York: Harper & Row, 1975), 37–58; Brody, "On the Humanity of the Foetus," in *Abortion: Pro and Con*, ed. Robert L. Perkins (Cambridge, Mass.: Schenkman, 1974), 69–90; Sumner, "A Third Way," in *The Problem of Abortion*, ed. Joel Feinberg, 2nd edn. (Belmont, Calif.: Wadsworth, 1984), 71–93; and Reiman, *Abortion and the Ways We Value Human Life* (Lanham, Md.: Rowman & Littlefield, 1999).

18 Although ancient Greek and Roman law was largely "indifferent to foeticide," some local jurisdictions prosecuted abortion "because the father's right to his offspring had been violated by the mother's action" (Ludwig Edelstein, *Ancient Medicine: Selected Papers of Ludwig Edelstein*, ed. Owsei Temkin and C. Lilian Temkin [Baltimore, Md.: Johns Hopkins University Press, 1967], 15–16). Such an action was considered wrong because of how it treats another person (the husband), not because of how it treats the fetus, which was not considered a person under the law.

19 Feldman, "From Occupied Bodies to Pregnant Persons," 272.

20 Ibid., 277–8.

21 Ibid., 278. Feldman echoes the famous analogy made by Judith Jarvis Thomson, which I will discuss shortly.

22 Thomson, "A Defense of Abortion."

23 Ibid., 59–63.

24 Thomson's almost exclusive focus on rights may be a product of the time in which she wrote her essay. "A Defense of Abortion" was published in fall 1971, just before *Roe v. Wade* was argued at the U.S. Supreme Court (13 Dec. 1971). The case justified abortion on the basis of a woman's right to control her own body.

25 Thomson, "A Defense of Abortion," 55–9.

26 David Boonin, *A Defense of Abortion* (Cambridge: Cambridge University Press, 2003), 154–67.

27 Thomson, "A Defense of Abortion," 62.

28 I mentioned in chapter 1 that, according to Kant, animals represent the world to themselves. Although Kant repeats this claim in several places (Ak 2:60, 11:52; CJ 464n; LM 28:276, 28:449), he also denies that nonhuman animals have consciousness. They sense the world and reproduce it imaginatively, but they do not organize the world according to rules; they do not engage in judgment. Instead of understanding, animals organize their sensations based on instinct, which is merely an "analogue of reason" (LM 28:449–50; see also LM 28:689–90).

29 Mary Anne Warren, "On the Moral and Legal Status of Abortion," in *The Problem of Abortion*, ed. Feinberg, 102–19.

30   H. Tristram Engelhardt confuses self-consciousness as a condition of subjectivity with practical reasoning as a condition of humanity. Although self-consciousness is a necessary condition of personhood, it is not sufficient for rational self-determination. See Engelhardt, "The Ontology of Abortion," in *Moral Problems in Medicine*, ed. Samuel Gorovitz et al. (Englewood Cliffs, N.J.: Prentice Hall, 1976), 318–34 (p. 331n57).

31   When Kant uses the term *Erfahrung* (experience), usually he is referring to sensible intuitions that have been organized by the understanding according to the categories. See CPR B147–8 and A177/B218. Although fetuses at a certain point in their development may feel things, they do not have objective cognitions.

32   Christine M. Korsgaard, "Fellow Creatures: Kantian Ethics and Our Duties to Animals," *Tanner Lectures on Human Values* 24 (2004): 79–110 (p. 96n49). This interpretation of Kant's approach to fetuses and children also appears in Otfried Höffe, *Medizin ohne Ethik?* (Frankfurt: Suhrkamp, 2002), 64–79, and Reinhard Brandt, "Kants Ehe- und Kindesrecht," *Deutsche Zeitschrift für Philosophie* 52, no. 2 (2004): 199–219.

33   Holly L. Wilson, "The Green Kant: Kant's Treatment of Animals," in *Environmental Ethics: Readings in Theory and Application*, ed. Louis P. Pojman and Paul Pojman, 5th edn. (Belmont, Calif.: Thomson Wadsworth, 2008), 65–72 (p. 69).

34   Stephen Schwarz, *The Moral Question of Abortion* (Chicago: Loyola University Press, 1990), 100–1. Patrick Lee and Robert P. George similarly claim that the fetus is a person. A person has the capacity to reason and to choose, but the person "is identical with the human organism, and therefore that subject comes to be when the human organism comes to be, even though it will take him or her months or even years to actualize the natural capacities to reason and make free choices" ("The Wrong of Abortion," in *Contemporary Debates in Applied Ethics*, ed. Andrew I. Cohen and Christopher Heath Wellman [Oxford: Blackwell, 2005], 13–26 [pp. 15–16]). This identification of the rational subject and the human organism depends on a very broad sense of what it means to have a capacity. As I will show, this argument collapses into an appeal to potential.

35   Fuat S. Oduncu, "Stem Cell Research in Germany: Ethics of Healing vs. Human Dignity," *Medicine, Health Care and Philosophy* 6, no. 1 (Mar. 2003): 5–16 (pp. 11, 12). Other philosophers who claim that membership in the species *homo sapiens* is morally decisive include Lee and George, "The Wrong of Abortion," 13–15, and A. Chadwick Ray, "Humanity, Personhood and Abortion," *International Philosophical Quarterly* 25 (1985): 233–45.

36   John M. Opitz, "Early Embryonic Development: An Up-to-Date Account," testimony before the President's Council on Bioethics, 16 Jan. 2003, bioethics. georgetown.edu/pcbe/transcripts/jan03/session1.html. See also Harold J. Morowitz and James S. Trefil, *The Facts of Life: Science and the Abortion Controversy* (New York: Oxford University Press, 1992), 51. Kant did not have specific numbers, of course, but he recognized that many embryos never come to term: "there is something so contingent about birth. How many millions of embryos are nipped in the bud or die at the earliest age?" (LM 29:918).

37   Warren, "On the Moral and Legal Status of Abortion," 110.

38   Oduncu, "Stem Cell Research in Germany," 12.

39   The latter counterexample comes from Marquis, "Why Abortion Is Immoral," 185.

40   Allen W. Wood, *Kantian Ethics* (Cambridge: Cambridge University Press, 2008), 98.

41   This distinction is made by Stephen Buckle, "Arguing from Potential," in *Embryo Experimentation*, ed. Peter Singer et al. (Cambridge: Cambridge University Press, 1990), 90–108.

42   Wood, "Kant on Duties Regarding Nonrational Nature," 197. See also Wood, *Kantian Ethics*, 102.

43   Like Wood, Reinhard Brandt argues that, for Kant, being a person does not mean that one acts or has acted freely. Rather, *when* or *if* one acts, then that person can be held responsible for what she does. The fetus is a person, then, because *when* the adult/former fetus acts – at 20 years old, or whenever – at that point she will be acting freely ("Kants Ehe- und Kindesrecht").

44   Respectively, these analogies are from Thomson, "A Defense of Abortion," 47, and Stanley I. Benn, "Abortion, Infanticide, and Respect for Persons," in *The Problem of Abortion*, ed. Feinberg, 143. See also Peter Singer, *Practical Ethics*, 2nd edn. (Cambridge: Cambridge University Press, 1993), 153.

45   See Aquinas, *Summa Theologica*, Q II-II, q154, a12, and Catholic Church, Sacred Congregation for the Doctrine of the Faith, *Persona Humana: Declaration on Certain Questions Concerning Sexual Ethics*, 9, www.vatican.va/roman_curia/congregations/cfaith/documents/rc_con_cfaith_doc_19751229 _persona-humana_en.html.

46   David S. Oderberg, *Applied Ethics: A Non-Consequentialist Approach* (Oxford: Blackwell, 2000), 32–40. See also David S. Oderberg, *Moral Theory: A Non-Consequentialist Approach* (Oxford: Blackwell, 2000), 178–83.

47   See Richard Werner, "Abortion: The Ontological and Moral Status of the Unborn," in *Today's Moral Problems*, ed. Richard A. Wasserstrom, 2nd edn. (New York: Macmillan, 1979), 51–74 (p. 65); Sumner, "A Third Way," 80n10; and Bonnie Steinbock, "Why Most Abortions Are Not Wrong," in *Advances in Bioethics*, ed. Rem B. Edwards and E. Edwards Bittar, vol. 5 (Stamford, Conn.: Jai, 1999), 245–67 (p. 252). The two different senses of "potential" that are being used here – the potentiality of the fetus versus the potentiality of the sleeping adult – can be untangled by using Aristotle's distinction between "first potentiality" and "second potentiality." The fetus has "first potentiality" because it may become a person, even though it has not yet exhibited the qualities of that thing. But a sleeping or comatose person has "second potentiality" because it has already exhibited the characteristics of personhood, even though it is not doing so at the moment (Daniel A. Dombrowski and Robert Deltete, *A Brief, Liberal, Catholic Defense of Abortion* [Urbana: University of Illinois Press, 2000], 78).

48   George W. Bush, "Transcript: Third Presidential Debate [between George W. Bush and John Kerry]," Arizona State University, Tempe, Arizona, 13 Oct. 2004, www.washingtonpost.com/wp-srv/politics/debatereferee/debate_1013.html. See also George W. Bush, "Address Before a Joint Session of the Congress on

the State of the Union," 2 Feb. 2005, frwebgate.access.gpo.gov/cgi-bin/getdoc. cgi?dbname=2005_presidential_documents&docid=pd07fe05_txt-9.pdf, and George W. Bush, "Proclamation 8339 – National Sanctity of Human Life Day, 2009," 15 Jan. 2009, georgewbush-whitehouse.archives.gov/news/releases/ 2009/01/20090115-1.html.

49 Carl Wellman, *Medical Law and Moral Rights* (New York: Springer, 2005), 143–4.

50 In chapter 4 I discussed the Catholic Church's similar moral objection to withdrawing treatment from PVS patients.

51 See chapter 1, note 10.

52 Centers for Disease Control, *Morbidity and Mortality Weekly Report 57*, no. SS-13 (28 Nov. 2008): 1–36 (p. 29), www.cdc.gov/mmwr/PDF/ss/ss5713.pdf.

53 Some have argued that there is a correlation between rates of violent crime and abortion, but it is not because getting an abortion or condoning abortion affects our character. Instead, the free availability of abortion is said to cause rates of violent crime to drop about seventeen years later, when the aborted fetuses would have developed into disadvantaged teenagers with poor social connections (fatherless, etc.), the sort of people who are most likely to become criminals. This may constitute a utilitarian argument in favor of abortion, but it is irrelevant for Kant. See Steven D. Levitt and Stephen J. Dubner, *Freakonomics: A Rogue Economist Explores the Hidden Side of Everything* (New York: William Morrow, 2005), 137–42.

54 American Psychological Association, Task Force on Mental Health and Abortion, *Report of the Task Force on Mental Health and Abortion* (Washington, D.C.: American Psychological Association, 2008), www.apa.org/ pi/wpo/mental-health-abortion-report.pdf.

55 As we saw in chapter 4, some philosophers have used Kant's theory of personhood to justify physician-assisted suicide for patients who are succumbing to dementia. When they are no longer persons, they have no dignity to respect. See Dennis R. Cooley, "A Kantian Moral Duty for the Soon-to-be Demented to Commit Suicide," *American Journal of Bioethics* 7, no. 6 (June 2007): 37–44.

56 John Locke, *Some Thoughts Concerning Education*, ed. John W. Yolton and Jean S. Yolton (Oxford: Clarendon Press, 1989), esp. §54 and §81.

57 Korsgaard, *Creating the Kingdom of Ends*, 341–2.

58 This distinction between a citizen of the world and a citizen of the state has odd implications. Kant says that an unmarried woman who kills her bastard child is deserving of death in a moral sense, but cannot legally be given the death penalty. This is so because the child is "born outside the law" and therefore is not a citizen of the state, but is "stolen into the commonwealth (like contraband merchandise)." Kant's analogy here is apt: for legal purposes, the child is not a person, so the crime cannot even be called murder (MM 336). Whether the child is a citizen of the world, not a citizen of the state, is what is at issue in this chapter.

59 Korsgaard, *Creating the Kingdom of Ends*, 351.

60 Interestingly, Kant's idealist successor Johann Gottlieb Fichte takes Korsgaard's approach (as opposed to Kant's) when it comes to recognizing the personhood

of others. According to Fichte, any object of my experience must be posited by me as an object of experience. The risk here, and the reason why Fichte is often considered a subjective idealist, is that the world generally and other people more specifically seem to be reduced to nothing but objects of consciousness that exist only for me and only as a result of my activity. In *The Vocation of Man*, however, Fichte writes that, practically, I am forbidden from treating other people merely as things, even though nothing in my experience warrants their status as autonomous agents with absolute value:

> I am aware of appearances in space to which I transfer the concept of myself; I think of them as beings like myself. Speculative philosophy, taken to its conclusion, has taught me or will teach me that these supposed rational beings outside of me are nothing but products of my own mind, that I just happen to be compelled, according to demonstrable laws of my thought, to present the concept of myself outside of myself and that, by the same laws, this concept can only be transferred to certain determinate intuitions. But the voice of my conscience calls to me: whatever these beings may be in and for themselves, you ought to treat them as self-subsistent, free, autonomous beings completely independent of you. . . . I will therefore always regard those beings as beings which exist for themselves and are there independently of me, as beings which set themselves purposes and carry them out. From this standpoint I will not be able to see them any other way, and that speculation will disappear before my eyes like an empty dream. (*The Vocation of Man*, trans. Peter Preuss [Indianapolis, Ind.: Hackett, 1987], 76)

No theoretical argument can be given for the personhood of some of my objects of experience. On Kant's view, I cannot even know in a theoretical sense that *I* am free. Instead, Fichte claims, my conception of others as moral agents follows from the practical injunction that I treat them as such.

61 Korsgaard, *Creating the Kingdom of Ends*, 352.
62 Ibid.
63 Wood, *Kantian Ethics*, 97.
64 Ibid., 95–105.
65 See David DeGrazia, *Taking Animals Seriously: Mental Life and Moral Status* (Cambridge: Cambridge University Press, 1996), esp. 166–210.
66 Wood, "Kant on Duties Regarding Nonrational Nature," 197.
67 Korsgaard, *Creating the Kingdom of Ends*, 341.
68 Reiman, *Abortion and the Ways We Value Human Life*.
69 Michael Tooley, "Abortion and Infanticide," in *Applied Ethics*, ed. Peter Singer (Oxford: Oxford University Press, 1986), 57–85, and Joel Feinberg, "The Rights of Animals and Unborn Generations," in *Rights, Justice, and the Bounds of Liberty: Essays in Social Philosophy* (Princeton, N.J.: Princeton University Press, 1980), 159–84 (pp. 178–80).
70 Warren, "On the Moral and Legal Status of Abortion." Nicole Hassoun and Uriah Kriegel argue that, if self-consciousness is necessary for personhood, then one can justify not only abortion but also infanticide. See Hassoun and

Kriegel, "Consciousness and the Moral Permissibility of Infanticide," *Journal of Applied Philosophy* 25, no. 1 (Feb. 2008): 45–55.

71   Reiman, *Abortion and the Ways We Value Human Life*, 104–8, and Warren, "On the Moral and Legal Status of Abortion," 117.

72   The American legal system is similarly inconsistent. Although a fetus that has not reached the point of viability can be legally aborted, in many states murdering a pregnant woman can result in two murder charges. Therefore, the fetus both is and is not a person under the law.

73   Rublack, "The Public Body," 69.

74   See R. M. Hare, "Possible People," in *Essays on Bioethics* (Oxford: Oxford University Press, 1996), 67–83, and "When Does Potentiality Count?" in *Essays on Bioethics*, 84–97.

75   Emmanuel Levinas, *Otherwise than Being, or, Beyond Essence*, trans. Alphonso Lingis (Pittsburgh, Penn.: Duquesne University Press, 1998).

76   Carol Gilligan, *In a Different Voice: Psychological Theory and Women's Development* (Cambridge, Mass.: Harvard University Press, 1982), and Nel Noddings, *Caring, a Feminine Approach to Ethics and Moral Education* (Berkeley: University of California Press, 1984).

77   Michael Sandel, *Liberalism and the Limits of Justice* (Cambridge: Cambridge University Press, 1982); Charles Taylor, "Atomism," in *Philosophy and the Human Sciences*, vol. 2 of *Philosophical Papers* (Cambridge: Cambridge University Press, 1982), 187–210; and Charles Taylor, *Sources of the Self: The Making of the Modern Identity* (Cambridge, Mass.: Harvard University Press, 1989).

78   Loren E. Lomasky, "Being a Person – Does It Matter?" *Philosophical Topics* 12, no. 3 (winter 1981): 139–52 (p. 150). See also Loren E. Lomasky, *Persons, Rights, and the Moral Community* (New York: Oxford University Press, 1987), 191–202.

79   In her book *Moral Status*, Mary Anne Warren does not make the value of the child contingent on its being wanted, as she does in "On the Moral and Legal Status of Abortion." Instead, she agrees with Lomasky that a child has "full moral status" because, when it is born, it "becomes part of the human social world" (*Moral Status: Obligations to Persons and Other Living Things* [Oxford: Clarendon Press, 1997], 217–18).

Conclusion: Emerging from Kant's Long Shadow

High towers and the metaphysically-great men who resemble them, around both of which is usually much wind, are not for me. My place is the fertile bathos of experience . . .
  – Immanuel Kant, *Prolegomena to Any Future Metaphysics* (373n)

Kant's practical philosophy continues to resonate with us because we are children of the Enlightenment. We believe that the moral community is composed of individual rights-bearers and that our obligations to one another are derived from what is required of us as particular agents in contact with other agents. Our duties follow from the individual choices we make or from the bare fact that rational beings deserve respect: we ought to keep our promises or repair bad things we have done, we ought to develop our talents, and we ought to help people, or at least not harm them. Certainly there is nothing objectionable about such duties. Kant rightly emphasizes the value of humanity. He also explains why it is wrong or unreasonable for the individual to make an exception of himself, to hold himself to a different moral standard than he applies to others. What we have seen over the course of this book, however, is that some of the theoretical assumptions underlying Kant's ethics have problematic implications and explanatory shortcomings. In closing, what I want to suggest, in the briefest of ways, is that a communitarian approach to ethics holds great promise for overcoming the limitations of Kant's practical philosophy.

Hegel charges Kant with formalism, claiming that the content of our moral obligations cannot be the result of rational deliberation by a solitary individual. Rather, moral reasoning can only be understood against culturally specific background conditions, and any moral ideal of universality

Kant and Applied Ethics: The Uses and Limits of Kant's Practical Philosophy, First Edition. Matthew C. Altman.
© 2011 John Wiley & Sons Inc. Published 2011 by Blackwell Publishing Ltd.

must take into account the social institutions in which it is instantiated. From a historical perspective, communitarianism amounts to a neo-Hegelian critique of Kantian political philosophy. For example, Michael Walzer claims that John Rawls neglects social reality in his pursuit of an ideal of justice. An appeal to what any rational agent would choose under certain contrived conditions (for example, from behind a veil of ignorance) cannot yield determinate values, only abstract principles. The relevance of those principles depends on how they are interpreted in a given social context.[1] In addition, philosophers such as Michael Sandel and Charles Taylor reject the Kantian subject. Instead of being separate moral agents who adhere to the demands of pure practical reason, we are defined and constituted by our communal attachments, by our ties to and recognition by others.[2] This is a Hegelian idea. The subject is essentially a social being, not a disembodied, autonomous end-setter who negotiates an atomistic social terrain populated by other individuals. This approach will better handle cases involving women in coercive situations, people with broader concerns for social justice, corporate entities, and those who are not (or not yet) rational.

Kant claims that any person can discover what is right if only he thinks about it in the right way. Everyone has the capacity to reason, so in principle, people at any time and place are capable of recognizing the categorical imperative if they consider ethics rationally, without being distracted by whatever people happen to believe as a matter of custom. Of course, Kant does not disregard history. He wrote extensively on how history is the progressive development of human culture toward perfection. However, Kant largely rejects the idea that our thinking, especially our moral thinking, is conditioned by our circumstances. To discover practical laws, we need not, and indeed should not, consult either social norms or history.

According to Kant, we as morally considerable and morally responsible beings are not people of different genders, races, ages, or nationalities. Rather, we (or some of us, at least) are rational beings who ought to conceive of ourselves as fellow legislators in a kingdom of ends. Bernard Williams has criticized Kant for this conception of the self. The Kantian subject is very different from the situated person who faces complex moral decisions in a culturally defined deliberative landscape:

> The very considerable consistency of Kant's view is bought at what would generally be agreed to be a very high price. The detachment of moral worth from all contingencies is achieved only by making man's characteristic as a moral or rational agent a transcendental characteristic; man's capacity to will freely as a rational agent is not dependent on any empirical capacities he may have. . . . Accordingly, the respect owed equally to each man as a member of the Kingdom of Ends is not owed to him in respect of any empirical characteristics that he may possess, but solely in respect of the transcendental characteristic of being a free and rational will.[3]

In theory, equality among rational beings is an important moral ideal, but in actuality, Kant's conception of personhood covers over contingent factors that shape a person's freedom and the possibility of recognition. There are empirical (biological and psychological) facts that are relevant for assessing responsibility, social conditions that can be more or less coercive, and historical circumstances that can shape how we see ourselves. The last four chapters, especially, have shown that all of these factors affect how we judge our own actions, who is held accountable, and the class of people with dignity. It is a laudable goal to strive for equal recognition under the moral law, but thinking of ourselves as essentially rational beings obscures the ways in which we are impacted unequally by contingent events. Social relations are not incidental to who we are such that, at any point, we can freely extricate ourselves from them and engage others (and ourselves) as we choose from an impersonal standpoint. Instead, our embeddedness in the world is integral to our identity as agents, our status as moral patients, and our ethical judgment.

Unlike Kant, Hegel claims that we do not merely produce our circumstances but are largely a product of our circumstances. Ethics does not simply govern social relations but actually emerges historically out of shared ethical traditions. This approach has some plausibility, since in the last hundred years or so we have begun to appreciate the social constitution of subjectivity: how our thinking is essentially related to language, how we are interpellated as subjects by others, and how our concepts of self-understanding emerge out of material relations. As we saw in chapter 8, even our conception of what is rational depends on how our expectations have been shaped by culture and society. According to communitarians, ethical principles derive their meaning and weight from traditional ethical practice. Ethics is a way of life rather than an impersonal way to judge a way of life.

Communitarians also reject Kant's singular focus on pure, formal constraints. Alasdair MacIntyre claims that ethics must begin with some shared view about what a good society looks like. The language we use to make sense of right and wrong is defined in relation to some historically contingent social ideal. Of course, members of a community can reflect on its ideal and debate its rightness, but any revised social arrangement will not be the result of applying formal principles to actual circumstances. Rather, we will arrive at a vision of the ideal society by reasoning about and discussing what we as a community take to be morally important, or the kind of society that we want to have. What results is not determinable in advance by an ideal, purely rational spectator, but is, rather, constructed through the process of intersubjective dialogue.[4] At this point, communitarianism begins to look like Jürgen Habermas's theory of communicative action, which emphasizes that engaging in linguistic speech acts commits the speaker to justify claims of moral rightness to others by appealing to reasons, all while situated within a shared cultural system of meaning, a "lifeworld [*Lebenswelt*]," that enables cooperation and mutual understanding.[5]

This conception of moral deliberation within a field of shared values deeply informs the work of Barbara Herman, but at its core the idea is more Hegelian than Kantian. Hegel follows Kant in claiming that morality is a matter of reasoning, but he understands reasoning differently. Kant's formal theory must be supplemented with an understanding of ethical life (*Sittlichkeit*), where people become agents only within particular social, linguistic, and cultural worlds. We are rationally constrained, but any reasoning is historically situated. One may even say that our deliberation occurs against certain rules of moral salience, which themselves can be revised but which are necessary to make moral judgments. For Hegel, ethical life is "intensely actual."[6] There is no view from nowhere.

This is not the place to defend communitarianism against its many critics, and I certainly do not mean to equate Hegel with a view that sometimes verges on relativism.[7] It suffices to note here that an ethic of mutual recognition within a shared space of reason-giving can better handle issues such as collective responsibility and our duties to moral patients who lack agency. Holding businesses accountable is important in its own right, despite the lack of a metaphysical subject who has inclinations and the capacity to reason. If we come to the point that we identify ourselves with living things in general rather than just rational beings – the expansion of moral considerability envisioned by Aldo Leopold and others – the direct consideration of nature and animals would make sense. The recognition of newborns and, perhaps, some late-term fetuses as members of the moral community would carry weight in our deliberations. The respect that we owe to newborns would not have to be justified by appealing to God's purposes or by deciding whether they have the requisite capacities.

As I noted at the beginning of this conclusion and at various points throughout the book, Kant's practical philosophy has had such a powerful impact on us because he gets so much right. The dignity of humanity and the value of autonomy have wide-ranging implications for some of the most pressing social issues of our time, including animal and environmental protections, health-care reform, physician-assisted suicide, the death penalty, and same-sex marriage. Kant's ethics serves as a corrective to moral theories that give too much weight to whatever positions we as a society happen to hold, and it asserts the absolute worth of persons against political expediency and economic efficiency. Nonetheless, we must reconceive what we mean by autonomy and personhood by transforming Kant's ahistorical and metaphysical concepts into more socially dependent, pragmatic concepts. Doing so runs the risk of the very relativism that Kant so strongly rejects.

The task now is to retain the compelling pieces of Kantianism – not to reject all of Kant's moral philosophy out of hand – as we attempt to formulate a more correct, Hegelian, approach.

Hegel himself understood Kantian universalism to be the starting point for arriving at the ethical life, which is a completion of rather than an alternative to Kantian morality.[8] For Hegel, the goal of the ethical life is rationality or universality – he more or less equates the terms[9] – but not in their abstract, Kantian form. For Kant, universality is opposed to particularity, in that (when necessary) we have to reject our inclinations in favor of what reason requires. Hegel's absolute universality overcomes this opposition by embodying what is universally required in the particular desires of the individual and by reflecting the practices of the community (*Gemeinschaft*).[10] In other words, the individual apprehends the meaning of what he does in the context of the community's expectations and institutions. This constrains the agent but also the community, because there are rational requirements that the community must meet in order for the self-conscious agent to be able to take on its expectations. Hegel's philosophy thus gives us a theory of moral judgment that does not amount to relativism while still taking seriously the agent's relation to others in a particular society at a particular time.

Ironically, some of the most interesting work currently being done on Kant's ethical theory incorporates elements of Hegelianism and communitarianism. Christine Korsgaard, Allen Wood, and Barbara Herman, in particular, are transforming what Kantianism implies about our recognition of nonpersons and our social embeddedness. As I have shown, these attempts chafe against the limits of Kant's philosophy. However, that alone does not amount to a criticism of Korsgaard, Wood, and Herman. It says more about Kant and the ways in which we have inherited his ideas and lived them out in our political and ethical lives.

Reading the epigraph of this conclusion strikes us as ironic, not only or even primarily because the sage of Königsburg claims to be immersed in "the fertile *bathos* of experience." Kant has become a towering figure in philosophy around whom there is the constant "wind" of scholarly activity, books and articles that attempt to further the Kantian philosophical program. To appreciate Kant's legacy, however, we must recognize not only his accomplishments but also his failures. For the most part, we are Kantians. When we call Kant's theory into question, we must be careful not to make him say what we wish he would have said. Instead, out of the struggle with the critical philosophy, we should take what works, perhaps find its basis not in the formal conditions of reason but in the act of deliberating with others in a community of rational beings. And if we go beyond Kant in our commitment to the ethical life, we should realize that it is only because of Kant that we are able to do so.

Notes

1   Michael Walzer, *Spheres of Justice* (New York: Basic Books, 1983).
2   Michael Sandel, *Liberalism and the Limits of Justice* (Cambridge: Cambridge University Press, 1982); Charles Taylor, "Atomism," in *Philosophy and the Human Sciences*, vol. 2 of *Philosophical Papers* (Cambridge: Cambridge University Press, 1982), 187–210; and Charles Taylor, *Sources of the Self: The Making of the Modern Identity* (Cambridge, Mass.: Harvard University Press, 1989).
3   Bernard Williams, "The Idea of Equality," in *Problems of the Self: Philosophical Papers, 1956–1972* (Cambridge: Cambridge University Press, 1973), 230–49 (p. 235).
4   Alasdair MacIntyre, *After Virtue* (Notre Dame, Ind.: University of Notre Dame Press, 1981).
5   Jürgen Habermas, *The Theory of Communicative Action*, trans. Thomas McCarthy, 2 vols. (Boston: Beacon, 1984, 1987).
6   G. W. F. Hegel, *Elements of the Philosophy of Right*, ed. Allen W. Wood, trans. H. B. Nisbet (Cambridge: Cambridge University Press, 1991), §156 (addition).
7   For a brief but valuable discussion of Hegel's divergence from communitarianism, see Allen W. Wood, *Hegel's Ethical Thought* (Cambridge: Cambridge University Press, 1990), 202–8.
8   Hegel, *Elements of the Philosophy of Right*, §135 (remark).
9   Ibid., §24 (remark).
10 Ibid., §§5–7 (remark). See also G. W. F. Hegel, *Logic*, vol. 1 of *Encyclopedia of the Philosophical Sciences*, trans. W. Wallace (Oxford: Oxford University Press, 1975), §163.

Bibliography

Aaltola, Elisa. "The Anthropocentric Paradigm and the Possibility of Animal Ethics." *Ethics and the Environment* 15, no. 1 (spring 2010): 27–50.

Abadie, Alberto, and Sebastian Gay. "The Impact of Presumed Consent Legislation on Cadaveric Organ Donation: A Cross Country Study." National Bureau of Economic Research (NBER) Working Paper no. W10604, July 2004. www.nber.org/papers/w10604.

Agus, Carol. "Fed Up with U.S. Women, Single Men Turning to Asia for Docile Mail-Order Brides." *Oakland Tribune*, 24 May 1984, D1, D3.

Allison, Henry E. *Kant's Theory of Freedom.* Cambridge: Cambridge University Press, 1990.

Althusser, Louis. "Ideology and Ideological State Apparatuses (Notes towards an Investigation)." In *Lenin and Philosophy and Other Essays*, trans. Ben Brewster, 127–86. New York: Monthly Review, 1971.

American Medical Association. *Code of Medical Ethics*, Opinion 2.20: Withholding or Withdrawing Life-Sustaining Medical Treatment. www.ama-assn.org/ama/pub/physician-resources/medical-ethics/code-medical-ethics/opinion220.shtml.

American Medical Association. *Code of Medical Ethics*, Opinion 2.211: Physician-Assisted Suicide. www.ama-assn.org/ama/pub/physician-resources/medical-ethics/code-medical-ethics/opinion2211.shtml.

American Medical Association. "Principles of Medical Ethics." www.ama-assn.org/ama/pub/category/2512.html.

American Medical Association. Report 7-A-05. Council on Ethical and Judicial Affairs. www.ama-assn.org/ama1/pub/upload/mm/369/ceja_7a05.pdf.

American Psychiatric Association. *Diagnostic and Statistical Manual of Mental Disorders.* 3rd rev. edn. Washington, D.C.: American Psychiatric Association, 1987.

Kant and Applied Ethics: The Uses and Limits of Kant's Practical Philosophy, First Edition. Matthew C. Altman.
© 2011 John Wiley & Sons Inc. Published 2011 by Blackwell Publishing Ltd.

American Psychological Association, Task Force on Mental Health and Abortion. *Report of the Task Force on Mental Health and Abortion*. Washington, D.C.: American Psychological Association, 2008. www.apa.org/pi/wpo/mental-health-abortion-report.pdf.

Anderson, Michelle J. "License to Abuse: The Impact of Conditional Status on Female Immigrants." *Yale Law Journal* 102, no. 6 (1993): 1401–30.

Anderson-Gold, Sharon. "Cosmopolitanism and Democracy: Global Governance without a Global State." Paper presented at the International Social Philosophy Conference, Portland, Oregon, July 2008.

Aquinas, Thomas. *Summa Theologica*. Trans. T. C. O'Brien. 60 vols. New York: McGraw-Hill, 1964–74.

Arluke, Arnold, Jack Levin, Carter Luke, and Frank Ascione. "The Relationship of Animal Abuse to Violence and Other Forms of Antisocial Behavior." *Journal of Interpersonal Violence* 14, no. 9 (Sept. 1999): 963–75.

Ascione, Frank R. "Battered Women's Reports of Their Partners' and Their Children's Cruelty to Animals." *Journal of Emotional Abuse* 1, no. 1 (July 1997): 119–33.

Ascione, Frank R. *Children and Animals: Exploring the Roots of Kindness and Cruelty*. West Lafayette, Ind.: Purdue University Press, 2005.

Ascione, Frank R., and Phil Arkow, eds. *Child Abuse, Domestic Violence, and Animal Abuse: Linking the Circles of Compassion for Prevention and Intervention*. West Lafayette, Ind.: Purdue University Press, 1999.

Axinn, Sidney. "Kant on World Government." In *Proceedings of the Sixth International Kant Congress*, ed. Gerhard Funke and Thomas M. Seebohm, vol. 2, 243–51. Washington, D.C.: University Press of America, 1998.

Bagemihl, Bruce. *Biological Exuberance: Animal Homosexuality and Natural Diversity*. New York: Stonewall Inn, 2000.

Baier, Annette C. *Moral Prejudices: Essays on Ethics*. Cambridge, Mass.: Harvard University Press, 1994.

Beccaria, Cesare. *On Crimes and Punishments, and Other Writings*. Ed. Richard Bellamy. Trans. Richard Davies, Virginia Cox, and Richard Bellamy. Cambridge: Cambridge University Press, 1995.

Becker, Kimberly D., Jeffrey Stuewig, Veronica M. Herrera, and Laura A. McCloskey. "A Study of Firesetting and Animal Cruelty in Children: Family Influences and Adolescent Outcomes." *Journal of the American Academy of Child and Adolescent Psychiatry* 43, no. 7 (July 2004): 905–12.

Bekoff, Marc. *The Emotional Lives of Animals: A Leading Scientist Explores Animal Joy, Sorrow, and Empathy – and Why They Matter*. Novato, Calif.: New World Library, 2007.

Bekoff, Marc, and Jessica Pierce. *Wild Justice: The Moral Lives of Animals*. Chicago: University of Chicago Press, 2009.

Belleau, Marie-Claire. "Mail-Order Brides in a Global World." *Albany Law Review* 67, no. 2 (winter 2003): 595–607.

Benn, Stanley I. "Abortion, Infanticide, and Respect for Persons." In *The Problem of Abortion*, ed. Joel Feinberg, 2nd edn., 135–44. Belmont, Calif.: Wadsworth, 1984.

Bergen, Raquel Kennedy. "Marital Rape: New Research and Directions." National Online Resource Center on Violence against Women, 2006. www.wcsap.org/MaritalRapeRevised.pdf.

Berlin, Isaiah. "Two Concepts of Liberty." In *Four Essays on Liberty*, 118–72. Oxford: Oxford University Press, 1969.

Bernasconi, Robert. "Who Invented the Concept of Race? Kant's Role in the Enlightenment Construction of Race." In *Race*, ed. Robert Bernasconi, 11–36. Oxford: Blackwell, 2001.

Bittner, Rüdiger. "Maximen." In *Akten des 4. Internationalen Kant-Kongress*, vol. 2, pt. 2, ed. Gerhard Funke, 485–98. Berlin: de Gruyter, 1974.

Black, Charles Jr. *Capital Punishment: The Inevitability of Caprice and Mistake.* 2nd edn. New York: Norton, 1981.

Blackstone, William. *Blackstone's Commentaries*. Ed. St. George Tucker. South Hackensack, N.J.: Rothman Reprints, 1969.

Boatright, John R. "Does Business Ethics Rest on a Mistake?" *Business Ethics Quarterly* 9, no. 4 (Oct. 1999): 583–91.

Boonin, David. *A Defense of Abortion*. Cambridge: Cambridge University Press, 2003.

Bordo, Susan. *Unbearable Weight: Feminism, Western Culture, and the Body.* Berkeley: University of California Press, 1993.

Bowie, Norman E. *Business Ethics: A Kantian Perspective*. Oxford: Blackwell, 1999.

Bowie, Norman E. "Kantian Capitalism." In *The Blackwell Encyclopedia of Management*, vol. 2, *Business Ethics*, ed. Patricia H. Werhane and R. Edward Freeman, 2nd edn., 285–8. Oxford: Blackwell, 2005.

Bowie, Norman E. "A Kantian Theory of Leadership." *Leadership and Organization Development Journal* 21, no. 4 (2000): 185–93.

Bowie, Norman E., and Denis G. Arnold. "Sweatshops and Respect for Persons." *Business Ethics Quarterly* 13, no. 2 (Apr. 2003): 221–42.

Brake, Elizabeth. "Justice and Virtue in Kant's Account of Marriage." *Kantian Review* 9 (May 2005): 58–94.

Brandt, Reinhard. "Kants Ehe- und Kindesrecht." *Deutsche Zeitschrift für Philosophie* 52, no. 2 (2004): 199–219.

Broadie, Alexander, and Elizabeth M. Pybus. "Kant's Treatment of Animals." *Philosophy* 49 (Oct. 1974): 375–83.

Brody, Baruch A. "On the Humanity of the Foetus." In *Abortion: Pro and Con*, ed. Robert L. Perkins, 69–90. Cambridge, Mass.: Schenkman, 1974.

Buckle, Stephen. "Arguing from Potential." In *Embryo Experimentation*, ed. Peter Singer, Helga Kuhse, Stephen Buckle, Karen Dawson, and Pascal Kasimba, 90–108. Cambridge: Cambridge University Press, 1990.

Bureau of Justice Statistics, United States Department of Justice. "Violence against Women: Estimates from the Redesigned National Crime Victimization Survey," 1995. bjs.ojp.usdoj.gov/index.cfm?ty=pbdetail&iid=805.

Bush, George W. "Address Before a Joint Session of the Congress on the State of the Union," 2 Feb. 2005. frwebgate.access.gpo.gov/cgi-bin/getdoc.cgi?dbname=2005_presidential_documents&docid=pd07fe05_txt-9.pdf.

Bush, George W. "Proclamation 8339 – National Sanctity of Human Life Day, 2009," 15 Jan. 2009. georgewbush-whitehouse.archives.gov/news/releases/2009/01/20090115-1.html.

Bush, George W. "Transcript: Third Presidential Debate [between George W. Bush and John Kerry]," Arizona State University, Tempe, Arizona, 13 Oct. 2004. www.washingtonpost.com/wp-srv/politics/debatereferee/debate_1013.html.

Callicott, J. Baird. "Animal Liberation: A Triangular Affair." *Environmental Ethics* 2, no. 4 (winter 1980): 311–28.

Callicott, J. Baird. *In Defense of the Land Ethic: Essays in Environmental Philosophy.* Albany: State University of New York Press, 1989.

Callicott, J. Baird. "Intrinsic Value in Nature: A Metaethical Analysis." *Electronic Journal of Analytic Philosophy* 3 (spring 1995). ejap.louisiana.edu/EJAP/1995.spring/callicott.1995.spring.html.

Calvo, Janet M. "Spouse-Based Immigration Laws: The Legacies of Coverture." *San Diego Law Review* 28, no. 3 (Aug.–Sept. 1991): 590–628.

Campbell, John Lord. *Lives of the Lord Chancellors and Keepers of the Great Seal of England from the Earliest Times till the Reign of King George IV.* 5th edn. London: John Murray, 1868.

Campbell, Rebecca, Sharon M. Wasco, Courtney E. Ahrens, Tracy Sefl, and Holly E. Barnes. "Preventing the 'Second Rape': Rape Survivors' Experiences with Community Service Providers." *Journal of Interpersonal Violence* 16, no. 12 (Dec. 2001): 1239–59.

Carr, Albert. "Is Business Bluffing Ethical?" *Harvard Business Review* 46, no. 1 (Jan.–Feb. 1968): 143–53.

Carruthers, Peter. *The Animals Issue: Moral Theory in Practice.* Cambridge: Cambridge University Press, 1992.

Catholic Church. *Catechism of the Catholic Church.* www.vatican.va/archive/catechism/p2s2c3a7.htm#I.

Catholic Church. Sacred Congregation for the Doctrine of the Faith. *Persona Humana: Declaration on Certain Questions Concerning Sexual Ethics.* www.vatican.va/roman_curia/congregations/cfaith/documents/rc_con_cfaith_doc_19751229_persona-humana_en.html.

Centers for Disease Control. *Morbidity and Mortality Weekly Report* 57, no. SS-13 (28 Nov. 2008): 1–36. www.cdc.gov/mmwr/PDF/ss/ss5713.pdf.

Chivian, Eric. "Environment and Health: 7. Species Loss and Ecosystem Disruption – the Implications for Human Health." *Canadian Medical Association Journal* 164, no. 1 (Jan. 2001): 66–9.

Chivian, Eric, and Aaron Bernstein, eds. *Sustaining Life: How Human Health Depends on Biodiversity.* Oxford: Oxford University Press, 2008.

Cholbi, Michael J. "Suicide Intervention and Non-Ideal Kantian Theory." *Journal of Applied Philosophy* 19, no. 3 (Dec. 2002): 245–59.

Climent, C. E., M. S. Hyg, and M. D. Ervin. "Historical Data in the Evaluation of Violent Subjects." *Archives of General Psychiatry* 27 (1972): 621–4.

Coalition against Trafficking in Women. *Coalition Report.* Philadelphia: Coalition against Trafficking in Women, 1992.

Cohen, Hermann. "Vernichtung der sittlichen Person." In *Hermann Cohens Schriften zur Philosophie und Zeitgeschichte*, vol. 2, ed. Albert Görland and Ernst Cassirer. Berlin: Akademie-verlag, 1928.

Constable, Nicole. *Romance on a Global Stage: Pen Pals, Virtual Ethnography, and "Mail-Order" Marriages*. Berkeley: University of California Press, 2003.

Cooke, Vincent M. "Kant, Teleology, and Sexual Ethics." *International Philosophical Quarterly* 31, no. 1 (Mar. 1991): 3–13.

Cooley, Dennis R. "A Kantian Moral Duty for the Soon-to-be Demented to Commit Suicide." *American Journal of Bioethics* 7, no. 6 (June 2007): 37–44.

Costanza, Robert, Ralph d'Arge, Rudolf de Groot, Stephen Farberk, Monica Grasso, Bruce Hannon, Karin Limburg, Shahid Naeem, Robert V. O'Neill, Jose Paruelo, Robert G. Raskin, Paul Sutton, and Marjan van den Belt. "The Value of the World's Ecosystem Services and Natural Capital." *Nature* 387 (15 May 1997): 253–60.

Dean, Richard. *The Value of Humanity in Kant's Moral Theory*. Oxford: Clarendon Press, 2006.

Death Penalty Information Center. "The Innocence List." www.deathpenaltyinfo. org/innocence-list-those-freed-death-row.

De George, Richard T. "Can Corporations Have Moral Responsibility?" In *Ethical Theory and Business*, ed. Tom L. Beauchamp and Norman E. Bowie, 2nd edn., 57–67. Englewood Cliffs, N.J.: Prentice Hall, 1983.

DeGrazia, David. *Taking Animals Seriously: Mental Life and Moral Status*. Cambridge: Cambridge University Press, 1996.

Denis, Lara. "From Friendship to Marriage: Revising Kant." *Philosophy and Phenomenological Research* 63, no. 1 (July 2001): 1–28.

Denis, Lara. "Kant on the Wrongness of 'Unnatural' Sex." *History of Philosophy Quarterly* 16, no. 2 (Apr. 1999): 225–48.

Denis, Lara. "Kant's Conception of Duties Regarding Animals: Reconstruction and Reconsideration." *History of Philosophy Quarterly* 17, no. 4 (2000): 405–23.

Department of Health and Social Security. *Report of the Committee of Inquiry into Human Fertilisation and Embryology*. Chairperson: Mary Warnock. London: HMSO, 1984.

Derrida, Jacques. *The Animal That Therefore I Am*. Ed. Marie-Louise Mallet. Trans. David Wills. New York: Fordham University Press, 2008.

de Waal, Frans. *Good Natured: The Origins of Right and Wrong in Humans and Other Animals*. Cambridge, Mass.: Harvard University Press, 1996.

De Wispelaere, Jurgen, and Lindsay Stirton. "Advance Commitment: An Alternative Approach to the Family Veto Problem in Organ Procurement." *Journal of Medical Ethics* 36, no. 3 (March 2010): 180–3.

Dombrowski, Daniel A., and Robert Deltete. *A Brief, Liberal, Catholic Defense of Abortion*. Urbana: University of Illinois Press, 2000.

Donaldson, Thomas. *Corporations and Morality*. Englewood Cliffs, N.J.: Prentice Hall, 1982.

Dula, Annette. "African American Suspicion of the Healthcare System Is Justified: What Do We Do about It?" *Cambridge Quarterly of Healthcare Ethics* 3, no. 3 (1994): 47–57.

Dyck, Arthur J. "An Alternative to the Ethic of Euthanasia." In *To Live and To Die: When, Why, and How*, ed. Robert H. Williams, 98–112. New York: Springer, 1973.

Edelstein, Ludwig. *Ancient Medicine: Selected Papers of Ludwig Edelstein*. Ed. Owsei Temkin and C. Lilian Temkin. Baltimore, Md.: Johns Hopkins University Press, 1967.

Egonsson, Dan. "Kant's Vegetarianism." *Journal of Value Inquiry* 31, no. 4 (Dec. 1997): 473–83.

Emerson, Ralph Waldo. *The Conduct of Life*. Vol. 4 of *The Collected Works of Ralph Waldo Emerson*. Ed. Alfred R. Ferguson. Cambridge, Mass.: Belknap, 2003.

Engelhardt, H. Tristram Jr. "The Ontology of Abortion." In *Moral Problems in Medicine*, ed. Samuel Gorovitz, Ruth Macklin, Andrew L. Jameton, John M. O'Connor, and Susan Sherwin, 318–34. Englewood Cliffs, N.J.: Prentice Hall, 1976.

Engels, Friedrich. *The Origin of the Family, Private Property and the State, in the Light of the Researches of Lewis H. Morgan*. Trans. Alec West. New York: International, 1972.

English, Jane. "Abortion and the Concept of a Person." *Canadian Journal of Philosophy* 5, no. 2 (Oct. 1975): 233–43.

Esty, Daniel C., Jack A. Goldstone, Ted Robert Gurr, Barbara Harff, Marc Levy, Geoffrey D. Dabelko, Pamela T. Surko, and Alan N. Unger. "State Failure Task Force Report: Phase II Findings." In *Environmental Change and Security Project Report*, 49–72. Washington, D.C.: The Woodrow Wilson Center, 1999.

Evan, William M., and R. Edward Freeman. "A Stakeholder Theory of the Modern Corporation: Kantian Capitalism." In *Ethical Theory and Business*, ed. Tom L. Beauchamp and Norman E. Bowie, 4th edn., 75–84. Englewood Cliffs, N.J.: Prentice Hall, 1993.

Eze, Emmanuel Chukwudi. "The Color of Reason: The Idea of 'Race' in Kant's Anthropology." In *Postcolonial African Philosophy: A Critical Reader*, ed. Emmanuel Chukwudi Eze, 103–40. Oxford: Blackwell, 1997.

Fanon, Frantz. *Black Skin, White Masks*. Trans. Richard Philcox. New York: Grove, 2008.

Favre, David, and Vivien Tsang. "The Development of Anti-Cruelty Laws during the 1800's." *Detroit College of Law Review* 1 (1993): 1–35.

Feinberg, Joel. *Harm to Others*. Vol. 1 of *The Moral Limits of the Criminal Law*. New York: Oxford University Press, 1984.

Feinberg, Joel. "The Rights of Animals and Unborn Generations." In *Rights, Justice, and the Bounds of Liberty: Essays in Social Philosophy*, 159–84. Princeton, N.J.: Princeton University Press, 1980.

Felch, Jason, and Maura Dolan. "DNA: Genes as Evidence; FBI Resists Scrutiny of 'Matches'." *Los Angeles Times*, 20 July 2008, A1.

Feldman, Susan. "From Occupied Bodies to Pregnant Persons: How Kantian Ethics Should Treat Pregnancy and Abortion." In *Autonomy and Community: Readings in Contemporary Kantian Social Philosophy*, ed. Jane Kneller and Sidney Axinn, 265–82. Albany: State University of New York Press, 1998.

Felthous, Alan R., and Stephen R. Kellert. "Childhood Cruelty to Animals and Later Aggression against People: A Review." *American Journal of Psychiatry* 144, no. 6 (June 1987): 710–17.

Felthous, Alan R., and Stephen R. Kellert. "Violence against Animals and People: Is Aggression against Living Creatures Generalized?" *Bulletin of the American Academy of Psychiatry and the Law* 14, no. 1 (1986): 55–69.

Fichte, Johann. *The Vocation of Man.* Trans. Peter Preuss. Indianapolis, Ind.: Hackett, 1987.

Fieldhouse, Heather. "The Failure of the Kantian Theory of Indirect Duties to Animals." *Animal Liberation Philosophy and Policy Journal* 2, no. 2 (2004): 1–9.

Fitzgerald, Amy J., Linda Kalof, and Thomas Dietz. "Slaughterhouses and Increased Crime Rates: An Empirical Analysis of the Spillover from 'The Jungle' into the Surrounding Community." *Organization and Environment* 22, no. 2 (June 2009): 158–84.

Foucault, Michel. "What Is an Author?" In *The Foucault Reader*, ed. Paul Rabinow, 101–20. New York: Pantheon Books, 1984.

Freeman, R. Edward. *Strategic Management: A Stakeholder Approach.* Boston: Ballinger, 1984.

French, Peter. *Collective and Corporate Responsibility.* New York: Columbia University Press, 1984.

French, Peter. "The Corporation as a Moral Person." *American Philosophical Quarterly* 16, no. 3 (July 1979): 207–15.

Freud, Anna. "A Psychoanalytic View of Developmental Psychopathology." In *The Writings of Anna Freud*, vol. 8, 57–74. New York: International Universities, 1981.

Friedman, Milton. "The Social Responsibility of Business Is to Increase Its Profits." *New York Times Magazine*, 13 Sept. 1970, 32–3, 122–6.

Frye, Marilyn. "Some Reflections on Separatism and Power." In *The Politics of Reality: Essays in Feminist Theory*, 95–109. Berkeley: Crossing, 1983.

Futterman, Laurie G. "Presumed Consent: The Solution to the Critical Organ Donor Shortage?" *American Journal of Respiratory and Critical Care Medicine* 4, no. 5 (1995): 383–8.

Gadamer, Hans-Georg. *Truth and Method.* Trans. Joel Weinsheimer and Donald G. Marshall. 2nd edn. New York: Continuum, 2004.

Gannon, John C. "Defining U.S. National Security for the Next Generation." Conference on the Role of Foreign Assistance in Conflict Prevention, United States Agency for International Development, 8 Jan. 2001. www.dni.gov/nic/speeches_definingsecurity.html.

Gauthier, Jeffrey A. *Hegel and Feminist Social Criticism: Justice, Recognition, and the Feminine.* Albany: State University of New York Press, 1997.

Gensler, Harry J. "A Kantian Argument against Abortion." *Philosophical Studies* 49, no. 1 (1986): 83–98.

Gibson, Kevin. "The Moral Basis of Stakeholder Theory." *Journal of Business Ethics* 26, no. 3 (Aug. 2000): 245–57.

Gilbert, Daniel R. Jr. "Respect for Persons, Management Theory, and Business Ethics." In *Business Ethics: The State of the Art*, ed. R. Edward Freeman, 111–21. Oxford: Oxford University Press, 1991.

Gilligan, Carol. *In a Different Voice: Psychological Theory and Women's Development*. Cambridge, Mass.: Harvard University Press, 1982.

Glodava, Mila, and Richard Onizuka. *Mail-Order Brides: Women for Sale*. Fort Collins, Colo.: Alaken, 1994.

Gobster, Paul H., and R. Bruce Hull, eds. *Restoring Nature: Perspectives from the Social Sciences and Humanities*. Washington, D.C.: Island, 2000.

Goering, Sara, and Annette Dula. "Reasonable People, Double Jeopardy, and Justice." *American Journal of Bioethics* 4, no. 4 (fall 2004): 37–9.

Goodpaster, Kenneth E. "On Being Morally Considerable." *The Journal of Philosophy* 75, no. 6 (June 1978): 308–25.

Goodpaster, Kenneth E., and John B. Matthews Jr. "Can a Corporation Have a Conscience?" *Harvard Business Review* 60 (Jan./Feb. 1982): 132–41.

Gostin, Lawrence O. "Meeting Basic Survival Needs of the World's Least Healthy People: Toward a Framework Convention on Global Health." *Georgetown Law Journal* 96 (2008): 331–92.

Grandin, Temple. "Behavior of Slaughter Plant and Auction Employees toward the Animals." *Anthrozoos* 1, no. 4 (1988): 205–13.

Greek, Jean Swingle, and C. Ray Greek. *What Will We Do If We Don't Experiment on Animals? Medical Research for the Twenty-First Century*. Victoria, B.C.: Trafford, 2006.

Gregor, Mary J. *Laws of Freedom: A Study of Kant's Method of Applying the Categorical Imperative in the "Metaphysik der Sitten"*. Oxford: Basil Blackwell, 1963.

Guadagnoli, E., C. L. Christiansen, W. DeJong, P. McNamara, C. Beasley, E. Christiansen, and M. Evanisko. "The Public's Willingness to Discuss Their Preference for Organ Donation with Family Members." *Clinical Transplantation* 13, no. 4 (Aug. 1999): 342–8.

Guyer, Paul. *Kant and the Experience of Freedom*. Cambridge: Cambridge University Press, 1993.

Habermas, Jürgen. *The Theory of Communicative Action*. Trans. Thomas McCarthy. 2 vols. Boston: Beacon, 1984, 1987.

Hardin, Garrett. "The Tragedy of the Commons." *Science* 162 (13 Dec. 1968): 1243–8.

Hare, R. M. "Abortion and the Golden Rule." *Philosophy and Public Affairs* 4, no. 3 (spring 1975): 201–22.

Hare, R. M. "A Kantian Approach to Abortion." In *Essays on Bioethics*, 168–84. Oxford: Oxford University Press, 1996.

Hare, R. M. "Possible People." In *Essays on Bioethics*, 67–83. Oxford: Oxford University Press, 1996.

Hare, R. M. "When Does Potentiality Count?" In *Essays on Bioethics*, 84–97. Oxford: Oxford University Press, 1996.

Hare, R. M. "Why I Am Only a Demi-Vegetarian." In *Singer and His Critics*, ed. Dale Jamieson, 233–46. Oxford: Blackwell, 1999.

Hassoun, Nicole, and Uriah Kriegel. "Consciousness and the Moral Permissibility of Infanticide." *Journal of Applied Philosophy* 25, no. 1 (Feb. 2008): 45–55.

Hayek, Friedrich A. *Law, Legislation and Liberty*. Vol. 2, *The Mirage of Social Justice*. Chicago: University of Chicago Press, 1976.

Hayek, Friedrich A. *The Trend of Economic Thinking: Essays on Political Economists and Economic History*. Vol. 3 of *The Collected Works of F. A. Hayek*. Ed. W. W. Bartley III and Stephen Kresge. Chicago: University of Chicago Press, 1991.

Health Resources and Services Administration, Division of Transplantation. "2005 National Survey of Organ and Tissue Donation Attitudes and Behaviors." Washington, D.C.: Gallup Organization, 2005. ftp://ftp.hrsa.gov/organdonor/survey2005.pdf.

Hegel, G. W. F. *Elements of the Philosophy of Right*. Ed. Allen W. Wood. Trans. H. B. Nisbet. Cambridge: Cambridge University Press, 1991.

Hegel, G. W. F. *Logic*. Vol. 1 of *Encyclopedia of the Philosophical Sciences*. Trans. W. Wallace. Oxford: Oxford University Press, 1975.

Hegel, G. W. F. *Phenomenology of Spirit*. Trans. A. V. Miller. Oxford: Oxford University Press, 1977.

Heide, Kathleen M. *Animal Cruelty: Pathway to Violence against People*. Lanham, Md.: AltaMira, 2003.

Herman, Barbara. "Could It Be Worth Thinking about Kant on Sex and Marriage?" In *A Mind of One's Own: Feminist Essays on Reason and Objectivity*, ed. Louise M. Antony and Charlotte Witt, 49–67. Boulder, Colo.: Westview, 1993.

Herman, Barbara. *Moral Literacy*. Cambridge, Mass.: Harvard University Press, 2007.

Herman, Barbara. *The Practice of Moral Judgment*. Cambridge, Mass.: Harvard University Press, 1993.

Hill, Thomas E. Jr. "Ideals of Human Excellence and Preserving Natural Environments." In *Autonomy and Self-Respect*, 104–17. Cambridge: Cambridge University Press, 1991.

Hoff, Christina. "Immoral and Moral Uses of Animals." *New England Journal of Medicine* 302, no. 2 (10 Jan. 1980): 115–18.

Hoff, Christina. "Kant's Invidious Humanism." *Environmental Ethics* 5, no. 1 (1983): 63–70.

Höffe, Otfried. "Kants kategorischer Imperativ als Kriterium des Sittlichen." *Zeitschrift für philosophische Forschung* 31 (1977): 354–84.

Höffe, Otfried. *Medizin ohne Ethik?* Frankfurt: Suhrkamp, 2002.

Jackall, Robert. "Looking Up and Looking Around." In *Moral Mazes: The World of Corporate Managers*, 75–100. Oxford: Oxford University Press, 1988.

Jedlicka, Davor. *American Men in Search of Oriental Brides: A Preliminary Study Released as a Courtesy to the Survey Participants*. Austin: University of Texas, 1988.

Johnson, Eric J., and Daniel Goldstein. "Do Defaults Save Lives?" *Science* 302, no. 5649 (21 Nov. 2003): 1338–9.

Johnson, Ericka. *Dreaming of a Mail-Order Husband: Russian–American Internet Romance*. Durham, N.C.: Duke University Press, 2007.

Joseph, Raymond A. "American Men Find Asian Brides Fill the Unliberated Bill: Mail-Order Firms Help Them Look for the Ideal Woman They Didn't Find at Home." *Wall Street Journal*, 25 Jan. 1984, 1.

Kant, Immanuel. "An Answer to the Question: 'What Is Enlightenment?'" In *Practical Philosophy*, trans. and ed. Mary J. Gregor, 11–22. Cambridge: Cambridge University Press, 1996.

Kant, Immanuel. *Anthropology from a Pragmatic Point of View*. Trans. Robert B. Louden. In *Anthropology, History, and Education*, ed. Günter Zöller and Robert B. Louden, 227–429. Cambridge: Cambridge University Press, 2007.

Kant, Immanuel. *Conjectural Beginning of Human History*. Trans. Allen W. Wood. In *Anthropology, History, and Education*, ed. Günter Zöller and Robert B. Louden. Cambridge: Cambridge University Press, 2007.

Kant, Immanuel. *Critique of Practical Reason*. In *Practical Philosophy*, trans. and ed. Mary J. Gregor, 133–271. Cambridge: Cambridge University Press, 1996.

Kant, Immanuel. *Critique of Pure Reason*. Trans. and ed. Paul Guyer and Allen W. Wood. Cambridge: Cambridge University Press, 1998.

Kant, Immanuel. *Critique of the Power of Judgment*. Trans. Paul Guyer and Eric Matthews. Ed. Paul Guyer. Cambridge: Cambridge University Press, 2000.

Kant, Immanuel. *Groundwork of the Metaphysics of Morals*. In *Practical Philosophy*, trans. and ed. Mary J. Gregor, 37–108. Cambridge: Cambridge University Press, 1996.

Kant, Immanuel. *Kants gesammelte Schriften*. 29 vols. Ed. Deutschen Akademie der Wissenschaften. Berlin: de Gruyter, 1902.

Kant, Immanuel. *Lectures on Ethics*. Trans. Peter Heath. Ed. Peter Heath and L. B. Schneewind. Cambridge: Cambridge University Press, 1997.

Kant, Immanuel. *Lectures on Metaphysics*. Trans. Karl Ameriks and Steve Naragon. Cambridge: Cambridge University Press, 1997.

Kant, Immanuel. *The Metaphysics of Morals*. In *Practical Philosophy*, trans. and ed. Mary J. Gregor, 353–603. Cambridge: Cambridge University Press, 1996.

Kant, Immanuel. *Observations on the Feeling of the Beautiful and Sublime*. Trans. Paul Guyer. In *Anthropology, History, and Education*, ed. Günter Zöller and Robert B. Louden, 18–62. Cambridge: Cambridge University Press, 2007.

Kant, Immanuel. "On a Supposed Right to Life from Philanthropy." In *Practical Philosophy*, trans. and ed. Mary J. Gregor, 605–15. Cambridge: Cambridge University Press, 1996.

Kant, Immanuel. "On the Common Saying: That May be Correct in Theory, But It Is of No Use in Practice." In *Practical Philosophy*, trans. and ed. Mary J. Gregor, 273–309. Cambridge: Cambridge University Press, 1996.

Kant, Immanuel. *On the Different Races of Human Beings*. Trans. Holly Wilson and Günter Zöller. In *Anthropology, History, and Education*, ed. Günter Zöller and Robert B. Louden, 82–97. Cambridge: Cambridge University Press, 2007.

Kant, Immanuel. *Prolegomena to Any Future Metaphysics That Will Be Able to Come Forward as a Science*. Trans. Gary Hatfield. In *Theoretical Philosophy after 1781*, ed. Henry Allison and Peter Heath, 29–169. Cambridge: Cambridge University Press, 2002.

Kant, Immanuel. *Religion within the Boundaries of Mere Reason.* Trans. George di Giovanni. In *Religion and Rational Theology*, ed. Allen W. Wood and George di Giovanni, 39–215. Cambridge: Cambridge University Press, 1996.

Kant, Immanuel. *Toward Perpetual Peace.* In *Practical Philosophy*, trans. and ed. Mary J. Gregor, 311–51. Cambridge: Cambridge University Press, 1996.

Kapparis, Konstantinos. *Abortion in the Ancient World.* London: Duckworth, 2002.

Kassalow, Jordan S. *Why Health Is Important to U.S. Foreign Policy.* New York: Milbank Memorial Fund and the Council on Foreign Relations, 2001. www.milbank.org/reports/Foreignpolicy.html.

Katz, Eric. "Is There a Place for Animals in the Moral Consideration of Nature?" *Ethics and Animals* 4, no. 3 (Sept. 1983): 74–87.

Kaufman, Alexander. *Welfare in the Kantian State.* Oxford: Oxford University Press, 1999.

Kaulbach, Friedrich. "Der Herrschaftsanspruch der Vernunft in Recht und Moral bei Kant." *Kant-Studien* 67 (1976): 390–408.

Keeley, Michael. "Organizations as Non-Persons." *Journal of Value Inquiry* 15, no. 2 (June 1981): 149–55.

Kekes, John. "Benevolence: A Minor Virtue." *Social Philosophy and Policy* 4, no. 2 (spring 1987): 21–36.

Kolata, Gina. "Some Scientists Doubt the Value of 'Genetic Fingerprint' Evidence." *New York Times*, 29 Jan. 1990, late edition, A1.

Korsgaard, Christine. *Creating the Kingdom of Ends.* Cambridge: Cambridge University Press, 1996.

Korsgaard, Christine. "Fellow Creatures: Kantian Ethics and Our Duties to Animals." *Tanner Lectures on Human Values* 24 (2004): 79–110.

Korsgaard, Christine. *The Sources of Normativity.* Cambridge: Cambridge University Press, 1996.

Krich, John. "Here Come the Brides: The Blossoming Business of Imported Love." *Mother Jones* 11, no. 2 (Feb./Mar. 1986): 34–7, 43–6.

Lacroix, Charlotte A. "Another Weapon for Combating Family Violence: Prevention of Animal Abuse." *Animal Law* 4 (1998): 1–32.

Langevin, R., D. Paitich, B. Orchard, L. Handy, and A. Russon. "Childhood and Family Background of Killers Seen for Psychiatric Assessment: A Controlled Study." *Bulletin of the American Academy of Psychiatry and the Law* 11, no. 4 (1983): 331–41.

Latham, Stephen R. "Kant Condemned All Suicide." *American Journal of Bioethics* 7, no. 6 (June 2007): 49–51.

Lea, Suzanne R. Goodney. *Delinquency and Animal Cruelty: Myths and Realities about Social Pathology.* El Paso, Tex.: LFB Scholarly Publishing, 2007.

Lee, Patrick, and Robert P. George. "The Wrong of Abortion." In *Contemporary Debates in Applied Ethics*, ed. Andrew I. Cohen and Christopher Heath Wellman, 13–26. Oxford: Blackwell, 2005.

Leibrick-Plehn, Larissa. *Hexenkräuter oder Arznei: Die Abtreibungsmittel im 16. und 17. Jahrhundert.* Stuttgart: Wissenschaftliche Verlagsgesellschaft, 1992.

Lempert, Richard. "Some Caveats Concerning DNA as Criminal Identification Evidence: With Thanks to the Reverend Bayes." *Cardozo Law Review* 13, no. 303 (1991): 303–41.

Leopold, Aldo. *A Sand County Almanac and Sketches Here and There*. Oxford: Oxford University Press, 1987.

Levinas, Emmanuel. *Otherwise than Being, or, Beyond Essence*. Trans. Alphonso Lingis. Pittsburgh, Penn.: Duquesne University Press, 1998.

Levitt, Steven D., and Stephen J. Dubner. *Freakonomics: A Rogue Economist Explores the Hidden Side of Everything*. New York: William Morrow, 2005.

Lewin, Louis. *Die Fruchtabtreibung durch Gifte und Andere Mittel: Ein Handbuch für Ärzte, Juristen, Politiker, Nationalökonomen*. Berlin: Stilke, 1925.

Light, Andrew. "The Case for Practical Pluralism." In *Environmental Ethics: An Anthology*, ed. Andrew Light and Holmes Rolston III, 229–47. Oxford: Blackwell, 2003.

Livingston, Margit. "Desecrating the Ark: Animal Abuse and the Law's Role in Prevention." *Iowa Law Review* 87, no. 1 (Oct. 2001): 1–73.

Lo, Yeuk-Sze. "Natural and Artifactual: Restored Nature as Subject." *Environmental Ethics* 21, no. 3 (fall 1999): 247–66.

Locke, John. *Second Treatise of Government*. Ed. C. B. Macpherson. Indianapolis, Ind.: Hackett, 1980.

Locke, John. *Some Thoughts Concerning Education*. Ed. John W. Yolton and Jean S. Yolton. Oxford: Clarendon Press, 1989.

Lockwood, Randall, and Frank R. Ascione, eds. *Cruelty to Animals and Interpersonal Violence: Readings in Research and Application*. West Lafayette, Ind.: Purdue University Press, 1998.

Lockwood, Randall, and Ann Church. "Deadly Serious: An FBI Perspective on Animal Cruelty." In *Cruelty to Animals and Interpersonal Violence: Readings in Research and Application*, ed. Randall Lockwood and Frank R. Ascione, 241–5. West Lafayette, Ind.: Purdue University Press, 1998.

Lomasky, Loren E. "Being a Person – Does It Matter?" *Philosophical Topics* 12, no. 3 (winter 1981): 139–52.

Lomasky, Loren E. *Persons, Rights, and the Moral Community*. New York: Oxford University Press, 1987.

Louden, Robert B. *Kant's Impure Ethics: From Rational Beings to Human Beings*. New York: Oxford University Press, 2000.

Luban, David, Alan Strudler, and David Wasserman. "Moral Responsibility in the Age of Bureaucracy." *Michigan Law Review* 90, no. 8 (Aug. 1992): 2348–92.

Lucht, Marc. "Does Kant Have Anything to Teach Us about Environmental Ethics?" *American Journal of Economics and Sociology* 66, no. 1 (Jan. 2007): 127–49.

Lynch, Tony, and David Wells. "Non-Anthropocentrism? A Killing Objection." *Environmental Values* 7, no. 2 (May 1998): 151–63.

MacIntyre, Alasdair. *After Virtue*. Notre Dame, Ind.: University of Notre Dame Press, 1981.

Marquis, Don. "Why Abortion Is Immoral." *Journal of Philosophy* 86, no. 4 (Apr. 1989): 183–202.

Mattas, Arthur J., John Arras, James Muyskens, Vivian Tellis, and Frank J. Veith. "A Proposal for Cadaver Organ Procurement: Routine Removal with Right of Informed Refusal." *Journal of Health Politics, Policy and Law* 10, no. 2 (summer 1985): 231–44.

Mendus, Susan. "Kant: 'An Honest but Narrow-Minded Bourgeois'?" In *Women in Western Political Philosophy: Kant to Nietzsche*, ed. Ellen Kennedy and Susan Mendus, 21–43. New York: Palgrave Macmillan, 1987.

Meng, Eddy. "Mail-Order Brides: Gilded Prostitution and the Legal Response." *University of Michigan Journal of Law Reform* 28, no. 1 (fall 1994): 197–248.

Midgley, Mary. *Animals and Why They Matter*. Athens: University of Georgia Press, 1983.

Mill, John Stuart. *Utilitarianism*. Ed. George Sher. Indianapolis, Ind.: Hackett, 1979.

Miller, Catherine. "Childhood Animal Cruelty and Interpersonal Violence." *Clinical Psychology Review* 21, no. 5 (July 2001): 735–49.

Morowitz, Harold J., and James S. Trefil. *The Facts of Life: Science and the Abortion Controversy*. New York: Oxford University Press, 1992.

Moustarah, Fady. "Organ Procurement: Let's Presume Consent." *Canadian Medical Association Journal* 158, no. 2 (27 Jan. 1998): 231–4.

Moyer, Jeanna. "Why Kant and Ecofeminism Don't Mix." *Hypatia* 16, no. 3 (summer 2001): 79–97.

Munzel, G. Felicitas. *Kant's Conception of Moral Character: The "Critical" Link of Morality, Anthropology, and Reflective Judgment*. Chicago: University of Chicago Press, 1998.

Murphy, Jeffrie G. "Does Kant Have a Theory of Punishment?" *Columbia Law Review* 87, no. 3 (Apr. 1987): 509–32.

Murphy, Jeffrie G. "Marxism and Retribution." *Philosophy and Public Affairs* 2, no. 3 (spring 1973): 217–43.

Nagel, Thomas. "Moral Luck." In *Mortal Questions*, 24–38. Cambridge: Cambridge University Press, 1979.

Narayan, Uma. "'Male-Order' Brides: Immigrant Women, Domestic Violence and Immigration Law." *Hypatia* 10, no. 1 (winter 1995): 104–20.

National Commission for the Protection of Human Subjects of Biomedical and Behavioral Research. "The Belmont Report: Ethical Principles and Guidelines for the Protection of Human Subjects of Research" (1979). ohsr.od.nih.gov/guidelines/belmont.html.

National Conference of Commissioners on Uniform State Laws. "Revised Uniform Anatomical Gift Act" (2006). www.law.upenn.edu/bll/archives/ulc/uaga/2009final.htm.

Nell [O'Neill], Onora. *Acting on Principle: An Essay on Kantian Ethics*. New York: Columbia University Press, 1975.

Nelson, Leonard. *System of Ethics*. Trans. Norbert Guterman. New Haven, Conn.: Yale University Press, 1956.

Nietzsche, Friedrich. *On the Genealogy of Morals*. Trans. Walter Kaufmann and R. J. Hollingdale. Ed. Walter Kaufmann. New York: Vintage, 1967.

Noddings, Nel. *Caring, a Feminine Approach to Ethics and Moral Education.* Berkeley: University of California Press, 1984.

Norton, Bryan G. "Environmental Ethics and the Rights of Future Generations." *Environmental Ethics* 4, no. 4 (winter 1982): 319–37.

Norton, Bryan G. "Environmental Ethics and Weak Anthropocentrism." *Environmental Ethics* 6, no. 2 (summer 1984): 131–48.

Norton, Bryan G. *Toward Unity among Environmentalists.* Oxford: Oxford University Press, 1991.

Nozick, Robert. *Anarchy, State, and Utopia.* New York: Basic Books, 1974.

Nussbaum, Martha C. *Frontiers of Justice: Disability, Nationality, Species Membership.* Cambridge, Mass.: Belknap, 2006.

Obama, Barack. "Renewing American Leadership." *Foreign Affairs* 86, no. 4 (July/ Aug. 2007): 2–16.

Oderberg, David S. *Applied Ethics: A Non-Consequentialist Approach.* Oxford: Blackwell, 2000.

Oderberg, David S. *Moral Theory: A Non-Consequentialist Approach.* Oxford: Blackwell, 2000.

Oduncu, Fuat S. "Stem Cell Research in Germany: Ethics of Healing vs. Human Dignity." *Medicine, Health Care and Philosophy* 6, no. 1 (Mar. 2003): 5–16.

O'Neill, Onora, *see also under* Nell

O'Neill, Onora. *Autonomy and Trust in Bioethics.* Cambridge: Cambridge University Press, 2002.

O'Neill, Onora. "Autonomy: The Emperor's New Clothes, The Inaugural Address." *Proceedings of the Aristotelian Society* 77 (2003): 1–21.

O'Neill, Onora. "Between Consenting Adults." *Philosophy and Public Affairs* 14, no. 3 (summer 1985): 252–77.

O'Neill, Onora. *Constructions of Reason: Explorations of Kant's Practical Philosophy.* Cambridge: Cambridge University Press, 1989.

O'Neill, Onora. "Ending World Hunger." In *Matters of Life and Death: New Introductory Essays in Moral Philosophy*, ed. Tom Regan, 3rd edn., 235–79. New York: McGraw-Hill, 1993.

O'Neill, Onora. "Environmental Values, Anthropocentrism and Speciesism." *Environmental Values* 6, no. 2 (May 1997): 127–42.

O'Neill, Onora. "Kant on Duties Regarding Nonrational Nature." *Proceedings of the Aristotelian Society for the Systematic Study of Philosophy*, supplement 72 (1998): 211–28.

O'Neill, Onora. "The Moral Perplexities of Famine Relief." In *Matters of Life and Death*, ed. Tom Regan, 1st edn., 260–98. Philadelphia: Temple University Press, 1980.

Opitz, John M. "Early Embryonic Development: An Up-to-Date Account." Testimony before the President's Council on Bioethics, 16 Jan. 2003. bioethics.georgetown.edu/pcbe/transcripts/jan03/session1.html.

Organ Procurement and Transplantation Network, United States Department of Health and Human Services. "Removal Reasons by Year." optn.transplant.hrsa.gov/latestData/rptData.asp.

Ozar, David T. "The Moral Responsibility of Corporations." In *Ethical Issues in Business: A Philosophical Approach*, ed. Thomas Donaldson and Patricia H. Werhane, 294–300. Englewood Cliffs, N.J.: Prentice Hall, 1979.

Papadaki, Lina. "Sexual Objectification: From Kant to Contemporary Feminism." *Contemporary Political Theory* 6, no. 3 (Aug. 2007): 330–48.

Parfit, Derek. "Energy Policy and the Further Future: The Identity Problem." In *Energy and the Future*, ed. Douglas MacLean and Peter G. Brown, 166–79. Totowa, N.J.: Rowman & Littlefield, 1983.

Parfit, Derek. *Reasons and Persons*. New York: Oxford University Press, 1986.

Pateman, Carole. *The Sexual Contract*. Stanford, Calif.: Stanford University Press, 1988.

Pellegrino, Edmund D., and David C. Thomasma. *A Philosophical Basis of Medical Practice: Toward a Philosophy and Ethic of the Healing Professions*. New York: Oxford University Press, 1981.

Perlmutter, Martin. "Desert and Capital Punishment." In *Morality and Moral Controversies: Readings in Moral, Social, and Political Philosophy*, ed. John Arthur, 7th edn., 124–31. Upper Saddle River, N.J.: Pearson Prentice Hall, 2005.

Perry, Constance. "Suicide Fails to Pass the Categorical Imperative." *American Journal of Bioethics* 7, no. 6 (June 2007): 51–3.

Petrick, Joseph A., and John F. Quinn. *Management Ethics: Integrity at Work*. Thousand Oaks, Calif.: Sage, 1997.

Piper, Adrian M. S. "Xenophobia and Kantian Rationalism." In *African-American Perspectives and Philosophical Traditions*, ed. John P. Pittman, 188–232. New York: Routledge, 1997.

Pippin, Robert B. *Hegel's Practical Philosophy: Rational Agency as Ethical Life*. Cambridge: Cambridge University Press, 2008.

Pitcher, George. "The Misfortunes of the Dead." *American Philosophical Quarterly* 21, no. 2 (Apr. 1984): 183–8.

Platt, Jean Gray, et al. "Special Project: Survey of Abortion Law." *Arizona State Law Journal* 67 (1980): 67–216.

Pogge, Thomas W. "Is Kant's *Rechtslehre* a 'Comprehensive Liberalism'?" In *Kant's "Metaphysics of Morals": Interpretive Essays*, ed. Mark Timmons, 133–58. Oxford: Oxford University Press, 2002.

Pogge, Thomas W. "Severe Poverty as a Human Rights Violation." In *Freedom from Poverty as a Human Right: Who Owes What to the Very Poor?* ed. Thomas Pogge, 11–53. Oxford: Oxford University Press, 2007.

Pogge, Thomas W. *World Poverty and Human Rights: Cosmopolitan Responsibilities and Reforms*. 2nd edn. Cambridge: Polity, 2008.

Pollack, Andrew. "Scientists Show That It's Possible to Create Fake DNA Evidence." *New York Times*, 18 Aug. 2009, late edition, D3.

Posner, Richard. "Animal Rights: Legal, Philosophical, and Pragmatic Perspectives." In *Animal Rights: Current Debates and New Directions*, ed. Cass R. Sunstein and Martha C. Nussbaum, 51–77. Oxford: Oxford University Press, 2004.

Price-Smith, Andrew T. *The Health of Nations: Infectious Disease, Environmental Change, and Their Effects on National Security and Development*. Cambridge, Mass.: MIT Press, 2002.

Rachels, James. "Active and Passive Euthanasia." *New England Journal of Medicine* 292, no. 2 (9 Jan. 1975): 78–80.

Radelet, Michael L., Hugo Adam Bedau, and Constance E. Putnam. *In Spite of Innocence: Erroneous Convictions in Capital Cases.* Boston: Northeastern University Press, 1992.

Radelet, Michael L., William S. Lofquist, and Hugo Adam Bedau. "Prisoners Released from Death Rows since 1970 because of Doubts about Their Guilt." *Thomas M. Cooley Law Review* 13, no. 3 (1996): 907–66.

Ramsey, Paul. "The Morality of Abortion." In *Moral Problems*, ed. James Rachels, 37–58. New York: Harper & Row, 1975.

Rawls, John. "Themes in Kant's Moral Philosophy." In *Kant's Transcendental Deductions: The Three "Critiques" and the "Opus Postumum"*, ed. Eckart Förster, 81–113. Stanford, Calif.: Stanford University Press, 1989.

Rawls, John. *A Theory of Justice*, rev. edn. Cambridge, Mass.: Harvard University Press, 1999.

Ray, A. Chadwick. "Humanity, Personhood and Abortion." *International Philosophical Quarterly* 25 (1985): 233–45.

Regan, Tom. *The Case for Animal Rights.* Berkeley: University of California Press, 1983.

Regan, Tom. "The Nature and Possibility of an Environmental Ethic." *Environmental Ethics* 3, no. 1 (spring 1981): 19–34.

Reiman, Jeffrey. *Abortion and the Ways We Value Human Life.* Lanham, Md.: Rowman & Littlefield, 1999.

Rolston, Holmes III. "Value in Nature and the Nature of Value." In *Philosophy and the Natural Environment*, ed. Robin Attfield and Andrew Belsey, 13–30. Cambridge: Cambridge University Press, 1994.

Ross, W. D. *The Right and the Good.* Indianapolis, Ind.: Hackett, 1988.

Rousseau, Jean-Jacques. *On the Social Contract.* Trans. Judith R. Masters. Ed. Roger D. Masters. New York: St. Martin's, 1978.

Rublack, Ulinka. "The Public Body: Policing Abortion in Early Modern Germany." In *Gender Relations in German History: Power, Agency, and Experience from the Sixteenth to the Twentieth Century*, ed. Lynn Abrams and Elizabeth Harvey, 57–79. London: University of London Press, 1996.

Rumsey, Jean P. "Re-Visions of Agency in Kant's Moral Theory." In *Feminist Interpretations of Immanuel Kant*, ed. Robin May Schott, 125–44. University Park: Pennsylvania State University Press, 1997.

Said, Edward W. *Orientalism.* New York: Pantheon, 1978.

Sandel, Michael. *Liberalism and the Limits of Justice.* Cambridge: Cambridge University Press, 1982.

Schaff, Kory. "Kant, Political Liberalism, and the Ethics of Same-Sex Relations." *Journal of Social Philosophy* 32, no. 3 (fall 2001): 446–62.

Scheler, Max. *Formalism in Ethics and Non-Formal Ethics of Values: A New Attempt toward the Foundation of an Ethical Personalism.* 5th rev. edn. Trans. Manfred S. Frings and Roger L. Funk. Evanston, Ill.: Northwestern University Press, 1973.

Scheman, Naomi. *Engenderings: Constructions of Knowledge, Authority, and Privilege.* New York: Routledge, 1993.

Schiebinger, Londa. *Plants and Empire: Colonial Bioprospecting in the Atlantic World.* Cambridge, Mass.: Harvard University Press, 2004.

Schönfeld, Martin. "The Green Kant: Environmental Dynamics and Sustainable Policies." In *Environmental Ethics: Readings in Theory and Application,* ed. Louis P. Pojman and Paul Pojman, 5th edn., 49–60. Belmont, Calif.: Thomson Wadsworth, 2008.

Schott, Robin May. "Feminism and Kant: Antipathy or Sympathy?" In *Autonomy and Community: Readings in Contemporary Kantian Social Philosophy,* ed. Jane Kneller and Sidney Axinn, 87–100. Albany: State University of New York Press, 1998.

Schott, Robin May. "The Gender of Enlightenment." In *What Is Enlightenment? Eighteenth-Century Answers and Twentieth-Century Questions,* ed. James Schmidt, 471–87. Berkeley: University of California Press, 1996.

Schott, Robin May, ed. *Feminist Interpretations of Immanuel Kant.* University Park: Pennsylvania State University Press, 1997.

Schröder, Hannelore. "Kant's Patriarchal Order." Trans. Rita Gircour. In *Feminist Interpretations of Immanuel Kant,* ed. Robin May Schott, 275–96. University Park: Pennsylvania State University Press, 1997.

Schwarz, Stephen. *The Moral Question of Abortion.* Chicago: Loyola University Press, 1990.

Schwarzschild, Steven S. "Kantianism on the Death Penalty (and Related Social Problems)." *Archiv für Rechts- und Sozialphilosophie* 71, no. 3 (1985): 343–72.

Sedgwick, Sally. "Can Kant's Ethics Survive the Feminist Critique?" In *Feminist Interpretations of Immanuel Kant,* ed. Robin May Schott, 77–100. University Park: Pennsylvania State University Press, 1997.

Serpell, James. *In the Company of Animals: A Study of Human–Animal Relationships.* Rev. edn. Cambridge: Cambridge University Press, 1996.

Shaw, William H., and Vincent Barry. *Moral Issues in Business.* 8th edn. Belmont, Calif.: Wadsworth, 2001.

Sheehy, Ellen, Suzanne L. Conrad, Lori E. Brigham, Richard Luskin, Phyllis Weber, Mark Eakin, Lawrence Schkade, and Lawrence Hunsicker. "Estimating the Number of Potential Organ Donors in the United States." *New England Journal of Medicine* 349, no. 7 (14 Aug. 2003): 667–74.

Shell, Susan M. "Kant's Conception of a Human Race." In *The German Invention of Race,* ed. Sara Eigen and Mark Larrimore, 55–72. Albany: State University of New York Press, 2006.

Sidgwick, Henry. *The Methods of Ethics.* New York: Dourer, 1966.

Siebert, Charles. "The Animal-Cruelty Syndrome." *New York Times Magazine,* 13 June 2010, 42–51.

Siminoff, Laura A., and Renee H. Lawrence. "Knowing Patients' Preferences about Organ Donation: Does It Make a Difference?" *Journal of Trauma* 53, no. 4 (Oct. 2002): 754–60.

Siminoff, Laura A., and Mary Beth Mercer. "Public Policy, Public Opinion, and Consent for Organ Donation." *Cambridge Quarterly of Healthcare Ethics* 10, no. 4 (fall 2001): 377–86.

Singer, Peter. *Animal Liberation.* Rev. edn. New York: HarperPerennial, 2002.

Singer, Peter. "Ethics beyond Species and beyond Instincts: A Response to Richard Posner." In *Animal Rights: Current Debates and New Directions*, ed. Cass R. Sunstein and Martha C. Nussbaum, 78–92. Oxford: Oxford University Press, 2004.

Singer, Peter. "Famine, Affluence, and Morality." *Philosophy and Public Affairs* 1, no. 3 (spring 1972): 229–43.

Singer, Peter. *Practical Ethics*. 2nd edn. Cambridge: Cambridge University Press, 1993.

Singer, Peter. "A Response." In *Singer and His Critics*, ed. Dale Jamieson, 325–7. Oxford: Blackwell, 1999.

Skidmore, J. "Duties to Animals: The Failure of Kant's Moral Theory." *The Journal of Value Inquiry* 35, no. 4 (Dec. 2001): 541–59.

Small, Michael, and Dirk Mathison. "For Men Who Want an Old-Fashioned Girl, the Latest Wedding March Is Here Comes the Asian Mail-Order Bride." *People Weekly*, 16 Sept. 1985, 127–9.

Soble, Alan. "Kant and Sexual Perversion." *The Monist* 86, no. 1 (Jan. 2003): 55–89.

Steinberg, David. "An 'Opting In' Paradigm for Kidney Transplantation." *American Journal of Bioethics* 4, no. 4 (fall 2004): 4–14.

Steinbock, Bonnie. "Why Most Abortions Are Not Wrong." In *Advances in Bioethics*, ed. Rem B. Edwards and E. Edwards Bittar, vol. 5, 245–67. Stamford, Conn.: Jai, 1999.

Steinfeld, Henning, Pierre Gerber, Tom Wassenaar, Vincent Castel, Mauricio Rosales, and Cees de Haan. *Livestock's Long Shadow: Environmental Issues and Options*. Rome: Food and Agriculture Organization of the United Nations, 2006.

Stiers, Gretchen A. *From This Day Forward: Commitment, Marriage, and Family in Lesbian and Gay Relationships*. New York: St. Martin's, 1999.

Stoeltje, Melissa Fletcher. "Customers Look to Russia for Love; Local Firm Puts Women on Web." *San Antonio Express-News*, 24 Dec. 2000, metro edition, 1A.

Strawson, P. F. "Freedom and Resentment." In *Studies in the Philosophy of Thought and Action*, ed. P. F. Strawson, 71–96. Oxford: Oxford University Press, 1968.

Subcommittee on Civil and Constitutional Rights. *Innocence and the Death Penalty: Assessing the Danger of Mistaken Executions*. Staff Report, Committee on the Judiciary, 103rd Congress. 1st Session (1993).

Sumner, L. W. "A Third Way." In *The Problem of Abortion*, ed. Joel Feinberg, 2nd edn., 71–93. Belmont, Calif.: Wadsworth, 1984.

Sylvan, Richard. "Is There a Need for a New, an Environmental, Ethic?" In *Proceedings of the XVth World Congress of Philosophy*, vol. 1, *Philosophy and Science, Morality and Culture, Technology and Man*, 205–10. Varna, Bulgaria: Sofia, 1973.

Tallichet, Suzanne E., and Christopher Hensley. "Exploring the Link between Recurrent Acts of Childhood and Adolescent Animal Cruelty and Subsequent Violent Crime." *Criminal Justice Review* 29, no. 2 (2004): 304–16.

Taylor, Charles. "Atomism." In *Philosophy and the Human Sciences*, vol. 2 of *Philosophical Papers*, 187–210. Cambridge: Cambridge University Press, 1982.

Taylor, Charles. *Sources of the Self: The Making of the Modern Identity*. Cambridge, Mass.: Harvard University Press, 1989.

Taylor, Paul W. *Respect for Nature: A Theory of Environmental Ethics*. Princeton, N.J.: Princeton University Press, 1986.

Teson, Fernando. "Kantian International Liberalism." In *International Society: Diverse Ethical Perspectives*, ed. David R. Maple and Terry Nardin, 103–13. Princeton, N.J.: Princeton University Press, 1998.

Thaler, Richard H., and Cass R. Sunstein. *Nudge: Improving Decisions about Health, Wealth, and Happiness*. New Haven, Conn.: Yale University Press, 2008.

Thompson, William C. "The Potential for Error in Forensic DNA Testing (and How That Complicates the Use of DNA Databases for Criminal Identification)." Paper presented at the national conference for the Council for Responsible Genetics, New York, June 2008. www.councilforresponsiblegenetics.org/pageDocuments/H4T5EOYUZI.pdf.

Thompson, William C. "Tarnish on the 'Gold Standard': Understanding Recent Problems in Forensic DNA Testing." *The Champion* 30, no. 1 (Jan./Feb. 2006): 10–16.

Thomson, Judith Jarvis. "A Defense of Abortion." *Philosophy and Public Affairs* 1, no. 1 (autumn 1971): 47–66.

Throop, William, ed. *Environmental Restoration: Ethics, Theory, and Practice*. Amherst, N.Y.: Humanity, 2000.

Tooley, Michael. "Abortion and Infanticide." In *Applied Ethics*, ed. Peter Singer, 57–85. Oxford: Oxford University Press, 1986.

Trials of War Criminals before the Military Tribunals under Control Council Law No. 10: Nuremberg, October 1946–April 1949. Vol. 2. Washington, D.C.: Government Printing Office, 1949.

United Nations Millennium Ecosystem Assessment Board. *Ecosystems and Human Well-Being: Current State and Trends*. Vol. 1. Ed. Rashid Hassan, Robert Scholes, and Neville Ash. Washington, D.C.: Island, 2005.

United States Census Bureau. "Poverty Thresholds 2010." www.census.gov/hhes/www/poverty/data/threshld/thresh10.html.

United States Department of Health and Human Services, Office of Inspector General. "Variation in Organ Donation among Transplant Centers," 2003. oig.hhs.gov/oei/reports/oei-01-02-00210.pdf.

U.S. Bishops' Pro-Life Committee. "Nutrition and Hydration: Moral and Pastoral Reflections." In *Ethical Issues in Modern Medicine: Contemporary Readings in Bioethics*, ed. Bonnie Steinbock, John D. Arras, and Alex John London, 7th edn., 429–35. Boston: McGraw-Hill, 2009.

Van den Haag, Ernest. "The Death Penalty Once More." In *The Death Penalty in America: Current Controversies*, ed. Hugo Adam Bedau, 445–56. New York: Oxford University Press, 1997.

Van den Haag, Ernest. "The Ultimate Punishment: A Defense." *Harvard Law Review* 99, no. 7 (May 1986): 1662–9.

Veatch, Robert M. *Transplantation Ethics*. Washington, D.C.: Georgetown University Press, 2000.

Velasquez, Manuel G. "Why Corporations Are Not Morally Responsible for Anything They Do." *Business and Professional Ethics Journal* 2, no. 3 (fall 1983): 1–18.

Villipando, Venny. "The Business of Selling Mail-Order Brides." In *Making Waves: An Anthology of Writing by and about Asian-American Women*, ed. Asian Women United of California, 318–26. Boston: Beacon, 1989.

Walton-Moss, Benita J., Jennifer Manganello, Victoria Frye, and Jacquelyn C. Campbell. "Risk Factors for Intimate Partner Violence and Associated Injury among Urban Women." *Journal of Community Health* 30, no. 5 (Oct. 2005): 377–89.

Walzer, Michael. *Spheres of Justice*. New York: Basic Books, 1983.

Warnock, Mary. "Do Human Cells Have Rights?" *Bioethics* 1, no. 1 (Jan. 1987): 1–14.

Warren, Mary Anne. "Moral Status." In *A Companion to Applied Ethics*, ed. R. G. Frey and Christopher Heath Wellman, 439–50. Oxford: Blackwell, 2003.

Warren, Mary Anne. *Moral Status: Obligations to Persons and Other Living Things*. Oxford: Clarendon Press, 1997.

Warren, Mary Anne. "On the Moral and Legal Status of Abortion." In *The Problem of Abortion*, ed. Joel Feinberg, 2nd edn., 102–19. Belmont, Calif.: Wadsworth, 1984.

Wellman, Carl. *Medical Law and Moral Rights*. New York: Springer, 2005.

Werner, Richard. "Abortion: The Ontological and Moral Status of the Unborn." In *Today's Moral Problems*, ed. Richard A. Wasserstrom, 2nd edn., 51–74. New York: Macmillan, 1979.

Wilkinson, T. M. "Individual and Family Decisions about Organ Donation." *Journal of Applied Philosophy* 24, no. 1 (Feb. 2007): 26–40.

Williams, Bernard. "A Critique of Utilitarianism." In *Utilitarianism: For and Against*, by J. J. C. Smart and Bernard Williams, 75–150. Cambridge: Cambridge University Press, 1973.

Williams, Bernard. *Ethics and the Limits of Philosophy*. Cambridge, Mass.: Harvard University Press, 1985.

Williams, Bernard. "The Idea of Equality." In *Problems of the Self: Philosophical Papers, 1956–1972*, 230–49. Cambridge: Cambridge University Press, 1973.

Williams, Bernard. *Moral Luck: Philosophical Papers, 1973–1980*. Cambridge: Cambridge University Press, 1981.

Wilson, Holly L. "The Green Kant: Kant's Treatment of Animals." In *Environmental Ethics: Readings in Theory and Application*, ed. Louis P. Pojman and Paul Pojman, 5th edn., 65–72. Belmont, Calif.: Thomson Wadsworth, 2008.

Wilson, Holly L. "Kant's Evolutionary Theory of Marriage." In *Autonomy and Community: Readings in Contemporary Kantian Social Philosophy*, ed. Jane Kneller and Sidney Axinn, 283–306. Albany: State University of New York Press, 1998.

Wilson, Holly L. "Rethinking Kant from the Perspective of Ecofeminism." In *Feminist Interpretations of Immanuel Kant*, ed. Robin May Schott, 373–99. University Park: Pennsylvania State University Press, 1997.

Wise, Stephen M. *Rattling the Cage: Toward Legal Rights for Animals*. Cambridge, Mass.: Perseus, 2000.

Wolff, Christian. *Von der Menschen Thun und Lassen, zu Beförderung ihrer Glückseeligkeit*. Ed. Hans Werner Arndt and Jean École. Hildesheim: Olms, 1976.

Wolff, Christian. *Von Gott, der Welt und der Seele des Menschen, auch allen Dingen überhaupt*. Ed. Charles A. Corr and Jean École. Hildesheim: Olms, 1976.

Wood, Allen W. *Hegel's Ethical Thought*. Cambridge: Cambridge University Press, 1990.

Wood, Allen W. "Kant on Duties Regarding Nonrational Nature." *Proceedings of the Aristotelian Society for the Systematic Study of Philosophy*, supplement 72 (1998): 189–210.

Wood, Allen W. *Kantian Ethics*. Cambridge: Cambridge University Press, 2008.

Wood, Allen W. *Kant's Ethical Thought*. Cambridge: Cambridge University Press, 1999.

World Medical Association. *Declaration of Helsinki: Ethical Principles for Medical Research Involving Human Subjects* (1964). www.wma.net/en/30publications/ 10policies/b3/index.html.

Yalom, Marilyn. *A History of the Wife*. New York: HarperCollins, 2001.

Zilney, Lisa Anne. *Linking Animal Cruelty and Family Violence*. Youngstown, N.Y.: Cambria, 2007.

Index

abortion, 7, 112n22, 163n20, 165,
   241–82
abstinence, *see* celibacy
aesthetic feeling, 56–9, 66, 69n20
agency, moral, 14–16, 23, 26–9, 31,
   36–7n2, 41n30, 45–7, 55, 59–60,
   70n27, 74–6, 91, 94–5, 109–10,
   118–25, 130, 132–4, 143, 177,
   179, 182–3, 186–7, 191n28,
   196–9, 204–10, 214, 215n2,
   217–40, 241–2, 250–3, 256, 262,
   265, 268, 273, 280–1n60, 283–7
   see also moral agents vs. moral
   patients
Althusser, Louis, 235
American Medical Association (AMA),
   87n5, 99–100, 106, 107
amphiboly, *see* fallacy
Anderson-Gold, Sharon, 177–8
animals, 13–45, 63–6, 75, 101–2, 110,
   142, 148, 151, 163n17, 219, 224,
   249–52, 257, 262, 265, 273,
   277n28, 286
   cruelty toward, 16–22, 32–4,
   37–8n9, 38–9n10, 43n58, 43n59,
   43n61, 69n21
   duties to vs. duties with regard to,
   16–18, 148

as "subjects of a life," 23
   see also experimentation, animal
anthropocentrism, 6, 13–16, 26, 33–6,
   43n56, 46, 48–53, 60–6, 67n2,
   110, 207–8
   and nonanthropocentrism, 60–6
   strong vs. weak, 61–2
apperception ("I think"), 98–100,
   249–51, 257–8, 262, 264,
   278n30
a priori philosophy, 32, 68–9n19, 72,
   87, 118, 124, 133, 134n1, 182,
   187, 194, 204, 213
Aquinas, Thomas, 258, 275n3
Aristotle, 275n3
autonomy, 2–4, 8n2, 11–12, 14–15,
   26, 30, 41n30, 45, 74–5, 90–5,
   99, 104–9, 111n6, 152, 186–8,
   189n4, 198–9, 210, 212–14, 227,
   230–1, 233, 250–1, 256, 262–5,
   267–8, 284, 286
   see also agency, moral; consent;
   patient autonomy
Axinn, Sidney, 88n18

Baier, Annette C., 1
beauty
   natural, 56–7, 59–60

Kant and Applied Ethics: The Uses and Limits of Kant's Practical Philosophy, First Edition.
Matthew C. Altman.
© 2011 John Wiley & Sons Inc. Published 2011 by Blackwell Publishing Ltd.

beauty (*cont'd*)
  as symbol of morality, 56–7, 62,
    69n20
Beauvoir, Simone de, 162n4
Beccaria, Cesare, 122, 130, 135n5,
    135n6, 137n19
  On Crimes and Punishments, 135n5
Bedau, Hugo Adam, 126
Belmont Report, 1–2, 4–5, 9n3, 108
beneficence, 4–5, 31, 55–6, 72–3,
    77–82, 85, 88n12, 100–1, 104,
    131–2, 137n21, 148, 150, 185,
    194, 197–204, 206, 209, 214,
    243, 270
Bentham, Jeremy, 42n50, 197
Bergh, Henry, 34
Berlin, Isaiah, 145
Bernasconi, Robert, 192n41
Bible, 16, 34, 49, 139, 158, 198
biocentrism, 25, 46, 48, 52, 66
  see also anthropocentrism, and
    nonanthropocentrism
bioethics, *see* abortion; health care;
    organ donation; patient autonomy;
    physician-assisted suicide; refusal
    of medical treatment; research
    ethics
Black, Charles, 137n20
Blackstone, William, 185
  *Commentaries on the Laws of
    England*, 185
Boatright, John R., 218, 232
Boonin, David, 246–9
Bordo, Susan, 188
Bowie, Norman E., 218, 225–7,
    228–9, 236n3, 237n13
Brake, Elizabeth, 149–51, 162n4, 176
Brandt, Reinhard, 279n43
Broadie, Alexander, 32
Brody, Baruch A., 277n17
Brown v. Board of Education, 164n25
Bush, George W., 260
business ethics, 79–80, 197, 227–40,
    286

Callicott, J. Baird, 13, 33, 41n33, 60,
    66–7n1

Campbell, John Lord, 43n58
capital punishment, 115, 117–38, 139,
    280n58
capitalism, 79–80, 168–9, 176, 184,
    208, 231, 233, 235
care ethics, 188, 273–4
Carruthers, Peter, 36–7n2
categorical imperative, 1, 4, 5, 15, 26,
    28, 32, 37n2, 55, 77, 128–30,
    151–2, 154, 182, 195, 204–5,
    213–14, 219, 222–5, 231–2,
    243–4, 269–70, 284
  formula of humanity, 15, 26, 37n6,
    53, 72–3, 87n5, 139, 142, 151–3,
    155, 162n6, 168–70, 203, 207,
    212–13, 222, 226, 232, 237n13,
    239n28, 244–6, 248–50
  formula of the kingdom of ends,
    118, 207, 226–7, 228–9, 284
  formula of universal law, 4, 53, 55,
    68–9n19, 73, 94, 118–19, 130,
    132, 153–4, 195, 199, 201–2,
    205, 222, 243–4, 258, 261, 270,
    276n11
categorical imperative procedure, 205,
    276n11
  contradiction in conception, 53,
    68–9n19
  contradiction in the will, 53, 55,
    68–9n19, 73, 95, 103, 122–3,
    130, 132, 137n19, 150, 153–4,
    163n20
categories of the understanding, 56,
    57–8, 124, 278n31
category of causality, 46–7, 124, 224,
    267–8
Catholic Church, 101–2, 112n22,
    191n23, 242, 258, 260, 275n3,
    280n50
celibacy, 154, 244
character (*Gesinnung*), 16–18, 20–1,
    39n12, 43n58, 57–62, 64, 101–2,
    112n22, 119, 150, 211, 223, 235,
    240n34, 260–1
charitable giving, 73, 81, 88n14, 101,
    194–216
  see also beneficence

children, 23, 54, 93, 154–5, 157,
161n2, 168, 175, 180, 242,
252–8, 262–75, 280n58, 282n79
chimpanzees, 14–16
choice, animal vs. free, 27–9, 75,
250–1, 262–3
Cholbi, Michael J., 94–5, 111n9,
111n10
citizens
obligations of and to, 72, 75–83, 85,
93, 105–6, 120, 163n10, 197,
223, 268, 280n58
passive vs. active, 23, 175, 185–7
of the world vs. of the state, 263–4,
280n58
citizenship
as good to be exchanged, 171,
173–5, 178, 186, 189n5
relevance/irrelevance of, 72, 81–6
civil society, 11, 78–9, 86, 88n20, 103,
104, 119–20, 122–3, 133, 135n7,
145–6, 147, 159, 163n10, 215n2,
223
civil unions, 160, 164n24
climate change, 52–3
coercion, 2, 78, 81, 92, 106–8,
169–70, 177–84, 198, 222
state, 77, 82, 86–7, 103, 118–20,
131–3, 146–51, 185
see also capital punishment;
punishment
collective responsibility, *see*
responsibility, collective
common sense, 32, 34–5, 42n50, 63–4,
66, 202
sensus communis, 56, 69n20
communitarianism, 165, 235, 273–4,
283–7
concepts, pure, *see* categories of the
understanding
concubinage, 184–5
consent, 8n3, 93–4, 106, 133, 148,
168–70, 180, 182–4, 198, 222,
232, 239n30, 244, 247–9
explicit vs. presumed, *see* organ
donation, opt-in vs. opt-out
informed, 2–4, 8–9n3, 184, 189n4

to the law and legal punishment,
77–80, 82, 86, 104–5, 109,
119–20, 122–3, 129–34, 134–5n4,
135n7, 145–6, 148, 215n2, 253–4
in marriage, 144–51, 167–72,
180–6, 191n23, 192n33
to medical treatment, 90–3, 95
tacit, 20–1, 106, 134–5n4, 135n7,
239n30
consequences, 54, 74, 91–2, 95–6,
191n28, 200–2, 230, 243, 257,
258, 280n53
consequentialism, *see* utilitarianism
conservation, environmental, 50, 57–8,
65–6
Constable, Nicole, 189n5
contract, 103, 147, 171, 184–5
see also marriage; social contract
convergence hypothesis, 60–3
Cooley, Dennis R., 96–8, 100
coordination maxim, *see* maxim,
coordination
corporate internal decision (CID)
structure, 220–3, 225, 227, 231,
233
corporate responsibility, *see*
responsibility, collective
cosmopolitanism, 72, 83–6, 88n18,
177, 192n41
coverture, 185–6

Dean, Richard, 30
Death with Dignity Acts (Oregon and
Washington), 91–2, 95, 97,
111n10
death penalty, *see* capital punishment
deception, *see* lying
Declaration of Helsinki, 8n2, 8–9n3,
9n8
De George, Richard T., 229–30
de Waal, Frans, 14–15, 36–7n2
deep ecology, 62
DeGrazia, David, 37n6
dementia, 96–100, 251, 262, 280n55
Denis, Lara, 39n12, 149
Derrida, Jacques, 26
Descartes, René, 27, 46, 62, 187, 188

dignity, 2–5, 14, 26–7, 30–1, 37n6,
    40–1n27, 53, 58, 74, 87n5, 91,
    96–102, 121–3, 134, 141–2,
    148–51, 158, 170, 179, 182, 184,
    188, 205, 207–8, 212–13, 223–6,
    249, 252–5, 258, 263, 266–8,
    280n55, 285
disinterested pleasure, *see* pleasure,
    disinterested
disposition, *see* character (*Gesinnung*)
DNA evidence, 126–7
Doctrine of Double Effect, 138n23
domestic partnerships, *see* civil unions
domestic violence, 34, 38–9n10, 173–5
    see also rape, marital
duties
    direct, 16–17, 21–6, 29–35,
        40–1n27, 45, 57, 82, 101–2, 180,
        245, 249, 251, 254–5, 257–8,
        260, 262, 264–7, 270, 274–5
    imperfect, 39n12, 73, 101, 153,
        203–4, 245–6, 270
    indirect, 16–19, 21–2, 29–34,
        39n12, 43n56, 50–3, 57, 59,
        101–2, 245, 251, 260–2, 266–7,
        269, 272, 274
    negative, 50, 55, 77, 81, 100
    perfect, 39n12, 246, 270
    positive, 50, 55, 72–3, 77–8, 87,
        100
    prima facie, 137n21, 142, 153
Dworkin, Andrea, 142, 162n4
Dyck, Arthur J., 93, 96

ecosystem, 47–8, 50, 52–3, 66
    services, 66
education, 173–4, 263, 265
    moral, 204–6, 208, 210
Egonsson, Dan, 19–21
Engelhardt, H. Tristram, Jr., 278n30
Engels, Friedrich, 168–9, 176, 183
English, Jane, 245
environmental ethics, 6, 11, 13–14, 16,
    25, 36, 45–70, 259
equality and inequality, 34, 39n15,
    78–80, 85, 88n12, 120, 122,
    147–9, 156–8, 159–60, 167,

    171–3, 185–6, 196–7, 208–9,
    212–14, 284–5
euthanasia, 91–2, 98
    passive vs. active, 99–100, 112n21
    see also physician-assisted suicide
Evan, William M., 217–18
experience (*Erfahrung*), 27–8, 56,
    249–51, 262, 270, 278n31
    see also representation (*Vorstellung*)
experimentation
    animal, 3, 9n7, 19, 39n15, 39n16
    human, 1–5, 189n4
    see also research ethics
Eze, Emmanuel Chukwudi, 192n41

fact of reason, 46, 87n8, 205, 224–5,
    264
fact/value distinction, 254, 269
    see also fallacy, naturalistic
factory farming, 19–22, 35, 52
faculty of desire
    (*Begehrungsvermögen*), higher and
    lower, 27–9, 75, 250
fallacy
    amphiboly, 18, 30, 39n13
    begging the question, 254–5, 264
    composition, 234
    false dichotomy, 226
    line-drawing, 263
    naturalistic, 31, 42n47, 152
Feinberg, Joel, 113n25, 266, 274
Feldman, Susan, 243–4, 245–6
feminism, 172–3, 175, 176, 190n9,
    190n15, 209, 255
feminist philosophy, 67n3, 140, 142,
    169, 188
Fichte, J. G., 280–1n60
    Vocation of Man, 280–1n60
fidelity, duty of, 232
    see also lying
forced marriage, *see* marriage, forced
formalism charge, 1, 195, 209–15,
    283–7
Foucault, Michel, 235–6
freedom, inner vs. outer, 78, 118–19
    see also liberty, positive vs. negative
Freeman, R. Edward, 217–18, 239n28

French, Peter, 220, 238n18
Freud, Anna, 69n21
Freud, Sigmund, 124, 142
Friedman, Milton, 218–19, 232–3
friendship, 149
Frye, Marilyn, 276n9
future generations, 53–6, 68–9n19,
    259

Gauthier, Jeffrey, 209
gay marriage, *see* marriage, same-sex
Genesis, *see* Bible
Gensler, Harry J., 243
George, Robert P., 278n34
Gibson, Kevin, 237n9, 239n28
Gilligan, Carol, 188, 273
global warming, *see* climate change
gluttony, 75, 143, 152
God, 16, 27, 30, 34, 129, 152, 158,
    224, 238n15, 267–70
    see also holy will
good, conditional and unconditional,
    16, 20, 23, 31, 65, 95, 99, 120,
    142–3, 148, 151, 156, 219, 247
good will, 28, 31, 65, 143, 176, 200,
    208, 219
Goodpaster, Kenneth E., 25, 219, 233
gratitude, 17, 59, 64, 70n27
    roots of, 58–9, 64, 70n27
Guyer, Paul, 39n12, 57

happiness, 94, 99, 111n9, 129, 140,
    143, 147–8, 155–6, 196, 198,
    200, 207, 225, 227, 233, 238n15,
    245, 247–9, 268, 269–70
Hardin, Garrett, 45
Hare, R. M., 40n20, 243, 271, 276n9
Hassoun, Nicole, 281–2n70
Hayek, Friedrich A., 77, 87–8n10, 90
health, 51–2, 73–5, 78, 80, 83–4, 93,
    96, 99–101, 103, 148, 153, 259,
    261, 271
    mental, 94–5, 111n10
health care, 6, 11, 71–89, 105, 206,
    209
Hegel, G. W. F., and Hegelianism, 1,
    146, 165, 176, 195, 198, 199,

201–2, 209–10, 214–15, 215n2,
    230–1, 235, 274–5, 283–7
Herman, Barbara, 17–18, 39n12, 55,
    72–5, 81, 94, 134n2, 142, 144–5,
    162n4, 204–6, 208, 211, 217,
    243, 276n11, 286–7
Herrera v. Collins, 137–8n22
Hill, Thomas E., Jr., 58–60, 64, 70n27
Hobbes, Thomas, 83, 104–5, 109,
    145
Hoff, Christina, 37n3, 37n6, 42n54
holy will, 30, 127, 224, 264
homosexuality, 115, 140, 144, 151–61,
    161n2, 163n17, 164n25
    see also marriage, same-sex
human subjects research, *see*
    experimentation, human; research
    ethics
humanism, *see* anthropocentrism
humanity, 1–2, 5, 14–17, 22, 26, 29,
    72–4, 96–102, 121, 131, 141–5,
    147–52, 156, 167–71, 180, 199,
    206–10, 212–13, 222, 225, 233,
    245, 247, 250, 255–6, 258,
    264–5, 270, 273, 286
    see also categorical imperative,
    formula of humanity
Hume, David, 211
hunting, 18, 20
Hutcheson, Francis, 269
hypothetical imperative, 28, 83, 212,
    269–70

incest, 157, 172, 245
inclination, 3–4, 14, 20, 26, 28, 31,
    56, 62, 76, 91, 94, 104, 109, 117,
    120, 124, 143, 148, 163n10, 169,
    178, 182, 188, 209–10, 223–5,
    228, 233, 248–9, 250, 270, 287
infanticide, 263–4, 266–71, 274,
    281–2n70
inheritance, 103–4, 168
inner sense, 123, 201, 250
intention, 74, 106–8, 123–5, 127,
    136–7n17, 138n23, 150, 176,
    197, 201, 205, 220, 230–1,
    233–4, 236–7n4, 237n9, 238n18

interest, 19, 25, 33–4, 39n15,
    40–1n27, 50, 54, 59, 66, 69n20,
    113n25, 163–4n21, 235, 266–7,
    271, 274, 276n9
  highest-order, 196, 229
international marriage agencies, *see*
    marriage, mail-order
intrinsic value, 13–16, 18, 23, 25, 33,
    37–8n9, 45, 48–9, 60–4, 95, 247

Jefferson, Thomas, 90
Johnson, Ericka, 178, 190n9
justice and injustice, 5, 76–81, 85,
    88n12, 105, 120–1, 145, 150,
    194–216, 229, 246–9, 284

Kant's works
  *Anthropology from a Pragmatic
    Point of View*, 111n9, 164n22,
    210–12, 249
  *Conjectural Beginning of Human
    History*, 49, 163–4n21
  Critique of Judgment, 46–50, 56,
    162n5; *Critique of Aesthetic
    Judgment*, 56; *Critique of
    Teleological Judgment*, 47
  Critique of Practical Reason, 46, 75,
    224, 250
  Critique of Pure Reason, 39n13, 46,
    224, 250
  *Groundwork for the Metaphysics of
    Morals*, 28, 31, 65, 72–3, 109,
    111n9, 118, 133, 152, 180, 182,
    187, 200, 206, 224, 250, 268
  Metaphysics of Morals, 39n16,
    88n12, 109, 133, 145, 147–52,
    157, 182, 187, 268; *Doctrine of
    Right*, 76, 118–19, 124–5,
    137n18, 215n2; *Doctrine of
    Virtue*, 59, 210
  Moralphilosophie Collins, 39n16,
    88n12, 92, 111n9, 144–5, 157
  *Observations on the Feeling of the
    Beautiful and Sublime*, 67n8,
    211
  *Prolegomena to Any Future
    Metaphysics*, 202

*Religion within the Boundaries of
    Mere Reason*, 224, 256
Kaufman, Alexander, 78
Keeley, Michael, 228
Kekes, John, 216n13
Korsgaard, Christine, 14, 22–32, 35,
    40–1n27, 41n30, 59, 243, 252–5,
    263–6, 276n11, 280–1n60, 287
Kriegel, Uriah, 281–2n70

land pyramid, 48
last man argument, 63–4, 260
Latham, Stephen, R., 98
league of nations, 72, 83–4, 88n18
    see also cosmopolitanism
Lee, Patrick, 278n34, 278n35
legality vs. morality, 3, 76–8, 86,
    103–5, 118–20, 124–5, 148–51,
    170, 229–30, 235, 280n58
Leibniz, Gottfried Wilhelm, 27, 39n14
Leopold, Aldo, 48, 52, 67–8n13, 286
    A Sand County Almanac, 52,
    67–8n13
Levinas, Emmanuel, 273
liberalism and libertarianism, 3, 11,
    67n2, 72, 77–80, 86–7, 87–8n10,
    92–3, 108–10, 113n27, 145–6,
    165, 169, 183–4, 235, 271
liberty, positive vs. negative, 145–6
lifeboat scenario, 20
Light, Andrew, 60–3
Livingston, Margit, 34, 43n56
Locke, John, 90, 92–3, 110n1, 145–6,
    147, 149, 263
logocentrism, 14–16, 36, 244
    see also anthropocentrism
Lomasky, Loren E., 274–5, 282n79
Louden, Robert B., 206, 208
love, 39n12, 56–7, 141, 149–51, 171,
    189n5, 198
Lucht, Marc, 60
lying, 2, 127–9, 136–7n17, 169–70,
    179, 181, 195, 233–4
    see also fidelity, duty of

MacIntyre, Alasdair, 285
MacKinnon, Catherine, 142, 162n4

Marquis, Don, 244–5
marriage, 139–93
  bourgeois, 168–9
  forced, 177, 180–2, 191n23
  mail-order, 167–93
  morganatic, 156
  polygamous, 156–7, 172
  same-sex, 7, 115, 139–64
Marx, Karl, 184, 231
  Marxism, 80, 89n23, 169, 183–4,
    208, 231
masturbation, 258
Matthews, John B., Jr., 219
maxim, 4, 16, 28, 36–7n2, 53–5, 59,
    68n17, 74, 76, 100–1, 118–20,
    128–32, 136–7n17, 138n23, 150,
    153–4, 176, 182, 191n28,
    194–216, 220–3, 225, 227,
    229–34, 243–4, 259, 261
  coordination, 153
meat-eating, *see* vegetarianism
medical ethics, *see* abortion; health
  care; organ donation; patient
  autonomy; physician-assisted
  suicide; refusal of medical
  treatment; research ethics
Mill, John Stuart, 145, 197, 240n34,
    269
miniride principle, 20
moral agents vs. moral patients, 15,
    37n3, 285–6
moral luck, 74, 87n6, 128, 136–7n17,
    137n18, 203
morality vs. legality, *see* legality vs.
  morality
Murphy, Jeffrie G., 134–5n4, 137n18

Naess, Arne, 62
Nagel, Thomas, 74, 87n6
natural and unnatural, 31, 42n47, 51,
    142–3, 151–8, 161n2, 175, 261,
    269–70
  see also fallacy, naturalistic;
  purposes/purposiveness, natural
natural law theory, 68–9n19, 152, 269,
    271
negligence, 199–204, 208, 214, 231–2

Nelson, Leonard, 40–1n27
Nietzsche, Friedrich, 124, 188, 235
Noddings, Nel, 273
non-identity problem, 53–4, 259
nonmaleficence, duty of, 4, 55, 72–3,
    77, 81–2, 85–6, 137n21, 199,
    232–3, 243, 276n11
Norton, Bryan G., 60–3, 65
Nozick, Robert, 77, 79, 82, 87, 90
Nuremberg Code, 1–5, 108
Nussbaum, Martha C., 32

Obama, Barack, 89n22, 113n29
Oderberg, David S., 259–60
Oduncu, Fuat S., 252–4
O'Neill, Onora, 43n56, 51, 62, 109,
    169, 177–8, 180, 182–4, 198,
    217, 220
organ donation, 102–9, 112n23,
    112–13n24, 113n29, 113–14n32,
    209
  mandated choice, 107–8
  opt-in vs. opt-out, 104–9
organism, 23–6, 47–8, 162n5
Ozar, David T., 237n11

Parfit, Derek, 54, 259
Pateman, Carole, 186
  The Sexual Contract, 186
paternalism, 90–2, 233
patient–agent parity thesis, 15, 37n3
  see also agency, moral; moral agents
  vs. moral patients
patient autonomy, 90–4, 99, 104–7,
    109–10
Pellegrino, Edmund D., 74
perfection, principle of, 27–9, 269–70
Perlmutter, Martin, 121
Perry, Constance, 97
persistent vegetative state (PVS), 98,
    100–2, 272
personification principle, 22, 24, 29,
    31, 257
physician-assisted suicide, 91–8, 99,
    111n10, 280n55
Piper, Adrian M. S., 193n43
Pitcher–Feinberg thesis, 113n25

plants, 14, 16, 24–5, 45, 48, 50, 66
pleasure, disinterested, 56–7, 60, 62
Pogge, Thomas, 81, 85, 124–5
polygamy, *see* marriage, polygamous
Posner, Richard, 35, 44n66
potential, argument from, 252,
    255–60, 266, 268–9, 271,
    278n34, 279n47
poverty, duty to reduce, 77–86, 88n12,
    105, 194–216
practical pluralism, 62–3, 65
practical standpoint, 224, 280–1n60
predisposition (*Anlage*), 143, 193n45,
    224–5, 256
preferences, 20, 22, 24–30, 41n30,
    207, 243, 257, 265, 271–2
    considered vs. felt, 61–2
pregnancy, 54, 96, 110–11n3, 162n3,
    245–9, 268–75, 282n72
presumed consent, *see* organ donation,
    opt-in vs. opt-out
property rights, 78, 80, 82, 87n1,
    92–3, 104–6, 119, 145–6, 149,
    170–1, 208, 215n2
    original acquisition, 146
    private, 55, 119, 168, 195, 215n2
    provisional, 146, 149, 215n2
    see also rights
prostitution, 169, 177, 182–5
punishment, 119–25, 127–33, 134–
    5n4, 135n7, 137n18, 146, 148–9,
    168–70, 175–6, 263
    see also capital punishment;
    coercion, state
purposes/purposiveness
    final, 49, 58–9
    intrinsic vs. extrinsic, 47
    natural, 22–31, 46–50, 58–9, 61,
        143–4, 151–6, 162n5, 162n6,
        163–4n21, 211, 261, 269
    without purpose, 56
Putnam, Constance E., 126
Pybus, Elizabeth M., 32

race and racism, 3, 5, 183, 192n41,
    193n45, 209, 211–14, 216n26,
    256

Rachels, James, 100, 112n21
Radelet, Michael L., 126
Ramsey, Paul, 277n17
rape, 96, 143, 179, 182–3, 191n31,
    192n32, 244, 246, 248
    marital, 150, 183, 192n33
Rawls, John, 150, 196–7, 199, 228–9,
    243, 284
    distribution principle, 196
    liberty principle, 196
    primary goods, 196, 229
    veil of ignorance, 284
reflective distance, 14–15
refusal of medical treatment, 90,
    98–102, 112n21
Regan, Tom, 18, 20, 23, 35, 41n30, 60
regulative principles, 47, 155–6, 162n5
Reiman, Jeffrey, 266–7, 274, 277n17
relativism, 35, 36–7n2, 44n66, 201,
    204–6, 208–9, 273–4, 286–7
reparation, duty of, 50, 79–81, 85,
    137n21
representation (*Vorstellung*), 27–9,
    56–8, 249–50, 277n28
reproduction, *see* sex, procreational
republican government, 72, 78, 83–4,
    88n18
research ethics, 1–5, 8n2, 8–9n3, 9n8,
    189n4, 253, 260
responsibility
    collective, 197, 217–40, 286
    legal, 14, 123–5, 229–30
    negative, 191n28
    role vs. individual, 218
restoration, environmental, 50, 55–6,
    60–1
retribution, law of, 7, 115, 117–38
right (*Recht*), 76, 82, 104, 118–20,
    124–5, 134–5n4, 144–6, 170, 175
rights, 20, 34, 40–1n27, 45, 71–2,
    77–80, 86, 87n5, 90–4, 103–8,
    110n1, 145–6, 170, 180, 208,
    246–9, 268, 271–5, 277n24, 283
    animal, 20, 31, 33–4, 40–1n27,
        43n56, 43n58
    to die, 91–5
    ethics, 54, 93

of fathers, 245, 277n18
legal, 43n56, 43n58, 103–4,
113–14n32, 140, 149, 160, 170,
175–6, 185–6, 229
to life, 246–9, 252–4, 272
natural, 146
to be punished, 121
as side constraints, 77
see also property rights
Roe v. Wade, 242, 261, 277n24
Rolston, Holmes III, 13, 25
Ross, W. D., 137n21, 232
Rousseau, Jean-Jacques, 93, 146, 147,
163n10
Routley, Richard, *see* Sylvan, Richard
rules of moral salience (RMS), 204–6,
286
Rumsey, Jean R., 186

same-sex marriage, *see* marriage,
same-sex
Sandel, Michael, 273, 284
Sartre, Jean-Paul, 162n4
Schaff, Kory, 144–5, 147, 151, 162n6
Scheler, Max, 1
Scheman, Naomi, 188
Schiavo, Terri, 99–100, 102
Schönfeld, Martin, 68–9n19
Schopenhauer, Arthur, 41n33
Schwarz, Stephen, 252–5
Schwarzschild, Steven S., 135n6
self-consciousness, *see* apperception
self-defense, 96, 138n23, 182, 246
self-interest, *see* inclination
self-preservation, 25, 96–8, 143, 182,
224, 259
sentience, 30, 45, 264, 271–2
sex, 140–5, 147–61, 162n3, 163–4n21,
167–71, 175, 178–9, 184, 244,
248, 261
procreational, 54, 143–4, 151–8,
161n2, 162n6, 163–4n21, 168–9,
211, 244, 258, 261, 267–9, 274–5
recreational, 152, 154–6
see also celibacy; homosexuality
Shaw, William H., 239n30
Shell, Susan M., 192n41

Sidgwick, Henry, 42n50, 263
Singer, Peter, 13, 18–20, 25, 33, 35,
39n15, 40n20, 44n66, 45, 81
Animal Liberation, 20
"Famine, Affluence, and Morality,"
81
Skidmore, James, 30
slavery, 93, 97, 98, 111n6, 111n15,
133, 147, 184–5, 244
slippery slope argument, 91–2, 96,
108, 112n22, 157–8, 264
social contract, 79, 82, 104–5, 119–20,
122–3, 130, 133, 134–5n4, 145–6,
185–6, 196
Socrates, 135n7, 270
Crito, 135n7
Euthyphro, 270
speciesism, *see* anthropocentrism
stakeholder vs. shareholder, 217–18,
232, 236n2, 239n28
state, function of, 72, 75–87, 88n12,
105, 109, 145–6, 170, 197,
222–3
see also citizens, obligations of and
to; citizenship, relevance/
irrelevance of; civil society;
coercion, state; social contract
state of nature, 109, 119, 145–7,
163n10
stealing, 72, 119, 121, 146, 179,
195–6
Steinberg, David, 112–13n24
stem cell research, 253, 260
stewardship model, 48–50
Strawson, P. F., 70n27
subjectivism, *see* relativism
sublimity, 57–8
suicide, 16, 23, 92–8, 100–1, 110–
11n3, 111n9, 111n10, 135n6,
137n19, 138n23, 143, 244,
268–70
see also physician-assisted
suicide
Sumner, L. W., 277n17
Sunstein, Cass R., 106–7, 113n29,
164n24
Sylvan, Richard, 49, 63, 67n2

talents, duty to develop, 16, 72, 100–1,
153, 237–8n14, 245–6
taste, judgment of, 56
taxation, 71–2, 75–80, 82, 85, 105,
197
Taylor, Charles, 273, 284
Taylor, Paul W., 25
teleology, natural, *see* purposes/
purposiveness, natural
Teson, Fernando, 88n18
Thaler, Richard H., 106–7, 164n24
Thomasma, David C., 74
Thomson, Judith Jarvis, 244–5, 246–9,
277n24
Tooley, Michael, 266, 274
transcendental idealism, 39n13, 124,
201, 224, 249–50
true needs, 55, 73–4, 134n2, 199
Turner v. Safley, 159–60
Tuskegee syphilis study, 1–3, 5, 9n5,
209

United States Citizenship and
Immigration Services (USCIS),
174–5
United States Congress, 126, 174–5,
225
United States Supreme Court, 66,
137–8n22, 159–60, 164n25, 242,
277n24
see also *Brown v. Board of
Education*; *Herrera v. Collins*; *Roe
v. Wade*; *Turner v. Safley*
universalizability, *see* categorical
imperative, formula of universal
law
unnatural, *see* natural and unnatural
utilitarianism, 18, 26, 33, 35, 39n15,
43n56, 54, 91, 191n28, 196–8,
200, 203, 207, 230, 233, 234–5,
240n34, 258, 264, 271–2, 276n9,
280n53

Van den Haag, Ernest, 126, 136n15
Veatch, Robert M., 107–8

vegetarianism, 19–22, 40n18, 40n20,
52
veil of ignorance, 284
Velasquez, Manuel G., 227, 238n18
violence graduation hypothesis, 17, 21,
38–9n10, 43n56, 57, 69n21
see also *animals, cruelty toward
virtue, 17, 58–60, 64, 101–2, 129,
211, 235, 238n15, 260
ethics, 33, 59, 235

Walzer, Michael, 284
Warnock, Mary, 34–5
Warnock Report, 244
Warren, Mary Anne, 37–8n9, 249,
254, 266–7, 274, 282n79
Wellman, Carl, 260
will, 2, 14, 23–4, 27–9, 41n33, 56, 74,
76, 94, 118–22, 130, 148, 151,
200–1, 220, 243, 250, 269–70,
284
see also *categorical imperative
procedure, contradiction in the
will; good will; holy will
Williams, Bernard, 1, 74, 87n6,
191n28, 207, 284–5
Wilson, Holly L., 252–4
withholding/withdrawing medical
treatment, *see* refusal of medical
treatment
Wolff, Christian, 27–9, 269
Wollstonecraft, Mary, 90
women
exploitation of, 156–7, 167–93,
245–6
Kant's views toward, 23, 158,
163–4n21, 164n22, 172–3, 175,
180, 185–8, 193n43, 211–14,
266, 269, 272, 275
see also *feminism; feminist
philosophy
Wood, Allen W., 16, 22–7, 29–32, 35,
49–50, 59, 162n4, 163–4n21,
213, 244, 255, 257, 265–6,
279n43, 287